PUBLIC ACCESS TO DOCUMENTS IN THE EU

All litigants before the General Court of the EU (GC), the Court of Justice of the EU (ECJ) or indeed before any EU body or agency will need to have full access to documents held by the European Union. Though the legislation regulating the field, Regulation 1049/2001, has been in force for some time, it is a complex field for all would be litigants. In this book the authors, both experienced practitioners in the area, clearly set out the documentation, access requirements and processes. They include a helpful glossary of terms, tables and appendices setting out the relevant legislation. This will be the seminal text for all practitioners who need to access documentation held by the EU.

Public Access to Documents in the EU

Leonor Rossi and Patricia Vinagre e Silva

·HART·
PUBLISHING
OXFORD AND PORTLAND, OREGON
2017

Hart Publishing
An imprint of Bloomsbury Publishing Plc

Hart Publishing Ltd
Kemp House
Chawley Park
Cumnor Hill
Oxford OX2 9PH
UK

Bloomsbury Publishing Plc
50 Bedford Square
London
WC1B 3DP
UK

www.hartpub.co.uk
www.bloomsbury.com

Published in North America (US and Canada) by
Hart Publishing
c/o International Specialized Book Services
920 NE 58th Avenue, Suite 300
Portland, OR 97213-3786
USA

www.isbs.com

HART PUBLISHING, the Hart/Stag logo, BLOOMSBURY and the Diana logo are trademarks of Bloomsbury Publishing Plc

First published 2017

British Library Cataloguing-in-Publication Data
A catalogue record for this book is available from the British Library.

ISBN: HB: 978-1-50990-533-1
ePDF: 978-1-50990-534-8
ePub: 978-1-50990-535-5

Library of Congress Cataloging-in-Publication Data

Names: Rossi, Leonor, author. | Vinagre e Silva, Patricia, author.

Title: Public access to documents in the EU / Leonor Rossi and Patricia Vinagre e Silva.

Description: Oxford [UK] ; Portland, Oregon : Hart Publishing, 2016. | Includes bibliographical references and index.

Identifiers: LCCN 2016034342 (print) | LCCN 2016035221 (ebook) | ISBN 9781509905331 (hardback : alk. paper) | ISBN 9781509905355 (Epub)

Subjects: LCSH: Records—Access control—European Union countries. | Public records—Access control—European Union countries. | Legal documents—Access control—European Union countries.

Classification: LCC KJE6071 .R67 2017 (print) | LCC KJE6071 (ebook) | DDC 342.24/0662—dc23

LC record available at https://lccn.loc.gov/2016034342

Typeset by Compuscript Ltd, Shannon
Printed and bound in Great Britain by CPI Group (UK) Ltd, Croydon CR0 4YY

Foreword

As a Professor of EU law at the prestigious Nova School of Business and Economics in Lisbon, Leonor Rossi is the type of jurist whose academic and professional background is particularly suited to understand, and explain, the links between legal principles and real life. This book owes much not only to her academic research but also to her interventions as a lawyer practising before the EU courts. That explains why, apart from our mutual respect and friendship, she has invited me on several occasions to explain some of my EU law cases to her students. I always enjoyed doing it.

Patrícia Vinagre e Silva added to their common venture the result of her experience and expertise as a practitioner in national and EU administrative law.

The invitation to write some words on *Public Access to Documents in the EU* was part of a surprise. In 2013, Leonor and Patricia confided to me that, it was their opinion that access to documents was an area of law 'fraught with misunderstandings'. I suggested then that misunderstandings were an excellent subject for the doctrine to dwell on.

After some months of silence, in 2014, the authors of this book wrote to me stating that they had worked on an answer to the challenge I had left them: the draft of a manuscript entitled *Public Access to Documents in the EU*. The surprise came with request, that in tribute to our long friendship I browse through it and write a dispassionate foreword.

In all, the book contains eight chapters devoted to the same theme: public access to documents in the EU. That is, in itself, a novelty, since access is usually confined to a mere section of broader discussions such as those concerning democratic principles in the EU.

The work takes into account the entirety of the case law delivered on this topic by the EU judicature (1995–2015) as well as the succession of normative instruments that led to the adoption of the so-called Transparency Regulation 1049/2001 and of the Aarhus Regulation 1367/2006.

The first chapter focuses on one main premise, that however constitutionalised may be the evolution of public access to documents of the EU institutions, in principle, the EU judicature is not empowered to address positive injunctions or orders to the institutions. The authors then propose that the legislative texts should more explicitly profess that, absent the possibility of such orders, access within the EU framework is a mere entitlement to deconstructive due process (annulment) rather than a substantive right or entitlement to request that documents be concretely handed over to any member of the public.

Chapter 2 opens the discussion concerning applicants with an account of the requirements both of legal personality and representation of any person by legal counsel. It then addresses applicants' profiles, contrasting the concept of applicants *by right* against that of applicants *by grace* in order to define access' scope *ratione personae.*

The third chapter describes the particulars of the development of a model crafted solely for the Council and the Commission into a model of institutional accountability that also embraces the European Parliament and all other EU institutions agencies and/or bodies.

Chapter 4 concerns the very notion of 'document'. The contrast between a document and information is explored but principally the consequences of the absence of quantitative and qualitative boundaries of that concept are brought to light. The discussion proceeds to so-called cumbersome applications, the legitimacy of the excessive burden clause and to the possibility of partial access. In addition, the authors propose that requests for access to databases be discussed separately. As a closing topic, Chapter 4 outlines the status quo of the absence of an institutional obligation to read documents before these are refused.

The fifth chapter dwells on the meaning of a 'No' as a response to a request for access. In first place, it addresses the legislative exceptions to the general principle that the widest possible access to documents authored or held by the EU institutions is to be granted to the public. Secondly, the consequences of presumptions within the access model are assessed.

Chapter 6 calls attention to the importance of negative silence within the context of the access policy. It then addresses the fact that no legal proceedings in which institutional silence was challenged by an applicant has ever proceeded to judgment before an explicit, albeit late, reply has been provided by the institutions. The discussion then focuses on the authors' view of how applicants should react to mandatory deadlines.

The seventh chapter departs from the previous style of micro-analysis of specific topics and outlines first, the many possible roles that Member States may choose to play within the access procedure. Here, the authors portray the initial applicant as a contender against possible interveners in order to secure the maximum share of the judicature's attention. Then, a statistical table on the times each Member State has intervened in access litigation allows the authors to trace foreign policy-oriented national profiles divided between pro-access and more conservative positions as regards the disclosure of documents and information. The same analysis is then made as regards institutions of the EU, focusing on whether they support one another, or not, within litigation. Finally, an account is given of private interveners including undertakings and associations even from the USA or China.

Chapter 8 wraps the discussion up by analysing how the access litigation proceeds beyond the General Court and comes before the European Court of Justice. It also casts light on the preponderant role of certain Member States in bringing appeals before the scrutiny of the ECJ even when initial applicants desist. The analysis shows how once litigation is set in motion, no one, not even the initial applicant, can predict when the dispute will come to an end and what proportions it may take on.

As the authors rightly write in an Epilogue to the work, the discussion of case law is sometimes a formidable task. I must say that they undertook this formidable task with exactitude and perspicacity, combining solid theoretical tools with a practical view on the whole range of topics they cover in their analysis.

Academics and practitioners will thus find in this book a great deal of information and a remarkable wealth of innovative and refreshing views on a subject whose importance has grown significantly in the last 20 years. I therefore strongly recommend it to readers who are looking for information and guidance in the whole of this field.

José Luís da Cruz Vilaça
President of chamber at the Court of Justice of the European Union
Former President of the Court of First Instance of the European Communities (1989–95)

Acknowledgements

First and foremost, our gratitude is to Hart publishing for choosing to support this book, and especially to Sinead Moloney and Emily Braggins who have worked with us for many months and have borne heroically all of the authors' requests for extensions of deadlines.

We owe a special word to Judge Cruz Vilaça for the encouragement to embark on this work, for his faith in our capacity to bring it to term, and for his generosity in writing the foreword to this book. To the members of his Cabinet who assisted us and welcomed us to the ECJ with such patience and grace, a word of gratitude is also owed.

We are also indebted to the Fundação para a Ciencia e Tecnologia (FCT) for research support and to Miguel Poiares Maduro and Nuno Garoupa for their comments and supervision of the seminal research project that would many years later allow us to ground this book.

To the Fundacion Rafael del Pino, our sincere thanks for making it possible to spend invaluable days at Harvard Law School. We thank Francisco Cabrillo, Rocio Albert and Fernando Gomez for their continued support, comments and patience, and we owe particular tribute to Steve Shavell, Director of the John Olin Center for Law and Economics at Harvard Law School, who encouraged us to engage in a fight against our own limitations when we were tired. We wrote the Epilogue in his honour.

In Lisbon, our colleagues John Huffstot and Vasco Santos helped us sail through many drafts and made sure we kept to a tight schedule. Miguel Sousa Ferro also read many versions of chapters and we are very grateful for his comments.

At Gouveia Pereira Costa Freitas and Associates many colleagues acquiesced to reading pages and pages on access to documents and a word in particular is owed to our colleague Susana Moreira who worked with us through the Tables of Cases and Bibliography.

Our research assistants at Nova SBE, Ana Rute Valente and Carolina Oliveira, also spent many hours helping to bring shape to this project. To them and to the students of EU Law at NovaSBE who held gainful discussions on these topics we leave our thanks and appreciation.

The Authors are greatly indebted to the head librarian at NovaSBE, Sean Story, as well as to Fabio Pappalardo, Bjarne Meyer and Afroditi Roumeliotou of the Library of the ECJ. Only the special temper of librarians can bear with such good humour all the requests of researchers.

Finally, to both of our families who have looked over our shoulder for many days and evenings and done without us so that we could complete this work and in particular to our children who have dropped toys and drawings into our materials (and that on occasion have drawn all over our materials!), who, in their oblivion of anything remotely connected to access to documents, with their joyous presence have kept us sane and made everything worthwhile.

Table of Contents

Table of Cases

European Union

Court of Justice, Case Number Order

Court of Justice, Name Order

Court of First Instance, Case Number Order

Court of First Instance, Name Order

Orders, Case Number Order

Orders, Name Order

Opinions, Case Number Order

Opinions, Name Order

1

The Normative Development of Access to Documents

I. INTRODUCTION

IN 1992, IN the wake of the Danish rejection of further EU integration, Miterrand suggested that a long-term oversight of the EU institutions lay in the lack of talking to (the) people.[1] In response to bitter criticism suggesting that there might be institutional autism two institutions of the EU (the Council and the Commission) produced codes of conduct governing access to the EU's internal documents. It was a long jump over an abyss: the perilous pit of rejection of the EU by its own constituent population. The purpose of this volume is to assess the robustness of the new legal rules that purport to signal to the international community that the EU institutions landed safely, and upright, on the other side of the precipice.

Within the new, access-embracing, legal framework the groundbreaking codes of conduct were the tip of the iceberg. Important certainly, but it is also true that they amounted to an incipient normative stage only of the European rules on access to documents. In fact, by the time the Treaty of Amsterdam came into force, a second constitutionalising stage would take over, and accordingly, access would be vested into Treaty articles of its own. Subsequently, and under a third stage of normative development that would hold well over a decade, access to documents would form the object of a European Regulation that is still in force today. A fourth stage, albeit limited to EU legislation on privacy, competition law and environmental law, describes the coming to terms with the subject of access to documents of other EU rules adopted and applied as sectoral laws that circumscribe the general law.

It might be said, and has been said, that the current framework is in need of reform, yet in the wake of the twentieth anniversary of its investiture as a European policy, access to internal documents in the EU is a cornerstone of the overall *acquis* of the Union that is both articulate and inescapable.

We propose to pay particular attention to the role of the EU courts in the shaping of the access to documents policy. Insofar as enforcement of these rules is concerned, over the last two decades both EU courts have together rendered judgment on more than 200 disputes concerning requests for documents. This valuable sample, admittedly not as extensive as might be wished, has played the fundamental role

[1] E Haywood, 'The European Policy of Francois Mitterand' (1993) 31(2) *Journal of Common Market Studies* 269–82.

of steering the practice of the institutions. Since this volume is intended to function as a handbook, the emphasis of this volume will be on the evolution through time (1994–2016) of the status quo of a series of access' conceptual parameters. Thus, attention will be paid, for each of the four abovementioned stages of its evolution, to the central issues of the specific phase, namely: applicant profile and institutions involved; documents that form the object of requests; exceptions relied on; instances of legal silence; legal costs; Member State intervention; and appeals.

Regarding the lexicon of access to documents, many an author has spent time on the difference between access and transparency as well as on the disjunction between the concept of documents and the information contained therein. We choose, on the one hand, to favour the practical dimension of access in a judicial setting rather than the more articulate teleology of transparency, and on the other, to qualify, here, as interchangeable (with the exception of Chapter 4) the concepts of document and information.

This being said, the task that we embark on is Herculean, and the authors, only human.

II. WIDE OR DEEP? HORIZONTAL OR VERTICAL PROFILES IN LEGAL DESIGN

One may easily be led to assume that it is very simple to obtain documents from the institutions of the European Union (EU). On the one hand, the law of the EU declares that a right of access to documents has been liberally bestowed upon many persons. On the other hand, the public might confuse the name of rights acknowledged by EU law, with rights of similar designation that exist within one or more legal systems of the Member States of the EU.

A. A Plain Proposition?

The law, often criticised for pervasively employing 'ponderous language as proof of its seriousness',[2] has chosen a curious approach for this access policy forged in Brussels. The words and terms on which the EU acknowledges a right of public access to the documents that it holds are, for once, plain. First, the law clarifies that it is by way of a mere application (dispensing with the requirement for the intervention of legal counsel) that the process of enforcement of such a right should commence. Next, it is stated that it is sufficient to submit the application by post or by e-mail to any institution of the EU identifying the documents one wishes to consult. Finally, the law promises the applicant that an answer will be provided within 15 days.

Subsequently, if a refusal is issued, an opportunity to engage the same institution higher up in the hierarchy is afforded. Indeed, a confirmatory application (once again dispensing with the intervention of legal counsel) requesting the same documents,

[2] The expression is coined by Steven Pinker in *The Sense of Style, The Thinking Person's Guide to Writing in the 21st Century* (New York, Penguin, 2014) 58.

and deliverable by post or e-mail, may be addressed to the body within the institution that is competent[3] to hear such internal appeals.

Should a second refusal be issued, the applicant becomes entitled either to engage the EU Ombudsman[4] by way of a simple complaint (that again dispenses with the intervention of legal counsel), and/or (in this case with the mandatory assistance of legal counsel) to engage the EU judicature. This last option must be carried out by way of an action lodged before the General Court[5] (GC) intended to have the judicature annul the institutional refusal to grant the applicant access to the contested documents. Should the GC not do as the applicant requests, the route to the highest judicial authority of the EU remains available, under the form of an appeal to the European Court of Justice[6] (ECJ).

While it is tempting to applaud simplicity in the language of the law, it is just as important to point out that simplicity is also a pitfall in disguise. After all, this legislation's main rhetorical target is the public in general. As a consequence, simple terminology, when employed by EU law in the description of broad advantages arising out of citizenship of the Union, may lead lay persons and/or novices to this litigation—less versed in the interpretation of ordinary words within a qualified context (ie what do 'person, institution, document, or No' mean for the law)—to misconceive what, in fact, the law has to offer. Where it occurs, that misconception will put a strain on the public's relationship with institutions,[7] and might even affect applicants' expectations regarding what legal counsel (practitioners) may obtain from the judicature, if and when litigation is pursued before the EU courts.

[3] Identifiable on a case-by-case basis, depending on which EU institution is involved.

[4] Thorought the book we have chosen not to explore the role of the EU Ombudsman as an alternative to litigation before the EU judicature.

[5] The GC is the new designation for the first instance court of the EU judicature. In fact, it was known as European Court of First Instance, or CFI, from 1988 until the coming into force of the Lisbon Treaty on 1 December 2009. Therefore rulings and orders of the first instance judicature will either be referred to as CFI (when delivered between 1989 and 1 December 2009) or as GC (when delivered post 1 December 2009). All cases lodged at GC (and/or CFI) level are identified by the letter T used as a prefix to the case's numerical reference; the choice of letter is inspired by the French term for first instance courts: *Tribunal*. The numerical reference identifies first, the order of lodging of the case within any year, and subsequently, the precise year of lodging of the case.

Still with regard to first instance rulings, as for the (much less frequent) involvement of the Civil Service Tribunal (CST), which deals mostly with staff cases where the CST is the first instance for litigation, the GC takes on the role of (final) appellate court. In such cases, the letter F is employed as a prefix to the numerical reference, and the choice of letter is inspired by the French designation for the civil service: *fonction publique*. The CST, due to the on-going revision of the EU judicial structure, is destined to disappear from the structure of the EU judicature shortly. See, as examples of references involving the CST, Case T-304/13P *Van der Aat a.o. v Commission*, which is the appeal of Case F-111/11 *Van der Aat a.o. v Commission*. Given that such cases are lodged as an appeal of a first instance ruling, the suffix P will be added, inspired by the French term for appeal: *pourvoi*.

[6] All cases lodged at ECJ level are identified, first, by the letter C as a prefix, inspired by the French term for high or supreme courts: *cour*. Secondly, they are identified by a numerical reference (following the same criteria employed for the GC). Thirdly, and if a case is lodged as an appeal of a first instance ruling, the suffix P will be added, inspired by the French term for appeal: *pourvoi*.

[7] The public may react with surprise when confronted with statements similar to that from Case T-436/09 *Dufour v ECB* [2011] ECR II-0772, para 72: 'The ECB argues that neither Decision 2004/258 nor European Union Law more generally provides for a right of public access to information'.

It is also important to keep in mind that the drafting of initial applications (and even of subsequent confirmatory applications) is often undertaken without the assistance of legal counsel. It is only when litigation[8] commences that the law dictates that a lawyer[9] take charge.

In the face of such apparent candour of the words that frame the offer made to the public (that it has[10] a right of access to documents) one cannot help but wonder if it is just as simple to enforce the offer. Therefore, and likewise simply put, it is the aim of this book to unravel the knot of what the EU promises.

B. Confusion and Misrepresentation

Turning to a distinct issue, the risk of confusion between what is offered by EU law versus the framework of national law, one should bear in mind that rights named 'access to documents' are acknowledged throughout the Member States of the EU. For this reason, members of the public (who are educated in the law of individual Member States) will often assume that if a right carrying the same name is acknowledged at EU level, its respective content, or at least its structure, is, and should be, identical to the national right. Intuitively (and misleadingly), the national standard acts as a ubiquitous measure of what the EU right should be, might be, or finally, might yet become. It plays the role of a *de lege ferenda* standard of comparison.

Although national law is undoubtedly the major source of inspiration for supranational solutions, understanding the law of the European Union often requires severance from the purely internal national mindset. A correct analysis of rights of EU law must be performed autonomously, focusing on what is effectively before us—*de lege data*—at that, specific and often different, normative level.

There are of course certain traits of the EU policies that are also present in national law and are treated in the exact same way at both levels. However, other traits of policies present both at the national and EU levels—and that moreover carry the same name, 'rights of access'—have parameters that vary from one framework (national law) to the other (EU law). The right of public access to documents (of the EU institutions)[11] being no exception it is consequently developed as a product of yet another layer of statute placed between the individual and the State. This occurs

[8] Litigation may only be commenced if it is a challenge to a refusal of a confirmatory application. For an early definition of challengeable measure, see T-106/99 *Meyer v Commission* [1999] II-03273, para 31. More recently, on the same topic, see C-127/13P *Strack v Commission* [not yet reported] para 36, *in fine*.

[9] With regard to admissible representation by a lawyer, the third para of Art 19 of the Statute of the Court of Justice includes a requirement which makes it necessary to engage a third person who is sufficiently detached from the client. On this point, see Case C-28/13P *Thesing and Bloomberg Finance v ECB* [not yet reported], order of the President of the ECJ, 6 November 2013; and also Case T-452/10 *ClientEarth v Council* [2011] II-00257, order of the GC, 6 September 2011. On the issue of the authority granted to an applicant's lawyer, according to Art 44(5) of the rules of procedure, see Case T-383/08 *New Europe v Commission* [not reported], order of the GC, 23 April 2009.

[10] eg Regulation 1049/2001, Art 1.

[11] For the EU, hereinafter 'access'.

despite the fact that it is placed beyond (and not beneath) national law, thus giving rise to inverted regionalism.[12] The results are different intensities of width and depth between Member State and EU law.

C. A Discussion for Applicants, Practitioners, Academics, Institutions and Judges

The discussion we propose to embark on is intended to facilitate many tasks: those of applicants, practitioners, academics, institutions and even of the judicature. The beneficiaries of the access policy (applicants) will be told the somewhat harsh truth about the practical significance of the *EU's* acknowledgement of such a right.[13] Practitioners will be reminded both of what applicants (clients) expect of them, of the substantial size of the case -law governing *access*, and of the more common pitfalls of the procedure. Academics (especially those interested in issues related to governance of institutions) will be exposed to an analytical discussion of the alignment of incentives in the access policy. The institutions and the judicature will hopefully gain a different view of the applicant person. For the authors of this book the applicant person (in the majority of cases) approaches both the institution and the judge with high expectations. Yet the applicant person is the same that, more often than not, turns away confounded.

We will begin by discussing the width and depth of the right of public access to documents of the EU institutions.

D. The Normative Width of Access

From a traditional standpoint, insofar as the width of any right is concerned, one way of measuring it is to count the persons involved. We inquire first about those who may ask for enforcement and second about those who are required to grant it.

The first group may be described as the basis of active legitimacy, and the second as the basis of passive legitimacy. Therefore, from this standpoint a right is wide either when (1) many persons (many potential applicants) are accorded an advantage; or when (2) many persons—or even only a single individual—are allowed to gain an advantage over many others (many potential addressees of requests).

Another way to measure a right's width is to ascertain whether that same right allows persons to ask others for many (types of) things. In this sense we define

[12] For a definition of inverted regionalism in EU Law the insightful JH Weiler, U Haltern and F Mayer, 'European Democracy and Its Critique, Five Uneasy Pieces' (1995) EUI Working Paper RSC No 95/11, 4 remind us that 'Even if the Union were to replicate in its system of governance the very same institutional set-up found in its constituent states, there would be a diminution in its specific gravity, in the political weight, in the level of control of each individual within the redrawn political boundaries, But, of course, the Union does not replicate domestic democratic arrangements'. See also, and in particular the discerning and groundbreaking analysis of F Lafay, 'L'accès aux documents du Conseil de l'Union: contribution à une problématique de la transparence en droit communautaire' (1997) 33 Jan–Mar (1) *Revue Trimestrelle de Droit Européen* 33, 37.

[13] A very wide perspective of access' utility is propounded by V Luszcz, 'Gunpowder for Court Battles: Litigant's Access to EU Institution Documents' (2012) 13 *EUZW* 488–94.

the scope or range[14] of things over which advantages are granted regardless of the number of persons involved.

Still, we would need to ask three further questions to fully understand access' status quo, and in order to define its width. Question (1) would regard the size of access' public; Question (2) would regard the number of EU institutions subject to access' rules, and Question (3) would focus on the types of documents covered by access, from the perspectives of their physical format subject matter and author.

i. Three Questions Regarding the Width of Access

1. Who are the persons who may ask for documents? Only natural persons or also legal persons? Only citizens of the EU or also third-country nationals? Do they have to provide explanations for their request or even demonstrate a legitimate interest?
2. From which institution(s) may the documents be requested? Only from the Commission and the Council or are other institutions subject to this request?
3. How many (kinds of) documents may be requested? Only documents printed on paper? Electronic versions? Audiovisual recordings? Within this third question, it is also important to consider two further issues
   - 3(a). How many types of subject matter may accessible documents be related to: Free movement? Competition law? Agriculture? Environment? International relations?
   - 3(b). Are only documents that the institution produces directly accessible? Or are documents produced by others and held by the institution also covered by the access policy?

As we will see,[15] access has been designed favouring its width within the EU framework. Even so, if a right is offered to many persons vis-à-vis many others, there is always the danger that many disputes will arise and the management of the right will become ungovernable: the respective judicature might be swamped. To deflect such dangers, the overall structure of a right (designed to be wide) is often re-calibrated into a manageable equilibrium through choices of policy that will place stringent bounds on that right's depth.

E. The Normative Depth of Access

When we say a right is deep we mean that the *results* of its enforcement are intense. We measure the remedial strength[16] and impact of the advantages given, rather than focus—as before—on the number of advantages offered.

[14] Lafay, 'L'accès aux documents du Conseil de l'Union' (n 12) employs the term '*étendue*', 68.

[15] See Chs 2, 4.

[16] Lafay (n 12) employs the term '*intensité*', 68. In the case law it is interesting to contrast the earlier terminology employed in Case C-5/93 *DSM v Commission* [1999] ECR I-4695, paras 2 and 36, which

When applied to access, we would ask two questions to define its depth.

Question (1) would regard the least that persons expect when they go to court, and Question (2) would regard the maximum expectation that persons who sue, entertain.

i. Two Questions Regarding the Depth of Access

1. If persons sue in court what is the minimum they might ask for? That the ruling of the court at least declares that the institution was wrong in refusing access to a document?
   1(a). One could go on to ask a sub-question: What happens if a court rules in their favour? Is it true that the decision to refuse access is annulled and thus a legal void is created retroactively? Does it follow logically that the institution must make another decision to replace the first?
2. If persons sue in court what is the maximum they might ask for? Is it feasible in EU law, as it is in national law, to request the court to order the institution to effectively grant access to a document previously denied?
   2(a). One could go on to ask a sub-question: What happens if a court rules in their favour? Do judges of the EU have power to address orders to the institutions?

To both questions—under the existing framework of EU access—a valid answer could not fail to recount that under EU law no injunction[17] is contemplated. In other words, while the EU judicature may declare that an institution wrongly denied access to a document, the same judges are not empowered to order the institutions to hand those same documents over to the applicant. Annulment of refusals is the

clearly carves out (positive) injunctions from the access model—'When exercising judicial review of legality under Article 173 of the Treaty (now, after amendment, Article 230 EC), the Community judicature has no jurisdiction to issue directions'—against a more recent and more intriguing approach in Case C-127/13P *Strack v Commission* (n 8) 145, considered below. It is not clear if the *Strack* formula is a hint that in the future (positive) injunctions might be clawed back into the model.

Whilst most requests for orders of disclosure arise within the main action for annulment, on occasion, applicants have attempted to lodge a principal action for annulment and at the same time lodge an ancillary urgent request for the disclosure of the contested documents. In such cases, the EU judicature has consistently dismissed all applications for interim relief, since to do otherwise would anticipate the decision of the courts in the main action. See eg T-610/97R *Carlsen a.o. v Commission* 1998] II-00485, order of the President of the CFI, 3 March 1998. As requests for these directions are issued under a framework of urgency, the references of such cases employ the letter R as a suffix. The reason is that this is inspired by the French term *référé* (*procédure d'urgence judiciaire*).

For an overview of the discussion of such directions as interim measures in judicial proceedings as an instrument of protection for individuals in EU law, see JL da Cruz Vilaça, *EU Law and Integration, Twenty Years of Application of Law* (Oxford, Hart, 2015) ch 5, 133.

[17] Only negative injunctive orders 'do not disclose' are included in the EU's legislative model for access. eg Case T-44/13 R *Abbvie v EMA* [not reported], Order of the President of the GC of 23 April 2013, in which, at point 2, the General Court ordered the European Medicines Agency not to disclose certain documents: 'The EMA is ordered not to disclose the documents referred to in point 1 of the operative part of this order'. For more on this, see Ch 7.

normative floor against which case law may be construed, but at the same time, it is also its normative ceiling.[18] Thus, access that is wide is not deep.

Its lack of depth balances the generosity of its width. Hence, although almost any person may request access to documents, if these are refused them, few persons bother to sue in court. In this context of 'undersuit'[19] what may appear to be a form of rational apathy[20]—when capable persons who should care don't react—is in fact a rational reaction to incentives.

F. The Name 'Access'

Having clarified that the remedies for access are shallow, our concluding remark to this introduction regards the purpose of this book. If within all legal systems, it is widely accepted that where there is no remedy there is no right, what is the significance of a shallow remedy for an important right? This is the main challenge of this volume: a frank discussion of whether it is correct to designate the accomplishments of the EU on public access to institutional documents as a right of access at all, since that system denies applicants injunctive relief.

An alternative would be to name the EU position as a 'right to annulment'. Or, as an alternative to opening the fundamental texts with the assurance to the beneficiaries that they have a right of access, rephrasing the founding legislative text in the following manner 'the public has a right to have illegitimate refusals annulled'.

In fact, since its inception, the EU framework has accorded many applicants judicial review over their right to have their requests dealt with by the institutions

[18] See, very recently, the rewording of what was, to date, a consistent position of the EU courts. In C-127/13P *Strack v Commission* (n 8) paras 145–47, the ECJ still excluded that it would be able to address orders to institutions, but rather intriguingly, added that this was so only in principle:

> 145 According to settled case law, the Courts of the European Union cannot, *in principle*, issue orders to an EU institution without encroaching upon the prerogatives of the administration (…).
>
> 146 Thus, contrary to the appellant's assertions, the EGC was right to hold, in paragraph 90 of the judgment under appeal, that, in accordance with Article 264 TFEU, it was only open to it to annul the contested act. In so far as the appellant's argument is based on Article 266 TFEU, it must be observed that that provision also does not provide for the possibility of issuing orders to the institutions.
>
> 147 That finding cannot be called into question by the appellant's arguments based on Article 47 of the Charter, since that article is not intended to change the system of judicial review laid down by the Treaties.

[19] 'Undersuit' may be defined as a socially inadequate level of suit where the private incentive to sue (since excessively low) is misaligned with the socially optimal incentive to do so. The concept is explored in S Shavell, *Foundations of Economic Analysis of Law* (Cambridge, MA, Belknap Press of Harvard University Press, 2004) Ch 4, 'Litigation and the Legal Process', 391: 'The plaintiff (applicant) would not usually be expected to treat as a benefit to himself the social benefits flowing from the suit, notably, its deterrent effect on the behavior of injurers (here the institutions)'.

[20] For examples of other fields of law in which private parties display deceptive levels of litigious inertia, see L Rossi and S Geraldes, 'Portugal, Article 234 and Competition Law' in B Rodger (ed), *Article 234 and Competition Law, An Analysis* (The Hague, Kluwer, 2008) 528–39; and L Rossi and M Sousa Ferro, 'Report on Portugal' in B Rodger (ed), *Competition Law, Comparative Private Enforcement and Collective Redress Across the EU* (The Hague, Kluwer, 2014) www.clcpecreu.co.uk

in accordance with the principles and procedures laid down.[21] As a consequence, refusals deemed illegitimate are removed by the EU courts (annulled) and replaced by the institutions. At most, the applicant is entitled to a *deconstructive due process* in which something illegitimate is removed. No more, no less. There is no entitlement to a *constructive due process* in which documents are literally 'handed over' to the applicant upon order of the courts.

To be sure, an entitlement to deconstructive due process is very different from an entitlement to a more intense legal instrument (injunctive relief, ie the empowerment of the judiciary to address orders to the institutions) by way of which one would finally and concretely, hold a document in one's hand. Therefore, one cannot but ask oneself if, by calling access in the EU context 'access', a misrepresentation[22] has in a certain sense been nurtured.

In this first chapter we return to access' *normative* origins and portray its development up to its present-day status. After all, comprehending the beginnings of the law—*as it* is—is a realistic point of departure.

III. TWO CODES OF CONDUCT FOR EUROPE

A. The Code of 1993

Chronologically, the normative development of access was born of an entanglement of acts that were simultaneously both inconspicuous and of dubious legal value. As a consequence, the investiture of access as a theme of EU law came about discreetly. First, the rules on how concrete requests from the public regarding access to documents should be dealt with by the EU institutions were laid down in a non-binding Code of Conduct of 1993.[23] That Code of Conduct (implemented by way of two Decisions) was the first instrument that could be relied on to challenge a refusal originating from a European institution before a court of law.

But it was *hors nomenclature*: when measured against the known range of *binding* instruments of EU law, it clearly did not fit. It was not a Treaty article, which would have been a prudent way to ground a policy. It was not a Regulation, which would have been a way to involve all EU institutions—with a legislative role—in the making of the policy. It was not a Directive, since, as such, it would not have been addressed to the EU institutions. It was not a Decision, although implementing Decisions were involved.

In comparison with the non-binding instruments of EU law with which the public was familiar, it also resembled a changeling. The Code of Conduct was neither a Recommendation, since it seemed to go beyond suggestion, nor an Opinion, since it was

[21] Case T-105/95 *WWF UK v Commission* [1997] ECR II-00313, para 34.

[22] The demand for remedies of greater strength on the part of the applicant has been quite evident from the outset, namely in Case T-50/96 *Primex Produckte Import a.o. v Commission* [1998] ECT II-3773 as well as in Case T-124/96 *Interporc v Commission* [1998] ECR II-231 (*Interporc I*).

[23] Code of Conduct, signed on 6 December 1993 by the Commission and the Council of Ministers on public access to Council and Commission Documents [1993] OJ L 340, 41; see Annex 1.

no proposed answer to any question. To put it bluntly, it was atypical. Therefore, no description of it was included among the list of expectable forms of EU acts contained in Article 189 of the treaty governing Europe in 1993.[24] The result was confounding. The nature of the Code of Conduct was elusive. Within the EU framework, no one knew exactly what a Code of Conduct meant. And, more importantly, since the Code of Conduct, as such, did not identify its own legal basis, neither was there a clear idea of what could be achieved through it.

> Code of Conduct 1993
>
> WHEREAS the said principles are without prejudice to the relevant provisions on access to files directly concerning persons with a specific interest in them;
>
> WHEREAS these principles will have to be implemented in full compliance with the provisions concerning classified information; …
>
> …
>
> [The Commission and the Council] HAVE agreed as follows:
>
> General principle
>
> The public will have the widest possible access to documents held by the Commission and the Council. 'Document' means any written text, whatever its medium, which contains existing data and is held by the Council or the Commission.

The Code of Conduct was geared for applications requesting two main types of documents: applications for published[25] documents and applications for internal documents. The latter, defined as 'documents which are not yet finalised or not intended for publication, irrespective of confidentiality rating'[26] were, understandably, much more coveted than the former.

Concretely, the Code of Conduct established simple administrative proceedings divided into two distinct and separate phases and added a further and subsequent option of recourse to the Union's judicature and/or Ombudsman to finally settle disputes.

The first phase of such proceedings consisted of an initial application for access to specific documents held by the Council or the Commission. Processing of initial applications had quite strict timings as the institution had only 30 days in which to reply. A second phase allowed applicants denied access in the first phase to lodge confirmatory requests. In its confirmatory response to the applicant, the institution—in case it wished to confirm refusal to the document—could rely on the same reasons

[24] The Treaty of Maastricht. For context on what the public might expect to be a right of legitimation of the EU vis-à-vis its citizens, see generally D O'Keefe, 'Union Citizenship' in D O'Keefe and P Towney (eds), *Legal Issues of the Maastricht Treaty* (London, Chancery Press, 1994) 87–107.

[25] No problems there. The applicant was simply told how and where to obtain them.

[26] European Commission, *Access to Commission Documents: A Citizen's Guide* (OPOCE, 1997) 15. The Guide confirms that internal documents were the object of the Code by stating at 6: 'The Commission understands that granting the public access not only to official publications, but also to *internal* documents, is an important component of its more ample information policy, allowing a vision as complete as possible of the activities of the Commission and of the European Union itself' (author's translation).

offered in the initial reply or, as an alternative it could put forth new and distinct reasons (among several typical exceptions listed). Another possibility was that the institution would alter the sense of the initial reply altogether, for example, by granting access to documents previously denied the applicant.

Whenever the second administrative phase was closed with a refusal the applicant would have to choose whether to lodge an action before the Union's courts or to address a complaint to the Ombudsman.

The normal arrangement would have been that as requests for access would be issued, some of the refusals would be challenged before the courts and the EU judicature would clarify both the meaning of and the scope of the Code's rules.

But things were not so simple. To add to the issue of the Code's cryptic form, confusion was soon further enhanced by an odd debut. The subject matter of the proceedings *Netherlands v Council*,[27] (the seminal case of the access litigation before the EU courts) was improbable. To be sure, it concerned the Code of Conduct, but it was not grounded, as would have been expected, on the grievances of an applicant that had been denied a document by the Council or the Commission.[28] Rather, it told the story of the Netherlands joined by the European Parliament voicing, in unison, their dissent with the Council's (alleged) improper choice of legal basis for the new policy.[29]

To unravel the knot and in order to understand the Netherlands' and the Parliaments' action—to understand why an EU institution and a Member State would go the length of challenging the Code's legal basis—one would have to retrace the normative steps that produced the text of the Code of Conduct. Indeed, to observe retrospectively how that first normative instrument was originated is quite revealing.

In truth, before a Code of Conduct even existed, the normative inspiration for an EU access policy had received its primary impetus from another uncommon act, a (mere) Declaration. The Declaration in question centred on the right of access to information, was numbered 17, and attached to the Final Act of the Treaty of Maastricht.[30]

[27] Case C-58/94 *Kingdom of the Netherlands v Council of the European Union* [1996] ECR I–02169.

[28] This came to pass only 3 months later in *Carvel I* when, on 19 May 1994, John Carvel and Guardian Newspapers Ltd sued the Council before the CFI. The respective ruling was issued on 19 October 1995: Case T–194/94 *Carvel and Guardian Newspapers v Council* [1995] ECR II–02765.

[29] To this effect, on 10 February 1994, the Kingdom of the Netherlands, supported by the European Parliament, challenged the Council's option before the ECJ. The Commission and the French Republic sided with the Council, intervening in support of the latter within the proceedings.

[30] On this point, Opinion of Advocate General Maduro, delivered on 18 July 2007 in Case C–64/05P *Sweden v Commission (IFAW)* [2007] ECR I–11389, para 34:

> The status of declarations annexed to Treaties remains relatively unclear. Although Article 311 EC provides that *protocols* annexed to the founding Treaties by common consent of the Member States 'form an integral part thereof' and therefore have the same legal value, the Treaty is silent on declarations. The preponderance of opinion refuses to recognize any binding legal effect for *declarations* included in final acts of Community treaties, seeing in them merely an expression of political commitment. The case law has long refused to take a stand on the matter. Only recently did it extend interpretative scope to declarations, thus falling into line with the accepted view in

From the Parliament's point of view this constituted an original sin and impeded the Code of Conduct from being acknowledged as having been grounded on a robust legal origin.

> Declaration on the Right of Access to Information
>
> The Conference considers that transparency of the decision-making process strengthens the democratic nature of the institutions and the public's confidence in the administration. The Conference accordingly recommends that the Commission submit to the Council, no longer than 1993, a report on measures designed to improve public access to the information available to the institutions.

Yet despite the issues raised regarding the legal significance of this very act, Declaration No 17's effects branched out, unrelentingly, along two substantive fields over which the European public came to gain scrutiny: (1) the decision-making of both Council of Ministers and Commission when acting as executive bodies; and (2) the work of the Council of Ministers when acting in a legislative capacity.

This would give rise to an intricate chronology of many legal acts of disparate nature, form and purpose, as portrayed in the following table.

Table 1.1: The First Chronology Of Access: The 1993 And 1995 Codes Of Conduct

7 February 1992	Treaty of Maastricht is signed Declaration No 17, on access to information is annexed
16 October 1992	Birmingham European Council Declaration 'A Community Close to Its Citizens'
12 December 1992	Edinburgh European Council
22 June 1993	Copenhagen European Council
5 May 1993	Communication of the Commission 'Public Access'
2 June 1993	Communication of the Commission 'Openness in the Community'
1 November 1993	Treaty of Maastricht enters into force Declaration No 17, on access to information is in force
6 December 1993	*Code of Conduct 1993* approved by Parliament and Commission
6 December 1993	Decision amending Council's Internal Rules of Procedure

(continued)

international law Article 31 of the Vienna Convention of the law of Treaties of 23 May 1969 states that a treaty is to be interpreted in the light of its context, which encompasses 'in addition to the text, including its preamble and annexes… any instrument which was made by one or more parties in connection with the conclusion of the treaty and accepted by the other parties as an instrument related to the treaty'. Declarations drawn up by the parties are thus included as bases of interpretation. Does this mean that the interpretation of a treaty thus given by common accord of the State Parties can go as far as to amend the stipulations in it? International law may have already provided a number of illustrations, in so far as the signatory States are a treaty's authentic interpreters, but that cannot be the case in Community law, given the rigid nature of the founding treaties which constitute the constitutional charter of the Communities.

Table 1.1: (*Continued*)

20 December 1993	Decision of the Council adopting the 1993 Code of Conduct
8 February 1994	Decision of the Commission adopting the 1993 Code of Conduct
10 February 1994	Case C–59/94 *Kingdom of the Netherlands and Parliament v Council* is lodged (ruled on 30 April 1996)
19 May 1994	Case T–194/94 *Carvel and Guardian Newspapers v Council* is lodged (ruled on 19 October 1995)
4 March 1994	Communication of the Commission 'Improved Access to Documents'
30 January 1995	Decision of the Council on Classified Information
2 October 1995	*Code of Conduct 1995* (specific to legislative activity of the Council) appears in Press Release
22 September 1995	Case T–174/95 *Svenska v Council* is lodged (ruled on 17 June 1998)
6 December 1996	Decision of the Council extending deadlines for responses
2 October 1997	Treaty of Amsterdam is signed
13 January 1998	Case T–14/98 *Hautala v Council* is lodged (ruled on 19 July 1999)
1 May 1999	Treaty of Amsterdam enters into force

B. Code of 1993—Administrative Tasks

Within eight months of the issuance of Declaration No 17, pursuant to a summit held in Birmingham on 16 October 1992, the European Council issued a second Declaration[31] stating that the Community institutions' work was to be opened to the public. Foreign Ministers and Commission alike were thereby invited to examine proposals stemming from the Danish Government on the subject of openness, and to report on them in the forthcoming European Council meeting that was to be held on 12 December in Edinburgh.

A later and crucial development of the Birmingham–Edinburgh sequence was set in place by a downstream meeting of the European Council in Copenhagen on 22 June 1993. On this occasion the European Council invited the Council of Ministers and the Commission to pursue their work on the basis of the principle of citizens having the fullest possible access to information.

As endorsement, two Communications of the Commission, a first of 5 May 1993 entitled *Public Access to the Institution's Documents*[32] together with a second of 2 June 1993 entitled *Openness in the Community*,[33] laid down a provisional framework to govern access to documents and proposed that concrete parameters for

[31] 'A Community Close to its Citizens' Bull EC 10–1992, 9.
[32] Communication 93/C 156/05 [1993] OJ 1993 C 156, 5.
[33] Communication 93/C 166/04 [1993] OJ 1993 C 166, 4.

public access to the executive activity of European institutions would be established normatively under an inter-institutional agreement.[34]

To enforce the promise, the Council of Ministers and the Commission approved a Code of Conduct on 6 December 1993.[35] The Code of Conduct, in turn, foreshadowed that both institutions would adopt, separately, and on the basis of their individual rules of procedure, Decisions[36] establishing concrete conditions of practical access of the public to their internal documents.

By way of a first step, each institution would resort to a Decision to introduce necessary changes into the existing rules of procedure, if that proved to be necessary.[37] Amending the existing internal rules of procedure was, at the time, more pressing for the Council since, principally, its activity as legislator had to be equated with the forthcoming principles of a more open European Union. The second step consisted of, once again by way of a subsequent Decision of each signatory institution, adopting the Code of Conduct, thus converting its contents into internal rules of each of its signatories.

Despite the one-year term defined for the drafting of a new practical framework—it was scheduled to be completed before 1 January 1994—only the Council of Ministers met the deadline. Accordingly, on 20 December 1993 the Council of Ministers' first concrete Decision on access was published in the Official Journal.[38] The Council's implementing act was soon followed by a corresponding Commission Decision that came about on 8 February 1994.[39]

A practical setback was that the duplication of Decisions was not germane to increase the policy's popularity with the public. Applicants would have to consult each Decision separately to identify, within each institution, the competent authority to which requests should be addressed.[40] However, identical standards were set regarding all other parameters for both institutions: the addressees, the concept of document, the time-limit for receiving a reply,[41] the internal pre-judicial appeal before any refusal became definitive, the list of exceptions to access, the abstract fee that could be charged for copies exceeding 30 pages, and even the two alternate authorities entrusted with the pacification of disappointed applicants.[42]

[34] On their nature, see F Snyder, 'Interinstitutional Agreements: Forms and Constitutional Limitations' in G Winter (ed), *Sources and Categories of European Union Law, A Comparative and Reform Perspective* (Baden-Baden, Nomos, 1996) 453.

[35] Annex 1.

[36] Typical binding acts of EU law described in the EC Treaty of Maastricht, Art 189.

[37] Decision 93/662/EC [1993] OJ L 303 revised the Council's Rules of Procedure.

[38] Decision 93/731, later amended by Decision 2000/527/EC [2000] OJ L 212.

[39] Decision 94/90 [1994] OJ L 46, 58.

[40] On 4 March 1994, a Communication of the Commission 94C/67/03, *Improved access to documents*, was issued, explaining the conditions for implementation of Decision 94/90, and was published in the Official Journal ([1994] OJ C 67, 5).

[41] Regarding deadlines, on 6 December 1996, the Council amended Decision 93/731 through Decision 96/705/EC ([1996] OJ L 325, 19) extending the existing deadline, if necessary, for an additional month.

[42] Indeed, under the new legal framework, definitive refusals originating from either institution could form the object of a complaint to the European Ombudsman or be challenged before the EU courts.

These implementing Decisions added a feature of great significance to the Code: a value for silence. It was determined that the absence of a timely answer was the equivalent of a timely refusal.[43] Thus, institutional inertia could not be opposed an applicant. And if it was, the silence was challengeable in court.

Council Decision 93/731

7(2). Failure to reply to an application within a month of submission shall be equivalent to a refusal, except where the applicant makes a confirmatory application, as referred to above, within the following month.

Commission Decision 94/90

2(4). Failure to reply to an application for access to a document within one month of application being made constitutes an intention to refuse access.

Failure to reply within one month of an application for review being made constitutes a refusal.

Implemented and further supplemented, the 1993 Code stood. It would prove to be—somewhat unexpectedly—a normative instrument that would spectacularly alter the relationship between the EU institutions and their public.

i. A Challenge to the Code of 1993

The dubious nature of the Code of Conduct was challenged almost immediately. Not by the public, to whom it was ultimately beneficial, but as we have stated,[44] by one of the Member States of the Union. Challenge to the Code's legal form was the motive behind the case of *Netherlands v Council*.[45] From the context it is clear that the Parliament had wanted to participate in the Code's drafting and, to be sure, a typical legislative EU act would have implied a role for the Parliament and would have caused less estrangement from the public. And in this light, the purpose of that first calling on the EU judicature is quite evident: an attempt to replace the Code by a Regulation. Through it, the Netherlands and the Parliament proceeded to question both the legitimacy of the Code and of all its subsequent implementing acts.

First, the 1993 Code of Conduct itself was challenged. Secondly, Decision 93/662/EC, introducing the amendment to Article 22 of the Council's rules of procedure that had been deemed necessary before the 1993 Code of Conduct could be adopted, was called into question. More importantly still, the Council's Decision adopting the 1993 Code of Conduct—Decision 93/731—was putatively labelled as a misuse of powers on the Council's part. The main grievance vis-à-vis the 1993 Code of Conduct was that—as a non-binding act—it could not purport to produce legal effects.

[43] See Ch 6.

[44] Case C-58/94 *Netherlands v Council* (n 27).

[45] E Chiti, 'Further Developments of Access to Community Information: Kingdom of the Netherlands v. Council of the European Union' (1996) 2 *European Public Law* 536.

As for the remaining implementing acts,[46] objections centred on the fact that both had been passed by the Council on the basis of Article 151(3) of the EC Treaty. That Treaty Article was the (only existing) basis that allowed the institution to adopt measures of internal organisation. Furthermore, Decision 93/731 had substantively 'copied and pasted' the terms of the 1993 Code of Conduct and, thus, transplanted what was written in the latter into internal rules of the Council.

Against this modus operandi of the institution, the Netherlands, for its part, argued that the Decisions of the Council went beyond the confines of its internal organisation. Since the rules were ultimately beneficial to the public, they were intended to have legal effects outside those (mere institutional) confines. The European Parliament argued instead that the principle of openness of the legislative process and access to connected legislative documents could not be treated as organisational matters purely internal to the institutions. Such a solution—binding Decisions reproducing a non-binding Code of Conduct—represented a misuse of the powers conferred on the institution by Article 151(3) TEC.

As the case before the ECJ progressed, the noise surrounding the challenge to the 1993 Code obscured the fact that yet another Council Decision had ensued, and once more on the basis of its revised rules of procedure. Pending the Council's adoption of more general rules on access, Decision 24/95 of 30 January 1995[47] laid out measures thought necessary to protect classified information held within the General Secretariat of the Council.

> Decision 94/95 of 30 January 1995 of the Secretary General of the Council
>
> Article 1
>
> This Decision lays down rules governing the arrangements for classifying information processed or prepared at the Council General secretariat enabling information so classified to be protected, whatever its origin, medium or stage of completion.
>
> Article 2
>
> 1. Information may be graded in one of the following categories:
>
> (a) SECRET...
> (b) CONFIDENTIEL...
> (c) RESTREINT...
>
> 2. LIMITE and SN documents shall not be classified information within the meaning of this Decision. The references LIMITE and SN shall apply to documents internal to the institution which are not intended for disclosure to the public.
>
> > The same shall apply to other information, for example General Secretariat in-house notes, documents or correspondence, subject, where appropriate, to special treatment where protection is warranted...
> >
> > Disclosure of such documents and information shall require the authorization of the Director-General responsible.

[46] In other words, the amendment to the Council's Internal Rules and the Decision which adopted the 1993 Code of Conduct (93/731).

[47] Later consolidated by Decision 27 July 2000, [2000] OJ C 239, 1–5.

3. Information shall be classified only insofar and for as long as necessary. Where the period of classification of information has not been laid down, a decision on its maintenance or declassification shall be taken after no more than five years.

The Council was once more—and consistently—construing the access policy on the basis of its own internal rules. This early option did not preempt a later understanding—common rules that would overarch all three institutions—from being set in place together with the Commission and the European Parliament.

Six months later, on 30 April 1996, the ECJ condoned the Council's choice. The ECJ proceeded primarily to save the substantive content and form of all three acts under challenge and thus indirectly acknowledged the appropriateness of the legal basis of Decision 94/95 as well.

Case C–58/94 *Kingdom of the Netherlands v Council*

24. … An action for annulment must be available [only] in case of all measures adopted by the institutions which are intended to have legal effects.

26. … The Code of Conduct merely foreshadows subsequent decisions intended, unlike the Code, to have legal effects.

27. … The Code is an act which is the expression of purely voluntary coordination therefore not intended in itself to have legal effects [and, as such, an act without legal effects may not be annulled, or, for that matter challenged].

38. … There is nothing to prevent rules on the internal organization of the work of an institution having such effects

40. … The Council is not guilty of any misuse of power.

Principally, the ECJ ruled that at the time there was no better alternative. Common rules that would straddle several institutions were certainly desirable but were not the *condition sine qua non* for a policy to commence. By way of the ruling what existed was preserved yet at the same time all players (the public, the institutions and Member States alike) were invited to work together (rather than against each other) to improve the policy's normative architecture. After all, an individual's right was under construction.

Hence, the prudent authority of the Court saved the policy and discouraged other applicants from challenging the corresponding implementing Decision of the Commission. Mollified by the ruling and in a constructive *volte face* the Parliament adopted the Code of Conduct,[48] becoming its third signatory institution.

Without intending to demean the ECJ's seminal ruling on these matters, with the benefit of hindsight one may emphasise that it is also true that the condoning of the 1993 Code of Conduct's legal basis by the ECJ on 30 April 1996 was greatly

[48] The European Parliament adopted the Code of Conduct by Decision 97/632 of 10 July 1997 [1997] OJ L 263, 25–29. On the details of the procedure, see A Guggenbuhl, 'A Miracle Formula or an Old Powder in New Packaging' in V Deckmyn and I Thomson (eds), *Openness and Transparency in the European Union* (Maastricht, EIPA, 1988) 12: 'It did so while at the same time adapting the exception protecting deliberations by stating that access to its documents may be refused in order to protect the confidentiality of deliberations of political groups or Parliament bodies meeting in camera. Access may also be denied to protect the confidentiality of the relevant services of the Parliament's secretariat'.

prompted by concurrent contemporary litigation, the *Carvel I* case, that had just taken place before the CFI.[49] Those proceedings had been concluded on 19 October 1995 (six months prior to the ECJ's ruling in *Netherlands v Council*). Therefore—regarding a request for access to documents pertaining to the Council's legislative activity—the public had already relied successfully before the CFI on the very legal basis that was also being challenged at ECJ level.

With its basis salvaged by the ECJ, the first objective of Declaration No 17—EU rules on public access to the executive activity of the Council and the Commission—was thus completed in less than two years (February 1992–December 1993). The next step in the normative development of access would take place in October 1997, by way of Article 255 of the Treaty of Amsterdam.

Table 1.2: Parallel Proceedings

	Lodged	Ruled on	Duration
Proceedings Before the CFI Case T–194/94 *Carvel and Guardian Newspapers v Council*	19 May 1994	19 October 1995	17 months
Proceedings before the ECJ Case C–59/94 *Kingdom of the Netherlands and Parliament v Council*	10 February 1994	30 April 1996	26 months

ii. Beyond the Code: Achievements of the Early Case Law

During the period that elapsed between the enactment of the 1993 Code of Conduct and the entry into force of the Treaty of Amsterdam on 1 May 1999, while not abundant,[50] the case law became an indispensable cornerstone of the access policy. Indeed, among other important clarifications, two of its early contributions are—in this context—particularly noteworthy since they inspired subsequent normative developments to the 1993 Code of Conduct.

The first contribution came forth in the *Svenska* ruling and centred on the scope, over all three pillars of the Union, of the competence of the EU judicature to rule on requests for access to documents.[51] It was thus clarified, as early as 17 June 1998, that no area of Union activity was immune to the openness obligations. The second

[49] Case T-194/94 *Carvel v Council* (n 28).

[50] C Naome, 'The Case-Law of the Court of Justice and of the Court of First Instance on Transparency from Carvel to Hautala II (1995–2001)' in V Deckmyn (ed), *Increasing Transparency in the EU?* (Maastricht, EIPA, 2002) 147–98.

[51] Case T–174/95 *Svenskajournalistforbundet v Council* [1998] ECR II–2289. See Ch 4. On this issue, see M Den Boer 'Steamy Windows: Transparency and Openness in Justice and Home Affairs' in Deckmyn and Thomson, *Openness and Transparency in the European Union* EIPA (n 48) 103.

contribution came in the *Hautala I* ruling[52] and founded the concept of partial[53] access. In that case, the CFI considered that, as a general rule, when access to any document was requested, the institutions were bound to consider, for each one, if it was feasible to expurgate the documents, or, literally, to 'separate out confidential parts' that would remain withheld, and to release the remaining parts to the public.

C. Code of 1995—Legislative Tasks

While it is indisputable that the overall activity of the Council of Ministers was greatly affected by the novel paradigm of public access to the internal documents of the European institutions, it is important to point out that the abovementioned Code of Conduct of 1993 was not an isolated achievement. In truth, chronologically, it was only the first instrument of its kind to forge practical rules of public access to the Council of Ministers' documents. Besides opening up the executive activity of institutions to the world, Declaration No 17 implicitly required the Union to produce new rules for public access in yet another part of institutional life: law-making.

Once again returning to the developments of the Edinburgh European Council, of 12 December 1992,[54] the Conclusions thereby produced, *Conclusions of the EEC on transparency and implementation of the Birmingham Declaration*, as well as addressing other subjects,[55] touched more specifically upon the role of the Council of Ministers as legislator. Six new principles were laid down that were to serve as guidelines for amendment of the Council of Ministers' rules of procedure in order to permit access to documents related to its legislative role.

As we have mentioned, the trumpeted revision ensued one year later, on 6 December 1993, by way of Decision 93/662.[56] The changes to Articles 5 and 7.5 in particular gave way to the drafting of a detailed procedure concerning the authorisation of the release of records of votes and votes within legislative acts.[57] What is less known is that almost two years later, on 2 October 1995, (17 days before the *Carvel I*[58] ruling on access to Council documents related to its legislative activity was rendered), a Decision of the Council (that was not published in the Official Journal) gave rise to a new Code of Conduct, specific to the institution's legislative role. This Code is referred to as the Code of Conduct of 1995.[59] Its main accomplishment was that the

[52] Case T–14/98 *Hautala v Council* [1999] ECR II-2489. The action was lodged as early as 13 January 1998 and the ruling was issued on 19 July 1999, 2 months after the entry into force of the Treaty of Amsterdam.

[53] See Ch 4.

[54] Portrayed within Table 1.1.

[55] The Council's executive activity.

[56] [1993] OJ L 304, 1–8.

[57] For further detail, see Guggenbuhl, 'A Miracle Formula or an Old Powder in New Packaging' (n 48) 17.

[58] Case T-194/94 *Carvel v Council* (n 28).

[59] Available in *Basic Texts on Transparency Concerning the Activities of the Council of the EU* (Luxembourg, Publications Office, Luxembourg, 2000) 53. The Code of 1995 is only marginally referred to in the literature; see generally M Nentwich, 'The EU Intergovernmental Conference 1996/1997' in A Follesdal and P Koslowski (eds), *Democracy and the European Union* (Berlin and New York, Springer, 1998) 93.

rules that had been previously amended in order for records of votes to be released were thereby extended to the statements and the minutes relating to the adoption of legislative acts of the Council.

Now the Union had two Codes of Conduct to regulate public access to the documents of the Council and the Commission, but as the second Code of Conduct of 1995 had been adopted by way of a Decision that was not published in the Official Journal, it is hardly surprising that it was never cited as the legal basis of any subsequent litigation.[60] In practice, the Code appeared only as part of a press release of the 1871st Council meeting (General Affairs) held in Luxembourg on 2 October 1995. No legal consequence was imposed vis-à-vis the Code due to its lack of publication, and in fact none was ever requested:

> Code of Conduct on Public Access to the Minutes and Statements in the Minutes of the Council acting as Legislator
>
> A (4) The Council is in favour of public access, in general, to the statements which it enters in its minutes when adopting legislative acts. When adopting such acts, the Council will therefore decide, in principle, that these statements are not covered by the obligation of professional secrecy, save in cases where, at the request of one of its members, the Council establishes it does not have the simple majority required by Article 5(1) of its rules of procedure to waive that obligation.
>
> In the case of a statement by one or more members of the Council, the Council will seek the agreement of the author(s) of the statement before deciding to make it available to the public...
>
> B (1) When adopting the minutes of its minutes, the Council will systematically examine the question of whether to make public the references to documents before the Council* and the decisions taken or conclusions reached by the Council which are contained in the minutes regarding the final adoption of its legislative acts. As regards statements in the minutes, the decision taken by the Council when adopting the legislation will determine whether they can be made available to the public, without prejudice of the Council Decision of 20 December 1993 on public access to Council documents.
>
> * The decision to make minutes public does not mean that the documents referred to therein will be made available to the public.[61]

Having remained for the most part in near oblivion, it did, nonetheless, leave a legacy: the role of the Council as legislator would always require separate attention[62] within access' general framework. The second objective of Declaration No 17 (access to

[60] On the internal institutional practice pursuant to the 1995 Code of Conduct, see H Brunmayer, 'The Council's Policy on Transparency' in Deckmyn and Thomson (n 48) 71.

[61] 10204/95 (Presse 271, 2 October 1995) 15–18.

[62] See section IV.C below for our comments on Art 207(3) TEC; Art 6 of the Preamble to Regulation 1049/2001 (Transparency Regulation) and Art 7 of the Preamble of Regulation 1367/2006 (Aarhus Regulation). Whilst the leading cases remain Joined Cases C-39/05P & C-52/05P *Sweden and Turco v Council* [2008] ECR I-04723, paras 45 and 46 and also Case C-350/12P *Council v Sophie in't Veld* [not yet reported] this area has attracted interest from the commentators. See, for an overview, S Lea and PJ Cardwell, 'Transparency Requirements in the Course of a Legislative Procedure, Council v Access Info Europe' (2015) 21(1) *European Public Law* 61–80. For the environmental area, see also T Schomerus, 'Access to Information on Legislative Proceedings: Case Note on the Judgement of the Court (2nd Chamber) of 18 July 2013, C-515/11' (2013) 10(4) *Journal for Environmental and Planning Law* 397–401.

documents of the institutions when acting in a legislative capacity) was thus implemented in just under four years (February 1992–October 1995). Ten months later, the Treaty of Amsterdam would further the normative development.

IV. TREATY ARTICLES FOR ACCESS

A. Article 1 TEU

As the first EU Treaty to touch upon the subject, the Treaty of Amsterdam (entered into force on 1 May 1999) embraced the access policy with remarkable enthusiasm. The institutions were so eager to engage the public that their commitment was drafted into the very first Article of the TEU.

> Article 1 TEU
>
> This Treaty marks a new stage in the process of creating an ever closer union among the peoples of Europe, in which decisions are taken as openly as possible and as closely as possible to the citizen

The principal accomplishment of the words chosen to ground the policy in the TEU was that the reference to the obligation of openness was made within an ample context: 'the Union'. In doing so, the Article normatively overcame the (previously alleged) insulation from public scrutiny of the second and third pillars of Union activity.[63] Two further articles in the TEC would complete the novel constitutional framework, both calling for sub-constitutional, joint normative detail from the Parliament, the Commission and the Council. Access was thus gifted with a constitutional ceiling to supplement the 1993 and 1995 Codes of Conduct and promised a new floor of ordinary legislative status.

B. Article 255 TEC

In contrast to the TEU's systematic option of placing access at the forefront of the constitutional text, the positioning of the theme in the TEC, albeit positive and novel, was less dramatic:

> It is striking that the citizen's right to obtain information on the Union's decision-making procedures, which from the perspective of democracy can be considered a highly fundamental matter, is regulated in a Title of the EC Treaty containing certain provisions which are 'common to several institutions'. The decision to place it here [Article 255] rather than for example in the section dealing with citizenship of the Union or general principles of the Union seems to have been an attempt to deny the fundamental status of the individual's right to information or to place it anywhere near on a par with, for example, the general principles laid down in Article 6. Instead the implication is still that the right of access

[63] See Ch 4. Prior to the normative (statutory) clarification, the issue of the transversal scope of access had been resolved in the case law by way of *Svenska* (n 51).

to documents is a matter concerning the internal functioning of a number of institutions themselves.[64]

Article 255 TEC

1. Any citizen of the Union, and any natural or legal person residing or having its registered office in a Member State, shall have a right of access to European Parliament, Council and Commission documents, subject to the principles and the conditions to be defined in accordance with paragraphs 2 and 3.

2. General principles and limits on grounds of public or private interest governing this right of access to documents shall be determined by the Council, acting in accordance with the procedure referred to in Article 189b within two years of the entry into force of the Treaty of Amsterdam.

3. Each institution referred to above shall elaborate in its own Rules of Procedure specific provisions regarding access to its documents.

Article 255 acted, as we have mentioned, as a supplement to the 1993 and 1995 Codes of Conduct that were still in force. Moreover, it is important to observe that Article 255 was accompanied by a separate Declaration to the TEC, Declaration No 35.[65]

While the Treaty Article was necessary and felicitous, the Declaration was rather less so. It might even be said that it was a catalyst of confusion. This holds true for two reasons: the first, its timing, and the second, the choice of wording it employed.

Declaration on Article 255 of the Treaty establishing the European

Community (ex 191a TEC)

The Conference agrees that the principles and conditions referred to in Article 191a(1) of the Treaty establishing the European Community will allow a Member State to request the Commission or the Council not to communicate to third parties a document originating from that State without its prior agreement.

Regarding the poorly chosen timing of the Declaration, it must not be forgotten that neither constitutional instrument (Treaty of Amsterdam or its Declaration No 35) revoked[66] the Codes of Conduct. Moreover, the Treaty limited itself to a mere enunciation of a general policy that was yet to be detailed. The existing Codes of Conduct, on the contrary, consisted of rules to be applied immediately: mainly detailed procedural rules about how requests for access were to be concretely dealt with.

It is simple to defend that the efficacy of the Declaration was clearly subject to a condition: that the Council, the Commission and the Parliament would, within a period of two years, determine *new* rules for access. In the same way it is simple to state (today) that it should have been understood that it was to shape the new rules for which the Declaration was intended. But because the 1993 Code of Conduct was formally still in force at the time the Declaration was enacted, the new measure

64 D Curtin, 'Democracy, Transparency and Political Participation' in Deckmyn and Thomson (n 48).

65 On the legal status of Declarations, see n 30 above.

66 This position is corroborated by Case T–191/99 *Petrie a.o. v Commission* [2001] ECR II-3677, para 36.

(in spite of its 'not yet' status) conflicted philosophically with the existing author's rule. Under such an arrangement the institutions were not empowered to disclose documents originating from third parties. Rather, the party requesting access was required to address its request directly to the author of the document.[67] The confluence of the Declaration (meant to govern the future) and the author's rule (which governed the present) engendered public suspicion, and suspicion within access—a context that purports to encourage transparency—is never productive.

As for the wording employed, given the context in which the institutions held the final word over self-produced documents only, the advent of a Declaration making references to the possibility that institutions might choose to release 'documents *originating from the Member States*' was, literally, chaotic. It brought on suspicion that some documents held by the institutions (at least those originating in the Member State) might—in the immediate future—become the subject of new rules.

Doctrine[68] was quick to protest—legitimately—that although a hiatus (that would last until the new rules came into force) was to be reckoned with, the mere confluence of the 1993 Code of Conduct, and Declaration No 35 inevitably raised doubts as to the meaning of a phrase of Article 255(1) of the Treaty itself: 'European Parliament, Council and Commission Documents'. The main point in issue was whether the Article's scope overarched incoming documents. That it was—at any rate—directed at the self-produced documents of the institutions was fairly clear.

At its early stage, the judicature kept a prudent distance from this doctrinal debate. In fact, while the 1993 Code of Conduct was in force the author's rule was consistently and simply upheld. Thus, in practice, because of the 'not yet' bound on its enforceability, Declaration No 35 was ignored. Accordingly, no comfort[69] was given to the hypothesis that some of the incoming documents might have been withdrawn from the 1993 Code's exclusionary rule and placed (too soon) under a novel procedure as sketched out in Declaration No 35.

Only at a much later stage would the judicature rule on this subject,[70] and as a result two crucial issues raised regarding the Declaration were finally clarified: namely its position in the hierarchy of EU law and the meaning of the phrase to 'to request the Commission or the Council'.

As a final remark regarding the normative contribution of Article 255, its part 2 foreshadowed comprehensive normative detail of ordinary level that was to replace the 1993 and 1995 Codes of Conduct within a period of two years. As a result, a Regulation numbered 1049/2001 of 30 May 2001 would become applicable from 3 December 2001.[71] Furthermore, the article's part 3 confirmed that it was through amendments to each institution's rules of procedure that, if necessary, specific practical provisions should be laid down.

[67] See Ch 2.
[68] Curtin, 'Democracy, Transparency and Political Participation' (n 64) 115.
[69] Case T–47/01 *Co-Frutta v Commission* [2003] ECR II–4441, para 59.
[70] By way of an interpretative ruling rendered, and that had as its object the new, common rules that the Treaty of Amsterdam had promised; Case C-135/11P *IFAW* [not reported].
[71] See section VII of this chapter for our discussion on Regulation 1049/2001.

C. Article 207(3) TEC

From another angle the Treaty of Amsterdam, via Article 207(3) TEC focusing specifically on the Council's *legislative* activity, supplemented the simple determinations of the 1995 Code of Conduct. This article engendered a revision of the Council's rules of procedure with a view to making public the records of its votes, minutes and statements.

> Article 207(3) TEC
>
> Whenever the Council is to act in its legislative capacity, the results of votes and explanations of votes as well as the statements in the minutes shall be made public.
>
> The Council is to itself define the cases in which it is to be regarded as acting in its legislative capacity.

In the same way that this had been significant for the *executive* activity, discussed above, the term 'whenever' extends the obligation laid down in the Article to legislative activity in all areas of Union competence, for example, within all three pillars, and does so textually.[72] As a result, the reining in of all European fields of activity under the cloak of access brought unity to the Union's policy and simplified its understanding by the public.

Nevertheless, and mostly because of the preponderant role of the EU courts, the material significance of an option laid down as Treaty-based, and therefore at the constitutional level, did not entirely live up to its constitutional clothes. First, since the constitutional rules were not the original stimulus of access, when they did come forth, the case law had been allowed a head start, and therefore an upper hand. Three-and-a-half years of prior litigation with accomplishments of the calibre of partial access are a significant inheritance, difficult to deflect or outshine. Secondly, the very first time an applicant attempted to use the constitutional leverage, the Court of First Instance postponed any concrete utility of that normative novelty. It ruled that the newly introduced Treaty articles did not have direct effect.[73] As such, without the adoption of subsequent legislative measures of ordinary status that the constitutional framework merely foreshadowed, Article 255 (at that moment) could not be (innovatively) used in court.[74] Thirdly, under such (suspended until the

[72] See Ch 4.

[73] In the fluctuating language of the Court, the wording employed is 'not directly applicable'; *Petrie* (n 66) para 34.

[74] The deliberate choice of not drafting the exceptions to the principle also at constitutional level was interpreted (too) enthusiastically by the applicant in *Petrie* (n 66); *cf* Guggenbuhl (n 48) 16, offers a more conservative reading of that absence:

> It is worth noting that while providing such general rules for the European Union and recognizing the fundamental nature of the right of Access to Documents, article 255.2 TEC does not at the same time make provision for the necessary exceptions. By not eliminating the decisions on the exceptions—both the current decisions [93/731 and 94/90] and the one to be adopted [ex Article 255 TEC] by the Council, article 255.2 TEC actually adds a layer of legal reference for the free access to documents. Transparency in this sense is not very well served.

legislative hiatus is overcome) status it was impossible to predict from the Treaty's scant words[75] if the new rules that it called for could alter the principle that annulment was access' ceiling.

Like a suddenly deflating balloon, the enthusiasm for the constitutional basis shrank and quickly departed.

Case T–191/99 *Petrie a.o. v Commission*

34 Contrary to the applicants' contention, Article 1, second paragraph, EU and Article 255 EC are not directly applicable. In this regard, as is clear from the judgment in Case 26/62 *Van Gend en Loos* [1963] ECR 1, the criteria for deciding whether a Treaty provision is directly applicable are that the rule should be clear and unconditional, in the sense that its implementation must not be subject to any substantive condition, and that its implementation must not depend on the adoption of subsequent measures which either the Community institutions or the Member States may take in the exercise of a discretionary power of assessment.

35 In this case, Article 1, second paragraph, EU is not clear in the sense required by the case law cited. It is likewise obvious that Article 255 EC is, by virtue of paragraphs 2 and 3 thereof, not unconditional and that its implementation is dependent on the adoption of subsequent measures. The determination of general principles and limits which, on grounds of public or private interest, govern exercise of the right of access to documents is a matter entrusted to the Council in the exercise of its legislative discretion.

36 It follows that the entry into force of Article 1, second paragraph, EU and Article 255 EC did not automatically render inoperative the provisions contained in Decision 94/90.

37 The applicants' argument that Decision 94/90 must be construed in accordance with the principles set out in Article 255 EC cannot be accepted. Because Article 255 EC does not lay down an unconditional obligation, the Commission could not, in advance of a determination by the Community legislature of the principles and limits to govern application of the article, deduce from it criteria for interpreting the provisions of Decision 94/90 that limit the right of access to documents.

38 It follows that the applicants' plea alleging failure to comply with Article 255(1) EC and Article 1, second paragraph, EU must be rejected as being unfounded.

D. Article 41 and 42 of the Charter of Fundamental Rights

The arsenal of access' soft constitutionality was not yet complete. Another atypical provision would concur in the design of the odd supra-legislative status it was accorded: the Charter of Fundamental Rights. The Charter, proclaimed on 7 December 2000, added two relevant articles to the normative status of access. Article 41

[75] On this point, see U Oberg, 'Public Access to Documents after the Entry into Force of the Treaty of Amsterdam: Much Ado about Nothing?' (1998) 2(8) European Integration Office On-line Papers 2 http://eiop.or.at/eiop/pdf/1998-008.pdf.

concerning the principle of sound administration, and Article 42 specifically dedicated to access to documents:

> Article 41
>
> Right to Good Administration
>
> 1. Every person has the right to have his or her affairs handled impartially, fairly and within a reasonable time by the institutions and bodies of the Union.
>
> 2. This right includes:
>
> — The right of every person to be heard, before any individual measure which would affect him or her adversely is taken;
> — The right of every person to have access to his or her file, while respecting the legitimate interests of confidentiality and of professional and business secrecy;
> — The obligation of the administration to give reasons for its decisions.
>
> 3. Every person has the right to have the Community make good any damage caused by its institutions or by its servants in the performance of their duties, in accordance with the general principles common to the laws of the Member States.
>
> 4. Every person may write to the institutions of the Union in one of the languages of the Treaties and must have an answer in the same language.
>
> Article 42
>
> Right of Access to Documents
>
> Any citizen of the Union, and any natural or legal person residing, or having its registered office in a Member State, has a right of access to documents of the institutions' agencies; in whatever form they are produced.

The new reference signified a further layer of institutional commitment, no doubt, and it is also true that in its aftermath applicants would add references to the Charter in their written submissions to the EU courts.[76] Articles 41 and 42 of the Charter were often pleaded together and were considered as intimately linked. However, there was an underlying *non sequitur* element that was inescapable: inclusion in the Charter (except for the inclusion of agencies alongside the Council, the Commission and the Parliament as parties to whom documents might be requested) brought no substantive improvement to the practical conditions already provided for in the 1993 Code, in the implementing Decisions or in Article 255 TEC. In this sense of practical neutrality, the concurrence of the Charter could be viewed as yet another dispersive, non-binding[77] red herring[78] in the normative development of this peculiar right.

[76] See generally G de Burca, 'The Drafting of the Charter of Fundamental Rights' (2001) 26 *European Law Review* 126. See also D Curtin and J Mendes, 'Article 42' in S Peers, T Hervey, J Kenner and A Ward (eds), *The EU Charter of Fundamental Rights, A Commentary* (Munich/Oxford/Baden-Baden, Beck/Hart/Nomos, 2014) 1099–119.

[77] See Ch 3. The Charter has since acquired binding legal status, namely with the entry into force of the Treaty of Lisbon.

[78] The ECJ has recently ruled that the Charter, and specifically Art 47 is unable to alter the nature of judicial review in an access to documents setting: Case 127/13P *Strack v Commission* (n 18) paras 145–47:

V. A CHALLENGE TO POST-AMSTERDAM IMPLEMENTING DECISIONS, PRE-REGULATION 1049/2001

In the aftermath of the Treaty of Amsterdam, access would not be granted either peace or stability. With a Regulation yet to come, the institutions were faced with a prior and more immediate task, the adoption of preparatory measures. It should be noted that in the meantime (December 1999) two Presidency Reports were adopted[79] within the Conclusions of the European Council meeting in Helsinki. They centred on the subject of developing the EU's means for military and non-military crisis management within the framework of a strengthened European security and defence policy. In order to implement these Conclusions, the Council (of Ministers) adopted three further Decisions on access.

The first was Decision 2000/23/EC[80] on the improvement of information on the Council's legislative activities and the public register of Council documents; the second was Decision 2000/C239/01[81] of the Secretary General of the Council/High Representative for the Common Foreign and Security Policy on measures for the protection of classified information applicable to the General Secretariat of the Council; and the third was Decision 2000/527/EC,[82] amending Decision 93/731/EC.

As had been the case with Decision 93/731 and Decision 94/95, their legal basis was the Council's powers of internal organisation.

Decision 2000/23/EC

Preamble...

2) Without prejudice to Council Decision 93/731/EC of 20 December 1993 on public access to Council documents(1) and to the principles and limits governing the right of access to documents to be adopted under Article 255 of the Treaty establishing the European Community:

— further efforts should be made to improve information on the Council's legislative activities as defined in Article 6 of its Rules of Procedure,

145 According to settled case-law, the Courts of the European Union cannot, in principle, issue orders to an EU institution without encroaching upon the prerogatives of the administration (see judgments in *Verzyck v Commission*, 225/82, EU:C:1983:165, paragraph 19, and *Campogrande v Commission*, C-62/01 P, EU:C:2002:248, paragraph 43).

146 Thus, contrary to the appellant's assertions, the EGC was right to hold, in paragraph 90 of the judgment under appeal, that, in accordance with Article 264 TFEU, it was only open to it to annul the contested act. In so far as the appellant's argument is based on Article 266 TFEU, it must be observed that that provision also does not provide for the possibility of issuing orders to the institutions.

147 That finding cannot be called into question by the appellant's arguments based on Article 47 of the Charter, since that article is not intended to change the system of judicial review laid down by the Treaties (see judgment in *Inuit Tapiriit Kanatami and Others v Parliament and Council*, C-583/11 P, EU:C:2013:625, paragraph 97).

[79] Annex IV to the Presidency Conclusions.
[80] Decision of 6 December 1999.
[81] Decision of 27 July 2000.
[82] Decision of 4 August 2000.

— measures should be taken to enhance further the performance of the public register of Council documents accessible on the Internet (http://ue.eu.int) since 1 January 1999,
— the Council's internal procedures for public access to its documents should be further rationalised by using information technologies and avoiding excessive bureaucracy.

Decision 2000/C239/01

Preamble...

(2) It is (therefore) necessary to amend Decision No 24/95 of the Secretary-General on measures for the protection of classified information applicable to the General Secretariat of the Council with regard to the grades of classification by adding the grade 'TRÈS SECRET/TOP SECRET' and by reinforcing internal arrangements, it being understood that this amendment is provisional pending the adoption of more complete measures in the near future.

Decision 2000/527/EC

Preamble ...

(6) Since the security and defence of the Union or of one or more of its Member States or military and non-military crisis management represent public interests which Decision 93/731/EC(2) is intended to protect, this should be specifically mentioned among the reasons justifying refusal of access to a document...

Decision 93/731 is hereby amended...

Decision 2000/23/EC(3) is hereby amended as follows:

1. The following shall be added as the second subparagraph of Article 2: 'The public register of Council documents contains no reference to documents classified TRÈS SECRET/TOP SECRET or SECRET or CONFIDENTIEL within the meaning of the Decision of the Secretary-General of the Council/High Representative for Common Foreign and Security Policy of 27 July 2000 on measures for the protection of classified information applicable to the General Secretariat of the Council, on matters concerning the security and defence of the Union or of one or more of its Member States or on military or non-military crisis management.'

As a consequence, another inter-institutional conflict took place. The Parliament—once—again came forth, insisting that normative developments to access should be made through common Regulations instead of by various Decisions of each institution. Accordingly, the Parliament attempted to have two of the Council's three implementing Decisions annulled. On 23 October 2000, an action for annulment was directed at Council Decision 2000/C239/01 and at Council Decision 2000/527. Case C–387/00 *Parliament v Council*[83] much resembled a behavioural replica of the earlier *Netherlands v Council*.

Case C–387/00 *European Parliament v Council of the European Union*

[83] Case C–387/00 *European Parliament v Council of the European Union* [2000] OJ C 355, 15.

The Parliament Claimed:

...

Infringement of an essential procedural requirement: the Legal basis for the Decisions at issue is inappropriate. Since Article 255 EC enshrined for the first time in primary legislation rights of access to documents of the Parliament, the Council and the Commission, the Council no longer has power to regulate such matters under the head of its powers of internal organization. Article 28(1) and Article 41(1) of the Treaty on European Union explicitly provide that rights of access extend also to documents concerning the common foreign and security policy and cooperation in the fields of justice and home affairs.

The obligation to lay down general principles and limits upon the rights of access to documents in accordance with the codecision procedure (Article 255(2) EC) is, admittedly, one that is to be complied with within a period of two years. However, that obligation came into effect as soon as the treaty of Amsterdam came into force, which necessarily excludes the adoptions of any unilateral measures laying down such general principles and limits.

Breach of the obligation to cooperate in good faith (Article 10 EC): despite the fact that the Commission adopted a proposal for a regulation, in accordance with Article 255(2) EC, and that the Parliament expected to collaborate closely with the Council and the Commission under the codecision procedure, the Council adopted the measures at issue without the knowledge of the Parliament.

Breach of the principle of institutional equilibrium: by adopting its decision unilaterally and without having regard to the procedures laid down in the Treaty, the Council also breached the principle of institutional equilibrium.

On 22 March 2002, the action was closed by an order of the Court of Justice and removed from the register without proceeding to the stage of a ruling. It should not be forgotten that although 18 months separated the closure of Case C–387/00 from its proposal, Regulation 1049/2001, enacted on 30 May 2001 (seven months after the lodging of the action), came into force on 3 December 2001, with the Parliament as one of its authors and as a consolidation measure[84] of all prior initiatives on the access topic.

By way of conclusion, with its origin in the Treaty of Amsterdam and its convergence at the moment from which Regulation 1049/2001 became applicable, a second chronology would unfold and assume relevance. It is summarised in Table 1.3.

[84] Regulation 1049/2001, Preamble (3). See generally S Peers, 'The New Regulation on Access to Documents: A Critical Analysis' (2001) 21(I) *Yearbook of European Law* 385–442. Regarding the institutional positions see:

1. Explanatory Memorandum to the Proposal for a Regulation of the European Parliament and the Council regarding public access to the European Parliament Council and Commission Documents (COM (2000) 30 final–COD 2000/0032).

II. Proposal for a European Parliament and Council Regulation regarding Public Access to Parliament, Council and Commission Documents, OJ C 177E, 26.6.2000; COM (2000) 30; Bull. 2–2000, point 1.9.2.

Table 1.3: The Second Chronology of Access: the Treaty of Amsterdam and Beyond

2 October 1997	Treaty of Amsterdam is signed
1 May 1999	Treaty of Amsterdam enters into force
25 August 1999	Case T–191/99 *Petrie v Commission* is lodged (ruled on 11 December 2001)
December 1999	Helsinki European Council Presidency reports on military and non-military crisis management
6 December 1999	Council Decision improvement of information on legislative activities and public register of documents
27 July 2000	Council Decision on the protection of classified information
4 August 2000	Council Decision amending Decision 93/731/EC
23 October 2000	Case C–387/00 *Parliament v Council* is lodged (removed from the register on 22 March 2002)
7 December 2000	Charter of Fundamental Rights is proclaimed
26 February 2001	Treaty of Nice is signed
30 May 2001	Regulation 1049/2001 is enacted
28 November 2001	European Parliament Bureau Decision on Access to Documents
29 November 2001	Council Decision 2004/840/EC
3 December 2001	Regulation 1049/2001 is applicable
5 December 2001	Commission Decision 2001/937/EC, ECSC, Euratom

VI. POST-AMSTERDAM ACHIEVEMENTS OF THE CASE LAW, PRE REGULATION 1049/2001

With the Treaty of Amsterdam in force, but before the advent of a Regulation to govern access, the principal contribution of the case law to the debate was the clarification that the Treaty articles, on their own, would be accorded no direct effect. This statement of the GC was issued in the *Petrie*[85] ruling. As a consequence of the ruling, in spite of their co-existence alongside the Treaty articles, the 1993 and 1995 Codes of Conduct would stand until a Regulation replaced them.

VII. A GENERAL FRAMEWORK—REGULATION 1049/2001

The month of May of the year 2001 is a landmark in the access theme. And it might be said that the enactment of Regulation (EC) No 1049/2001 of the European Parliament and of the Council of 30 May 2001 regarding public access to European Parliament, Council and Commission documents (hereinafter Regulation

[85] Case T-191/99 *Petrie a.o. v Commission* (n 66).

1049/2001)[86] embodied, on many fronts, a renaissance of the access policy. It was a keenly awaited legislative instrument of ordinary status and represents a common and thorough response of the Parliament, the Council and the Commission to the access theme.

As a first comment, Regulation 1049/2001 proved to be notably resilient. It would endure well over a decade of growing case law, the entry into force of two subsequent Treaties (Nice and Lisbon) and a failed attempt at reform.[87] Indeed, as we write, in 2016, it is still in force.[88] This resilience may alternatively reflect the appropriateness of the solutions adopted within Regulation 1049/2001 or could also signify that once a first Regulation was adopted the institutions were unable to agree again to further reform.

Although this legislation will be discussed in detail over the subsequent chapters, we will briefly comment here on its three more important normative contributions. First, in relation to the Treaty-based provisions, the advent of an implementing act under the typical form of a Regulation filled the normative gap that the Treaty of Amsterdam had opened. Secondly, its dimension was confined to an attractive six-page format, which in spite of its discreet length, spanned not only the background to the Regulation but also purpose, beneficiaries and scope; exceptions; relations with the Member States; procedure; treatment of sensitive documents; registers; annual reports; implementation; and even the relationship with the historical archives of the EEC and the EEA. Thirdly, it was a chance to start anew: a rare opportunity to normatively embrace selected achievements of the prior case law (partial access) and a good excuse to innovate on[89] or even discard altogether[90] less cherished characteristics of the pre-2001 model. Injunctive relief (understood as the power of the judicature to address (positive) orders to the institutions) was kept outside the EU scheme and was simply not mentioned.

As a final remark, Regulation 1049/2001 encouraged conforming self-regulation on the part of each institution by way of amendments to existing rules of procedure.[91] Accordingly, the Regulation's three signatory institutions effected amendments to their rules of procedure. On 28 November 2001, the Parliament was the first institution to comply and adopted Bureau Decision on public access to European Parliament documents.[92] One day later, on 29 November 2001, the Council adopted Decision 2004/840/EC.[93] The Commission, for its part, adopted Decision 2001/937/EC, ECSC Euratom, on 5 December 2001.[94]

[86] [2001] OJ L 145.

[87] See generally HR Kranenborg, 'Is it Time to Revise the European Regulation on Public Access to Documents?' (2006) 12(2) *European Public Law* 251–74. See also I Harden, 'The Revision of Regulation 1049/2001 on Public Access to Documents (2009) 2 *European Public Law* 239–56.

[88] On this resilience, see M Maes, 'Le droit d'accès aux documents des institutions europénnes: ou en est la revision du règlement 1049/2001?' (2014) 3 *Revue du Droit de L'Union Européenne* 475–97.

[89] Innovation occurred regarding: active legitimacy; the classification of purpose of inspections, investigations and audits as a public interest exception, and more stringent deadlines were introduced.

[90] The so-called author's rule was set aside.

[91] Regulation 1049/2001, Art 17 of the Preamble, and Art 18 of its core.

[92] [2001] OJ C 374, 1.

[93] [2001] OJ L 313, 40.

[94] [2001] OJ L 345, 94.

A. Selected Achievements of the Prior Case Law Drafted into Regulation 1049/2001

It is also important to emphasise that Regulation 1049/2001 was not a mere theoretical and self-important normative exercise. In fact, two case law-originated principles were incorporated in it. These both enriched the novel framework for access and consolidated (eight years of) experience arising from the litigation into the normative level. First, Article 4(6) of Regulation 1049/2001 embraced the *Hautala*-ruling-based inheritance of partial access[95] as a normative requirement. Secondly, and credibly it was in the wake of the *Svenska*[96] ruling that Article 8 of the Preamble to Regulation 1049/2001 made an explicit reference to the requirement that the full application of the Regulation was to be ensured over 'all activities of the Union'. It was an important addition. In contrast with the Treaties' mere allusion that this was so, the Regulation was definitive on the subject. The matter was, finally, harmoniously resolved at all three levels: in the case law, in the Treaty and now at the ordinary normative level as well.

B. Normative Changes Introduced by the Regulation to the Pre-2001 Model

If it is true that on the one hand, Regulation 1049/2001 took inspiration from lessons learned between 1993 and 2001, on the other hand notable changes were introduced that completely upset the paradigm that had governed the policy over the previous (eight) years.[97]

The first notable change was that active legitimacy was (theoretically) restricted.[98] The 1993 Code of Conduct's inclusive general concept of the public was abandoned in favour of a two-tier reference to applicants in Article 2 of Regulation 1049/2001. In Article 2, a first category of applicants identified *by right*,[99] is contrasted with a second category characterised as applicants *by grace of the institution.*[100]

The second notable change was performed via Article 4, this time pertaining to the exceptions. What reads today 'as the protection of the purpose of inspections, investigations, and audits' is inspired by a similar set of exceptions that enjoyed a very different status under the 1993 Code of Conduct. In fact, according to the previous rules, audits were not included at all in the list of exceptions. At the time of the 1993 Code of Conduct, two mandatory exceptions (within the 'public interest' heading) for investigative proceedings in general were foreseen solely 'as

[95] Case T–14/98 *Hautala v Council* (n 52).

[96] Case T–174/95 *Svenskajournalistforbundet v Council* [1998] ECR II–2289 (n 51).

[97] See generally on the effects of the new paradigm J Heliskoski and P Leino, 'Darkness at the Break of Noon: the Case Law on Regulation No 1049/2001 on Access to Documents' (2006) 43 *Common Market Law Review* 735–81.

[98] See Ch 2.

[99] Regulation 1049/2001, Art 2(1): 'citizens of the Union and natural or legal persons residing or having their registered office in a Member State'.

[100] Regulation 1049/2001, Art 2(2): 'any natural or legal person not residing or having its registered office in a Member State'.

regards inspections and investigations'. With the advent of the new rules a part of the old public interest heading was first redrafted[101] and then reclassified by Regulation 1049/2001.[102]

Thirdly, the length of deadlines was altered. Via Article 7 these were shortened to 15 days in contrast to the Code of Conduct's more generous concession (30 days). Fourthly, a notable innovation that indeed amounts to a purposeful *volte face* in policy was the abandonment of the so-called author's rule. Regulation 1049/2001 embraced the novel idea that all documents held by the institutions were covered by the EU policy. The new rule was laid down in Article 2(3), and further by Article 4(4) and 4(5). This new option (foreshadowed by Declaration No 35 attached to the Treaty of Amsterdam) under which the institutions would retain final control over the fate of any document transmitted to them, would later bring about significant tension between the institutions and the Member States.[103] From another angle, albeit equally seriously, the departure from the author's rule would additionally give rise to intense conflict within the realm of EU competition law, namely regarding access to documents transmitted to the institutions by private persons under leniency proceedings.[104]

C. Treaty of Nice

Just as Regulation 1049/2001 began to acquire increasing stability and to receive input from the judicature, the almost contemporary appearance of a new Treaty for the EU on the horizon—the Treaty of Nice—represented a double threat to progress made: new (and contradictory) rules would have rendered previous lessons learned completely obsolete, and much in the same way new (even if merely additional) rules would require another round of adaptation from the public, the institutions and judicature alike.

Interestingly, the Treaty of Nice neither added new and contradictory rules to the access policy nor, for that matter, added any new and merely complementary ones to it. The Treaty of Nice entered into force on 1 February 2003, and simply left the content of the references to access in both TEC and TEU unchanged. In fact the result of the desire to keep the old references pristine was so remarkable that even the numbers of the Treaty articles remained constant. In the TEU it was again—just as it had been under the Treaty of Amsterdam—Article 1 to ground the access policy. In the TEC, access was kept under the umbrella of Article 255.

> Article 1 of the TEU of the Treaty of Nice
>
> This Treaty marks a new stage in the process of creating an ever closer union among the peoples of Europe, in which decisions are taken as openly as possible and as closely as possible to the citizen.

101 See Ch 5.
102 See Ch 5.
103 See Ch 4.
104 See Ch 7.

Article 255 TEC of the Treaty of Nice

1. Any citizen of the Union, and any natural or legal person residing or having its registered office in a Member State, shall have a right of access to European Parliament, Council and Commission documents, subject to the principles and the conditions to be defined in accordance with paragraphs 2 and 3.

2. General principles and limits on grounds of public or private interest governing this right of access to documents shall be determined by the Council, acting in accordance with the procedure referred to in Article 251 within two years of the entry into force of the Treaty of Amsterdam.

3. Each institution referred to above shall elaborate in its own Rules of Procedure specific provisions regarding access to its documents.

D. Failed Attempt at Reform

Between the entry into force of the Treaty of Nice and the entry into force of the Treaty of Lisbon and its aftermath, a number of attempts of reform of the framework of Regulation 1049/2001 came to populate the access normative background, but none has been successful. The first of these is linked to the tentative advent of the Constitutional Treaty signed in 2004.[105] Under the Treaty, Article 42 of the Charter of Fundamental Rights[106] would have been extended to all institutions and bodies of the Union. Moreover, access to the executive activity-related documents would have been regulated through Article I–50(3) and Article III–399, which drew on Article 255 TEC but also established that certain institutions would be subject only to access obligations when exercising their administrative tasks.

On the legislative role of the institutions, Article I–50 would have laid down a requirement for public meetings of the Council when discussing and voting on a draft legislative act, and finally Article II–399(2) would have called for publication of documents related to legislative proceedings. The entire project having been abandoned, the proposed rules nonetheless served as an inspiration for the subsequent framework of access within the Treaty of Lisbon.[107]

As a second reference to an attempt at change, on 9 November 2005 the Commission established a European Transparency Initiative.[108] However, neither this specific initiative nor subsequent follow-up attempts of renewal have been successful in recasting the ever resilient Regulation 1049/2001.

105 [2004] OJ C 310/1.

106 Renumbered as II-102.

107 See section VII.E below.

108 European Commission, Green Paper on the European Transparency Initiative, COM(2007) 127-Final (not published in the Official Journal).

E. Treaty of Lisbon

Notably, the Treaty of Lisbon would not attempt to alter access' parameters either. In fact, the policy that has consistently been drafted into both TEU and TEC since the Treaty of Amsterdam has not been treated differently under the latest Treaty governing the EU, which entered into force on 1 December 2009. Access remains at the forefront of the TEU, enshrined into the very first Article and in the following terms:

> Article 1 TEU
>
> This Treaty marks a new stage in the process of creating an ever closer union among the peoples of Europe, in which decisions are taken as openly as possible and as closely as possible to the citizen.

Still within the TEU, on another front, Article 16(8) replicates the recurrent dichotomy between access related to the executive role of the institutions versus a 'special attention criteria' reserved for access related to the legislative role of the EU institutions and, accordingly establishes that:

> Article 16(8) TEU
>
> The Council shall meet in public when it deliberates and votes a draft legislative act. To this end, each Council meeting shall be divided into two parts, dealing respectively with deliberations on Union legislative acts and non-legislative activities.

As for access' current position within the TFEU, Article 15(3) has succeeded Article 255 of the TEC as the main Treaty provision that serves as a concrete basis for access:

> Article 15 TFEU (ex Article 255 TEC)
>
> 1. In order to promote good governance and ensure the participation of civil society, the Union institutions, bodies, offices and agencies shall conduct their work as openly as possible.
>
> 2. The European Parliament shall meet in public, as shall the Council when considering and voting on a draft legislative act.
>
> 3. Any citizen of the Union, and any natural or legal person residing or having its registered office in a Member State, shall have a right of access to documents of the Union institutions, bodies, offices and agencies, whatever their medium, subject to the principles and the conditions to be defined in accordance with this paragraph.
>
> General principles and limits on grounds of public or private interest governing this right of access to documents shall be determined by the European Parliament and the Council, by means of regulations, acting in accordance with the ordinary legislative procedure.
>
> Each institution, body, office or agency shall ensure that its proceedings are transparent and shall elaborate in its own Rules of Procedure specific provisions regarding access to its documents, in accordance with the regulations referred to in the second subparagraph.
>
> The Court of Justice of the European Union, the European Central Bank and the European Investment Bank shall be subject to this paragraph only when exercising their administrative tasks.

The European Parliament and the Council shall ensure publication of the documents relating to the legislative procedures under the terms laid down by the regulations referred to in the second subparagraph.

F. Achievements of the Case Law under Regulation 1049/2001

While the normative development of access from Treaty to Treaty has been gentle and conservative, the accomplishments of the case law that developed on the basis of Regulation 1049/2001 are at once numerous, innovative and vigorous. They will be commented on by area of influence in Chapters 2–8, with special emphasis accorded to Chapter 5 (Exceptions). It is, however, not untimely to present a synopsis of the backbone of the combined contributions to this debate from the EU judicature.

It is striking how some issues addressed by the case law stand out, and even more striking how the normative context of access as it stands today cannot be fully understood without a prior understanding of them. Free from any temporal order in their address, four problematic issues may be identified: two of which are settled, two of which are not.

The first problematic issue concerns the deadlines established in Regulation 1049/2001. More precisely, it concerns their imperative nature when the deadline is established vis-à-vis an institution. The issue gave rise to the highly controversial *Co-frutta v Commission*[109] ruling of 19 January 2010 and was subsequently resolved and more adequately settled only 10 months later with the (no less controversial) *Ryanair v Commission*[110] ruling of 10 December 2010.

The second problematic issue centred on the sensitive possibility that the EU institutions be granted the final word over the possibility of release to the public of documents originating in the Member States. This was especially pressing in cases—as occurred in the *IFAW*[111] proceedings—in which Member States specifically requested that the institution not release the document. Normative basis held insufficient, it took Advocate General Maduro's Opinion favouring a teleological approach,[112] to overcome the contrasting views on the point. The ECJ concurred with the Advocate General and left the Member States with no choice other than the surrender of their voiced claims for autonomy. The feat was accomplished in spite of a significant setback for the Member States: they were not to be acknowledged veto power over the destiny of self-originating documents.[113]

[109] Joined Cases T–355/04 & T–446/04 *Co-frutta v Commission* [2010] ECR II–00001 (*Co-frutta II*).

[110] Joined Cases T–494/08 to T–500/08 & T–509/08 *Ryanair v Commission* [2010] ECR II-5723. As late as May 2014, the issue of their 'imperative nature' has been discussed once again and clearly confirmed in AG Kokott's Opinion delivered on 22 May 2014 in Case C–127/13 P *Strack v Commission* [not yet reported] para 40.

[111] Case C–64/05P Joined Cases C-39/05P and C-52/05P *Sweden and Turco v Council IFAW* (n 30).

[112] Opinion of AG Maduro in Case C–64/05P Joined Cases C-39/05P and C-52/05P *Sweden and Turco v Council, IFAW* (n 30).

[113] A Barav, 'Opacité et Transparence, ou, le droit d'émpecher, la jurisprudence em matière d'access aux documents provenant des États Membres detenues par les institutions communautaires' in *Chemins D'Europe, Mélanges em Honneur de Jean-Paul Jacqué* (Paris, Dalloz, 2010) 29–62; P Cabral, 'Member

The third problematic issue, to this day governed by fluctuating criteria, is the answer to the question of whether the institutions must actually and concretely examine a document before they take definitive decisions on its release to the public. This third issue was examined in the *Turco*[114] proceedings that rose through the ranks of the EU judicial system in a striking manner.[115] From ECJ's final judgment a tripartite test, known as the three-limbed *Turco* test, may be derived. The test serves as a benchmark to assess the propriety of the institution's examination of the contested documents. Its subsequent popularity with the ECJ has, however, been somewhat inconstant.[116]

The fourth and final issue, possibly the most problematic of all, lies in the advent of an incipient (and ever-growing) theorisation of presumptions[117] (controversially described as rebuttable) within the access context. This novel approach has been resorted to by the institutions in the fields of access to documents related to judicial proceedings[118] and access to competition proceedings (State aid, merger control, and more recently, concerted practices).[119] Access to leniency documents has also taken on a life of its own and does not cease to attract attention from commentators.[120] Less justifiably, it has somewhat simplistically, also been accepted by the EU judicature when applied by the institutions to environmental files.[121]

State Documents in EC Law' (2006) 31(3) *European Law Review* 378–89. For an account of an interesting *volte face* in the case-law, see V Tourrès, 'Droit d'accès aux documents jurisdictionels: um pas vers la transparence? Trib EU, 27 Fevrier 2015, Breyer / Commission, aff. T-188/12' (2015) 1 *Revue des affaires européennes* 195–204.

[114] Case T–84/03 *Turco v Council* [2004] ECR II-4061 (*Turco I*).

[115] See Ch 7. The Kingdom of Sweden, which had supported the applicant in first instance, proceeded to lodge an independent State appeal against the first instance ruling. The independent appeal was subsequently joined with Mr Turco's (applicant at first instance) own appeal and decided together by the ECJ: Joined Cases C-39/05P and C-52/05P *Sweden and Turco v Council* (2008) ECR–I 4723 (*Turco II*).

[116] *cf* Case C-365/12P *Commission v EnBW (EnBW II)* [not reported], the judgment of the Court, 12 February 2014 (and the Opinion of AG Villalon).

The issue's importance has very recently been revived through Advocate General Eleanor Sharpston's Opinion rendered on occasion of the *Council v Sophie in't Veld* proceedings (n 62) on the subject of access and international relations; Case C–350/12P, Opinion of Advocate General Eleanor Sharpston, 13 February 2014 [not yet reported].

[117] See Ch 5.

[118] Joined Cases C-514/07 P, C-528/07 P and C-532/07 P *Sweden v API ASBL and Commission* [2010] ECR I-08533 (*API II).*

[119] In the field of State aid, see Case C-139/07 P *Commission v Technische Glaswerke Ilmenau* [2010] ECR I-5885 (*TGI II*); In the field of Concerted Practices, see *EnBW II* (n 116), involving Regulation no 1/2003 and 773/2004. For 3 structured and incisive overviews of the presumptions in competition law, see K Jurimae, 'The Interaction between the EU Transparency Policy and The Enforcement of EU Competition Law, Who Should Strike the Balance and How Should it be Struck?' (2012) *European Competition Law Annual* 365–95; O Speltdoorn, 'The Technische Glasweke Ilmenau Ruling, a Step Backwards in Transparency in EU Competition Cases?' in *Constitutionalising the EU Judicial System, Essays in Honour of Pernilla Lindth* (Oxford, Hart, 2012) 439–72; K Lenaerts, 'The Principle of Transparency and its Limits in the Context of Competition Investigations' (2014) 4 *Osterreichische Zeitschrift fur Kartellrecht* 123–26.

[120] See eg D Mandrescu, 'Access to Leniency Programme Documents Based on the Transparency Regulation: The European Commission v EnBw Energie Baden-Wurtrenberg AG' (2015) 42(3) *Legal Issues of Economic Integration* 301–15.

[121] Joined Cases C-514/11 & C 605/11 *LPN and Finland v Commission* [not reported].

By contrast, Advocate General Sharpston's Opinion rendered in the abovementioned[122] *Sophie in't Veld* proceedings has, for the moment, kept at bay recent attempts at extension of this practice to the field of international relations.[123]

VIII. RULES GOVERNING SPECIAL TOPICS

While it is undoubtedly the main normative instrument on access, Regulation 1049/2001 does not stand as sole normative governor of the subject. On occasion it encounters concurrent law of the EU that deals with public access to internal documents (under a variety of normative forms) and which must be reasoned with and taken into account.

A. The Exceptions in Article 4 of Regulation 1049/2001

A first threshold of normative concurrence with Regulation 1049/2001 is foreshadowed by the Regulation itself. Indeed its Article 4 provides for a series of exceptions to its own application.[124]

> Regulation 1049/2001, Article 4—Exceptions
>
> 1. The institutions shall refuse access to a document where disclosure would undermine the protection of:
>
> (a) the public interest as regards:
> — public security,
> — defence and military matters,
> — international relations,
> — the financial, monetary or economic policy of the Community or a Member State;
>
> (b) privacy and the integrity of the individual, in particular in accordance with Community legislation regarding the protection of personal data.
>
> 2. The institutions shall refuse access to a document where disclosure would undermine the protection of:
>
> — commercial interests of a natural or legal person, including intellectual property,
> — court proceedings and legal advice,
> — the purpose of inspections, investigations and audits, unless there is an overriding public interest in disclosure.
>
> 3. Access to a document, drawn up by an institution for internal use or received by an institution, which relates to a matter where the decision has not been taken by the institution, shall be refused if disclosure of the document would seriously undermine the institution's decision-making process, unless there is an overriding public interest in disclosure.

[122] Case C–350/12P *Council v Sophie in't Veld* (n 62).

[123] See generally GM Lentner, 'Access to Documents of the Institutions: Transparency of International Negotiations: Council of the Union v Sophie in't Veld, ECJ (First Chamber) Judgment of 3 July 2014, C-350/12P' (2014) 4 *European Law Reporter* 123–29.

[124] See Chs 4 and 5.

> Access to a document containing opinions for internal use as part of deliberations and preliminary consultations within the institution concerned shall be refused even after the decision has been taken if disclosure of the document would seriously undermine the institution's decision-making process, unless there is an overriding public interest in disclosure.
>
> 4. As regards third-party documents, the institution shall consult the third party with a view to assessing whether an exception in paragraph 1 or 2 is applicable, unless it is clear that the document shall or shall not be disclosed.
>
> 5. A Member State may request the institution not to disclose a document originating from that Member State without its prior agreement.
>
> 6. If only parts of the requested document are covered by any of the exceptions, the remaining parts of the document shall be released.
>
> 7. The exceptions as laid down in paragraphs 1 to 3 shall only apply for the period during which protection is justified on the basis of the content of the document. The exceptions may apply for a maximum period of 30 years. In the case of documents covered by the exceptions relating to privacy or commercial interests and in the case of sensitive documents, the exceptions may, if necessary, continue to apply after this period.

Accordingly, the so-called 'right of access to documents' will fall away if disclosure of a document would undermine the protection of one or more of nine concurrent concerns of the EU. Article 4, in fact, consists mainly of a list of equally meritorious interests that are both nurtured by the EU and are the object of specific rules on public access, that are often quite disconnected from Regulation 1049/2001. As such, it is on a case-by-case basis that prevalence or capitulation of these is determined versus the interest served by disclosure of documents.[125]

B. The Environmental Law of the EU

A second threshold of normative concurrence with Regulation 1049/2001 may be identified: it is the case of environmental EU law. By contrast to what has been said above regarding other areas of EU law, this relationship has been construed as a normative development to Regulation 1049/2001. It is the latest theme to be regulated by a specific statute on access, concurrent but coordinated with Regulation 1049/2001. Not surprisingly, any rules or judgments delivered within its context generate great expectation[126] in the public.

There are three reasons that explain this. First, the discussion of environment together with access is (relatively) new. Second, and differently from the interests protected by the list of exceptions within Article 4 of Regulation 1049/2001, protection of the environment principally calls for more access, not less. Finally, the nature of environmental applicants also matters. These consist mainly of NGOs that have,

[125] The issue of the intensity and enforcement in the case law of each of the exceptions established in Regulation 1049/2001's Art 4 will be discussed individually throughout Chs 4 and 5.

[126] For an early perspective of what role environmental law would play within the access framework, see S De Abreu Ferreira, 'The Fundamental Right of Access to Environmental Information in the EC: A Critical Analysis of WWF-EPO v Council' (2007) 19 *Journal of Environmental Law* 399–408.

since the early days,[127] inveterately prodded and probed the EU institutions about the validity of the reasons for refusing to disclose documents. Furthermore, they have—of late—come to assume a role that is comparable to that of sentinels, and bellicose ones at that. They are ever watchful over the concrete day-to-day practice of the Institutions related to the concession of documents to the public, and are just as eager to take matters before the EU courts.[128]

As a normative option, access to environmental information has been addressed by reference to two separate thresholds that should not be confused. While it is true that both resulting instruments are inspired by the Aarhus Convention[129] their individual purposes are quite divergent. One threshold (the main focus of our discussion)—established under the form of a Regulation[130]—is addressed to the EU institutions that function within stringent limitations to access (annulment as a ceiling) and is not intended to have any effect whatsoever on Member State law. It is known as the Aarhus Regulation, that is in fact Regulation (EC) 1367/2006 on the application of the provisions of the Aarhus Convention on Access to Information, Public Participation in Decision-making and access to Justice in Environmental matters to Community institutions and Bodies dated September 6, 2006. It lays down a framework that principally seeks to facilitate a wider dimension of access to (environmental) information.

A second threshold—established under the form of a Directive[131]—has been addressed solely to the Member States and its aim is to approximate, where possible, the rules governing access to environmental information of disparate national fora. Both of these instruments will be commented on in Chapter 5.

C. An Outlier—The Council of Europe's Convention on Public Access to Official Documents

It is worth noting that on 18 June 2009 a Convention on Access to Official Documents was signed within the Council of Europe's legal framework of reference. But it is equally important to clarify that given its distinct and legal setting (pertaining to issues that are governed exclusively by Council of Europe rules) it is not apt to deploy efficacy on EU law. Therefore it is not to be considered a normative development to the EU framework on access. Having left the reference, we choose not to address the instrument in further detail.[132]

[127] Case T-105/95 *WWF UK* (n 21).

[128] See Ch 2.

[129] Although the European Community signed the Convention on Access to Information, Public Participation in Decision-making and Access to Justice in Environmental Matters as early as 1998, the process was concluded only in 2005: [2005] OJ L 124/1.

[130] Regulation 1367/2006 [2006] OJ L264/16 (Aarhus Regulation). See Annex 4.

[131] Directive 2003/4/ EC on public access to environmental information [2003] OJ L 41/26.

[132] Available at: www.coe.int/en/web/conventions/full-list/-/conventions/treaty/205

IX. CONCLUSIONS

The excursion along this normative development has brought to light the many normative acts that sought to foster the legitimation of the EU institutions vis-à-vis their public by way of the construction of an access policy. There are 23 normative contributions that have helped build the current status quo, and it is true that, taken together, they form a notable accomplishment.

From the origins of rather general Communications and Declarations the EU has today not only successfully grounded its access policy at the forefront of its constitutional concerns, but has also provided practical rules to ground its practice and laid down judicial (and non-judicial) remedies to ensure its enforcement.

This notwithstanding, it is also evident that the irreconcilable rational selfishness of actors involved is a great hindrance to the affirmance of a robust right of access to documents within the EU. The institutions will fight each other in order to secure (a louder) voice within the policy. The Member States (who voted for the policy) will fight the Institutions in order to secure final control over the destiny of self-produced documents. The individuals' right under construction rises from difficult battlefields.

Access seems to soldier on, nonetheless.

It does so in a way of its own, of course, since what exists in the EU is a certain form of access. That is very different from saying that in the EU access exists, and that it has been normatively laid down under a certain form.

Throughout the seven chapters that follow a practice-oriented analysis will be undertaken, focusing principally on the existent case law regarding seven topics. The first three topics focus on access' protagonists and on the object of requests for disclosure: *Applicants* (Chapter 2) who may ask *Institutions* (Chapter 3) for *Documents* (Chapter 4). The two subsequent chapters address refusals, and refusals come in two forms: the first is valid reasons to say 'No' explicitly, *Exceptions* (Chapter 5), the second, *Silence*, that means 'No' (Chapter 6). The two closing chapters are addressed from a fairly metric-oriented standpoint. First, the issue of why the *EU Member States* (albeit involved) are not to be considered main protagonists, as well as the role of other actors (Ch 7). Lastly, *Appeals*, their structure and their measure of success are discussed (Ch 8).

2

Applicants

I. INTRODUCTION—BY RIGHT OR BY GRACE?

LEGAL PERSONALITY, IS indispensable if one has in mind to engage the institutions of the EU by way of a request for access to documents.[1] Moreover, it is also important to have a clear idea of who are the lawyers one may count on if and when litigation before the EU courts proves necessary. The main point to keep in mind is that for the purpose of representation before the EU judicature, first, one must engage a lawyer who is competent to plead in one of the national jurisdictions of the EU. Secondly, and subject to satisfying the previous condition, one may not engage as legal counsel someone who is not sufficiently detached from oneself so as not to qualify as an independent third party. Take, for example, one of the applicant's trustees,[2] or legal counsel already bound to the applicant by way of a permanent employment contract, a so-called 'in-house lawyer'.[3]

Once these two issues are settled, anybody who is a person must still fit the shape of *beneficiary* (discussed below) before one may go on to apply for documents, thus becoming an *applicant*.

The main point of the discussion on applicants is, as we will see, that the access policy has an extremely generous point of entry. Or, in other words, that a great many persons are enabled by the law to request documents. Moreover, no filters have been put in place to help manage a, potentially endless, influx of requests. In fact, within the EU system—differently from most legal systems of the Western legal tradition—persons who ask for documents are not obliged to give reasons for wanting to consult them.[4] Such a model makes it so simple to approach the

[1] This is true at least as of the entry into force of Regulation 1049/2001. Legal personality (the ability to be the titleholder of rights and duties) is a quality that is inherent to natural persons (ie human beings). It is in addition a quality that is acknowledged, once certain requirements have been met, to bodies wishing to take legal form under private or public law. These bodies then become legal persons. There have been instances in which the EU judicature has refused to protect bodies that have been refused access to documents for the sole reason that they are not legal persons. See generally (for public law) Case T-236/06 *Landtag Schleswig Holstein v Commission* [2008] ECR II-00461, order of the CFI of 3 April 2008; and Case C-281/08P *Landtag Schleswig Holstein v Commission* [not yet published] order of the ECJ, 24 November 2009. Also (for private law) Case T-383/08 *New Europe v Commission*, order of the CFI, 23 April 2009.

[2] Statute of the ECJ, Art 19; and Case C-573/11P *ClientEarth v Council* [not yet reported] order of the ECJ, 9 November 2011.

[3] Case C-28/13P *Gabi Thesing and Bloomberg v ECB* [not reported], order of the ECJ, 6 November 2013 in respect of Media Legal Defence Initiative and Guardian News and Media Ltd.

[4] Regulation 1049/2001, Art 6(1).

institutions that, ultimately, these could come to face an ungovernable, quantitative, burden. The institutions might not be able to process all of the incoming requests within the deadlines laid down by the law.

At the same time, it is also true that within the access to documents litigation that is fashioned as a mere review of the legality of institutional decisions the EU courts—again differently from most legal systems in the Western Legal tradition—are not empowered to address (positive) orders to the EU institutions, as in 'do this, do that'. This means that even if the EU court was to voice the opinion that a document had been illegitimately refused an applicant—and this is frequently the case—the same EU court could not compel any EU institution to provide the applicant with that document.

This narrow judicial exit point to the policy (the less significant measure of judicial protection available) acts as a counterweight to the generous point of entry. Persons who are refused documents by the EU institutions—even illegitimately—will have low incentives to sue, since their remedial expectation[5] is extremely limited.

Curiously, the interplay of the policy's generous point of entry coupled with the limited judicial protection made available to applicants, remains fascinating. Above all else it reveals a great deal about the reasons behind requests. Indeed, concerning applicants, the case law tells stories of curiosity, determination, need, quixotical attempts to make the policies' limits budge, and even, on occasion, of twinkles of naughtiness. Moreover, all this transpires from judgments rendered in regard to persons that are obliged to reveal only the bare minimum about themselves.[6] As we embark on the analysis of this part of the subjective dimension of access it is never redundant to point out that the case law only develops when problems arise, when refusals are handed down and, generally, when applicants are not satisfied. In all other circumstances documents are asked for and handed over, and there is nothing more to talk about.

Every now and then unpublished[7] documents of the EU institutions are disclosed (pursuant to a request for access) if no objections are entertained regarding their unveiling. In such a setting the issue of rights or duties is not—necessarily—disputed. The institution acts by grace. A prayer is answered.

For this to take place two conditions must be satisfied. First, that there be no uneasiness regarding the subjective dimension of the request (what that particular person is going to do with the documents). Second, that there be no uneasiness regarding the request's objective dimension either (what any person could do with those particular documents).[8]

[5] S Shavell, *Foundations of Economic Analysis of Law* (Cambridge, MA, Belknap Press of Harvard University Press, 2004) explores the issue of remedial expectations using the term 'Expected Gross Return' (EGR).

[6] That this unsettles institutions is obvious in a Note to the Heads of Unit responsible for access to documents in the Commission, dated 19 March 2014, in which the General Secretariat points out that 'The Commission has been increasingly confronted with cases where applicants seem to hide behind false identities'; available at: www.asktheeu.urg/eu/request/1337/response.

[7] Hereinafter 'documents'. It is never superfluous to clarify that the rules on access in EU law exist to govern requests for unpublished, internal or incoming documents that previously (and in the vast majority of cases) have never been made available to the public. This point is further explored in Ch 4 and Ch 5.

[8] See Chs 4, 5.

However, the normal arrangement is a little more complex. In the foreground of any institutional reaction[9] to requests for disclosure of documents an assessment will be carried out taking into account that persons, when requesting access to documents of the EU institutions, may be doing more that expressing a passing fancy or whim. In fact they may be—and often are—relying on normative entitlement: on a right to ask for access. This chapter addresses the many facets of the concerns that are implicit to the subjective dimension of requests.

Requesting an EU institution for access to its documents is not the same as being enabled by law to do so. Anyone *can* ask. It is fairly uncomplicated to write a letter to an institution, to send an electronic message or to make a phone call and do so. However, in the present context, it is relevant to inquire who—by law—*may* ask and—entitlement asserted—also expect the institution to give the request consideration.

Once the opportunity (to request access) is laid down in the law and ascribed to one or more persons[10] identifiable as 'beneficiaries', such persons are the only persons who enjoy legal standing[11] to (choose to) address a request to the institutions to the effect that document disclosure be considered. Distinguishing itself from this more abstract concept of beneficiaries, another term—'applicant'—is habitually employed to describe persons who (being beneficiaries) do exercise that opportunity. Once a beneficiary applies for documents, thus becoming an applicant, the institution concerned becomes the 'addressee' of a request for disclosure. And, having received the request, the same institution will carry out a double assessment: first, to establish if the request originates from a beneficiary and, secondly, to establish if there are no objective reasons[12] that justify the non-disclosure of the documents requested.

A. Persons, Beneficiaries and Applicants

An inaugural task thus arises and consists of understanding the concrete dimension of access' subjective ambit, its universe of beneficiaries, or, in simpler words, all persons to whom this opportunity is attributed. If one considers that access is a policy of the EU, it is remarkable that the 1993 Code of Conduct, singular in many aspects as mentioned in Chapter 1,[13] was no less singular in its choice of designation for the (group of) persons that were to be allowed to request access to documents of the EU institutions.

[9] The institutions may opt between disclosure, refusal (Ch 5) or silence (Ch 6). Silence is of course an aggressive choice, but a legitimate form of institutional conduct, nonetheless. It is often considered and, on occasion, undertaken.

[10] See eg Case C-281/08P *Landtag Schleswig Holstein v Commission* (n 1) on the capacity of a regional parliament to be a party to legal proceedings.

[11] Regarding the phrase 'legal standing', an equivalent Latin expression—*locus standi*—is often employed. Regarding the universe of beneficiaries, the phrase 'scope *rationae personae*' may be employed as a synonym.

[12] See Ch 5.

[13] See Ch 1.

The expression employed therein was the 'public'. A plebeian term. A superfluity of imprecision.[14]

1993 Code of Conduct

> The public will have the widest possible access to documents held by the Commission and the Council.

Owing to the preference for such a wide ambit, legal standing (to choose to address a request to the institutions to the effect that document disclosure be considered) appeared wholly unconstrained. No condition as to the beneficiaries' nationality, residence, domicile, or even (in the case of legal persons) place of registration of their principle seat. No condition stemming from the public or private nature of the applicant. Conjecture was of course inevitable. Was the government of a Member State or any administrative authority within a Member State part of the public? Was another EU institution (signatory or not) part of the public? Was any institution of any international organisation part of the public?

At first glance, the entire world[15]—its private and public component parts alike—had been invited to enjoy the greater openness of the institutions of the EU. Moreover, since at the time the Code was published there was no case law (on access) to help identify categories of subjects who might be excluded from the Code's ambit, uncertainty hovered.

As a contentious issue of the access policy, legal standing and its contours reached the GC in 1995.[16] On that occasion, the GC, normally a source of clarification, exacerbated the problem (or at any rate offered no helpful contribution) since it chose to adopt fluctuating language. In *Svenska*, to designate the Code's beneficiaries four different terms were employed interchangeably: 'any person', 'citizens', 'the public' and 'members of the public'. Instead of proposing an unambiguous reading of the figure's subjective ambit, the GC merely echoed that access had been accorded to the public at large:

Case T–174/95 *Svenskajournalistforbundet v Council*

> 65. In the case of Commission Decision 94/90/ECSC, EC, Euratom of 8 February 1994 on public access to Commission documents (OJ 1994 L 46, p. 58, hereinafter 'Decision 94/90), the Court has already held that from its overall scheme, it is clear that Decision 94/90 is intended to apply generally to requests for access to documents, and that, by virtue of that decision, any person may request access to any unpublished Commission document, and is not required to give a reason for the request (Case T–124/96 *Interporc v Commission* [1998] ECR II–0000, paragraph 48).
>
> 66. The objective of Decision 93/731 is to give effect to the principle of the largest possible access for citizens to information with a view to strengthening the democratic character

[14] The 1993 Code's choice of words was echoed *ipsis verbis* by its implementing Decisions 93/731 and 94/90. Even today—with the benefit of hindsight—it would be hazardous to attempt an explanation of the exact meaning that was to be gleaned, in 1993, from those words.

[15] J Schwarze uses the expression '*Quivis ex populo*' at 340 in 'Access to Documents under European Union Law' (2015) 2 *Rivista Italiana di Diritto Pubblico Communitario* 335–44.

[16] Case T–174/95 *Svenska* [1998] ECR II-02289.

of the institutions and the trust of the public in the administration. Decision 93/731, like Decision 94/90, does not require that members of the public must put forward reasons for seeking access to requested documents.

Imprecise or not, in practical terms the choice of terminology would prove to be innocuous. There is no record in the case law that the EU institutions ever refused to release documents on the basis the failure of an applicant to fall within the definition of the public.[17] What is more, in the case law there was no massive interference of non-EU members of the public[18] in the Union's affairs. It also reveals that applicants were predominantly private individuals[19] and not public bodies since no Member State of the EU,[20] other EU institution, non-EU government, administrative authority or international organisation[21] lodged any action for annulment (of a refusal to disclose documents) before the EU judicature. These actors of a public nature clearly did not self-identify as applicants.[22] Instead, they preferred the role of interveners,[23] or even appellants[24]—more shielded positions, from which—albeit still exposed—they could exert their influence[25] from the sidelines.

B. A Geo-political Contraction of Access?

That is why when a new normative definition of the subjective ambit ensued,[26] one possible reading is that it underwent an unnecessary contraction.[27] As a result of the

[17] 'Legal standing to request documents' is not to be confused with an applicant's failure to qualify as addressee of a decision of refusal, *conditio sine qua non* of entitlement to bring annulment proceedings before the EU judicature. On this point, see *Svenska* (n 16).

[18] While the 1993 Code of Conduct was in force, only in Case T-106/99 *Meyer v Commission* [1999] II-03273 did a (contested) refusal relate to a request for documents of the EU institutions originate from 'outside' the EU. In fact, a farmer residing in one of the Overseas Territories (Uturoa on the Island of Raitea, French Polynesia), Karl L Meyer, requested documents of the Council. The geographical origin of the request did not affect the applicant's standing in any way.

[19] The expression 'private individuals' encompasses both natural and legal persons. For legal persons, proof of existence in law must be adduced; see eg Case T-383/08 *New Europe v Commission* [Not reported] order of the CFI, para 19.

[20] Except for the Netherlands which chose to engage the Commission on the basis of Regulation 1049/2001; Case T-380/08 *Netherlands v Commission* [Not reported].

[21] Not to be confused with non-governmental organisations (NGOs).

[22] There are, of course, exceptions; in Case C-406/06 it is clear that the *Landtag Schleswig-Holstein* incorrectly self-identifies as an applicant State.

[23] Ch 7. For a technical approach to the subject of intervention, see T Materne, 'La Procedure en Intervention devant la Cour de Justice de l'Union Européenne' (2013) 29 *Cahiers de Droit Européen* 77–131. For a more metric-oriented analysis, see MPF Granger, 'When Governments Go to Luxembourg, The influence of Governments on the Court of Justice' (2004) 29 *European Law Review* 1–31.

[24] Chs 7, 8. There is no prerequisite that the Member State qualify as a *defeated party* at first instance. Consequently, they may appeal, to the ECJ, another applicant's first instance defeat.

[25] Ch 7.

[26] This occurred pursuant to the entry into force of the Treaty of Amsterdam and Regulation 1049/2001.

[27] In this sense, see S Peers, 'The New Regulation on Access to Documents: A Critical Analysis' (2001) 21(I) *Yearbook of European Law* 391: 'A limitation of the personal scope of applicants would represent a lowering in standards compared to the previous rules, which allowed *any* person to apply'.

However, it is true that if one were to consider that in *Svenska* (n 16) the Court, in fact, employed the term 'citizens' as a synonym for 'the public' then some comfort could be accorded to doctrinal claims to the effect that legal standing beyond the EU-origin might not have been a certainty. In this sense,

new wording the inclusive general concept of 'the public' was abandoned in favour of a two-tier reference to applicants. In Regulation 1049/2001, a first category of beneficiaries *by right* is contrasted with a second category of beneficiaries *by grace of the institutions*:

> Regulation 1049/2001, Article 2
>
> Beneficiaries and scope
>
> 1. Any citizen of the Union, and any natural or legal person residing or having its registered office in a Member State, has a right of access to documents of the institutions, subject to the principles, conditions and limits defined in this Regulation.
>
> 2. The institutions may, subject to the same principles, conditions and limits, grant access to documents to any natural or legal person not residing or not having its registered office in a Member State.

Since it was not a response to any over-burdening of the institutions, one less flattering explanation is that the divergence was no more than a subsequent preferential endowment of EU citizens and residents. An alternative interpretation could be that it consisted, in fact, of a preventive stance of the institutions with the purpose of organising priorities and which was possibly intended to function (only) in the event that an ungovernable amount of non-EU requests should compete for institutional attention alongside EU-originating ones.

C. Applicants by Right

Conjectures aside, what is true today is that beneficiaries pursuant to Article 2(1) of Regulation 1049/2001 become applicants by right. They are always entitled to legal standing to request access. Thus, the right to request access may not be refused them, and in consequence, their requests for disclosure of documents must always be given subsequent consideration by the institutions of the EU.

If an EU institution refuses an applicant access to documents, that applicant may call upon the EU judicature[28] for protection. However, from a procedural point of view, a first refusal from an EU institution is not sufficient ground for any applicant to call on the GC. Indeed, Article 7 of Regulation 1047/2001 states that once a request for access is rejected (either tacitly or explicitly) the addressee of the refusal may lodge a confirmatory application with the institution concerned. A confirmatory application is, in essence, a second chance. It gives the institution time to reconsider the points of divergence with the applicant's request carefully before conflict

the Treaty of Amsterdam may be read as bringing forth a generous concession; D Curtin, 'Democracy, Transparency and Political Participation' in V Deckmyn and I Thomson (eds), *Openness and Transparency in the European Union* (Maastricht, EIPA, 1988) 112: 'One positive feature of the formulation used however is that the Article [255 TA] applies not only to Union citizens but much more widely to any natural or legal person residing or having its registered office in a Member State'.

[28] As has been noted, we are not discussing the (alternative) role that the Ombudsman plays in such cases.

becomes unavoidable. The judicature, for its part, has clarified that a first decision on access is not definitive.[29] And thus consequently, that only a response to a confirmatory request[30] may be challenged in court.

D. Applicants by Grace

On the other hand, beneficiaries pursuant to Article 2(2) of Regulation 1049/2001—at the most—might become applicants by grace. Within this second setting, it is on the basis of absolute[31] institutional discretion that legal standing to request access might be conceded them. However, if legal standing is acknowledged them—but only if—such a concession is made, non-EU applicants become no different from their EU counterparts. And consequently, the institutions will be bound to accord such requests for disclosure of documents the same consideration that is owed to EU-originating requests.

A point of law that has not been clarified—since it was never disputed—is the status of beneficiaries pursuant to Article 2(2) of Regulation 1049/2001 in regard to Article 7(1) and (4) and Article 8(3) of Regulation 1049/2001. With this framework in mind, it might be said that persons[32] that are unable to produce an EU connection criteria under Article 2(1), should be prepared to respond to multiple and sequential challenges of the(ir) very right to request access.

> Regulation 1049/2001
>
> Article 7 Processing of Initial Applications
>
> 1 [...] An acknowledgement of receipt shall be sent to the applicant.
>
> 4 [...] Failure by the institution to reply within the prescribed time-limit shall entitle the applicant to make a confirmatory request.
>
> Article 8 Processing of Confirmatory Applications
>
> 3 [...] Failure by the institution to reply within the prescribed time-limit shall be considered a negative reply and entitle the applicant to institute court proceedings against the institution and/or make a complaint to the Ombudsman under the relevant provisions of the EC Treaty.

When such persons are addressed a first refusal (a tacit or explicit refusal that expresses institutional reserve in regard to the concession of legal standing to the beneficiary and/or to the merits of the request) the law is silent as to a succession of hypotheses that flow from this.

For the sake of argument, and only in regard to this second class of persons (Article 2(2)), it is important to divide the analysis of a first refusal into two possible

[29] Case C-127/13 *Strack v Commission* [not yet reported] para 36 and see further Ch 7.

[30] ibid 36 and further Ch 7.

[31] Thus rendering the merit of such a choice unamenable to judicial review.

[32] ie persons who have yet to be acknowleged as beneficiares in order to subsequently qualify as applicants.

component parts. First, a non-definitive position of the institution may be gleaned in regard to the (discretional) concession of legal standing to request access. Second, a non-definitive assessment of the objective conditions of merit that may justify a refusal will be laid out.

i. Silence on the Concession

From another angle, in the hypothesis that the institution is silent, neither the status of beneficiary nor the subsequent status of applicant have been acknowledged, since there has been no enabling act. Even an acknowledgement of receipt is inadequate to that effect. Therefore, a restrictive interpretation of the law would suggest that there is an absolute bar to the possibility that a person who holds only an abstract expectation to become a beneficiary may lodge a confirmatory request. In consequence, access to Article 8 is barred.

Again for the sake of further argument, and admitting that such a candidate to beneficiary does lodge a confirmatory request, more contentious issues could arise. If once again the institution is silent, it is academically questionable whether silence (on the merits) within Article 8(3) (which, for applicants, will open the door to court proceedings in regard to the merits) has the same meaning in regard to a mere candidate to beneficiary who has, in fact, never previously been conceded any form of legal standing. In sum, such a person is very probably barred from challenging the merits of the reply.

ii. The Concession, Revoked

Again academic, but worth exploring, would be the situation in which legal standing is explicitly acknowledged (in the first response from the institution) and yet, the response to the confirmatory decision explicitly revokes it. If one takes into account that the GC itself has stated that a first response is a temporary, non-definitive, position on the merits of requests, then the same reasoning could be extended to the issue of the definitive character, or not, of the concession of legal standing.

Untried as these hypotheses may be, their phantom hovers over all persons unable to demonstrate an EU connection criterion.

E. The (Ir)relevance of Reasons for Requests

It is now important to add that if there was a geo-political contraction of access' subjective ambit aimed at discriminating positively in favour of EU Europeans it also was, from its inception, rendered ineffectual. A concurrent principle of access' framework made that condition so easy to circumvent that as an obstacle—if it was an obstacle at all—it was no more than trivial. To illustrate this point, we must return to the role of the EU judicature.

It is undisputed that the GC was not forthcoming with regard to the normative endorsement of the term 'the public'.[33] Yet the same GC had played a fundamental and meritorious role regarding another perplexing characteristic of this EU policy. A remarkable omission in the 1993 Code had also required the Court's examination,[34] namely the absence of any compulsion to the effect that any applicant, EU or non-EU, was to state reasons for requests of access. With the purpose of singling out the Court's position on the extent to which applicants are required to provide explanations for their requests for disclosure of documents, a second examination of the *Svenska*[35] ruling sheds light on two departures from classical standards of EU law.

First, it is clear that in *Interporc*,[36] grounding its reasoning on the interpretation of the 1993 and 1994 Communications of the Commission,[37] the GC had voiced the opinion that institutions were not entitled to enquire as to why any applicant had chosen to request a document. Thus, it excused applicants—all applicants—from providing (private) reasons for their requests. In a second departure from standard prerequisites, the GC stated that applicants' interest in bringing about an annulment of a refusal of access was asserted by inherence (and arose automatically) once any refusal was addressed to the applicant. In this manner the GC waived the requirement for applicants—as addressees of a refusal—to prove that that very refusal had adversely affected their individual position before they could challenge it in court. In other words, a second exemption would ensue: applicants were now also excused from proving what is known as direct and individual concern.[38] A brave new world was in the making.

T-174/95 *Svenskajournalistforbundet v Council*

> The applicant is the addressee of the contested decision and, as such, is not obliged to prove that the decision is of direct and individual concern to it. It need only prove that it has an interest in the annulment of the decision.

[33] Case T-124/96 *Interporc* [1998] ECR II-231; *Svenska* (n 16).

[34] The 2 (early) leading cases on this topic were the *Svenska* (n 16) and *Interporc* (n 33) proceedings. Although *Svenska* was lodged in 1995 and *Interporc* in 1996, the judgment in *Interporc* was rendered 4 months prior to *Svenska*. Therefore *Svenska* draws on *Interporc* and not vice versa.

	lodged	judgment
Svenska	1995	17 June 1998
Interporc	1996	6 February 1998

[35] Case T–174/95 Svenska (n 16).

[36] *Interporc* (n 33) para 48.

[37] Ch 1, s III.A,

[38] On this point, see Case T-623/13 *Union Almacenistas*, with regard to the complaint, 'failure to take into account situation of the applicant'. The severe consequences of this option will be further explored in Chs 4 and 5. It was an option that has proved difficult to reconcile with the necessary role of applicants both within access' objective ambit (the identification of types of documents and their content (Ch 4) and the so-called balancing tests and/or overriding public interest test related to exceptions to document disclosure (Ch 5).

> 65 In the case of Commission Decision 94/90/ECSC, EC, Euratom of 8 February 1994 on public access to Commission documents the Court has already held that from its overall scheme, it is clear that Decision 94/90 is intended to apply generally to requests for access to documents, and that, by virtue of that decision, any person may request access to any unpublished Commission document, and is not required to give a reason for the request (Case T-124/96 *Interporc v Commission* [1998] ECR II-00231, paragraph 48).
>
> 66. The objective of Decision 93/731 is to give effect to the principle of the largest possible access for citizens to information with a view to strengthening the democratic character of the institutions and the trust of the public in the administration. Decision 93/731, like Decision 94/90, does not require that members of the public must put forward reasons for seeking access to requested documents.
>
> 67. It follows that a person who is refused access to a document or to part of a document has, by virtue of that very fact, established an interest in the annulment of the decision.

It was thus established that asking for documents without offering reasons was legitimate, and if disclosure of documents was refused, the refusal was, of itself, sufficient ground for litigation. Moreover, since the institutions could not demand from any member of the public that they explain why they wanted a document or how being impeded from accessing it was detrimental to them, even more pressure was placed on the outer bounds of access'—already implausibly generous—ambit of beneficiaries.

A universal, impersonal[39] right began to take form, one without limits. Since no reasons were required, any member of the public could request access to documents to satisfy their own private concerns (or interests) whether explicit or not. But at the same time any member of the public could also address to the institutions requests for access on behalf of any anonymous client. And thus from the initial superfluity of imprecision, a superfluity of (potential) customers emerged.

With this option embedded, the early case law on the lack of compulsion to state reasons was normatively grafted into Regulation 1049/2001 as Article 6(1). Therefore, it easily annihilated the same Regulation 1049/2001's contraction of access' subjective ambit. The non-EU applicant had only to ask that an EU-based applicant render a favour: a request for access to be addressed to the institutions on behalf of a non-EU applicant,[40] without stating as much:

> At any rate, a limitation to EU citizens and residents would be easy to circumvent, since people who are interested enough in EU affairs to apply for the institutions' documents are likely to have contacts in the EU who could request the documents on their behalf, so there would be little point in trying to enforce such a rule.[41]

Two detrimental consequences would ensue pursuant to such behaviour: on the one hand, official statistics (with regard to both the geographical origin of requests and to the type of applicant) would be thwarted. On the other hand, it might even degrade

[39] There was no link to (direct and) individual concern.

[40] This is, of course, distinct from representation by legal counsel.

[41] S Peers, 'The New Regulation on Access to Documents: A Critical Analysis' (2001) 21(I) *Yearbook of European Law* 385–442, 391.

access' raison d'être: with what was conceived as a political, trust-enhancing, opportunity of an infinity of beneficiaries versus the EU administration being reduced to an otherwise bare economic advantage of the more privileged beneficiaries. They now had the further—yet somewhat dubious—opportunity of acting as service providers or facilitators to the less fortunate.

II. A SMALLER(ER) VERSION OF REVERSED *ERGA OMNES*

The access policy has thus drawn a generous circle to include beneficiaries within. It has been said that the 1993 Code of Conduct's subjective ambit was more generous. Possibly this is true. And if indeed the expression 'the public' were taken to have simply meant the EU's public at large, then it may also be said that—within the period governed by the 1993 Code of Conduct—the EU, when offering an opportunity to 'the public', attributed a right to all beneficiaries conceivable.

That a universal criterion would be required in order to identify the beneficiaries of a right, especially when the provider of the same is a geographically limited institution (such as the EU) is unprecedented. It is a case of one organisation, according a right to all persons (in the world as it is known) and its mirror image is that all those persons can demand the consummation of such a right from that single organisation. It creates a perilous[42] All versus One relationship.

With the same amplitude of effects, the rights that we are more familiar with (at least within the Western legal tradition) are, for example, the rights of property. These enjoy status towards the world at large. Attributed by governments to their subjects, they must be respected by all persons (in the world as it is known). In other words, the proprietor may successfully assert a claim to the property versus any member of mankind. As a result, a more feasible One versus All relationship ensues. This is known as *erga omnes*[43] governance of rights. Literally it means '[defendable in court] versus mankind'.

Therefore, what the 1993 Code of Conduct is purported to have laid down was a reversed form of an *erga omnes* right. Indeed, access offered by the EU to the public, is not to be claimed (in court) versus any Member State or versus any other individual. Much to the contrary it may only be claimed versus (component parts[44] of) one organisation: the EU. Consequently, what is brought about is not a One versus All relationship. Instead, an All versus the EU position arises.

[42] This is especially true from a quantitative standpoint, in the sense that the amount of requests to be promptly handled could become ungovernable.

[43] The expression *erga omnes* has been quoted by B Driessen, *Transparency in EU Institutional Law* (Alphen aan den Rijn, Kluwer, 2012) 44, 45, as being known to the EU *acquis*, but within a distinct context. Therein it is argued that the expression access *erga omnes* serves to illustrate that if access is granted, it is on the basis of an objective assessment only. Thus, the conditions held to determine that a document may be (objectively) disclosed to one applicant are the same that will justify its release to any other applicant. Access to which only a handful are privy does not take place. Therefore '[all] documents released enter the public domain and become publicly available'.

[44] See Ch 3.

By way of a single, simple, opening statement to a Code of Conduct, the world had been pitted against the EU, sole bearer of a prodigious burden. Notably, with the advent of the Treaty of Amsterdam and Regulation 1049/2001, the (new and) conditional status of the many beneficiaries by grace of the institutions weakened the *erga omnes* prior dimension of access' subjective ambit. The concession of access to any person is still a possibility, admittedly. However, beyond the EU-origin one can no longer rely on that concession as a certainty. Certainty lies—today—in a small(er) version of what was once offered.

III. PROFILES

The discussion of *whom* applicants must address when requesting documents is undertaken in Chapter 3 and subsequently, the discussion about *what it is* that applicants may request is found in Chapter 4. However, at this point, we have taken a moment to distinguish applicants according to profiles.

If applicants are not required to offer reasons for their requests, and furthermore since it is relatively simple to establish a (required) EU connection, the universe of persons who do lodge requests for documents will, very probably, be extremely diverse. And yet, if one is to comprehend hidden patterns within the case law, the classification of applicants according to a series of profiles is prescribed. Therefore, in spite of the fact that all applicants are to be treated on equal terms once their legal standing to request access is asserted and acknowledged, it is worthwhile to (try to) call them by different names.

There are many ways of drawing profiles of applicants. By way of example, and on the basis of incidents arising within the case law, three benchmarks seem to be relevant. Taken separately, but discussed sequentially, they reveal to a good measure the principal 'types' of users that have enabled the access policy of the EU to function and develop. A first, and simple criterion (A) is to approach the discussion of applicants on the basis of the (given) names of categorisations that are found in official statistics. A second option (B) would be to commence from an assumption: the 'typical' applicant understands the policies' limitations and therefore—rationally—only requests annulment from the EU courts. Finally, (C) it is important to spend some time discussing applicants that continue to request injunctions from the EU courts.

A. Names from the Statistics

The EU Commission, Council and Parliament very meritoriously provide extensive information in their annual reports about the application of Regulation 1049/2001. These annual reports were first published in 2003[45] and are an indispensable source of inquiry into the development and practice of the access policy.

[45] The first report for the Commission was: 'Report from the Commission on the application in 2002 of Regulation (EC) No 1049/2001 of the European Parliament and of the Council regarding public access to European Parliament, Council and Commission documents. COM (2003) 216 final, 29 April 2003'.

The annual reports relate to a single institution, therefore the normal arrangement is that every year three distinct reports (one for the Commission, one for the Council, one for the Parliament) are drafted and made available on each institution's website. In these reports, besides copious data regarding requests for access that do not reach the EU courts,[46] data are made available for each year as per the number (and identification) of access-related cases lodged by applicants against the applicable institution before the EU courts. Furthermore, the institution will also indicate if it has resolved to appeal[47] any first instance condemnation.

From a comparison of the annual reports of all three institutions it emerges that the Commission, in particular, is the addressee of the vast majority of requests for access. Therefore it comes as no surprise that the vast majority of legal actions lodged by applicants—to the effect that decisions refusing access are annulled—are lodged versus the Commission.

In the light of this greater intensity of the Commission's role, focusing solely on Commission-originating information regarding the type of beneficiaries of access that tend to engage the EU judicature, it emerges that the institution resorts to a categorisation[48] to identify and qualify applicants. These are divided into six categories: academics; Civil Society (interest groups/industry/NGOs); public authorities (non-EU); other EU institutions; journalists; not specified.

Subsequently, rates of litigation are calculated, per year, per category as a percentage of the overall number of actions lodged. It is also important to state that the Commission does not provide data within the same format from year to year which makes long-term interpretation spanning several years more difficult.

Minor adversities aside, a closer look at the Civil Society heading reveals that, under that heading, three sub-categories have been grouped: interest groups, industry and NGOs. What is immediately conspicuous is that these categories of applicants differ from the point of view of their nature, their purposes, their (private) reasons to request access, and even their economic resilience. The last aspect, for that matter, is the *conditio sine qua non* that must be satisfied before litigation is even attempted.[49] Therefore although the institution is generous enough to provide

The first for the Council was: www.consilium.europa.eu/uedocs/cmsUpload/EN-AR-02.pdf. The first for the Parliament was: PE 324.992/BUR of 23 January 2003: www.europarl.europa.eu/RegWeb/application/registre/simpleSearch.faces?language=EN.

[46] For a critical analysis of these figures, see L Cotino, 'Theory and Reality of Public Access to EU Information' in D Curtin, AE Kellerman and S Blockmans (eds), *The EU Constitution: The Best Way Forward?* (The Hague, TMC Asser Press, 2005) 233–44.

[47] When this takes place, the institution itself becomes an applicant, naturally only within proceedings that take place before the ECJ. The institution is not requesting documents. Much to the contrary, the institution applies to the ECJ to the effect that, as the final court of the EU, it annul a ruling of the GC. The so-called contested ruling of the EU's first instance court will have ordered the annulment of a decision refusing to disclose documents, made by the very institution that is now an applicant and which was addressed to one of access' beneficiaries.

[48] Source of the Categorisation: Commission's Annual Reports on the application of Regulation 1049/2001 for 2008, 2009, 2010, 2011, 2012.

[49] While for natural persons legal aid (accorded under the strictest of conditions) is available from first instance, until July 2015, legal persons had to overcome the first instance hurdle by way of independent means. For the latter, before July 2015 financial support was available only at the stage of an appeal to the ECJ. See Rules of Procedure of the ECJ, Arts 155 and 116 and Rules of Procedure of the General Court, Arts 146 to 150.

the information in regard to that category's (Civil Society) performance as per rates of litigation for that year, it might be the case that—at a given moment in time and within that broad category—the industry is more indolent while its non-Industrial component (NGOs and/or interest groups) is sparring against one or several institutions, or vice versa.

What is in fact crucial is that it is of no avail merely to plot the number of times that a given sub-category is lodging actions. The objective of doing so is to subsequently find a connection to an objective influential factor that would shed light on the frequency of litigation.

By way of a simple example, if one were to adopt a more articulate breakdown of the Civil Society Group it would be possible to refine the available information further in regard to two different queries.

The first, of more general purpose, would be: from 1993–2013,[50] which category of applicants, overall, is the most assiduous in lodging actions for annulment? This would shed light on whom the access policy is, overall, most attractive and useful to.

The second, aimed at better understanding the tensions that exist within a given categorisation, would be: within the Civil Society, which sub-group is more industrious? Industry, NGOs or interest groups?

i. Who most Calls on the EU Courts?

In regard to the first question, and as we have mentioned, the official reports on the access policy are written on a yearly basis (and only since 2002). Therefore, first, it would be necessary to control for the period 1993–2001 and, subsequently to add together data spanning from 2002–13. While this is certainly feasible, and has been done,[51] an overwhelming exponent of the Civil Society[52] category emerges. That the main protagonist of a policy offered to the public is the Civil Society comes as no surprise, yet the conclusion is somewhat lacking in detail. Who is the Civil Society? What is the data revealing about applicants?

If one were to single out eight applicant categories rather than six,[53] at least a refinement of conclusions would be facilitated. The difference in regard to the Commission's option would be twofold: on the one hand regarding the Civil Society, the industry would become an independent category and NGOs would be merged with interest groups into a new category: non-industry.[54] On the other hand a new category, 'prisoner', would be introduced. Therefore, by way of example the following alternative break-up could be adopted: journalists; public authorities (non-EU); industry; non-industry (merging NGOs and interest groups); other EU institutions; not specified; academics; and prisoners.

[50] The entire lifespan of access.

[51] It has been done (authors' own computation).

[52] Over 20 years, 1993–2013, out of 216 actions in total, 132 are ascribed to the Civil Society (96 industry+36 non-industry).

[53] Other options are, of course, possible and just as valid.

[54] Cross-referencing applicants to a category 'interest groups' on the sole basis of applicants' names or designation is not possible.

This approach would be especially informative since with a single glance it would become evident that, overall, in seeking the aid of the judicature, the most industrious beneficiary of the policy is, literally, the industry.

Table 2.1: Nature of the applicant 1994–2013

Journalist	6
NON-EU	13
NON-Industry	36
Industry	96
Other EU institutions	3
Not Specified	35
Academic	16
Prisoner	2

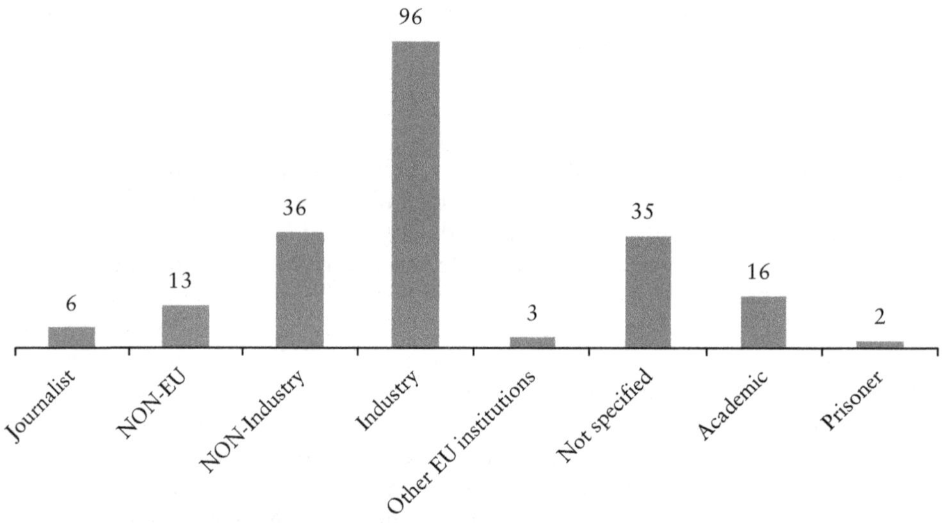

Source: L Rossi, AR Valente (own computation).

ii. Divergences in Purpose

The first query served to identify access' most industrious beneficiary. That having been accomplished, and given that the Commission's data on rates of litigation between 2008–12 suggests that the rate of litigation of the Civil Society group as a whole is constant, the second, more specific, query would be: what was the distribution of rates of litigation (for that period) within the group when comparing its industrial v non-industrial components (the latter taken to mean NGOs and interest groups)?

On the basis of consultation of all the applications for actions for annulment, orders[55] and judgments pertaining to actions lodged between 2008 and 2012, the following conclusions were drawn: first, from the information available in the case law it was impossible to understand which applicants should be categorised as an interest group.[56] However, it was somewhat less difficult to identify a dividing line between industry and non-industry (NGOs and interest groups together). Having compared their activity within each separate year, it emerges that while the category Civil Society (taken globally) may be constant (as a percentage of all litigation lodged versus the Commission in a given year), within the category itself there is significant variance.

Peaks of litigation are identifiable regarding the industry during the year 2008, and again during the year 2012, while the same is true for the non-industry (NGOs and interest groups) in 2010 and 2011.

Table 2.2: Industry v Non-industry per year

	Industry	Non-industry
2008	15	4
2009	2	2
2010	3	9
2011	11	11
2012	16	2

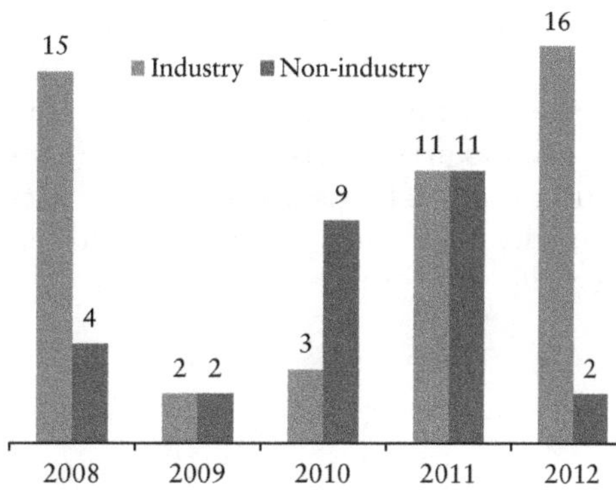

Source: L Rossi, AR Valente (own computation).

iii. Industry

One explanation might be that an objective factor accounts for peaks of litigation from the *Industry* in 2008 and 2012, namely parallel competition proceedings. In

[55] The term 'order'—here—is used to identify as a typical act that the judicature resorts to within the case law. Generally these consist in acts that fall short of a judgment. By way of example and—inter alia—decisions on costs, the removal of a case from the Register, decisions not to proceed to judgment of the merit of a case etc. It is not used in the sense of pointing in the direction of availability of (positive) injunctive relief which, as has been noted, is absent from the EU's access policy of the EU.

[56] As the institutions do not provide information about which specific cases are ascribed to each category.

2008 it is highly likely that the Commission's investigation of Ryanair[57] prompted that undertaking to attempt to access documents via Regulation 1049/2001 in order to bolster its defence. In the same sense, in 2012, it is highly likely that the so-called Car Glass Cartel[58] parallel proceedings triggered a rampage from the industry (defendants and their competitors alike) towards the opportunities arising from Regulation 1049/2001.

iv. Non-industry

Regarding the non-industry (NGOs and the interest groups), the prediction of what could have accounted for such an outbreak of litigious activity in 2011 is far less immediate. Still, the answer may well lie in the necessity for applicants categorised as non-industry—possibly less economically resilient than industry-originating applicants—to secure a certain interpretation of rules of procedure. In sum, and inter alia, they sought to obtain several assurances from the Court.

First, that—as was already the case for applicants—deadlines in general and, in particular, those laid down in Article 8 of Regulation 1049/2001, should be ruled to be imperative for the institutions as well. Secondly, that applicants were not to be rebuked for challenging implied decisions. Thirdly, that the discomforts arising from express decisions issued after implied decisions were to be borne by the institutions.[59] The visible retreat of this type of applicants from the Courts in 2012[60] is equally coherent with the assumption made above: by then, those precedents had been adjusted[61] to their satisfaction.

[57] It is clear from the opening paras (1–3) of the judgment rendered in Joined Cases T–494/08 to T–500/08 & T–509/08 *Ryanair v Commission* [2010] ECR II-5723 that:

> Between 2002 and 2006 the Commission received several complaints concerning alleged State Aid granted to [Ryanair] by the operators of [eight] airports. In addition the Commission received, on 26 January 2007, the Commission received a notification from the French authorities concerning contracts concluded by the Pau-Béarn Chamber of Commerce with [Ryanair] and one of its subsidiaries. In each case, the Commission initiated formal investigation procedures in respect of aid, allegedly granted to Ryanair]. Summaries of those Decisions, informing parties concerned of the possibility of submitting their comments were published in the [OJEU]. By letters of June 2008 [Ryanair] requested the Commission to grant it access, under Regulation 1049/2001, to the files concerning the State Aid allegedly granted to it by the operators of [those eight] airports.

[58] By way of illustration many requests are linked to a competition investigation (Comp 39.125 Carglass) namely and inter alia, Case T-421/12 *Wurtembergische Gemeinde Versicherung v Commission* [not reported]; Case T-462/12 *Pilkington Group v Commission* [not reported]; Case T-465/12 *ACG Glass Europe a.o. v Commission* [not reported]; Case T-476/12 *Saint Gobain Glass Deutschland v Commission* [not reported].

[59] Ch 6. By way of example it is worth mentioning that 10 out of the 13 actions lodged before the GC during 2010 are procedure-related, namely, Cases T-17/10, T-36/10, T-120/10; T-167/10; T-180/10, T-291/10, T-300/10; T-301/10; T-449/10 and T-511/10.

[60] Table 2.2, Year 2012.

[61] See Ch 6.

v. Preponderance of Name

There is a lesson to be learned from these disparate interpretations of the same data. Although there is no room in the access policy to hear their (private) reasons, each and every applicant fights with a purpose. Therefore, purpose is seminal. Although all applicants have uniformly asked for documents, some will be content with annulment, others will accept nothing short of an injunction and others, who will not surrender the requirement that a process be equitable, seek to enforce procedure. In spite of what the access policy is—normative choices and judicial precedent—the purpose behind litigation reveals what the public needs access to be. Trust cannot be enhanced if an abyss remains between one and the other.

B. Those who Seek Annulment

When we speak of the purpose of litigation it is conventional to suppose that victorious applicants will return home satisfied since they have been vindicated in court. As a famous Englishman, Lord Patrick Devlin, once said, litigation seeks the removal of a sense of injustice. Thus while it is to be expected that unsuccessful applicants will lodge appeals before a higher court[62] it is less obvious that successful applicants in first instance will pursue their dispute further.

i. Meeting again at the Baseline Court

Curiously, this kind of perseverance of successful applicants was observable from the outset as a distinctive feature of the access litigation. Although perplexing, there is a structural explanation for these occurrences. Owing to the functional consequence of *mere* annulment being granted to applicants as maximal remedy, when examining any request for annulment, the GC is confined to *cassation*[63] *or* affirmation[64] of the institutions' decisions. In consequence, with the conspicuous exception of requiring the institutions to produce the contested documents in order that the courts—but never the applicant—examine them,[65] the EU judicature lacks the power to order the institutions to act in (positively) any other manner. The Court is limited to the issuance of (temporary) negative orders (*de non facere, de non dare*) with regard to instances of interim relief, when it is sought by an applicant against disclosure. Whilst the judicature may, thus, order the institutions not to disclose and/or publish

[62] As was the case of *Van der Wal I* (here the ECJ); Case T-83/96 *Van der Wal v Commission* [1998] II-00545.

[63] The Court rules that the institutional decision refusing access is tainted and it is annulled.

[64] The Court rules that the institutional decision refusing access is untainted and, therefore it is upheld.

[65] There has been growing interest in this possibility. In fact, appeals have been lodged against judgments of the GC on the grounds that the first instance court, having made assertive statements about the contested documents, had not examined the same. On this point see inter alia Opinion of AG Villalon in Case C-135/11P *IFAW v Commission* [not reported] para 73 and the respective judgment in Case C-135/11P *IFAW v Commission* [not reported] paras 74–77.

documents, the opposite kind of instructions, ie positive orders (*de facere*, *de dare*), remain barred.

ii. A Model without Injunctive Orders

More concretely, the EU courts' powers are greatly restricted on three occasions: (1) in the event of institutional inertia the EU courts are unable to prompt the institution to decide; (2) in the face of an institution's refusal to hand over documents to an applicant the EU courts may not instruct the institution to do so; and finally (3) in the event that the EU courts themselves are in possession of the contested documents they may not, of their own motion, make them available to applicants.

Within the type of framework just described, if an institutional refusal to grant an applicant access to documents is annulled either by the GC or the ECJ, the successful applicant does not—inherently—leave the courtroom in possession of the contested documents. Rather, a novel duty arises vis-à-vis the institution involved: it must decide anew on the (old) request for access, taking the Court's ministrations into account.

iii. One Exception at a Time

One must bear in mind that the exceptions to access laid down in the Code of Conduct were profuse (11), and are no less profuse under Regulation 1049/2001. The Courts have held consistently that an institution may base a refusal to grant access simultaneously on more than one exception, but are not obliged to do so even when several exceptions apply concurrently.[66] Consequently, the institutions have declared that for reasons of procedural economy, more often than not they will put forth a single reason to ground their position. This is a delicate issue and it is important to clarify the legitimacy of the institutional argument.

If an exception—any exception—is deemed applicable (and overriding),[67] it is—alone—sufficient to uphold a refusal to grant access. Therefore, it is enough that the institution successfully pleads one (among several viable alternatives) to secure the support of the judicature.

In any case, if a first exception is rejected by the GC, it is highly probable—and often true—that the new decision on the old request, will, in substance, consist of the advent of a second (or third or fourth...) exception to justify the (initial) refusal.

Case C-41/00P *Interporc v Commission*, Opinion of AG Philippe Leger

63 In the view of *Interporc*, such a practice amounts to preventing citizens from asserting their right of access to documents. The Commission's behaviour, it contends, undermines the effectiveness of that right, inasmuch as individuals would be obliged to bring legal actions until such time as the Commission had, as it were, exhausted all possible grounds for refusal and was no longer in a position to justify a further decision to refuse access.

[66] Case T-105/95 *WWF UK v Commission* [1997] ECR II-00313, para 61.
[67] See Ch 5.

> The appellant maintains that the Commission's conduct is an abuse and that from the time it examined the making of the first request for access to documents it should have analysed all foreseeable grounds for refusal in such a way that it would no longer have been possible, subsequently, to refuse the request for access on new grounds under the Code of Conduct.

When this comes to pass—and it did[68]—a successful applicant at first instance might, in spite of an initial annulment, be forced to overcome the new hurdle. Thus subsequent actions will be brought, regarding the same dispute, to challenge new reasons before the (same) baseline court. An 'infinite loop' appears on the applicant's horizon. An extremely vexing one.

> John Carvel
>
> Request for Documents of the Council: An Account of the Guardian Case in Openness and Transparency in the European Union[69]
>
> On the Relationship between the Case T 194/94 (*Carvel I*) and Case T-19/96 (*Carvel II*)
>
> We secured the judgment at the Court of First Instance in October 1995.
>
> A month later the Council took a fresh decision on the material in question. It handed over the contested documents minus a few items ... on the grounds that their disclosure might harm the EU's international relations.
>
> It was then that I discovered that [in fact] they had not sent the 'decisions' as I had asked but instead a press release which did not even give a complete list of the decisions taken.
>
> We had to lodge a second application to the Court and engage in acerbic correspondence before getting the documents in dribs and drabs.
>
> We had said in our second application to the Court that we would withdraw it as soon as the Council provided the missing documents.

[68] Notably regarding 3 applicants: the first, Carvel lodged proceedings T-194/94 *Carvel and Guardian Newspapers v Council* [1995] ECR II–02765 (*Carvel I*). After the institution's initial refusal was annulled the applicant received a fresh refusal from the institution: disclosure of part of the contested documents could also undermine the EU's international relations. In consequence, the applicant lodged Case T-19/96 *Carvel v Council* [1996] ECR II-01519 (*Carvel II*).

The second and possibly most notable applicant to fall under this category was Interporc, (who had been a co-protagonist in Case T-50/96 *Primex Produkte a.o. v Commission* [1998] II-03773 (the Commission appealed the ruling but proceedings C-417/98P (not reported) were closed with an order of the ECJ of 10 May 2000)), successfully challenging a separate decision of the Commission singlehandedly in the subsequent T-124/96 *Interporc I* proceedings (*Interporc v Commission* [1998] ECR II-231). As a result, Interporc was fully successful and managed to have the Commission's second decision annulled. A legal void was thus created and the Commission issued a third decision (of 23 April 1998) on the matter. The third decision of the Commission—a new refusal based on different grounds—was, in turn, challenged before the GC on 9 June 1998 in Case T-92/98 [1999] II-03521 (*Interporc II*): this time only partial success ensued, on 7 December 1999.

It was only at this stage that Interporc (three times prior protagonist before the GC) lodged an actual appeal before the ECJ in Case C-41/00P [2003] ECR I-02125 (*Interporc III*).

The same repetition is observable in Case T-188/98 *Kuijer v Council* [2000] ECR II-01959 (*Kuijer I*), where, following full success of the applicant, a subsequent Case T-211/00 *Kuijer v Council* [2002] ECR II-00485 (*Kuijer II*), was lodged, regarding the initial dispute, again before the GC, to counter a new refusal of the Council based on different reasons.

[69] EIPA 1998, 63.

> In the end we got what we wanted, although we had to bear our own legal costs in the second stage because that is the penalty for withdrawers.

iv. The Abyss of the 'Infinite Loop'

It is important to clarify that this repetitive feature, rather than being the applicant's choice of legal strategy, is a feature imposed on the applicant. In truth it is a functional consequence of two characteristics of access' procedure. First, institutions are permitted to invoke only one exception at a time. Second, the lack of depth or intensity of effect that goes hand in hand with the legislative option that judicial competence is—*de lege data*—confined to mere annulment.

C. Those who Seek Injunctions

In spite of enduring judicial clarity on this point since 1996, some applicants do not accept that judicial review of institutional refusals to grant access has been fashioned as mere cassation or annulment. So they put their shoulder to the judges' (lack of) empowerment and push, as many times as they can manage and as loudly as they are permitted to voice their concerns. Of course the result of such requests is that the judicature inveterately holds the applicant to have capitulated in regard to that head of claim's merit.

It would be overly hasty to assume that they—applicants or their legal counsel—do not understand the rules of procedure, in other words that there is procedural illiteracy. Or worse, to suggest it is a form of obstinate autism to the effect that the current normative framework and judicial precedent come with stringent limitations. It is no cry of simpletons.

The first to have comprehended this were the judges, who in their constant firmness of making clear to applicants that the place beyond annulment is not to be ventured into have been tactful in their self-restraint.[70] Repeatedly they have passed on a subliminal signal that it is the current stage of EU law that does not empower the judicature to go further in the protection of the applicants' right.

D. Those who Enforce Procedure

By way of conclusion of the analysis of beneficiaries' reaction to the opportunities arising from the policy, it is worth mentioning that an especially assertive category of applicants has addressed arguments against the establishment within the EU law of access of precedents that are unduly restrictive.

[70] Although the possibility remains within the discretion of the courts, the EU courts have, recently, adopted a more forthcoming position on the concrete examination of contested documents by the judicature.

The binding judicial precedent, being exactly what we know it to be, occasionally moves on. When the precedent budges, concessions are made. But, it is also true that more often than not, judicial concessions made to either of access' *dramatis personae* (to the institutions[71] or to the applicants)[72] have devastating effects on the status of the counterpart. However, at times the judicature—albeit bringing about a radical change of framework—manages nonetheless to strike a quasi-moral balance between rivals (here, institutions and applicants). One of the parties may nurture preference for a different solution but does not dare protest. A new precedent arises.

i. For whom the Deadline Tolls

Such was the case with deadlines, on the surface a factually unexciting topic. Uncomplicated as they may appear—either a deadline exists or it does not, and if it exists there are only two options to consider: either the deadline is mandatory, or it is not—deadlines do pertain to the ambit of basic requirements of procedural certainty and security, in sum, procedural decency, which is, of course, a highly contentious issue.

For the moment[73] it suffices to say that when, on 19 January 2010, (a rather unexpected and idiosyncratic) decision of the GC threatened to accord the institutions tolerance regarding the tempo within which they were to reply to requests,[74] a quasi-mutiny of applicants took place. At the origin of the troubles was an undertaking (*Co-frutta*) who, in 2004, had lodged an action against the silence of one of the institutions. And when the late answer came, the applicant would not accept it.[75] It stated as much. The GC did not welcome the impertinence.

> Joined Cases T-355/04 and T-446/04 *Co-frutta v Commission*
>
> 52 The applicant claims that to accept that the Commission still has the possibility of adopting an express decision after adopting an implied decision of refusal would encourage the Commission to ignore the mandatory deadlines fixed by the legislation on access to documents. That would constitute, according to the applicant, a manifest infringement of the principle of legal certainty and would oblige citizens to bring two actions for annulment, one against the implied decision and the other against the express decision—the situation in which the applicant finds itself.
>
> Findings of the Court
>
> 58 In the field of access to documents, the legislature specified the consequences of failure to comply with the time-limits laid down in Article 8(1) and (2) of Regulation No 1049/2001, by providing, in Article 8(3) thereof, that such failure on the part of the institution is to give the applicant the right to institute judicial proceedings.

[71] eg the acknowledgement of (allegedly) rebuttable presumptions. On this point, see Ch 5.

[72] eg when the GC enforced an individual examination of hundreds of documents; Case T-2/03 *Verein Für Konsumenteninformation v Commission* [2005] ECR II-00121.

[73] This issue will be further explored in Ch 6.

[74] Joined Cases T-355/04 and T-446/04 *Co-frutta v Commission* [2010] ECR II–00001 (*Co-frutta II*).

[75] ibid.

59 In that context, the consequences which the applicant wishes to attribute to the Commission's failure to comply with the time-limits laid down in Article 8(1) and (2) of Regulation No 1049/2001 must be considered to be disproportionate. There is no legal principle which results in the administration losing its power to respond to an application, even outside the time-limits laid down for that purpose. The mechanism of an implied refusal decision was established in order to counter the risk that the administration would choose not to reply to an application for access to documents and escape review by the courts, not to render unlawful every decision which is late. On the other hand, the administration is required, in principle, to provide—even late—a reasoned response to every application by a citizen. That approach is consistent with the function of the mechanism of the implied refusal decision, which is to enable citizens to challenge inaction on the part of the administration with a view to obtaining a reasoned response.

60 Contrary to the assertions of the applicant, such an interpretation does not affect the objective pursued by Article 253 EC of protecting the rights of citizens and does not permit the Commission to disregard the mandatory time-limits fixed by Regulation No 1049/2001 and Decision 2001/937. Compensation for any loss occasioned by failure to comply with the time-limits for responding can be sought before the General Court, in the context of an action for damages.

ii. Late Answers, the Fox in the Henhouse

The Court's position was dangerous to access' beneficiaries. As addressees of the institutions' Decisions they would have to react to late answers that would be sent to them after they had challenged implied refusals. The GC's solution moreover, pointed to an avenue that applicants did not care to tread: the cumbersome pleadings of the action for damages. Pursuing compensation was not their purpose. Applicants' purpose overlooked, the GC was off the mark.

Curiously, applicants did not desert the policy. After the initial numbness, a period during which the rather iniquitous interpretation exerted unnecessary offence upon pending cases,[76] applicants (of all categories) rose from the ashes and returned to plead in court that an imposition of fair play would be ruled. With resolution, and among other grievances placed before the judicature, applicants continued to drop actions for annulment of silence onto the court's agenda.

The stakes were perilous: for the applicants, for the institutions, for the court. The first would not surrender that they were to be treated, at least, in accordance with the more congenial interpretation of rules laid down. The second were now under scrutiny, their behaviour questioned, their own legitimation overshadowed by accusations of abuse. Last but not least the court was tested. Self-restraint of

[76] Issued on 19 January 2010, the *Co-frutta* judgment worsened equally offensive precedents that gave credit to so-called '*holding replies*' from the institutions, namely the order of 1 December 2006, in Case T-203/06 *Eurostrategies sprl v Commission* [Not reported]. The *Co-frutta* ruling was moderately mitigated in the order of 17 June 2010 in Case T-359/09 *Jurasinovic v Council* [2010] II-00114, and despite consistent signalling that the precedent was not to endure (10 December 2010, *Ryanair* (n 57) and, in the same sense, the order of 8 April 2011 in Case T-291/10 *Martin v Commission)*, the rulings' effects were projected as far as 9 September 2011 into Case T-29/08 *Liga para Protecção da Natureza v Commission* [2011] ECR-II-06021 (*LPN*) para 46.

the judicature had been accepted as fatuous while there was a *secundum legem* backing;[77] conversely, when measured against this different framework it was an option that carried greater risk. Disenfranchising applicants from automatic protection against the breach of imperative deadlines is difficult—or even impossible—to justify over time. A court that makes justice too hard to attain will enjoy no sympathy and, as a consequence, will not be in demand either. It is true that access is a relatively shielded area of EU law. Yet a Union that does not uphold legal certainty risks the desertion of even its most enthusiastic supporters.

10 months after the failed route of its tolerance coupled with the suggestion to the applicant that relief lay in the civil action for damages, the Court subtly embarked on a different remedial approach to tardiness. Questioned repeatedly on the issue, first, the Court made no further mention of the civil action. Secondly, it stated[78] and subsequently confirmed,[79] as many times as was necessary, and with the simplicity of new yet compulsive argument, that deadlines (after all) were very much alive.[80]

iii. Stratagems of Many Kinds

As a concluding sub-topic within the discussion of the enforcement of procedure by applicants, although it may opportune to commend their resilience, it is also true that, on occasion, they venture down thought-provoking behavioural paths as well. It is not our purpose to judge the opportunity of legitimate methods employed to enforce own rights, yet there are two episodes worth mentioning for the simple reason that they call our attention to the policy's exposure to multiplying effects.

a. One Document, Many Applicants

In the first place, what comes across is that when, over an extended period, multiple beneficiaries of the policy flock to the same practitioner in order to challenge various institutional refusals regarding access to the same documents, the repeated coincidence both of documents sought and practitioner may give rise to many separate actions that share the same object. Although the actions will be lodged in a trickle spread out over a significant period of time, all of them will share the purpose of assessing the possibilities of disclosure of the same papers. An example may be drawn from the *Aid N 715/99* affair. That was a case of eight actions for annulment

[77] eg no statutory empowerment to grant injunctions.

[78] In Joined Cases T–494/08 to T–500/08 & T–509/08 *Ryanair v Commission* (n 57).

[79] Among others, in Case T-36/10 *Internationaler Hilfsfonds a.o. v Commission* ([2011] ECR II-01403, order of the GC of 24 March 2011; Case T-291/10 *Anne Martin v Commission* [not reported], order of the GC of 8 April 2011; Case C-208/11 P *Internationaler Hilfsfonds a.o. v Commission* (not published), order of the ECJ of 15 February 2012. Again, very recently the new understanding was evoked in Case C-127/13P *Strack v Commission* [not yet reported], in the Opinion of AG Kokott of 22 May 2014, para 32.

[80] This new approach will be further explored in Ch 6. However, there are exceptions; see eg Case T-214/13 *Typke v Commission* [not yet reported], in which in spite of institutional tardiness, the entirety of the costs were imposed on the applicant.

challenging the refusal of the same documents[81] lodged by a single practitioner representing seven clients over a number of years.[82]

The pattern[83] is thought-provoking. Whilst the same applicant would possibly be barred from challenging sequential refusals to grant access to the same document in the guise of a chain reaction, since an applicant's track record would easily be traceable and joinder (or a declaration that the successive actions are devoid of purpose) would swiftly ensue, any document may be requested an infinite number of times. This is true both if the applicant is different and if the moment in time of the requests and challenges to refusals are spread out.[84] We have a situation of one document, many applicants.

b. Many Documents, One Applicant

From another angle, the *Ryanair* joined cases, lodged six years later, also reveal the system's heavy dependence on applicants' procedural options.

After a first action lodged by the undertaking *Ryanair* on 7 November 2008, it was but seven days later that the same undertaking, on 14 November 2008, lodged seven actions for annulment[85] of seven further refusals to grant access to documents. It might be said of the episode that it was more brutal than the *Messina* follow-on actions since it was not as sequential (ie not so spread out over time). Yet, on the other hand the multiplying effect sought by the same applicant was immediately visible (since the applicant is the same) and could be more swiftly addressed by the Court.

All of the actions shared the same subject matter: applications for annulment of the Commission's implied decisions refusing to grant Ryanair access to certain

[81] Annulment of the Commission's decision refusing the applicant access to certain documents relating to the State aid scheme which was the subject of the Commission's Decision of 2 August 2000 (State Aid N 715/99—Italy (SG 2000 D/10574)). Those proceedings, lodged on 18 March 2002, came to an end on 17 September 2003.

[82] Case-T-76/02 *Mara Messina v Commission* [2003] ECR II-03203; Case T-139/03 *Nuova Agricast v Commission* [not reported]; Case T-151/03 *Nuova Agricast v Commission* [2005] ECR II-01967; Case T-287/03 *S.I.M. SA srl v Commission* [not reported]; Case T-295/03 *Poli Sud v Commission* [not reported]; Case T-297/03 *Tomasetto Achille v Commission* [not reported]; T-298/03 *Bieffe v Commission* [not reported]; Case T-299/03 *Nuova Fa.U. Di v Commission* [not reported].

[83] The Court declared Case T-151/03 to be devoid of purpose and the later cases were not litigated to the end.

[84] The fact that different applicants share the same legal counsel is no bar to new proceedings. Having refused a document once, the institution is not obliged to maintain this position over time.

[85] Cases T-494/08; T-495/08; T-496/08; T-497/08; T-498/08; T-499/08; T-500/08 and T-509/08:

> By means of this application the applicant seeks annulment of the Commission implied decision rejecting the applicant's request, pursuant to Regulation No 1049/2001 of the access to documents relating to State aid procedures concerning the presumed State aid granted through an agreement with the operator of Aarhus airport. The said decision was followed by the express decision of 9 October 2008. The annulment of the express decision is alternatively sought by the applicant in the present case.

documents relating to procedures for reviewing State aid allegedly granted to that undertaking by the operators of eight airports.[86]

c. Eyes Wide Shut

It is clear from the subsequent ruling of the GC that a significant administrative congestion was placed on the Commission. The total of 377 documents requested by that single applicant was spread out over eight separate—yet simultaneous—requests for access. Furthermore, eight simultaneous confirmatory requests had to be dealt with by the institution as well. Consequently, the GC agreed to mitigate the severity with which it judged the Commission's ability to respond promptly. Yet this was conceded only insofar as the alleged discomfort to the institution would not be unduly impacted on the applicant (impinging on Ryanair's statute-based expectations of institutional compliance with deadlines).

The fact that many documents may be requested by one applicant or that the same documents may be requested many times by many different applicants is, ultimately, a characteristic of the policy, not of the applicants. Equidistant from both applicant and Commission, in regard to both episodes just mentioned, the Court has read applicants' conduct with 'eyes wide shut'. In sum, the strategy of any beneficiary when legitimate, however burdensome, is no excuse for the institutions to stray from the procedural security that applicants were promised.

IV. CONCLUSIONS

It is only after the acknowledgement of a person's entitlement to ask for documents (ie when a person is acknowledged the status of beneficiary) that the procedure for requesting access to documents is adequately set in motion. Thus by way of conclusion to the debate on legal standing and its connection with the irrelevance of private reasons, it appears that applicants would do well to articulate their requests keeping two tenets in mind. First, that a connection criterion to the EU-origin of the request for access is discernible. Second, that explanations for the request are not to be volunteered.

Two other difficulties that are well known to applicants should be remembered. In the light of the current status quo, there seems to be no practicable alternative to mere annulment or to invocation of exceptions on a one-at-a-time basis. These are limitations that even the judicature is in no position to counter. In consequence, there is no evading these characteristics unless Regulation 1049/2001 and the forces at play between the EU institutions, access' beneficiaries, and the judicature are profoundly recast. Uncomfortable as they may be, these enduring characteristics of the policy shed light on what—today—access is.

[86] Namely, of Aarhus (Denmark) (Case T-494/08), Alghero (Italy) (Case T-495/08), Berlin-Schönefeld (Germany) (Case T-496/08), Frankfurt-Hahn (Germany) (Case T-497/08), Lübeck-Blankensee (Germany) (Case T-498/08), Pau-Béarn (France) (Case T-499/08), Tampere-Pirkkala (Finland) (Case T-500/08) and Bratislava (Slovakia) (Case T-509/08).

Applicants have nonetheless earned their day in court. An important territory has been secured: if it is true that a deadline after all, is just a date, it is also a date beyond which there are consequences. For everyone. Ultimately, what the judicature imposed was dignity as a paramount value of EU law. Courtesy of *Ryanair*, and the related follow-on actions, unless there are compelling reasons to depart from this principle, the institutions are to be treated according to the same criteria that govern applicants. That everyone must abide by the deadlines is a rule of public order that—for the time being—is not negotiable.

In regard to legitimate tactics employed by applicants, a question remains, a quantitative one. What is a 'document'? An entire file? A single page? Each single page? And although the answer to the question is better addressed in Chapter 4, an interesting task for the GC and ECJ may just have been identified: that they take care with the incentives that rulings provide in regard to applicants' more subtle stratagems. The rulings would do well to—at least—steer applicants also, since the policy may not be able to accommodate every kind of legitimate strategy. What does indeed emerge from the case law as appropriate? A single applicant who through a single request seeks to consult 100 pages? A single applicant who through 100 requests seeks to consult distinct single pages (of an extensive file)? 100 applicants that separately (in a concerted manner) seek to consult the same, single page?

3

Institutions

I. INTRODUCTION—COMPONENT PARTS OF A CENSUS

WHO IS BOUND to disclose documents of the EU? In Chapter 2 we discussed the subjective perspective of who are the persons that request documents. In the present chapter the discussion is still confined to the subjective perspective, but it regards whom applicants request documents from. We turn our attention to the component parts of the EU that may be counted as valid addressees of applicants' requests for access.

For many decades, accountability to the public was not a cardinal value in the activity of the EU institutions. Thus, when the EU made a promise to act differently, and in spite of having summoned up the courage to commit to a model of openness, sceptical words were heard. It would be difficult—or so it was said—to bring the European civil servant to conform to an access policy:

> The lack of appropriate information can also be explained by the absence of a truly administrative culture in the field of information and communication among the civil servants of the EU institutions. It is indeed not at all common for an official of these institutions to consider himself 'at the service of' the citizens, to easily abandon the status of European diplomat or 'kingpin' of Europe, and to slip on the shoes of an information officer or even a clerk for the European Union citizens.[1]

Principally, the admonition identifies the Achilles heel of the access policy: the inexperience of the EU institutions in managing (even their own) people.[2] The EU faced the challenge of changing its own internal procedures and of doing so widely, horizontally; hence, in order to become an actual policy, the access principles needed to be implemented into the practice of civil servants across the entire board of EU institutions, agencies and similar bodies. Further, although the rules on access identified the public as the policy's sole beneficiary, it was clearly apparent that in 1993 the EU was itself in need of legitimation.

Although this was not voiced, it was the EU that, first and foremost, would reap the benefits—popular support—of such a policy's success. Further, in spite of the fact that in 1993, as today, the Commission, the Council of Ministers and the Parliament were the most visible face of the institutional EU, the EU was and is composed of a

[1] A Guggenbuhl, 'A Miracle Formula or an Old Powder in New Packaging' in V Deckmyn and I Thomson (eds), *Openness and Transparency in the European Union* (Maastricht, EIPA, 1988) 26.

[2] Here understood as all persons coming into contact with the EU administration.

larger institutional collective. In 1993, its principal structure consisted of six main institutions and two advisory bodies.[3] To support this main structure, a myriad of agencies, bodies and other committees was attached.

A. Implementation: Top-down

The EU had then to opt whether to implement the policy bottom up, from the base to the vertex, or whether to choose a top-down model of implementation. The first option would signify that access would be imposed first onto the agencies, bodies and committees, and then work its way up into the institutions. The alternative would rely on example from the top as a catalyst for the policy's advancement over the EU's lower ranks.

At the basis of this choice one principal issue mattered: the project had to thrive. Access was not to be experimented with and abandoned. Access would either exist within the EU organisation or be left alone. The EU was well aware that there would be no second chance to make an adequate first instalment. With regard to beginnings, and the urgency of a new relationship with the public, a discreet debut was deemed preferable. Still, however discreet, that debut needed robustness. Therefore, to ensure it would succeed, the project was saddled immediately onto two of the EU's principal heavyweights, and therein enforced to the smallest detail. As a start, there was to be access—at least—in the Council and in the Commission.

That place of impact (the vertex of the Union), whilst barely sufficient as a foundation for an entire policy, was at the same time so strong in symbolism that with regard to the remnant components of the EU, even the Parliament's inclusion was expendable in the earliest stage. The Parliament could be—and was—cajoled into tagging along later. And if further down the line a position of neophyte to the policy could be arranged for the Parliament, then the same strategy could be employed regarding other EU institutions, bodies, agencies and committees.

It is as a consequence of that understanding—access as a top-down and inspirational sequence—that the policy was first implemented into the more prominent institutions. Subsequently, Europe's lower segments, the agencies, bodies and committees, would find it impossible to refuse to conform to new-age principles already practised by the (higher) institutions.

i. First-movers Secure a Foothold

One last comment regarding this advancement strategy is that as time elapsed the case law built up. The top-down imposition of the access policy did not merely

[3] The institutional framework is currently laid down in Art 13 TEU. The institutions are the European Commission, the Council of Ministers, the Parliament, the European Central Bank, the Court of Auditors and the Court of Justice. The European Council came to be the seventh EU institution, but that addition is recent and special. Since the early days the advisory bodies have been the European and Social Committee and the Committee of the Regions.

consist of bringing the component parts of the EU under the wing of a set of rules. The later any component of the EU was reined in, the more intense would be the burden flowing from access' judicial *acquis*. As such, early movers into the policy had a better chance of contributing to the policy's very shaping. The mirage of influence worked a powerful incentive to commit to the new rules. Such a trade-off would prove interesting to observe, for example, regarding the early involvement in the policy of the European Central Bank (ECB) and of the European Data Protection Supervisor (EDPS).[4]

B. No Enumeration

Having clarified that the top-down advancement was a choice, one cannot help but wonder what might have been if a contemporary imposition of the access policy over all of the EU's component parts had been feasible. The price that was paid for the policy's advancement as a disjointed smattering of ripples was that it was never decreed that an official census of access-compliant bodies should be taken throughout the structure of the EU. Therefore, no exhaustive list was ever provided to the EU's public with the indication of all the components of the EU that requests for documents could be addressed to. The burden of an inventory would fall—and does to this day fall—upon persons coming into contact with the EU administration. Ironically, those same persons are the policy's intended beneficiaries.

The task of inventory, however, has become more and more overwhelming with the passing of more than 20 years since 1993. It was one thing, in 1996, to identify the third signatory of an inter-institutional agreement (the Parliament) in an age in which the media would pay considerable attention to any such development. It is another quite different task to know whether a remote agency or temporary committee of the EU is subject to rules of access, and if so, which part of those rules is applicable. Adherence to the access policy has reached a stage of such dispersion among the component parts of the EU that today the difficulties inherent in such a compilation exceed by far what may be required of access' beneficiaries.

C. Distinct Periods of Advancement

The goal of this chapter is not to write a list. Rather, we seek to retrace the three strategic and principal periods in the advancement of the access policy over the remaining component parts of the EU, since it was implemented for the Commission and for the Council of Ministers. These periods consist, first, of the one taking place under the 1993 Code of Conduct (1993–2001), second, of the one taking place under Regulation 1049/2001 but before the advent of the Treaty of Lisbon (2001–09), and third of the period that, albeit co-governed by Regulation 1049/2001, was opened with the advent of Article 15 TFEU.

[4] See Ch 7.

Regarding the necessary steps towards a more widespread embrace of the access policy, several methods were open to the EU. There was indeed a question to be answered for each element of the EU: whether or not to come under access' roof. Of course, at the outset the EU had to opt between two alternatives. An extension of institutional coverage could be accomplished either by *imposing* subsequent encompassment into the policy or by *encouraging* the policy's embrace on a voluntary basis.

Ultimately, it was the fact that the EU did not unequivocally opt for one or the other route that brought about a somewhat dispersed pattern of protagonists until the entry into force of the Treaty of Lisbon in 2009.

II. INSTITUTIONS THAT WERE SIGNATORIES TO THE CODES OF CONDUCT

In order to retrace the order of the advancement of the access policy, we must first turn to the 1993 Code of Conduct. It was, after all, with that Code that access became a policy instead of a promise. Although from its title it would appear that only the Council and the Commission signed the same—as has been noted—the Parliament became its third (and final) signatory institution by way of a later, separate Decision in 1997.[5]

What is central to our analysis is that between December 1993 and December 2001, formally, the Code's entire orbit spawned an extremely exclusive group of institutions, numbering three. During that period it was therefore quite straightforward to monitor any developments in the number of access' potential addressees of requests. Beyond the 1993 Code of Conduct, with the passing of the years and the arrival on the scene of many other potential addressees of requests for access to EU documents, this ease of global observation would gradually fade.

Yet during this first period, and curiously, access' turf stretched beyond the terrain of the 1993 Code of Conduct. It was not exclusively governed by the 1993 Code of Conduct, and by the Council of Ministers', the Commission's and the Parliament's implementing Decisions. In 1998, the Court of Auditors[6] adopted its own rules on access. During the next year the European Central Bank[7] followed suit.

A. All Quiet in the Early Case Law

Curiously, this extension of influence of the 1993 Code's main rules over other parts of the EU is not discernible from the early case law. In fact, there are no cases on the subject of access to documents involving the opposition of the public versus these

[5] [1997] OJ L 263/27–29.
[6] [1998] OJ C 295/1.
[7] [1999] OJ L 110/30.

newcomers. This notwithstanding, what is true is that before the advent of Regulation 1049/2001, five institutions[8] had, in fact, embraced access as a policy.

B. Reining in the Committees

The early case law nonetheless played an extremely important role in the policy's expansion too. First in *Rothmans*,[9] a position later confirmed in *British American Tobacco*,[10] the EU judicature sanctioned the absorption into the access policy of any EU body of poor[11] formal structure and under the control of any EU institution already subject to access:

Case T-188/97 *Rothmans v Commission*

57. 'Comitology' committees have their origin in Article 145 of the EC Treaty (now Article 202 EC), which provides that the Council may confer on the Commission, in the acts which the Council adopts, powers for the implementation of the rules which the Council lays down. These committees established pursuant to the 'comitology' decision are composed of representatives of the Member States and are presided over by a Commission representative.

58. According to the 'comitology' decision, the committees established under that decision, such as the Customs Code Committee, assist the Commission in performing the tasks conferred on it. Furthermore, under the terms of the Committee's internal regulation, the Commission provides the secretarial services for the Committee, which means that it draws up the minutes which the Committee adopts. In addition, it appears that this Committee, in common with the other 'comitology' committees, does not have its own administration, budget, archives or premises, still less an address of its own.

59. In light of the above findings, the Committee cannot be regarded as being 'another Community institution or body' within the meaning of the Code of Conduct adopted by Decision 94/90. Since it is also not a natural or legal person, a Member State or any other national or international body, such a committee does not belong to any of the categories of third-party authors listed in that Code.

Case T-111/00 *British American Tobacco*

37. It must be emphasized that the deliberations of the Committee on Excise Duties, and the documents of that committee, are to be regarded as being the deliberations and documents of the Commission. The main task of the committee, which was constituted in pursuance of a Community act, is to assist the Commission, which presides over it and provides its secretariat. The Commission thus draws up the minutes which the committee adopts. In

[8] We are adopting here a broad definition of institution, as the Court of Auditors (CA) is formally regarded as a 'body' of the EU.

[9] Case T-188/97 *Rothmans v Commission* [1999] ECR II-02463.

[10] Case T-111/00 *British American Tobacco v Commission International (Investments) Ltd v Commission* [2001] ECR II-02997.

[11] See *a contrario*, Case T-439/08 *Joséphidès v Commission and EACEA* [2010] ECR II-00230, followed by Case C-626/10P *Joséphidès v Commission and EACEA* [2011] ECR I-00169 and also Case T-578/13 *Luxembourg Pamol a.o. v Commission* [not yet reported].

> addition, it appears that this committee does not have its own administration, budget, archives or premises, still less an address of its own. Consequently, the committee is not a natural or legal person, nor a Member State or any other national or international body, and cannot be regarded as another Community institution or body within the meaning of the code of conduct (see, to that effect, Case T-188/97 *Rothmans v Commission* [1999] ECR II-2463, paragraphs 58 and 59).

These two successive rulings absorbed the entire sample of so-called 'comitology committees' into the Commission, but the logic of the ruling could be extended well beyond. Any entity, however temporarily adjunct to a main institution, would no longer be able to withhold own or self-produced documents from public scrutiny. Those own or self-produced documents were, after *Rothmans*, attributable, concerning authorship,[12] to the main institutions served by temporary bodies. From this, it is easily discernible that to impose (literally) a Code of Conduct that binds the controlling institution on the controlled body is both advised and incontestable. It would have been much more unlikely—had the policy been advanced bottom-up—for the judicature to attempt the reverse (ie for the judicature to attempt the imposition of principles governing the controlled body, on the entirety of the controlling institution).

III. INSTITUTIONS INCLUDED UNDER REGULATION 1049/2001

The advent of Regulation 1049/2001, portrayed as a structural betterment of the 1993 Code of Conduct, was a golden opportunity to lay down clear rules to govern the encompassment of more (than three) institutions within access' formal area of imposition. Obviously, either the Regulation itself would include a list of institutions, agencies, bodies and committees from whom access could be requested or a mechanism of gradual adherence to Regulation 1049/2001—voluntary or otherwise—could have been laid down. As the EU committed to both alternatives, we will discuss them one at a time.

A. By the Regulation itself

i. Institutions

Regulation 1049/2001 lists three institutions that it covers, but makes no further attempt either to close that list or make it longer. At the heart of the absence of a list within Regulation 1049/2001 lies the wording of the Treaty of Amsterdam: Article 255 of the Treaty, while indeed novel, was not more ambitious in terms of institutions than the 1993 Code of Conduct. Moreover, in spite of the fact that both the ECB and Court of Auditors were clearly willing to commit to the new rules

[12] This issue is continued in Ch 4.

(or at least to some version of them), only the same trinity to have formally adopted the access rules of 1993 would feature within the title of Regulation 1049/2001, the 1993 Code of Conducts' first statutory replacement. The Regulation's title 'public access to European Parliament, Council and Commission Documents' named only the Council, the Commission and the Parliament. Consequently, only these three institutions directly adopted implementing rules in 2001.[13]

As for the Regulation's body of text, although slightly more optimistic, it was tainted with the ineffectual ambiguity that ultimately leads to less innovation than has been promised. Voluntary adherence[14] to Regulation 1049/2001 by other institutions, for example, is not excluded but nor is it concretely promoted. Article 1 clearly restricts the scope of the access rules 'to European Parliament, Council and Commission (hereinafter referred to as "the institutions") documents'.

ii. Agencies, Bodies and Committees

It is only with regard to EU agencies that, in the eighth recital of the Regulation, there is a hint that the principles of Regulation 1049/2001 should be applied beyond the institutional trinity. Nonetheless, the statement is rather vague:

> Regulation 1049/2001, Recital (8)
>
> In order to ensure the full application of this Regulation [1049/201] to all activities of the Union, all agencies established by the institutions should apply the principles laid down in this Regulation.

It is not said that the Regulation itself will be applied to the agencies, only its principles are considered. It is also not said if the provision is directed at all agencies already established at the time of the rules' entry into force or reserved for all those yet to be established.

At the same time, a Joint Declaration[15] adopted together with the Regulation includes, at paragraph 1, a reference to the intention that agencies and similar bodies of the EU created by the legislator should have rules on access, which conform to the rules of the Regulation.[16] The Joint Declaration is in accordance with the eighth recital of the Regulation but also goes beyond it, since, besides the agencies, the Joint Declaration refers to EU similar bodies as well.

A second tier of new potential addressees is then identified in the Joint Declaration's paragraph 2: the institutions and bodies not covered by paragraph 1. These are, differently from those enumerated in paragraph 1, called on to adopt internal rules on access which take account of the principles and limits of the Regulation.

[13] For the Commission, Decision [2001] OJ L345/94. For the Council of Ministers, Decisions [2001] L313/40 and later [2009] OJ L 325/35 and for the Parliament, Decision [2001] C374/1, which underwent revision by Decision [2011] C284/32.

[14] Discussed below, at II.B.

[15] [2001] OJ L 173/5.

[16] B Driessen, *Transparency in EU Institutional Law, a Practitioner's Handbook* (Alphen aan den Rijn, Kluwer, 2012).

Once again the wording is unfortunately broad as we encounter two expressions. Rules on access that (1) conform to the Regulation and rules on access that (2) take account of the principles and limits of the Regulation. There is no clarification of the practical significance of either expression, and, more crucially, there is no clarification regarding what the practical consequences would be if the institutions, agencies and bodies failed to adopt such rules.[17] Legal paternalism is present in Regulation 1049/2001, but it is light and quite insubstantial.

Another Regulation seems to have added a layer of guidance to this issue. Council Regulation (EC) No 58/2003 of 19 December 2002[18] lays down the statute for executive agencies to be entrusted with certain tasks in the management of Community programmes, in particular Article 23(1),[19] pursuant to which an executive agency shall be subject to the Regulation when it receives a request for access to a document in its possession.

Driessen[20] has compiled a notable table describing the agencies covered by the access policy, the legal basis of their rules on transparency, as well as their specific implementing rules. A detailed overview of the access-status of the remaining bodies and joint undertakings of the EU is also included in that discussion. This bird's eye observation of agencies' and bodies' post-2001 internal rules seems to suggest that, in fact, as a general rule, agencies and bodies established post-2001 have been conferred with rules on access.[21] This is arranged by way of the agencies' internal rules either in the form of a reference to Regulation 1049/2001 itself or by way of a reference to the Regulation's principles.

In practice, one can expect that, in principle at least, agencies and bodies established after 2001 will include a mechanism for communicating with the public regarding requests for access. Furthermore, one might expect the underlying philosophy to be 'access unless'. Accordingly, within each set of rules, if there is no reference to Regulation 1049/2001 a list of exceptions must be made available at the outset, as well as indications with regard to existing means of redress against an institutional refusal to grant access.

[17] The question was, regrettably, left unresolved by the judgment in Case T-496/13 *McCullough v Cedefop* [not yet reported].

[18] [2003] OJ L 11, 1.

[19] Regulation 58/2003, Art 23:

> Access to documents and confidentiality
>
> 1. Executive agencies shall be subject to Regulation (EC) No 1049/2001 of the European Parliament and of the Council of 30 May 2001 on public access to European Parliament, Council, and Commission documents when it receives a request for access to a document in its possession.
>
> The Steering Committee shall adopt any special rules needed to implement these provisions no later than six months after the setting-up of the executive agency.
>
> 2. The members of the Steering Committee, the director and members of staff, and all persons involved in the activities of the executive agency shall be required, even after their duties have ceased, not to disclose information of the kind covered by the obligation of professional secrecy.

[20] The situation as it stands until June 2012; Driessen, *Transparency in EU Institutional Law, a Practitioner's Handbook* (n 16) 17 ff.

[21] ibid, 29. Most institutions and bodies have decided either to follow the Regulation or to adopt rules largely similar to it.

B. By the Institutions Voluntarily

The ECB and CA, who had been first-movers with regard to adopting own internal rules on access, pursuant to and inspired by the 1993 Code of Conduct, also adopted new rules inspired by Regulation 1049/2001. This took place for the ECB in 2004[22] and for the CA in 2005.[23] Even so, both institutions remained outside the Regulation's title and confined to the half-light of voluntary adherence to the access principles, and it is rather disappointing that their commitment was not pulled into the more visible, formal framework of the new Regulation.

As significant bodies of the EU, the European Investment Bank (EIB) 2002, the Economic and Social Committee (EESC) 2003 and the Committee of the Regions (CR) 2003 also adapted their internal rules to reflect Regulation 1049/2001.

Another interesting case of voluntary, post-2001, *rapprochement* to the access policy is that of the European Data Protection Supervisor (EDPS). In 2002,[24] its internal rules generally committed to compliance with Regulation 1049/2001. However, this adherence, in itself noteworthy, is no different from the case of any other EU component that chooses to formally adapt its internal rules to access. More interesting than its statutory support of the policy, was its active participation in *Bavarian Lager.*[25] In that case, whilst not a principal party to proceedings (no EDPS-held documents were sought), the EDPS, in the role of intervener,[26] made its support of the applicant's position clear. At stake were two conflicting rights and two conflicting Regulations. On the one hand, the general interest of the protection of personal data was measured against a specific applicant's interest in access to documents. On the other, Regulation 1049/2001 was pitted against its contemporary, Regulation 45/2001,[27] which ensures the protection of privacy within EU law. The EDPS came forth to argue that (in that specific case) access could prevail.

The participation of such a specialised body in the debate on access, and moreover before the courts, on the one hand enriched the discussion of the topic. On the other, it shows that access has construed a position amongst the priorities of the EU, and that it has to be reasoned with and taken into account.

22 ECB, [2004] OJ L80/42. Specific exceptions with regard to access to ECB documents were included in the 2004 model. In addition, the 2004 model was amended in 2011 to accommodate a further exception.

23 CA, [2005] OJ C96/1.

24 Decision [2002] OJ L 138/1.

25 T-194/04 *Bavarian Lager v Commission* [2007] ECR II-04523.

26 See Ch 7.

27 Regulation 45/2001 [2001] OJ L 8/1–22 and Corrigendum [2007] OJ L 164/36–36. For an overview of the personal data issues, see V Tilli, 'An Everlasting Challenge for the European Union in Constitutionalising the EU Judicial System' in *Constitutionalising the EU Judicial System, Essays in Honour of Pernilla Lindth* (Oxford, Hart, 2012) 473–85. However, the case law has come to a *volte face* in Case-C-615/13P *ClientEarth and PAN Europe v EFSA* [not yet reported].

C. By Article 15 TFEU

On 1 December 2009[28] a second—and heavier—dose of paternalism augmented Regulation 1049/2001's effectual area of incidence. On this occasion it did so significantly. It was the advent of the Treaty of Lisbon and in particular of Article 15 TFEU:

> Article 15 TFEU
>
> In order to promote good governance and to ensure the participation of civil society, the Union's institutions, bodies and agencies shall conduct their work as openly as possible.
>
> The European Parliament shall meet in public, as shall the Council when considering and voting on a draft legislative act.
>
> Any citizen of the Union, and any natural or legal person residing or having its registered office in a member State, shall have a right of access to documents of the Union's institutions, bodies, offices and agencies, whatever their medium, subject to the principles and to the conditions to be defined in accordance with this paragraph.
>
> General principles and limits on the ground of public or private interest governing this right of access to documents shall be determined by the European parliament and the Council, by means of regulations, acting in accordance with the ordinary legislative procedure.
>
> Each institution, body, office or agency shall ensure that its proceedings are transparent and shall elaborate in its own Rules of Procedure specific provisions regarding access to its documents, in accordance with the regulations referred in the second subparagraph.
>
> The Court of Justice of the European Union, The European Central Bank and the European Investment Bank shall be subject to this paragraph only when exercising their administrative tasks.
>
> The European Parliament and the Council shall ensure publication of the documents relating to the legislative procedures under the terms laid down by the regulations referred in the second subparagraph.

On this occasion all of the EU institutions, bodies, offices and agencies were finally covered by the policy. However, an exception was made for the ECJ (including the GC and the Civil Service Court), ECB and EIB. It does not mean that they were left outside the EU rules on access, only that the exercise of their non-administrative tasks was withdrawn from public scrutiny.

IV. PRACTICAL CONSEQUENCES OF THE POLICY'S ADVANCEMENT

In this section we examine what, in practice, may happen to any component part of the EU when it embraces the access policy and, concomitantly, an applicant is unhappy with an institutional reply to a request for access: court proceedings.

[28] The date of entry into force of the Treaty of Lisbon.

This is a task that makes sense in the first aftermath of the entry into force of Article 15 TFEU (as we write, June 2016). It tells the story of some component parts of the EU other than the Council or the Commission that have been taken to court by applicants for refusing to grant them access to documents. We do not seek to compile an exhaustive list of all the elements of the EU to which this has happened. Unless the ECJ is able to provide a search engine that can infallibly identify all the cases in which Regulation 1049/2001 and/or the practical arrangements for its implementation is discussed, that task is virtually impracticable.

Instead, by discussing a sample of such cases of our own selection,[29] our purpose is to identify, on the one hand, what changes in the structure of litigation if the defendant is different from the Council or the Commission, and, on the other, what stays the same.

A. The EACEA

An unexpected victim of access' public was forced to appear before the GC at the side of the Commission in 2008:[30] an agency, specifically, the Education Audiovisual and Culture Executive Agency[31] (EACEA). It was at the hand of Kalliope Agapiou Joséphidès that the first signal of practical consequences of the access policy beyond the Council, the Commission and the Parliament came to light. In this case, inter alia,[32] the applicant (unsuccessfully) disputed the EACEA's independence from the Commission. The applicant wrongly assumed that the EACEA would not be able to independently handle confirmatory applications for access to documents without (at least) the supervision of the Commission.[33] Moreover, the GC ruled that requests for access should be handled according to the internal rules of the EACEA that implement Regulation 1049/2001[34] (and not in accordance with the corresponding rules for the Commission).[35]

This is an important sign that relationships of control of one institution over another agency, body or committee must be well clarified before the lodging of court proceedings is attempted. The caution rings especially true for the identification of

[29] If, however, a reader comes across any such case that we have not discussed we would be grateful for a notification.

[30] Case T-439/08 *Joséphidès v Commission and EACEA* (n 11) followed by Case C-626/10P *Joséphidès v Commission and EACEA* (n 11).

[31] The EACEA adopted implementing provisions of Regulation 1049/2001 on 13 June in 2005 (AE/2005/CD03/D-Ifinal).

[32] It is interesting to note that here the Court interpreted a request for the production of documents (para 27) as a measure of organisation and inquiry (para 170).

[33] Case T-439/08 *Joséphidès v Commission and EACEA* (n 11) para 42.

[34] ibid, para 31 (available only in French): 'les modalités de traitement par la Commission d'une demande d'accès aux documents n'est pas applicable à l'EACEA. En effet, celle-ci est une entité juridique distincte de la Commission, disposant de son propre règlement intérieur, et elle est tenue de fixer elle-même les modalités de mise en œuvre du règlement n° 1049/2001. Par ailleurs, l'article 4 de la décision du comité de direction prévoit précisément la compétence du directeur de l'EACEA pour traiter des demandes confirmatives'.

[35] Case T-439/08 *Joséphidès v Commission and EACEA* (n 11) para 43.

situations in which measures adopted pursuant to delegated powers are nonetheless still attributable to the delegating institution. According to the CFI, this takes place when 'the author of a measure exercises a merely advisory competence or the measure of which annulment is sought is conditional upon the prior agreement of the delegating institution'.[36]

In *Joséphidès*, the applicant was rebuked both for wrongly assuming a relationship of control of the Commission over the EACEA and for lodging proceedings against defendants *ad abundantiam*. It would have sufficed to institute proceedings against the EACEA without involving the Commission.

B. The EP and the ECB

In 2009, it was the turn of two institutions' prior commitment to access[37] to have visible practical consequences: the European Parliament and the European Central Bank.

The EP (the third institution to come under the 1993 Code of Conduct and subsequently of Regulation 1049/2001) became the fourth[38] EU institution to have an own decision—refusing an applicant access to self-held documents—challenged before the EU judicature. *Dennekamp*[39] introduced the EP into the access litigation and also called for the joint application of Regulation 1049/2001 and of Regulation 45/2001. As to the outcome of its debut, the EP was successful. In 2010, however, the *Egan and Hackett*[40] case, again calling for the joint application of Regulation 1049/2001 and of Regulation 45/2001, proved to be a bittersweet adventure for the EP. Lately (2015) the EP has been dealing with several cases within which the significant amount of documents requested is possibly the most striking aspect.[41]

The year of 2009 also implied practical consequences on the access front for yet another EU institution, the ECB. The institution was introduced into the litigation by *Dufour*,[42] and saw a decision of its executive board annulled, as a consequence. As had happened with the EP, the ECB had hardly been allowed time to recover from the first blow before another of its decisions was challenged before the EU judicature. In fact, in 2010, documents held by the ECB were sought. Thesing & Bloomberg Finance[43] challenged a refusal of the ECB to disclose documents related to the government deficit of one of the Member States. The action had the added sparkle of having (also) been lodged by an applicant established in the USA. Access'

[36] Case T-578/13 *Luxembourg Pamol a.o. v Commission* (n 11) paras 53 and 69.
[37] The Parliament since 1997 and the ECB since 1999 (section I and section III.B).
[38] Until then only the Commission and the Council of Ministers had been taken to court.
[39] Case T-82/09 *Dennekamp v EP* [2011] ECR II-00418.
[40] Case T-190/10 *Egan and Hackett v EP* [not reported].
[41] Cases T-136/15 *Europaiki Dynamiki v EP* [not yet reported]; T-540/15 *De Capitani v EP* [not yet reported]; T-640/15 *Kristan v EP* [not yet reported], which is linked to 28 other actions against the Parliament, all sharing the same object and legal counsel (N Pirc Musar).
[42] T-436/09 *Dufour v ECB* [2011] ECR II-07727.
[43] Case T-590/10 *Thesing & Bloomberg Finance v ECB* [not reported].

infinite public was beginning to show. The ECB's debut was also a felicitous one, and accordingly it was at the instigation of the applicants that the case cruised on into appeal in 2013. However, on the basis of two technicalities,[44] it was dismissed.

Still in 2013, an (oddly) connected pair of actions for annulment—*Hoepner*[45] and *Versorgungswerk der Zahnarztekammer Schleswig-Holstein*—[46] were lodged against the ECB's refusal to grant access to an annex for a swap agreement of 2012 between the Eurosystem and the Hellenic Republic.

Re-treading the argument, stratagems[47] are often employed within the access litigation by applicants. For example, in the *Versorgungsverk* proceedings, the ECB (unsuccessfully) pleaded that the same action be considered inadmissible since Olaf Hoepner, legal counsel to the Versorgungsverk, had previously requested the contested documents in his own name. And more. Olaf Hoepner had also lodged an action for annulment against the ECB's prior refusal to grant him access to the same documents but had, finally, desisted.[48] It is not surprising that the GC ruled that the Versorgungswerk's action was admissible (despite a previous request for the same documents that ended up before the EU judicature). Indeed, the applicant in Case T-70/13 had withdrawn the action before the GC had a chance to examine its merits.[49] However, the fact that the contested documents were identical in both actions and the evident duplicity of the role of Olaf Hoepner, first as applicant (in Case T-70/13) and later as legal counsel to someone else who was seeking access to the same contested documents (in Case T-376/13)—albeit entirely legitimate—is striking.

On the one hand, it gives credit to the perplexities and voiced concerns of the Commission as to the real identities[50] of applicants within each, single, request for access to documents. On the other hand, and more importantly even, it shows how the access policy has been construed in a very different way from the national procedures governing access with regard to its principal class of beneficiaries: a public that need not offer reasons[51] for requests, and whose reasons (for requesting) are not to be probed. Finally, the problem repeats itself whether the defendant institution is a principal one such as the Council or the Commission or whether it is a more specialised neophyte such as the ECB.

44 Order of the ECJ, 14 February 2014, Case C-28/13P *Thesing and Bloomberg v ECB* [not reported].

45 Case T-70/13 *Hoepner & Causaconsilio Koch & partner: Rechstanwalte v ECB*, removed from the register on 20 March 2013 [not reported].

46 Case T-376/13 *Versorgungswerk der Zahnarztekammer Schleswig-Holstein v ECB* [not yet reported].

47 See Ch 2.

48 Case T-70/13 *Hoepner & Causaconsilio Koch & partner: Rechstanwalte v ECB* (n 45).

49 Differently, as in orders of the GC and the ECJ (respectively 12 March 2008, Case T-443/07, paras 9–10 and 29 June 2009, Case C-225/08P, para 60) *Nuova Agricast v Commission*, that successive actions (in which judgment is rendered) lodged against what is considered to be one and the same refusal to grant documents will be *ex officio* barred by the judicature.

50 See Ch 2. The system allows for theoretical models of (some form of) deceit. Principally, and without being penalised for it, persons may pose first as applicants and later as initiators of litigation. In truth they may be acting as mere facilitators of another person's (whose identity remains anonymous) quest for documents.

51 This infinitely wide notion of public *cum* beneficiary of the (impersonal) EU access policy ultimately calls into question the stringent limitations laid down as to interventions (within EU access proceedings; see Ch 7) on the basis of the concept of 'interest in the outcome of the case'.

C. The EFSA

In 2010, an authority joined the players. In fact, 2010 was rife with judicial solicitations for the newcomers to the access policy. It was also the turn of the European Food Safety Authority (EFSA)[52] to defend itself before the GC. In *Cosepuri*,[53] the EFSA (successfully) refused access to documents related to a call for tenders concerning a shuttle service. The ruling is extremely rich in clarifications with regard to the access policy.[54] Besides its other merits, of particular interest to the present discussion is that the ruling states (in spite of the EFSA's own rules on access) that Regulation 1049/2001 is concomitantly applicable if an authority relies on it in its response to an applicant.[55] The ruling adopts a harmonious interpretation approach of practical arrangements for the application of Regulation 1049/2001 (within each agency, body or committee) with regard to the Regulation itself.

Victorious debut notwithstanding, the EFSA's access ordeal was not over, not by a long shot. The authority came before the GC again in 2011, this time at the instigation of ClientEarth and Pesticide Action Network Europe,[56] with regard to the joint application of Regulation 1049/2001 and Regulation 45/2001. The unsuccessful applicants at first instance proceeded to challenge[57] the corresponding ruling of the GC. Two points are worthy of note. The first is that the EDPS has come forth in an unprecedented[58] display of support for another EU authority. The second, worth following up, is that Advocate General Villalon has not entirely ruled out a reversal of the first instance proposition.[59] Indeed, on 16 July 2016, the ECJ set the GC's judgment aside.

The EFSA is further involved in the access litigation by way of Luxembourg Pamol and Luxembourg Industries,[60] two undertakings seeking to secure confidential

[52] The EFSA adopted a Decision concerning access to documents on 16 September 2003.

[53] Case T-532/10 *Cosepuri, Soc Coop p.a. v EFSA* [not reported] (which was joined with Case T-339/10 seeking annulment of the tender).

[54] ibid. The clarifications covered (1) the inability of the Court to grant an order for the production of documents, paras 76–77. The request was (questionably) interpreted as a request for an order to grant access; (2) the absence of a provision in either Regulation 1049/2001 or in the Financial Regulation giving primacy to one over the other, para 85, 'Even if, as EFSA maintains, Article 100(2) of the Financial Regulation contained a specific rule concerning access to documents, it is common ground that Regulation No 1049/2001 and the Financial Regulation have different objectives and do not contain any provision expressly giving one regulation primacy over the other. Therefore, it is appropriate to ensure that each of those regulations is applied in a manner which is compatible with the other and which enables a coherent application of them'; (3) the obligation for the institution to verify (before refusal) the existence of an overriding public interest, para 91 and, finally, (4) that presumptions of harm (in disclosure) have also cropped up in the field of access of tenderers to the bids of others, paras 98–100.

[55] ibid, para 85 *in fine*: 'Furthermore, it should be noted that, in the present case, EFSA expressly relied in particular on Regulation No 1049/2001 in refusing to grant access to the documents at issue'. The EFSA implemented own rules in 2003.

[56] Case T-214/11 *ClientEarth and Pesticide Action Network Europe v EFSA* [not reported].

[57] Case C-615/13P *ClientEarth and Pesticide Action Network Europe v EFSA* [not yet reported].

[58] See Ch 7.

[59] Opinion of AG Villalon in Case C-615/13P *ClientEarth and Pesticide Action Network Europe v EFSA* of 14 April 2014 [not yet reported].

[60] Case T-578/13 *Luxembourg Pamol a.o. v Commission* (n 12) an action (seeking confidential treatment of data) inititated by two companies, one established in Cyprus and the other in Israel.

treatment of information related to pesticides. They rely inter alia on the argument that company know-how and product registration strategies amount to confidential data or information of commercial interest on the basis of Article 4(2) of Regulation 1049/2001.[61] The EFSA referred to the Commission, for consultation[62] and the latter suggested that the EFSA refuse to accord confidential treatment to the contested documents. Curiously, rather than any decision of the EFSA, it was the Commission's suggestion that was challenged since (in the applicant's view) according to the law[63] the final decision on these matters is the responsibility of the Commission. Whilst interim relief against the release of the contested documents was successfully sought,[64] the GC ultimately dismissed the main action since it took the view that the contested act, a decision (refusal to grant confidential treatment) notified by letter of the EFSA, was not attributable to the Commission.[65]

The applicant has been rebuked both for wrongly assuming a relationship of control of the Commission over the EFSA and for not identifying the defendant properly. The Commission should not have been singled out as the defendant. Consequently, the proceedings should have been lodged against the EFSA (and only against the EFSA).

D. The ECDC

2012 brought a centre into the limelight, namely the European Centre for Disease Prevention and Control.[66] Ioannis Ntouvas,[67] a former legal assistant and legal officer[68] of the ECDC, successfully argued that inadequate reasoning had been offered to ground the refusal to grant him access to the final audit reports carried out on the ECDC by the Commission's Internal Audit Service. Interestingly, the applicant requested access from the ECDC to a document produced and originating

[61] ibid, para 50.

[62] ibid, paras 14–16.

[63] ibid, para 16: 'in accordance with Article 14 of Directive 91/414, that question (confidential treatment) fell within the responsibility of the Commission'.

[64] Incidentally, and in clear contrast to settled case law on the lack of competence of the EU judicature to issue (positive) orders to the institutions, the instruction of the GC to the Commission comes quite close to a *de facere* command. Admittedly, it is issued with the purpose of a standstill order—'not publish'. However, the fact that it is directed to the vertex of a chain-of-command, 'the Commission shall ensure that the EFSA does not', muddies the waters considerably; ibid, order of 14 February 2015: 'the European Commission shall ensure that EFSA does not publish a version of the peer review report and final addendum thereto concerning the inclusion of the active substance potassium phosphonate that is more detailed than the redacted version included in the letter of Luxembourg Pamol (Cyprus) Ltd and Luxembourg Industries of 25 February 2013, as set out in Annex A3 to the application in the main proceedings'.

[65] ibid, judgment of the GC of 3 June 2015.

[66] There is mention of an 'Internal Procedure on Public Access to Documents' based on Regulation (EC) 851/2004, Art 20(2), which establishes the Centre for Disease Prevention and Control, in which there is a remission to Regulation 1049/2001.

[67] Case T-223/12 *Ntouvas v ECDC*.

[68] ibid, para 18.

from another institution. This model might represent the beginning of a practice of cross-requests.

E. The EMA

In 2013, another American[69] applicant AbbVie[70] (alongside one from the UK) forced another agency, the European Medicines Agency (EMA),[71] to defend an own decision concerning access to documents. However, it was not a decision to refuse access. It was a decision to grant 'someone else' access to documents connected to the applicant. Ultimately the applicant applied for discontinuance of the proceedings. However, one cannot but wonder what might have taken place, had the 12 prospective interveners[72] (authorised to submit their opinions to the GC) concretely argued the substance of the case.

Still, from the *Abbvie* proceedings a (successful) request for interim relief[73] emerged against the EMA's decision to grant access. The agency reacted and, in turn (successfully) appealed[74] the order of the GC, which was set aside.

Of very similar structure were the subsequent *Intermune*[75] proceedings, also challenging the EMA's management of information. This time it was an international trinity of applicants[76] (once again a US-based applicant among them) who sought to impede the release of information (previously submitted by the applicants to the EMA, and which was not already in the public domain) to Boehringer Ingelheim, their competitor.

In this case also, successful interim relief for the applicants[77] was granted at first instance, only to be set aside on appeal[78] by the EMA. Once more, given the identical structure to *AbbVie*,[79] there was no opportunity (for the public) to observe the prospective interveners' arguments.

[69] As before, in *Thesing & Bloomberg* (see section IV.B above).

[70] Case T-44/13 *AbbVie Inc and AbbVie Ltd v EMA* [not yet reported].

[71] The agency adopted internal rules for the implementation of Regulation 1049/2001 on 19 December 2006 (EMEA/MB/203359/2006 Rev 1). It is not to be confused with the European Medicines *Association*, also identified as EMA (and currently involved in litigation against the Commission: Case C-100/14P).

[72] (1) In support of the applicant (AbbVie) who wished to withold the documents from prying eyes: European Federation of Pharmaceutical Industries and Associations (EFPIA) established in Switzerland; Pharmaceutical Research and Manufactuirers of America established in the USA; EuropaBIO; Biotechnology Industry Organization established in the USA; Intellectual Property Owners Association established in the USA. (2) In support of the defendant (EMA) who wished to release the documents: Portuguese Republic; European Ombudsman; Republic of Slovenia; Bureau Européen des Unions de Consommateurs (BEUC); Republic of Finland; Kingdom of Denmark, and French Republic.

[73] ibid, order of the President of the GC 25 April 2103.

[74] Case C-389/13PR *EMA v AbbVie* [not yet reported].

[75] Case T-73/13 *InterMune UK a.o. v EMA* [not yet reported].

[76] ibid; InterMune UK Ltd; InterMune Inc, established in the USA; and InterMune International AG, established in Switzerland.

[77] ibid.

[78] Case C-390/13PR *EMA v InterMune UK a.o.* [not yet reported].

[79] See above.

F. The Cedefop

In 2013, Colin McCullough,[80] a former personal assistant to the Director of the European Centre for the Development of Vocational Training[81] (Cedefop), made a serious accusation. Allegedly, the Cedefop has failed to adopt practical arrangements for implementing Regulation 1049/2001.[82] Moreover, to bridge this gap, the applicant proposed that the respective detailed rules adopted by the Commission should be applied by analogy. In its judgment, the GC avoided addressing the issue of non-adoption of implementing measures altogether.[83]

With regard to the applicable statute, in *McCullough*[84] (differently from *Cosepuri*)[85] there is no rivalry between Regulation 1049/2001 and the specific practical arrangements for its implementation or other rules on access. Besides the detailed rules of the Commission[86] that cover all executive agencies, there are allegedly no specific rules (to which only the Cedefop is subject) of implementation of Regulation 1049/2001. Therefore, the proceedings could gainfully have clarified what the default framework in such cases might be.

On the one hand, if a relationship of control of the Commission over the Cedefop had been proven, it is not difficult to suppose that, if necessary, the detailed rules of the Commission might have been considered as an adequate framework in default. *In casu*, and from what may be gleaned from the application and judgment, the applicant has both identified an internal addressee for his (confirmatory) request for documents and obtained a (negative) decision from that addressee. It appears that 'the Acting Director of Cedefop' has refused the applicant access to the contested documents. Therefore, here, in contrast to *Joséphidès* (one defendant too many) and to *Luxembourg Pamol* (wrong defendant altogether), the defendant has been correctly identified.

On the other hand, even if the accusation (no detailed implementation) was grounded, the courts could still draw on *Cosepuri*[87] inasmuch as there was reliance on Articles 4(1)(b) and Article 4(3) of Regulation 1049/2001 in the response to the applicant. The entire *acquis* construed around the latter might also have contributed to close the gap. What this precedent might have clarified (and avoided doing) was the question of how sufficient, per se, Regulation 1049/2001 is in the management

[80] Case T-496/13 *McCullough v Cedefop* (n 17).

[81] On the Cedefop's website an electronic form making a reference to rights of access based on Regulation 1049/2001 and TFEU, Art 15 is available to the public.

[82] Fourth plea in law of the application.

[83] Worthy of note is that in Case T-496/13 *McCullough v Cedefop* (n 17), the GC did, however, respond to the applicant's sharp criticism of the EU system of judicial protection of private parties. Conscious of a certain wearying of it by applicants, the GC—and not without a modicum of solicitude—provided lengthy and detailed observations on plausible explanations for the inability of the EU judicature to issue orders to the institutions; paras 15–28. The GC also went on to discuss the limits of the (simple) presumption of veracity of statements made by institutions; paras 49–58.

[84] ibid.

[85] Case T-532/10 *Cosepuri, Soc. Coop. p.a. v EFSA* (n 53) para 85, *in fine*.

[86] See section III.A.ii; Regulation 58/2003, Art 23.

[87] Case T-532/10 *Cosepuri, Soc. Coop. p.a. v EFSA* (n 53) para 85, *in fine*.

of the remaining issues of an access to documents practice (such as the correct identification of an addressee of a confirmatory request) if no further detailed rules are available.

G. The EASO

Another interesting incident (Case T-617/14)[88] has opposed the European Asylum Support Office (EASO) against a German organisation, Pro Asyl Bundesweite Arbeitsgemeinschaft fur Flüchtlinge eV, who wishes to access reports concerning the situation of refugees in Bulgaria. The EASO informed the applicants that their request would be examined both on the basis of Regulation 1040/2001 as well as on the basis of the internal rules of the Office (Decision no 6 of the Management Board[89] on access to its internal documents). However, the case was closed by order of the GC of 14 July 2015[90] for reasons of procedure.

V. ECJ DOCUMENTS—SAME PERSON, DIFFERENT HATS

Finally, a word on the role of the ECJ as an addressee of requests for access is called for. It is interesting to note that the ECJ kept both the 1993 Code of Conduct and Regulation 1049/2001 at bay. Curiously the ECJ's initial *rapprochement* to access came before the Treaty of Lisbon and at the hand of environmental rules laid down in Regulation 1367/2006.[91] The Treaty of Lisbon would complete the ECJ's subjection to the access policy whilst, nonetheless, and as has been noted above, granting it a significant amount of insulation[92] from the bite of Regulation 1049/2001.[93]

As the EU institution that it is—just another player of the access policy—the ECJ would be discussed as just another potential addressee of requests for access to self-held documents.

[88] [Not yet reported].
[89] 20 September 2011.
[90] Available only in French/German [not reported].
[91] See Regulation 1367/2006, Art 2(1)(c) and Recital 7, which states:

> The Aarhus Convention defines public authorities in a broad way, the basic concept being that wherever public authority is exercised, there should be rights for individuals and their organisations. It is therefore necessary that the Community institutions and bodies covered by this Regulation be defined in the same broad and functional way. Under the Aarhus Convention, Community institutions and bodies can be excluded from the scope of application of the Convention when acting in a judicial or legislative capacity. However, for reasons of consistency with Regulation (EC) No 1049/2001 of the European Parliament and of the Council of 30 May 2001 regarding public access to European Parliament, Council and Commission documents, the provisions on access to environmental information should apply to Community institutions and bodies acting in a legislative capacity.

[92] Below.
[93] See generally C Amalfitano, 'L'accesso ai documenti in possesso della Corte di Giustizia dell'Unione Europea nell'esercizio delle sue funzioni amministrative' in *Scritti in Onore di Giuseppe Tesauro* (Naples, Editoriale scientifica, 2014) vol 2, 781–806.

Still, inescapably the ECJ (as a whole) is the EU judicature too. Thus, although this conjecture is for now merely academic, if any action for annulment against a refusal to disclose documents is lodged against the EU judicature (GC ECJ or CST), both the CFI and the ECJ will (at some stage) inevitably become judges of their own behaviour. In this odd context, judicial review becomes very unconventional.

On this point it is important to recall, first, that all actions for the annulment of an institutional refusal must commence before the GC Therefore, whenever either the CST or the ECJ are involved (as refusing institutions) the judge at first instance will, in fact, always be independent from the refusing institution. On appeal, the same holds for the CST. With regard to the ECJ the situation will be different, of course, unless no applicant or defendant appeals … thus blocking the ECJ's power of judicial review (of its own behaviour) altogether.

Secondly, whilst for the GC there is no detachment at first instance between judge and refusing institution, the appeal route to the ECJ is always available. In fact, as a rule, the GC operates under constant (threat of) *ex post* control by the ECJ. Consequently, the framework now brought about by the access policy is not overly worrying.

VI. DIFFERENT GUARDIANS, SAME DOCUMENTS

The abolition of the author's rule by Regulation 1049/2001 brought much more 'noise' into the access policy than had existed under the Code of Conduct. Before that rule disappeared Member States managed the release of Member State documents and private parties managed the release of private parties' documents. After that rule disappeared the institutions were forced to find a way to manage the release not only of own documents but also of all incoming documents.

In addition, a potentially schizophrenic characteristic of the post-Regulation 1049/2001 framework is that there is no impediment for an applicant to request from a certain institution access to the documents of another. Still, the affected counterpart (who authored the documents) might deploy interim relief to impede such release of information. As an alternative, the affected counterpart might intervene in support of an institutional refusal to disclose those documents.

Hypothetical layers build up. Curiously, institutions, Member States and private parties alike are not only bound to manage the release of incoming documents. They must also control what is being proposed to be done with the documents of which they are authors by the (other) institutions of the EU.

It is quite clear that the abolition of the author's rule principally sought to encompass in the access policy information produced by the Member States and/or private parties on which the EU bases (many) substantive decisions. The new framework anticipated (and prepared for) cross-requesting of documents produced by either Member States or private parties to specific EU institutions. What the new framework possibly underestimated was the procedural mayhem from (the now feasible) cross-requesting of documents of one institution to another. It is manageable, yet likely to create tension.

VII. CONCLUSIONS

In spite of a top-down and sequential strategy of the advancement of the access policy over the EU's component parts, the number of principal institutions of the EU under the wing of the access policy as laid down by the 1993 Code of Conduct (three formally, plus two less formally) suffered no alteration with the advent of Regulation 1049/2001. Furthermore, although through *British American Tobacco*[94] the EU judicature sanctioned encompassment into the policy of any body under significant control of a participating, main institution, no further formal reference to this groundbreaking inclusion was made.

Moreover, both from its title and from its body of text, only three main EU institutions are clearly straddled by Regulation 1049/2001. As for voluntary adherence of further EU (main) components, it was neither prohibited nor instigated. In fact, there seems to have been no effort by Regulation 1049/2001 even to acknowledge the ECB and CA's own, and prior, internal rules on access of 1998. What Regulation 1049/2001 accomplished instead was to open a period of influence over EU agencies and bodies. In spite of this, all references in regard to the intention of expanding the Regulation's area of influence over EU agencies and bodies were rather vague. Regulation 58/2003 adds a layer of reference for the executive agencies, but neither Regulation states what is to be done in the event that an agency keeps the rules of access at a distance.

Article 15 of the TFEU, very differently, sweeps the access policy over the entirety of the remaining component parts of the EU that had, as yet, not come under its direct area of influence. The drawing of a circle of addressees of requests for access, commenced in 1993, was completed 13 years later, in 2009. However commendable, the legislative route of inclusion left it to the judicature—as *McCullough* might have shown—to bridge the gaps in the law that create divides between applicants and institutions.

Finally, relationships of control of the principal institutions of the EU over its remaining component parts must be properly understood before documents are requested and proceedings are lodged against refusals of access to the same. It is relatively simple to observe which part of the EU notifies refusals to applicants. Another very different issue is to identify, well in advance of the lodging of court proceedings, which part of the EU decided to say 'no'.

[94] Case T-111/00 *British American Tobacco v Commission* (n 10).

4

Documents

I. INTRODUCTION—A POLICY OF BITES AND PIECES?[1]

MONEY IS NO key to the access policy. First-mover litigants[2] play the game in order to gain access to documents,[3] and seldom seek compensation[4] when they challenge institutional refusals. Institutions, for their part, scrutinise each time whether they can disclose the document in question fully or whether there is an exception foreseen in Article 4 of Regulation 1049/2001 which applies.[5]

If this is true, the foreground to access to documents disputes brought before the judicature is quite intuitive: applicants have asked institutions for access to documents, and the institutions have refused their application(s).[6] But what concretely do applicants crave? What *is* a document?

The answer is startlingly ambiguous. The main reason for such incertitude is that 'document' is a word (and also a concept) without clear qualitative or quantitative boundaries. *Qualitative* boundaries regard what *bits* of our world might be considered a document. *Quantitative* boundaries, differently, pertain to the different *sizes* of documents.

We will first address access' *qualitative* boundaries. To explore these we will consider two main points. First, the legislator's approach: document (rather than

[1] This title, which casts light on the concept of 'document' as a layered construction and, in particular, as straddling electronic forms of stored information, rewords D Curtin, 'The Constitutional Structure of the Union: *A Europe of Bits and Pieces*' (1993) 30(1) *Common Market Law Review* 17–69.

[2] Applicants, invariably.

[3] The present chapter concerns documents that are to be made publicly available as a consequence of an application for access. Case T-115/13 *Dennekamp*, para 67 [not yet reported] made clear that Regulation 1049/2001 and Regulation 45/2001 provide, with limitations, *erga omnes* disclosure of documents.

[4] On the occasions when compensation has been mentioned in the access litigation it has been kept to symbolic levels and is not argued as a principal plea. It is argued as an ancillary plea in Case C-127/13 *Strack v Commission* [not yet reported]; Joined Cases T-3/00 and T-337/04 *Pitsiorlas v Council and ECB* [2007] ECR II-4779, para 290; and Case T-436/09 *Dufour v ECB* [2011] ECR II-07727. Applicants, in fact, have consistently refused to adopt a liquidated damages approach to access, or in other words, to the monetarisation of this right. In spite of some rather infelicitous nudging by the first instance judicature in this direction as a solution for the breach of mandatory deadlines (in Case T-47/01 *Co-frutta* [2003] ECR II-04441; Case T-29/08 *LPN* [2011] ECR II-06021) the access litigation remains focused on a single issue: whether there is to be disclosure or not.

[5] Here, of course, we disregard the (distinct) role of institutions as 'eccentric' players. In that capacity, on occasion, institutions come forth to support applicants (Ch 7).

[6] Confirmatory applications (with the exception in *Strack* (n 4); see Ch 6).

information) as the legal object of the right of access. Then, we will give an account of the judicial approach to this legislative text. As for the *quantitative* boundaries of the concept of document, first and foremost, an analysis of the judicial approach is indispensable since on this topic guidance from the law is extremely succinct, or even absent altogether. A last section of this chapter explores the access policy's very own elephant in the room: most of the times no one reads (the contested) documents.

In the aftermath of the excursus it will be simpler to understand refusals.[7]

II. QUALITATIVE BOUNDARIES—THE OBJECT OF THE ACCESS POLICY, LEGISLATOR'S APPROACH

With the purpose of defining a document in its *qualitative* dimension, if asked to answer the following question spontaneously: 'What is a document?' most people would state that it is a piece of paper that is first, headed, second, has an official stamp on it (somewhere) and, third, states something relevant.

In reality, within the specific context of access' defining conceptualism, such a tentative description falls short of what is actually being offered to the policy's beneficiaries. For EU law, 'document' is a name that fits many more bits and pieces of our world. Today, for example, within the specific context of Regulation 1049/2001, it also embraces information stored in forms such as an image or even sound recording.[8]

Touching on this qualitative analysis of documents, the point that is most central to the present discussion is that although in the access context the term 'document' is a pliant concept that fits many information-carrying media (meaning here the plural of medium), not all (coveted) information is stored in a document.

Practitioners are trained to manage these subtleties, but it is wrong to dismiss as irrelevant that this legislation's main rhetorical target is the public in general. With regard to terminology employed by EU law in the description of broad advantages arising out of citizenship of the Union, persons—less versed in the interpretation of ordinary words (ie 'document') within a qualified context—might thus misconceive what, in fact, the law has to offer. In the access to documents context specifically, it is almost certain that the intended beneficiaries will confuse an entitlement to *documents* (what they are indeed being offered) with an entitlement to *information* (what they logically desire to be offered).

With the purpose of addressing the consequences of this issue, we will break down the EU legislator's definition of a 'document', into its several component parts.

[7] Ch 5, 'Exceptions' (valid reasons to say 'no' explicitly) and Ch 6, 'Silence' (which means 'no').

[8] Inter alia, Case T-436/09 *Dufour v ECB* (n 4) para 91, *in fine*: 'a document [...] may contain words, figures or any kind of symbol, but also images and sound recordings, such as the words of a speaker, or visual recordings such as films'.

A. Definition that Expands over Time

The main point to keep in mind is that, without doubt, the definition of document broadens from the 1993 Code of Conduct[9] to Regulation 1049/2001. As a result, under Regulation 1049/2001 it should be possible to access more (types of) document(s) than before. Wording this same idea differently, under Regulation 1049/2001 the object of the access policy has become more capacious.

That said, in the law, and already since 1993, a *document* was never merely intended to designate *paperwork* that the public might have wished to consult. Accordingly, at the time, the Code of Conduct[10] stated that what the public was entitled to apply for was *written text*:

> Code of Conduct
>
> A Document means any written text, whatever its medium, which contains existing data and is held by the Council or the Commission.

That first definition, whilst admittedly confined to '[things] *written*', also opened up the world of microfiches, compact disks and e-mail[11] to the public's scrutiny. Almost a decade later, Regulation 1049/2001 severed the earlier definition's confinement to writing. *Content* replaced *written text* as the pivotal concept around which applications might revolve and thus, a 'document', in the access context, came to cover more bits and pieces:

> Regulation 1049/2001, Article 3(a)
>
> A Document shall mean [...] any content whatever its medium (written on paper or stored in electronic form or as a sound, visual or audiovisual recording) concerning a matter relating to the policies, activities and decisions falling within the institution's sphere of responsibility

Interestingly, there is no indication that the definition's new version was in any way a response to needs identified in the case law.[12] It was no surprise then that, in spite

[9] It is important to make the caveat that the 1993 Code of Conduct focused textually on access to 'the internal documents' of the EU. At the time that expression was taken to mean documents *ab initio* not intended for publication. Today, by contrast, so-called 'internal' documents are somewhat insulated from public scrutiny by Art 4(3) of Regulation 1049/2001, which lays down an exception (to access) related to the institutional decision-making process. For more on this point, see Ch 5.

[10] 1993 Code of Conduct, General Principle.

[11] And any other media (ie plural of medium) for written material that we are able to remember existed at the time. The nature of the storage medium on which content is saved is irrelevant to the question of whether that content does or does not constitute a document (qualitatively) and adapted to the post-Regulation 1049/2001 framework; Case T-436/09 *Dufour* (n 4) para 90.

[12] There is no prior (judicial) record of a document being refused because certain information had been stored only, and eg, as a sound recording. However, it is interesting to observe such occurrences in proceedings disassociated from the 1993 Code of Conduct and Regulation 1049/2001 and pursuant instead to special rules (Regulation EEC 4064/89) that pre-date an EU access policy for 'any person'. This was in proceedings regarding access to the file by the defence in an accusatorial, competition law-driven, context, Case T-211/95 *Endemol Entertainment BV v Commission*, in which, at para 86, the Court declares legitimate the fact that information gathered by the Commission by telephone was not (rearranged on another medium in order to be) communicated to the applicant, and furthermore, at para 94, clarifies that the EU administration is not always obliged to draw up minutes of hearings for the benefit of the defence's access to the file and may limit itself to recording the same on audio-cassettes.

of the advent of new wording under Regulation 1049/2001, there was no stampede of applications seeking sound recordings and/or images. Indeed, most applications made today still refer to (some form of) written text, printed on paper.[13] This points to a more contained, and prevailing, practice that survives the more ambitious legal framework.

B. The Textual Preference for Document Over Information

Settled as it is that it is documents (and not something else) that embody the policy's object, the law has always imposed on applicants a requirement that they identify (the contested) documents adequately, rather than requiring that applicants identify what information[14] they seek.

Once again backtracking to the 1993 Code of Conduct, although in the Code the definition of 'document'[15] might have been read as implying that access to data[16] was the policy's focal point, other articles in the Code made clear that the policy's object was anchored elsewhere.

> Code of Conduct—processing of initial applications
>
> An application for access to a document will have to be made in writing, in a sufficiently precise manner; it will have to contain information that will enable the document or documents concerned to be identified.

This promoted the logical condition that information, in order to be sought via the Code of Conduct, needed to have been consigned (*ex ante* application) into written text and subsequently into some form of medium that would have allowed that written text to be conveyed. Again logically, that same condition—the prior consignment of information sought (regardless of whether it is stored as writing, sound, or image) into a conveying medium—also holds true post-Regulation 1049/2001.

> Regulation 1049/2001, Article 6
>
> Applications
>
> Applications for access to a document shall be made in any written form, including electronic form, in one of the languages referred to in Article 314 of the EC Treaty and in a sufficiently precise manner to enable the institution to identify the document [...].

[13] There are exceptions of course, as in Case T-436/09 *Dufour* (n 4), in which access was sought to an entire database.

[14] Special care should be employed with regard to requests for *environmental* information, under the Aarhus Regulation 1367/2006, since in the textual reference there is to 'information (...) in environmental matters' rather than documents (see Ch 5). This point is an interesting angle from which to approach Case T-245/11 *ClientEarth a.o. v ECHA* [not yet reported].

[15] Above (s II.A): 'Written text which contains existing data'.

[16] At present, on the basis of Case T-436/09 *Dufour* (n 4) 169, there is no doubt that 'data do not constitute a document so long as they are contained in a database and that they may be classified as such only once they have been extracted from the database in order to be formally set down in another printed or printable document'. Furthermore, the term 'printable' must also be understood broadly so that the courts' assertion may be applied by analogy to images and/or recordings.

> If an application is not sufficiently precise, the institution shall ask the applicant to clarify the application and shall assist the applicant in doing so, for example, by providing information on the use of the public registers of documents.

It follows that information may not be applied for in isolation from a documental context. In corroboration, the text of Article 6 of Regulation 1049/2001 also, and in line with the Code of Conduct before it, is categorical in the imposition of a burden of precision onto the applicant so as to enable the institution to identify the document(s) in question.

Textually, both versions of the law stood and stand to protect a (mere) right of access to *documents*. And, notwithstanding the fact that the concept of document is instrumental, here, for public access to *information*[17] to become practicable, a pre-existing document (containing the information sought) would appear to be a *conditio sine qua non* of any institutional obligation to disclose information.[18]

C. The Functional Implications of the Legislative Definition

For the reasons set out above, only when content (stored as writing, sound or image) is consigned to any medium able to convey it, does a 'document' exist today.

The next important issue to clarify is that although throughout the book we have considered (and still do consider) that the concepts of 'contested document' and 'information sought' are (for the most part) interchangeable, it should not be forgotten that, conceptually, access to *documents* might be (in fact) distinct[19] from access to *information*.[20] We will, thus explore this distinction in depth, with the purpose of drawing out two theoretical boundaries, namely, first, the bounds of institutional duties and, secondly, the terminus of judicial competence.

[17] See the reasoning of the GC in *Dennekamp* (n 3) para 71, in which the applicant's right of access to documents must be protected 'for European citizens *to know* which MEPs had a personal interest in the additional pension scheme when called upon to take decisions regarding its management'.

[18] In this sense, see Case T-436/09 *Dufour* (n 4) para 88 'the expressions "medium", "stored", "recording", "drawn up" and "held" used in that definition indicate, implicitly but clearly, that what was contemplated was content that is saved and may be copied or consulted after it has been generated. Material that is not saved does not, therefore, consitute a document, even if the [institution] has knowlege of it'.

Further on the point, *Dufour*, para 89: 'Thus where the views expressed at an [institutional] meeting are neither recorded by sound or audiovisual recording nor formally set down in minutes, there can be no question of there being any document to which an application for access may be made, even if those who attended the meeting have a precise recollection of the tenor of their discussions'. Also, Case T-264/04 *WWF European Policy Program v Council* [2007] ECR II–911, paras 76–78. Very recently, the ruling in Case T-245/11 *ClientEarth a.o. v ECHA* (n 14) also concurs that pre-existing documents (only) represent the limit of the access policy.

[19] This interchangeability of concepts has been a practical concession to applicants made by both the institutions and the judicature but it is not intended to be unlimited.

[20] Moreover, this conceptual partition, however subtle, could—in the extreme—serve as a basis for drawing the boundaries of the competence of the judicature (in terms of access).

i. One, Two, Three

Functionally, we believe that the blueprint of Article 6 of Regulation 1049/2001 allows us to infer three theoretical implications, which differ in consequence. The first implication (a) lends contextual[21] protection to applicants since the law gives no room for institutions to redact information arbitrarily. Concomitantly, a second (b) and a third (c) implication restrict this right of applicants to the mere inspection and/or copying of existing original documents.

a. One

More specifically, a first implication—no arbitrary redaction—might be held to prescribe that even if it is accepted that what applicants ultimately desire is information, they are entitled to have it communicated to them only 'as it was arranged'[22] on the respective medium. Thus, in principle, the information contained in a given document may not be conveyed to applicants in decontextualised form (such as a deliberate omission of dates, of signatures, or by alteration of systematic position in a longer text). At least, not without the applicant being informed that such a (legitimate)[23] redaction was undertaken.

b. Two

A second implication (b)—no mandatory redaction—might in turn be held to prescribe concomitantly that, in principle, there is no obligation for the institutions to explain[24] the information contained in a certain document. Therefore, the institutions are, for their part, not bound to interpret, highlight or clarify the content of complex or lengthy documents. They are simply bound to allow applicants to 'consult them on the spot or to ensure that applicants receive a copy including, where available, an electronic copy, according to the applicant's preference'.[25]

c. Three

A third implication (that is also concomitant to the first two)—no obligation to draw up ad hoc documents—would then prescribe that if the content (ie information) applied for has not been pre-arranged into a medium, the institutions are not bound (subsequent to the applications for access) to compile that information into

21 See (a) below.

22 The expression in Case T-436/09 *Dufour* (n 4) para 70 is 'the documents covered [...] must be capable of being transmitted to the applicant *as they are*, without anything being done to their content or form'.

23 Except where the redaction was undertaken upon request from the applicant (as in the case of a database as in *Dufour*), or when only partial access may be granted without procuring harm to a competing interest (s IV.A below).

24 Although some clarification might be necessary in cases of partial access (see s IV.A below).

25 Regulation 1049/2001, Art 10(1).

some sort of medium and create an ad hoc document[26] so that applicants may gain access to the latter.

Regulation 1049/2001 in this aspect is necessarily distinct from other rules of EU law that are open to a different (and opposite) interpretation, namely Regulation 17/62 (and also, for example, Regulation 4064/89) pursuant to which the EU judicature obliged the Commission to stay true to a self-imposed duty, inter alia, to draw up tables of contents of lengthy (investigative and accusatorial) files. Indeed, the judicial catalyst for this specific duty is Case T-7/89 *Hercules Chemicals v Commission*[27] paragraphs 53 and 54:

> Undertakings are informed of the contents of the Commission's file by means of an annex to the statement of objections or to the letter rejecting a complaint, *listing all the documents in the file and* indicating documents or parts thereof to which they may have access.

These lists of documents are necessary to bring to light incriminating evidence (*à charge*) and exculpatory evidence (*à décharge*) that underlie any decision to issue a Statement of Objections vis-à vis any natural or legal person.

Both Regulations pertain to proceedings that pressupose both an adversarial nature and an accusatorial role on the part of the EU administration. Whilst the wording is often ambiguous (ie documents in their favour), from a teleological standpoint the related rulings of the EU judicature seek much more to grant the accused access to evidence (ie information) than mere access to documents: 'all documents, whether in their favour or otherwise, which it has obtained during the course of the investigation, save where the business secrets of other undertakings, the internal documents of the Commission or other confidential information are involved'.[28]

[26] Case C-127/13 P *Strack v Commission* (n 4) paras 39–47:

> 46 Neither Article 11 of Regulation No 1049/2001 nor the obligation of assistance in Article 6(2) thereof, can oblige an institution to create a document for which it has been asked to grant access but which does not exist.
>
> 47 In the light of all of the foregoing, the judgment under appeal must be set aside in so far as, by that judgment, the General Court held that the Commission was obliged to create a non-existent document and thereby annulled the Commission decision of 24 July 2007 refusing access to the extract of the register concerning refusals of confirmatory applications for access to documents.

Case T-245/11 *ClientEarth a.o. v ECHA* (n 14) confirms this position. However, it is still necessary, first, to point out how on the basis of *Dufour* (n 4) paras 150–53:

> when applied to a case involving databases, in the event of an application for access designed to have the ECB carry out a search of one or other of its databases using search criteria specified by the applicant, the ECB is obliged to accede to that request, [only] if the search called for can be carried out using the search tools available for the database in question.

[27] Case T-7/89 *Hercules Chemicals v Commission* [1991] ECR II-1711.

[28] Further on this point, Case T-175/95 *BASF Coatings AG v Commission* [1999] ECR II-01581, para 50 draws a distinction with regard to Case T-7/89 *Hercules Chemicals v Commission*, para 54; Joined Cases T-10/92, T-11/92, T-12/92 and T-15/92 *Cimenteries CBR and Others v Commission* [1992] ECR II-2667, para 38; Case T-65/89 *BPB Industries and British Gypsum v Commission* [1993] ECR II-389, para 30; Case T-30/91 *Solvay v Commission* [1995] ECR II-1775, paras 59 and 81.

D. *Blind Man's Buff?*[29] The (Im)possible Specificity of Applications

The inferable absence of an institutional duty to create ad hoc documents[30] is an interesting (and troubling) angle from which to discuss applications (for access) that are not document-specific, or in other words, that are not framed in terms of 'I request access to Documents X, Y, and Z'.

As a preliminary remark, it should be noted that before they draft a request to access specific documents in any file, applicants are not invited to consult even a synoptic table of contents that might function as a menu from which to pick and choose.[31] As a consequence, applications for documents come forth at a time in which (in the vast majority of cases) applicants are, literally, hoodwinked. They have no prior cognisance either of what documents are contained in the EU's files, or of what information is consigned in them. Therefore, it is inevitable that initial applications (and even most confirmatory applications) are served on the EU by a player groping in the dark.[32]

Case T-436/09 *Dufour v ECB*

> 29 [...] Account must also be taken of the fact that, in adopting (rules on access to documents), the legislature was conscious of the difficulty in identifying documents which arises, first and foremost, for citizens seeking information. In most cases, they do not know which documents contain the information and must therefore rely on the administrative authorities which hold the documents and thus the information also (see, by analogy, judgment of 10 September 2008 in Case T-42/05 *Williams v Commission*, not published in the ECR, paragraph 71).

This is the best explanation for the fact that many applications come forth framed as follows: 'Access is sought to all documents on Subject X' or even 'Access is sought to a list of X on subject Y'. However, because they seem to target *information* rather than specific *documents*, such applications do not appear to conform to the requirements of Regulation 1049/2001's Article 6.

On this point, however, the institutions (well aware that the applicant is unsighted at the time of the drafting of the initial application) often cooperate in seeking some way of fitting the application to a feasible analysis of such requests.

Yet, by behaving in this manner, the institutions have, at the same time and unintentionally, allowed the requirement of precision laid down in the law to be eroded. Again, a pause for further introspection is necessary.

[29] For an explanation of the *Blind Man's Buff* game, see, inter alia, AB Gomme, *The Traditional Games of England, Scotland and Ireland* (London, Forgotten Books, 2012).

[30] Time and again confirmed in the case law.

[31] This is often true of *national* rules of administrative law, which, however, are not the subject of this book.

[32] This circumstance renders any imposition on applicants of the burden to identify an overriding public interest in disclosure of (the contested) documents (and not the contested information), particularly open to critique; see Ch 5.

i. A Document (Implicitly) Identified by the Applicant?

When in their applications applicants target information, it might be checked, first, whether the applicant also specifies (even in an implied fashion) that access is ultimately being sought to a particular document; for example, by reference to information contained in a specific report, in specific minutes of a specific meeting that, obviously, have *ex ante* already been consigned to medium: 'I want to know the names[33] of the persons mentioned in the *minutes of meeting x*'. If this is true, whilst what is first mentioned in the application is information, access is ultimately also being sought to documents (in the example given above, the minutes of meeting x). In this case, the greater relevance of the part of the application that concerns access to a document might be held to absorb the part of the application that targets (mere) information.

ii. A Document Identifiable by the Institution?

In addition, in other cases, whilst the information sought in an application is also clearly identified, the medium on which it might be embodied is less clear. For example: 'all objections raised[34] during all the meetings held in November 2012 concerning the forthcoming Directive on the Quality of Drinking Water'.

In such cases, (again) it might be considered whether, in spite of the vagueness of the application, the institution is able to identify (among all the documents that it holds) those that would meet the applicant's needs. Let us admit, for example, that (although the applicant has no cognisance of the fact) those meetings are mandatorily recorded in minutes.[35] Here, the imperative (institutional) duty to assist[36] applicants compels the institution to acknowledge an (underlying and implied) application 'to the minutes of the meetings, held by the institution'. Moreover, that (implied) re-framing of the application absorbs any relevance of the concrete terms of the request that refer solely to information sought.

What is important to point out is that these (internal) choices of the institutions are hardly ever clarified or even remotely perceptible to the public. This keeps the discussion at the levels of precision that are required as to the drafting of applications down to the bare minimum.

[33] Issues pertaining to the relevance of privacy and personal data will be disregarded for the time being and discussed separately in Ch 5. Another version of this example could be 'I want to know the names of all the chemical components mentioned in Report X'. Case T-245/11 *ClientEarth a.o. v ECHA* (n 14) is extremely relevant to the analysis.

[34] cp *Dennekamp* (n 3) (all docs); and *LPN* (n 4) (access to the file).

[35] *A contrario*, Case T-221/95 *Endemol v Commission* [1999] ECR II-02199.

[36] Case T-436/09 *Dufour* (n 4) para 30. When the burden of identification of the document is not overwhelming.

iii. Cross-referencing and Compiling—Beyond the (Outer) Limit of Institutional Duty?

One final, and even more complex, situation arises when an applicant frames an application for access as one that seeks information that requires the cross-referencing of two limbs. For example 'a list of names of the persons who attended the meeting concerning drinking water held on 12 December 2012 and who are (concomitantly) employed by DG ENV'.[37]

What is the purpose of asking for a list? Is it that a list is known to exist and that is what is wanted or is there also an (implicit) application that the applicant's interlocutor (here, the institution) draws up a list in order to satisfy the terms of that request? With regard to the first scenario, if such a list is known to exist the application for access may be dealt with in accordance with the possibilities considered for subheading (ii) above.

We will now turn to the situation in which such a list does not exist prior to the application. On this point, it is very important that the EU judicature takes the time to clarify more precisely[38] whether this is an attempted exercise of a right that is not unconditionally acknowledged in EU law: access to information.

Truly, in spite of the possible existence of many documents with regard to each individual limb of the request (because what the applicant is seeking is information that presupposes cross-referencing) at the time of the request, there is no document containing such cross-referencing.

Coming back to our example of a list of 'persons who attended meeting X and are also employed by department Y', those names are certainly retrievable on the basis of two separate lists, but in all likelihood do not pre-exist as a *single* list (a series of names or other items written or printed together in a meaningful grouping or sequence so as to constitute a record). For this reason, even if the institution is in possession of an unconnected variety of different documents (say, invitations to the meeting and a directory of all employees of DG ENV) that, if cross-referenced, would cast light on whether certain names might be considered as fitting the applicant's request, it is questionable that it falls to the institution to undertake those additional, successive and multiple steps.

Case T-436/09 *Dufour v ECB*

> 149 An application for access that would require the [institution] to create a new document, even if the document were based on information already appearing in existing documents held by the institution, is not an application for partial access and does not come within the parameters of [the EU rules on access to Documents].

[37] The exact same reasoning could well be applied to an application for access to 'a list of the names of chemical components considered dangerous for human health identified in the reports produced by Committee X'.

[38] Case T-245/11 *ClientEarth a.o. v ECHA* (n 14) para 247 whilst not dwelling on the distinction between document and information does draw the line between existing documents and documents that have yet to be drawn up.

First, it is questionable whether we may devise any duty for institutions to cross-reference data held. Equally debatable is the devising of a duty to compile a list of names (identified through cross-referencing) for the applicant.

In fact, in all cases in which a list does not pre-exist an application, when applicants request that specific information be conveyed to them under that form, applicants are not asking to access a document, they are asking the institution to draw one up. At the same time it is only applications for (pre-existing) documents that fit the EU access policy and come within its scope.[39] By way of conclusion, the point that such applications do not qualify as applications for access to documents at all may well be a defensible one.

iv. Documents that Contain Names v Names (Contained) in Documents

In the case law, a hint that these matters have yet to be discussed at a more structured level has come up in *Dennekamp*.[40] In that case, the terms of the application consisted, inter alia, of a request to be granted access to two lists:

> Case T-115/13 *Dennekamp v Parliament*
>
> 5. in 2012 [...] (I) all documents showing which current MEPs were also members of the additional pension scheme; (II) a list of names of MEPs who were members of the scheme after September 2005; (III) a list of names of the members of the scheme for whom the Parliament paid a monthly contribution; (IV) all documents related to the financial position of the scheme since 2009.

Ultimately, the GC annulled the European Parliament's refusal to grant the applicant's request, but not because the applicant was barred from accessing certain documents; rather, the EP's decision was annulled

> insofar as access is thereby refused to the names[41] of Members participating in the additional pension scheme of the European Parliament who, as members of the Parliament's plenary, actually took part in the votes on that additional pension scheme held on 24 April 2007, 22 April 2008 and 10 May 2012.

The paragraphs that precede the ruling are worth reading carefully.

First they touch upon a required specificity of (initial applications and) confirmatory applications:

> Case T-115/13 *Dennekamp v Parliament*
>
> 95–96 Yet the applicant did not refer in the confirmatory application only to votes resulting in amendments being made to the management of the additional pension scheme but to any vote in which the European Parliament or one of its bodies decides on the scheme in one way or another.

[39] In the same sense, Case T-245/11 *ClientEarth a.o. v ECHA* (n 14).

[40] Case T-115/13 *Dennekamp v Parliament* (n 3).

[41] Also on this (dangerous) terminological path, in Case T-245/11 *ClientEarth a.o. v ECHA* (n 14) in para 1 of the final ruling whereby the GC '[a]nnuls the ECHA decision of 4 March 2011 insofar as it refused to disclose *information* requested by point 1'.

However, and at variance with the same, the Court proceeds to concede the applicant a surprising margin of non-specificity too, which in turn waives the requirement of the documental basis of requests:

> Case T-115/13 *Dennekamp v Parliament*
>
> 110 [...] for the purpose of bringing to light the potential conflicts of interest of MEPs voting on the additional pension scheme, the applicant was, as a matter of law, entitled merely to show that they were in that situation because of their dual role as MEPs and as members of the scheme. [...] More specifically, the applicant cannot be criticised for not having himself identified the body within the Parliament that was required to decide on the scheme, and thus the group of MEPs concerned, before requesting that the names of the relevant MEPs be transferred.
>
> 111 A contrary interpretation would mean that the applicant was required to apply, initially, for access to documents identifying those bodies within which the additional pension scheme had been voted upon, and, in the light of the result obtained, to apply, secondly, for access to the documents identifying the MEPs who actually took part in the vote on that point, and then to the documents identifying the MEPs participating in the scheme. There is nothing in Regulation No 1049/2001 to require an applicant for access to the documents held by an institution or body of the European Union to adopt that approach, nor can it be inferred from the application of Regulation No 45/2001 with respect to documents containing personal data.

This ruling is obviously an approach of first instance and moreover it is still raw.[42] However, what comes across as indisputable is that a cross-referencing task has (and unless this point is appealed) been imposed on the EP.

v. Coupling 'No Duty to Draw up' with 'Excessive Burden'—A Tactic for the Future?

For the present there is little solace that may be obtained from the remaining case law. Indeed, there is one case[43] in which an institution refuses the application on the grounds that (although it does hold the documents that would enable a list to be drawn up) there is no list that combines a first and a second limb of an application.

In addition, aside from a slightly different scenario primarily regarding databases,[44] the institutions have addressed the problem of 'having to draw up documents' usually with regard to cases concerning applications that are worded in a very general manner and which target existing documents that are part of extensive files. On occasion, the institutions have objected to being required to draw up tables of contents of the files themselves.

However, this point has been argued solely under the very general 'excessive burden' excuse,[45] and arguably differently from cross-referencing, a table of contents

[42] The ruling was delivered on 15 July 2015.

[43] Case T-245/11 *ClientEarth a.o. v ECHA* (n 14).

[44] Case T-436/09 *Dufour* (n 4).

[45] On this point, see Case T-2/03 *VFK* [2005] ECR II-00121 para 130: 'the Commission stated in its defence that drawing up a table of contents [with regard to a file comprising 47,000 pages] would have been a disproportionate task'.

merely requires copying and/or reproducing titles or, at the most, providing a spurious common explanation, applicable to entire sets of documents, grouped under the same title.[46]

In fact, and with regard to applications by way of which access is sought to lists of a different nature (ie that may only be drawn up after cross-referencing), the coupling of the 'excessive burden' argument with a different objection—that the application targets information that (*ex ante* application) has not been pre-consigned into a single document—has been neither consitently[47] explored nor, for that matter, adequately exploited.

This has all taken place with regard to a framework in which the law contains a clear textual confinement to documents that is quite distinct from acknowledging a right of access to information.[48]

As a consequence, if the judicature takes to requiring the drawing up of lists (that presuppose institutional cross-referencing of documents held)[49] the law's approach and the approach of the judicature might become irreconcilable. This is because the judges of the EU would thus threaten to extend the protection of applicants well beyond the legislator's intention,[50] and, if accepted, would lead to an empowerment of the judicature well beyond the text of the law and thus *contra legem*.

E. Provenance Matters: The Origin of Documents as a Qualitative Boundary

Having settled that the substance of 'documents' reaches well beyond paper, and that requests for access must (as far as it is feasible) be document-specific, we will now discuss how in the passage from the Code of Conduct to Regulation 1049/2001 another qualitative aspect of the definition of document was affected.

This time the change did not concern any intrinsic trait of documents, but rather it focused on their provenance. From this angle—the origin of documents—the (new) definition of 'document' in Regulation 1049/2001 brought implications (and complications) for the relationships between the players[51] of the access policy.

i. Some Documents (those Drawn up by the Institutions)

Under the governance of the 1993 Code of Conduct[52] many documents related to the activity of the EU were protected from access' bite. Indeed, to render the rights

[46] See the discussion in sections IV.C.iii and IV.D below on categories of documents and presumptions of harm respectively.

[47] Again, Case T-245/11 *ClientEarth a.o. v ECHA* (n 14) is the only precedent in which both arguments are combined.

[48] Again, a caveat must be made for environmental information.

[49] There might be a suggestion in this direction in Case T-115/13 *Dennekamp* (n 3) para 94.

[50] See recently ibid, para 94.

[51] This perspective is discussed in detail in Ch 7.

[52] Although in time, it would be clarified that all three pillars of EU activity were subject to public scrutiny via the access policy (see section III.A.iii below).

emerging from the Code of Conduct a dead letter, it would suffice to demonstrate that any person[53] other than the EU had authored any document (access to which was being requested of the EU institutions).

In very broad lines,[54] the understanding at the time was that it was not the task of the EU to take decisions with regard to documents that it held but that had been authored by others. Applications with such an object would simply be refused, and it would have been useless[55] to plead the contrary. At this time, the definition of 'document' was narrow: it comprised only (and intuitively) written text, produced by the EU:

> Code of Conduct
>
> The public will have the widest possible access to documents held by the Commission and the Council. [...]
>
> When the document held (...) was written by [another] the application must be sent direct to the author.

ii. All Documents (in Possession of the Institution)

At a later stage of the EU access policy (December 2001), the abovementioned simplistic approach to applications for incoming documents (automatically refused) was replaced by a different practice, in accordance with a new framework. The author's rule faded out with the advent of Regulation 1049/2001. Withdrawing author's discretion over documents transmitted to the EU institutions, by way of Article 2(3), the new rules asserted the EU's authority over all documents held:

> Regulation 1049/2001, Article 2(3)
>
> This Regulation shall apply to all Documents held by an institution, that is to say, Documents drawn up or received by it and in its possession, in all areas of activity of the EU.

This amounted to a quasi-revolution. The first consequence was that the EU institutions were plunged into a bitter and lengthy conflict with eccentric[56] players of the access policy: the authors of documents.[57] The second consequence of the rule's disappearance, more central to the present discussion, was that yet again, the concept of document (disclosable via the EU access policy) was expanded. The policy came to straddle (and does to this day) not only documents drawn up by the EU but also each and every type of content, whatever its medium that has ever been transmitted (even as a mere copy, or even as a mere annex) by any person, undertaking, party, body, institution, organisation or country to the institutions of the EU.

[53] We are using the term in a very broad sense, meaning to cover any entity or body.

[54] For a more detailed discussion, see Ch 7.

[55] Case law before *Interporc/Messina/Petrie*.

[56] Ch 7. The term 'eccentric' here means both that certain players are not at the centre of the policy since they are not its main protagonists, and it also means that they are wildcards. One never really knows what to expect from them in terms of litigious choices.

[57] Ch 7. This is especially true when the author of a document is the Member State.

Table 4.1: The Expansion of the Definition of Document

	Object	Medium	Provenance
Code of Conduct 1993	Written text containing data Stored as: Writing	(consigned to any basis)	Drawn up by the institutions
Regulation 1049/2001	Content Stored as: Writing, sound recording, image, audio-visual recording	(consigned to any basis)	Drawn up by the institutions or held by the same.

III. QUALITATIVE BOUNDARIES—THE OBJECT OF THE ACCESS POLICY, THE JUDICIAL APPROACH

Having explained how, first, the change of the policy's object from written text to content was mostly inconsequential, secondly, that no player seemed overtly interested in pursuing the theoretical distinction between 'document' and 'information',[58] and finally how the definition of 'document' in the 1993 Code of Conduct was expanded by the abolishment of the author's rule in Regulation 1049/2001, we now turn to a different question: was (or is) the access policy confined to limited sections of EU activity?

A. Jurisdiction

This problem is related to the breadth of the EU enterprise within which documents are produced in practice. It is important to approach this point having in mind first that there was not much guidance to be had from the 1993 EU provisions for the access policy. Secondly, that on 19 October 1995 a ruling of the GC (CFI) in *Carvel I*[59] definitively annulled a decision whereby the Council had refused the applicants access to decisions adopted by the Justice and Home Affairs Council.

i. Carvel I, *Jurisdiction is not an Issue*

At the time, no objection had come forth regarding the jurisdiction of the CFI to adjudicate on access to documents falling under Title VI of the Treaty of Maastricht. The issue of jurisdiction was simply not called into question. Possibly it went unchallenged because the principal issue in *Carvel I* (the requirement for a true balancing of competing interests by the EU institutions) absorbed all of the concerns of protagonists and commentators alike.

[58] The scarcity to this day of litigation (from the institutions) on this point is surprising.
[59] Case T-194/94 *Carvel and Guardian Newspapers v Council* [1995] ECR II-02765.

ii. Svenska, *Jurisdiction is Discussed*

The ruling in *Carvel I* notwithstanding, until 17 June 1998,[60] the EU institutions advertised the opinion that the access policy had been thought of as straddling only the so-called first pillar of the Maastricht Treaty. Consequently, the significance of the tripartite structure of the EU with regard to the access policy called for the judicature's introspection in a separate, subsequent conflict: the *Svenska* proceedings. These were lodged on 22 September 1995, less than a month before the *Carvel I* ruling came to be delivered. They, inter alia, pinpointed the issue of the (alleged) lack of competence of the EU judicature to rule on access proceedings outside the first pillar. In the proceedings, the French and UK Governments—with a guarded echo in some doctrine[61]—also came forth to argue that the second and third pillars of Union activity, being outside the EC Treaty, were possibly insulated from public scrutiny. Only the intervention of the GC (at the time called CFI) put an end to these deliberations:

> Case T-174/95 *Svenska Journalistforbundet v Council of the European Union*
>
> 85. The fact that the Court has, by virtue of Article L of the EU Treaty, no jurisdiction to review the legality of measures adopted under Title VI does not curtail its jurisdiction in the matter of public access to those measures. The assessment of the legality of the contested decision is based upon its jurisdiction to review the legality of decisions of the Council taken under Decision 93/731, on the basis of Article 173 of the EC Treaty, and does not in any way bear upon the intergovernmental cooperation in the field of Justice and Home Affairs as such. In any event, in the contested Decision the Council itself drew the applicant's attention to its entitlement to appeal under Article 173 of the EC Treaty.
>
> 86. The fact that the documents relate to Title VI is only relevant insofar as the contents of the documents might possibly come within the scope of one or more of the exceptions provided for in Decision 93/731. That fact is thus relevant only to the examination of the substantive lawfulness of the decision taken by the Council and not to the admissibility of the application as such.

iii. Jurisdiction (on Access) Asserted Over All Three Pillars

It is important to point out that the clarifications of *Svenska*[62] of 17 June 1998, two and a half years after the *Carvel I* ruling rendered on 19 October 1995, could not have contradicted the factual circumstance of the earlier ruling in the *Carvel I* proceedings. It is undeniable that within the latter, the EU judicature had, unhindered,

[60] The date of the *Svenska* ruling, Case T-174/95 *Svenska Journalistforbundet v Council* [1998] ECR II-02289.

[61] D Curtin, 'Democracy, Transparency and Political Participation' (Maastricht, EIPA, 1998) 116: 'One very positive feature of the Amsterdam Treaty is the fact that the Third Pillar (justice and home affairs) now contains a parallel provision on access to documents (Article 41 TA) applying the new Article 255 TA to the provisions relating to the relevant areas. This represents a very significant opening up of this sensitive area of policy-making'.

[62] As previously stated with regard to Case C-58/94 *Netherlands v Council.*

annulled a refusal to documents that reflected decisions adopted by the Justice and Home Affairs Council. It would be highly unlikely, if not unthinkable, that the CFI would concur with some Member States (albeit heavyweights such as France and the UK) in calling into question that existing status quo.

The conclusion that must be drawn is that this discussion of the width[63] of the access policy should have been closed down one month after it had begun. At least since 19 October 1995, any discussion of the policy's borders (in terms of pillars) was rendered superfluous. In hindsight it might be said that from its inception the access policy was always of the same size as the EU project. It comprised the documents not only connected to one pillar, but also those connected to a second, and yet another.

IV. QUALITATIVE *CUM* QUANTITATIVE BOUNDARIES: TOPICS NOT COVERED BY THE LAW, THE JUDICIAL APPROACH

Having addressed the issue of the *qualitative* boundaries of the concept of EU documents, both from the point of view of the substance of documents (intrinsic traits) and from the point of view of their provenance (authors), our discussion has reached this stage without even a hint of what a document might be from a *quantitative* point of view.[64]

This is because leaving that (unsolved) conceptual query at the sidelines, applicants, institutions and judicature preferred to focus on details of the policy that apparently touch only upon a document's *qualitative* boundaries (what type of substrate (paper, disk, microfilm, image) is eligible as a document). Some of the details, however, also relate to the *quantitative* boundaries of the concept of document (the size of documents), but do so less perceptibly.

First, we will address two qualitative *cum* quantitative boundaries: partial access and non-existence of documents. Secondly, we will assess a quantitative boundary only, namely, cumbersome applications and, finally, we will turn to a related qualitative *cum* quantitative boundary: categories of documents.

All four topics have in common that there was no clear basis in the 1993 Code of Conduct to address them.

A. Partial Access

The discussion concerning partial access focuses on implications for the access policy that arise from the relationship between the entire document and its constituent parts, this regardless of whether a document is taken to mean an entire file or a single page.

[63] Identified as Question 3(a) in Ch1, section II.D.i, 'Three Questions regarding the Width of Access'.
[64] ie is only an entire file or report a document? Or is each page of the file or report a document in its own right?

At the core of partial access a main choice must be made: if there are *parts* of a text, recording etc, that should not be released to the public (for example for reasons of public order), and also parts of the same text the release of which to the public is harmless, would that imply that the entire document is to be withheld?

i. Censure as an Opportunity

In practice, partial access consists of the *blanking out* of allegedly contentious and/or sensitive segments of documents, before the latter are disclosed to the public. On the one side, the conceptualisation of partial access expands the definition of (disclosable) document. The harm that the disclosure of a mere segment of it would bring about does not taint its remaining parts. And so, documents that would have been automatically withheld because of the existence of even half a dozen (harmful) words[65] contained in them, remain available for the public's scrutiny.

ii. Censure without Thresholds

However, it is also true that, once the judicature qualifies partial access (the blanking out of contentious segments) as a justifiable option of the institutions, the latter might more easily arrange that many parts of many documents be withheld from the scrutiny of the public. For example, there are many instances in which only the titles of the documents (applied for) are released to applicants. With regard to this specific practice two positions may be gleaned.

a. At the Least, (Disclose) the Title!

On the one hand, it might be said that even if everything but the title of a document is harmful, then at least the document's title must be released. Those who defend this position call for a standard of institutional analysis that always evaluates if at least partial disclosure is feasible. This view also lends strong support to the acknowledgement of a horizontal requirement of a concrete examination of each (single) document before it is refused. Abiding by such standards, however, would not leave much room for presumptions of harm[66] to be invoked in order to 'dispense the institutions of a specific and individual examination of the documents applied for',[67] before refusals are handed out.

b. Still, is the Title Enough?

On the other hand, it is also true that by way of partial access (ie access to the title of a document, only) the institutions become empowered to resort to censure. Moreover it is censure practically without measure or limitation, since it is extremely

[65] Or sound bites or pixels...
[66] See section IV.D.
[67] Joined Cases C-514/11P and C-605/11P *LPN and Finland*, para 21 [not reported].

difficult to subject the adequacy of the amount of specific passages blanked out to judicial review.[68] In addition, by responding to an application for a document by disclosing its title, the EU institutions, prima facie, do discharge themselves of all the obligations imposed on them by Regulation 1049/2001. In sum, there is yet to be a case in which a *de minimis* measure of access is actually held to be, *ipso facto*, in breach of the law.

Coming back to the example used above of an application for access to 'a list of names',[69] in the extreme, the applicant might end up with access to the title of the list but without access to a single name contained in the list.

Ironically, a person who ultimately seeks information contained in a document ends up with the document without having access to the information.

iii. However Lessened, it Remains a Tale of Access to Documents

What is at stake here is a very subtle issue. It is no longer a controversy regarding what would allow us to classify anything (take a piece of paper with written text) as a document.[70] Quite distinctly, when any document is disclosed partially, a line of analysis that is practically absent from the on-going discussion would focus on what proportion of the document must, however, be kept available in order (for that measure of disclosure) to qualify as meaningful disclosure or access. Indeed, whilst in theory partial access—regardless of the proportion of document hidden—is access, in practice this example at the extreme may lead us to question the qualification of these (lessened) bequests to applicants, as access to documents at all.

Still, it is not acceptable to conclude that, ultimately, partial access is the foundation of access to information (as opposed to access to documents). What continues to root the example into the access to documents policy is that—because there is an underlying duty for the institutions to preserve context—the information is passed on as a redacted version of the original document.

For the reason just mentioned, and to stress this somewhat narrowing trait (of partial access), we have opted to include it among the structural aspects of the policy that help keep it contained.

iv. The Judicial Approach: Mecklenburg *and* Hautala

Finally, we turn to the judicial approach with regard to the admissibility of partial access. Owing to silence on this matter in the 1993 Code of Conduct, it was left to the judicature to decide if, and on what terms, partial access might fit into the access policy.

At the origins of the discussion, Heidi Hautala, an applicant for documents, and coincidentally a Finnish member of the European Parliament, argued that the

[68] It is unheard of that either ECJ or GC have ever ventured so deep as to challenge the institutions' choice of (obliterated) passages.

[69] A list of names that is known to pre-exist an application for access and which is held by the institution.

[70] Case T-436/09 *Dufour* (n 4) paras 93 and 94.

possibility of partial access was teleologically (albeit not textually) contemplated by Article 4(1) of Decision 93/731[71] adopting the 1993 Code of Conduct. Her reasoning was inspired on the *Mecklenburg* case law of the ECJ from 1998[72] interpreting the wording of a Council Directive[73] on the freedom of access to information on the environment.[74]

Decision 93/731, Article 4(1)

Access to a Council document shall not be granted where its disclosure could undermine:

Using the words 'its disclosure' as a starting point, it was argued—circuitously—that for each document applied for, the institutions were bound to consider the possibility of separating out its confidential parts, and to release the remainder to the public, even where a document did relate to one of the mandatory exceptions. The Swedish Government, intervener in the proceedings in support of the applicant, drew the same argument from prior institutional practice.[75]

The defendant institution (the Council) objected, adducing that to introduce (a right of applicants also to) partial access and requiring the institutions to consider the feasibility of that option, with regard to every application, would entail adaptation (ie redaction) of documents. This would, the Council maintained, inevitably bring about access to fragmentary information and not access to documents with respect to their original form, which was what the rules textually protected.

However, making no distinction between document and information, the CFI (now GC) ruled that in 1993 a general principle of access to documents had been established. And thus (with the exception of cases in which the volume of the document or the passages to be removed would give rise to an unreasonable[76] amount of administrative work), the Council, and therefore any institution, was obliged to examine whether access might be granted to only parts of the document. In other words, it became incumbent on the institutions to establish whether within a document—covered by an exception—there are particular passages that may be released to the public. The central thread of this procedural obligation of the institutions is that those passages merely contain information unable to undermine the competing interest that has been asserted by the institution.

Case T-14/98 *Hautala v Council*

78. Decision 93/731 does not expressly require the Council to consider whether partial access to documents may be granted. Nor (...) does it expressly prohibit such a possibility.

85. Furthermore, the principle of proportionality requires that derogations remain within the limits of what is appropriate and necessary for achieving the aim in view.

(...)

71 [1993] OJ L 340, 43.

72 Case 321/96 *Mecklenburg v Kreis Pinneberg* [1998] ECR I-3809, para 25.

73 A Directive is an act addressed to Member States only.

74 Council Directive 90/313/EEC of 7 June 1990 on the Freedom of Access to Information on the Environment [1990] OJ L 158, 58. (See ch 5.) See also Case C-93/09 *Land Hessen* [2010] ECR I-11063.

75 Case T-14/98 *Hautala v Council* [1999] ECR II-2489, para 53: 'Secretary General's report on the implementation of Decision 93/731 for the Years 1994 and 1995, Document 8330/96, p.12'.

76 With the proviso that on the basis of Case T-436/09 *Dufour* (n 4) paras 175–76 'the mere mention of the "significant burden of work" [...] is manifestly insuficient to justify rejection of that application'.

87. Accordingly, Article 4(1) of Decision 93/731 must be interpreted in the light of the principle of the right to information and the principle of proportionality. It follows that the Council is obliged to examine whether partial access should be granted to the information not covered by the exceptions.

v. Epilogue: The Law Changes

This principle (that applicants may be granted access to parts of documents) would be drafted into the subsequent normative framework (Article 4(6) of Regulation 1049/2001). The new law, moreover, implicitly requires the institutions to carry out such an analysis.

However, it must be noted that Article 4(6) makes no mention of blanking out or redacting parts of documents:

Regulation 1049/2001, Article 4(6)

If only parts of the requested document are covered by any of the exceptions, the remaining parts of the document shall be released.

Therefore partial access, on the one hand, enters Regulation 1049/2001 as an analysis of two types of documents. First, within the (entire) set of contested documents it calls for the choosing and picking of those that (after all) are *not* covered by the exception relied on by the institution. Secondly, within the subset of documents that *are* covered by exception, it calls for an analysis with the purpose of fishing out harmless excerpts. On the other hand, it survives post 2001, via case law engendered pre-2001,[77] as a horizontal duty of redaction (where feasible) of documents that *are* covered by the exceptions.

Partial access, as a principle, would later redouble its importance in the *Turco*[78] judgment. In its judgment in that case, in the guise of a mandatory procedural requirement,[79] the so-called 'harm test' or '*Turco* test' was described by the ECJ as a three-stage examination incumbent on the institutions:

Case C-39/05 *Sweden and Turco v Council*

38 First, the Council must satisfy itself that the document which it is asked to disclose does indeed relate to an exception (legal advice) and, if so, it must decide which parts of it are actually concerned and may, therefore, be covered by that exception.

40 Second, the Council must examine whether disclosure of the parts of the document in question which have been identified as relating to that exception (legal advice) 'would undermine the protection' of that advice.

44 Third and last, if the Council takes the view that disclosure of a document would undermine the protection of that exception (legal advice) as defined above, it is incumbent on the Council to ascertain whether there is any overriding public interest justifying disclosure

[77] Case T-14/98 *Hautala v Council* (n 75).

[78] Case C-39/05P *Sweden and Turco v Council* [2008] ECR I-04723, paras 37–45.

[79] ibid. As per para 37 the requirement certainly holds for any situation regarding Art 4(2) of Regulation 1049/2001.

> despite the fact that its ability to protect competing interests (seek legal advice and receive frank, objective and comprehensive advice) would thereby be undermined.

The characterisation of partial access as a procedural requirement also comes across quite impressively in *VFK*.[80] A further development of this institutional duty came to light in *Int'Veld v Commission*,[81] in which the requirement for the institutions to examine whether partial access is feasible was extended to documents related to the so-called 'trilogues', informal negotiations between the EP, the Council and the Commission aimed at reaching early agreements on new EU legislation. Recently, in *Miettinen*,[82] (no doubt encouraged by the pre-legislative connection and the fact that the contested document had been made publicly available in two Member States),[83] the *Turco* test has been revived for cases regarding public access to legal advice concerning proposals for a Directive.

However, concomitantly, from 29 June 2010,[84] partial access (less as a principle and mainly as a procedural requirement incumbent on the institutions) would be set aside—or at least gravely disregarded—by the growing case law on (allegedly) rebuttable presumptions[85] (in disclosure).

Although we will return in more detail to the detachment between partial access-and presumption of harm,[86] it is important to keep two things in mind. First, with particular incidence in cases involving access to pre-legislative documents,[87] the judicature continues to affirm partial access as a fundamental principle of the access policy. Secondly, and following on from the principle's affirmation, where presumptions of harm are concomitantly affirmed, by way of mere twists to a paragraph, or by juxtaposition of successive paragraphs, terms such as 'but' and 'however' are simply inserted into rulings and proceed to dispense the institutions, not only from the requirement to identify harmless parts of documents likely to satisfy the applicant's interests, but even from any type of examination[88] of the contested documents.

B. Institutional Allegations that Documents Do Not Exist

A very different discussion, that regarding non-existence, is related to the qualitative and quantitative boundaries of documents since it both relates to a substrate (a piece of paper, a disk, a recording) subtracted from the access policy and concomitantly defines a size zero for (contested) documents. The case-by-case analysis

[80] See section IV.C ('Cumbersome applications').

[81] D Chalmers, G Davies and G Monti, *European Union Law, Text Cases and Materials* (Cambridge, Cambridge University Press, 2014) 414; Case T-529/09 *Int'Veld v Commission*, Judgment of 4 May 2012 [not reported].

[82] Case T-395/13 *Miettinen v Council* [not yet reported].

[83] ibid, para 6.

[84] Case C-139/07 P *Commission v TGI* [2010] ECR I-0000; Case C-514/11P *LPN and Finland* (n 67) para 21.

[85] Below, for further discussion. See also Ch 5.

[86] Below, for further discussion, see section IV.B.ii.

[87] Case T-395/13 *Miettinen v Council* (n 82) para 46.

[88] See Ch 5.

of non-existence is indispensable when the institutions allege that a document that has been applied for does not exist.

Once again resorting to the aid of examples, let us imagine that an applicant requests access to certain minutes of a meeting, but in the meeting no minutes were kept. It is important to distinguish two different situations here.

i. Documents No Longer Held

One first situation would be the case in which an institution refuses access because a document once held by the institution has, for example, been returned to its author and no copy of the same has been kept.[89] This example (albeit analogous in consequence) is not an instance of non-existence. The document exists (somewhere). However, it is simply not in the possession of the EU. Moreover, since institutional allegations in this sense are to be believed,[90] it is not the existence of the (contested) document that is relevant. What becomes central is that the criteria of Article 2(3) of Regulation 1049/200—possession—are not met.

Case T-496/13 *McCullough v Cedefop* (our redaction)

> 50 Where the institution declares that it is not in possession of the documents requested [a rebuttable] presumption [of veracity of that statement] must be applied

ii. Veritable Non-existence and/or Lack of Cognisance

Non-existence (genuinely), for the law and for the EU judicature, is a quite different case. It certainly includes the case of an institution clearly stating that a document (as identified by the applicant) does not exist.[91] But it has also been accepted to include situations in which an institution alleges that it is unsure[92] of whether a document (again, as identified by the applicant) exists or not.

Finally, as stated above with regard to lack of possession, allegations by the EU institutions claiming non-existence of documents are supported by a presumption that the truth is being told.

Case T-496/13 *McCullough v Cedefop*

> 49 It follows from the terms of Article 2(3) of Regulation No 1049/2001 that an EU institution or body clearly cannot accede to an application for access to documents which do not exist.

[89] By analogy, and on the basis of Case T-436/09 *Dufour* (n 4) para 128 deleted data, future content or content that has not yet been recorded, are not subject to the EU rules on access.

[90] See recently Case T-496/13 *McCullough v Cedefop* [not yet reported] para 4: 'The CEDEFOP [...] stated that it was not in possession of the minutes of the KMS, following the audit carried out by the European Commission's internal audit service ("the IAS") and the European Anti-Fraud Office (OLAF), raising the issue of whether those minutes even existed and noting that all the relevant documents had been sent by OLAF to the competent Greek authorities'. See also judgment of 19 January 2010 in T-355/04 and T-446/04 *Co-Frutta v Commission* EU:T:2010:15, para 155.

[91] See Case T-123/99 *JT's Corporation v Commission* EU:T:2000:230, paras 56–58; and Case T-311/00 *British American Tobacco v Commission* EU:T:2002:167.

[92] Case T-496/13 *McCullough v Cedefop* (n 90) para 4.

> 50 It is case law that a presumption of legality attaches to any statement of the institutions relating to the non-existence of documents requested. Consequently, a presumption of veracity attaches to such a statement. That is, however, a simple presumption which the applicant may rebut in any way by relevant and consistent evidence

These presumptions only hold *juris tantum* admittedly (until the opposite is proven in court). However, it would be very difficult for an applicant[93] to demonstrate in court that the opposite is true: either that the document does exist, or that the institution does know of its existence and/or does have it in its possession.[94]

It is questionable whether this last aspect expands or contracts the definition of a document. On the one hand, (since the mere allegation of non-existence is sufficient to ground a refusal appropriately), this would seem to bring about a contraction in the number of documents subject to the policy. On the other hand, it is difficult to ignore that such documents, in spite of allegations that they might not exist, are in some cases the contested ones, and are the object not only of applications but also of court proceedings. Therefore, it would be precipitous to ascribe the figure definitively to the contraction of the definition of document.

[93] Even in instances in which statements of the institutions have been challenged, it has been necessary for the judicature to lend the applicant a hand: Case T-311/00 *British American Tobacco* (n 92) paras 12 and 65:

> The Court also observes that it was only after it ordered the summoning of witnesses and after one of those witnesses proffered written evidence that the Commission was able to find and send to the applicant, on the day before the hearing fixed for hearing the witnesses, the relevant sets of minutes of the cancer experts committee. In addition, almost 21 months after the initial application for access and after having repeatedly denied its existence, the Commission also found a document which it produced to the applicant only minutes before the hearing on 5 March 2002.

In addition, the standard of proof (that an institution has made an untruthful allegation) is high (para 39):

> The Court notes that the applicant has produced no relevant or, *a fortiori*, consistent evidence within the meaning of the judgment in *JT's Corporation* v *Commission*, cited above, to throw doubt upon the Commission's assertion that neither it nor the cancer experts committee is in possession of sets of minutes of committee meetings assessing the international scientific research, at which the application for access was directed.

[94] Case T-496/13 *McCullough v Cedefop* (n 90) para 5: 'The applicant disputed Cedefop's observation that it was questionable whether the KMS minutes existed, claiming that he was the rapporteur for that steering group and had himself drafted those documents'; and para 35: 'The third plea alleges that Cedefop's denial of the existence of the KMS minutes is suspect'. Still, at para 47:

> In this plea, the applicant submits, primarily, that the Acting Director of Cedefop is not sincere when he asserts in the contested decision that it is questionable whether the KMS minutes ever existed, since he was the Deputy Director for part of the period in respect of which those documents were requested and he was involved in all the KMS activities and meetings. The applicant also submits that the statements made in the initial decision contradict those made in the contested decision, since the Acting Director of Cedefop first stated that the KMS minutes are no longer in Cedefop's possession following the audit carried out by the IAS and OLAF, then that it is questionable whether those documents ever existed.

C. Cumbersome Applications and Categories of Documents

A further issue that must be addressed is how the institutions may deal with applications for 'lengthy documents or for a large number of documents'. Because with regard to this analysis there are two main items that are easily confused, a first step is to detach them.

The easier of the two to single out is what may generally be called a cumbersome application, which imposes a substantial amount of work on the institutions, and might (or not) come to be considered disproportionate. With regard to this figure, it is the law that (in a manner somewhat lacking in thoroughness) attempts to provide the judicature with basic guidelines.

The second item, the concept of a category of document, is in fact a complementary criterion that the judicature has adopted and adjusted in order for the institutions to deal with two different hindrances. In the first place, the concept of category has clearly been shaped to address the threat of excessive quantities of work for the institutions. Second, and much more subtly, it has also been creatively salvaged to address applications framed imprecisely. Gainfully, the substantive discussion we have just outlined, in parallel, sheds light on applicants' strategies with regard to the terminology employed in the drafting of applications.

i. Cumbersome Applications: 'It's the Quantity, Stupid!'[95]

As a starting point to this discussion of documents from a quantitative point of view, no one knows what a document is. If a document is one page of a larger file, two pages of a larger file, 20 pages of a larger file or even 20,000 pages of a very lengthy report, is absolutely unclear. To this day, the circumstance that any application pertains either to one or more documents (further interpreted to mean either a page or an entire file or to one or 1000 pages) has been left entirely up to the applicant.

Case T-436/09 *Dufour*

> 109 Acceptance of that premiss would give rise to the question of what size of content is required in order to constitute a document within the meaning of [the EU rules on access to documents]. In other words, if it were to be admitted, for example, that a figure or a single word were not sufficient for that purpose, it would then be necessary to establish whether a sentence, a whole paragraph or some other larger piece of text might be necessary for that purpose. Given that the author of [these rules] decided not to set any minimum threshold for the size of content required in the definition set out in Article 3 of [Regulation 1049/2001], the Courts of the European Union cannot themselves assume that task.

As a result, nothing in the law impedes an applicant from drafting a single application the object of which, in physical, quantitative terms, amounts to a truckload of documents. Take the case of an applicant who by way of a single application identifies 3000 documents. The same is true of all applications that are framed in terms

[95] This title rephrases the notorious statement of the US Presidential campaign, '*It's the Economy, Stupid*' coined by James Carville in 1992.

of 'all documents regarding X'. However unexpected the outcome, in such cases applicants may also end up with a truckload of documents delivered to their door.

Admittedly it is also true that if the law required applicants to lodge an individual application for each single document, we might be facing truckloads of applications placed at the door of the institutions, instead of having one application that asks for 10 or 1000 documents at a time.

And so, it has fallen to the judicature, in as far as this is possible, to strike a balance on the one hand between the practicability of the rules involved, and on the other, that the levels of specification and robustness of the rules' impositions on the players must be taken into account.

Indeed, all outcomes that presuppose truckloads of anything travelling back and forth between applicants and institutions would bring disastrous consequences for the access policy. Without the judicature's tactful arbitrage, the functioning of the institutions might easily be compromised, and at the same time the entire framework of a general right of access might be undermined in the process.

Although the judicature does impose the burden of proof of the (disproportionate) scale of the task onto the institutions,[96] the law offers up no further guidance on this point. Always in regard to what is imprecisely described as 'a very long document or to a very large number of documents' what the law does, in three of its articles, is to open a door for informal negotiations that have as their object assorted details of the procedure. First, the law speaks of the negotiation of a fair solution, secondly, of a (single) extension of the deadlines for reply, and thirdly, indicates that for applications totalling fewer than 20 A4 pages, copies are free.

Regulation 1049/2001

Article 6(3)

In the event of an application relating to a very long document or to a very large number of documents, the institution concerned may confer with the applicant informally, with a view to finding a fair solution.

Article 7(3)

In exceptional cases, for example in the event of an application relating to a very long document or to a very large number of documents, the time-limit provided for in paragraph 1 [15 working days] may be extended by 15 working days, provided that the applicant is notified in advance and that detailed reasons are given.

Article 10(1) *in fine*

Consultation on the spot, copies of less than 20 A4 pages and direct access in electronic form or through the register shall be free of charge.

With regard to illuminating contributions from the judicature on this point, there has been no judicially-set threshold with regard to the qualification of any document as lengthy or not.[97]

[96] Case T-436/09 *Dufour v ECB* (n 4) para 122.

[97] Conversely, what we do find are instances in which the judicature opts for joinder of multiple actions lodged by a single applicant (Ryanair), which have come forth prima facie as challenging distinct refusals

ii. Leading Case

It remains that the leading case on so-called 'cumbersome applications' is possibly still *Verein für Konsumenten.*[98] In that case, the applicant framed the application broadly. What was sought was access to 'the administrative file relating to the Lombard Club decision'. Moreover, it is observable in paragraph 17 of the ruling that 'excluding internal documents, that file contains more than 47 000 pages'. After extending the deadline once to reply in accordance with Article 7(3),[99] and after inter alia dividing the documents into 11 categories,[100] the Commission refused the applicant's application in its entirety adding that 'a detailed examination of each document, which was necessary for any partial consultation, would have represented an excessive and disproportionate amount of work for it'.

The judicature, *in casu*, opted to enforce a strict interpretation of the need for partial access[101] to be considered in the policy,[102] but did not provide any guidance, for example, on what might fit into a distinct legal requirement: *that the institutions confer with the applicant with a view to finding a fair solution.*[103]

That—much-needed—judicial contribution would come forth at a much later stage, within the *Strack* proceedings. The explanation offered up, albeit tardy, is instrumental to the understanding of whether (in cases regarding lengthy documents or a large number of documents) the deadlines of Regulation 1049/2001 are, or

for access handed down with regard to separate applications for distinct documents. These cases may be read as a sign of little tolerance on the part of the judges of the EU for applicants who attempt to lend a multiplying effect to the impact of their grievances. Consequently, the judges occasionally correct the vexatious partitioning of applications and lodging of actions. In this way, it is made clear that since the institutional reaction to a set of similar and identifiable documents has to be coherent, a single application for their entirety would suffice to engage the institutions, as would, where appropriate, a single action to contest their refusal.

[98] Case T-2/03 *VFK* (n 45). More recently, Case T-436/09 *Dufour v ECB* (n 4) also brings a significant contribution to the discussion.

[99] See section IV.C.i.

[100] See section IV.C.iii.

[101] Regulation 1049/2001, Art 11.

[102] Case T-2/03 *VFK* (n 45) para 130:

> However, it is not apparent from the reasons for the contested decision that the Commission assessed, in a concrete, specific and detailed manner, on the one hand, the other conceivable options for limiting its workload and, on the other, the reasons which could allow it to avoid carrying out any examination rather than adopting, where appropriate, a measure less restrictive of the applicant's right of access. In particular, it is not apparent from the contested decision that, as regards the identification of documents contained in a file arranged in chronological order, the Commission specifically examined the option of asking the banks involved in the Lombard Club file to provide it with the dates of the documents submitted by them, which might possibly have enabled it to find some of them more easily in its file. In addition, although the Commission stated in its defence that drawing up a table of contents would have been a disproportionate task, the examination of that option is not mentioned at all in the contested decision and therefore cannot be considered to have been specifically examined. Finally, it is likewise not apparent from the contested decision that the Commission evaluated the amount of work involved in identifying, then examining, individually and concretely, the few documents most likely to satisfy immediately and, where appropriate, partially in the first instance the applicant's interests.

[103] Regulation 1049/2001, Art 7(3).

are not, imperative and/or negotiable as part of the fair solution to cumbersome applications.

Case C-127/13P *Strack*

21 The Commission claims that no implied refusal could be deemed to exist on expiry of the time-limits laid down in Article 8 of Regulation No 1049/2001 since, first, the appellant refused to find a fair solution in accordance with Article 6(3) thereof and, second, since the application for access to the relevant documents concerned a manifestly disproportionate number of documents, the Commission was not obliged to comply with the time-limits laid down in that regulation in the interests of good administration.

26 In the case of an application relating to a very long document or to a very large number of documents an extension of 15 working days of the time-limit laid down in Article 8(1) of that regulation is authorised in exceptional cases. Although, in such a case, Article 6(3) allows the institution concerned to find a fair solution with the applicant seeking access to documents in its possession, that solution can concern only the content or the number of documents applied for.

28 Thus, an institution may, in exceptional circumstances, refuse access to certain documents on the ground that the workload relating to their disclosure would be disproportionate as compared to the objectives set by the application for access to those documents. However, reliance on the principle of proportionality cannot allow the time-limits laid down by Regulation No 1049/2001 to be changed without creating a situation of legal uncertainty.

30 [...] the appellant's wish to remain within the time-limits laid down by Regulation No 1049/2001 cannot, in the light of the findings set out in paragraphs 24 to 28 of the present judgment, mean that the Commission had no opportunity to reach a fair solution.

Thus, whilst the judicature does not (or cannot) commit to a quantitative approach to the definition of document, it has ruled that regardless of the concrete dimension of the quantitative burden imposed on the institutions, the deadlines consigned in the law may not be set aside. Notably, not only can they not be set aside without the agreement of the applicant, but a moral imperative (for the institutions not to do so) is also said to hold in spite of any (naïve) agreement of the applicant in that sense.

Advocate General Kokott trumpets such a warning to the applicant:

Case C-127/13P *Strack*, Opinion of AG Kokott

34. Where an applicant allows himself to be put off by the Commission, he risks, as a result, an action brought against a subsequent, express decision being dismissed because it is directed against a decision which merely confirms a previous decision. He must even fear the Commission relying on the time-limit for bringing proceedings against the implied refusal being exceeded, even though the Commission has previously repeatedly availed itself of further extensions to the processing time-limits.

35. Even if the Commission were to refrain from claiming that proceedings had been initiated out of time, or if it were to be barred from raising that objection because to do so would be to act in bad faith (*venire contra factum proprium*), the action brought would not necessarily be admissible. This is because the courts may examine of their own motion whether the time-limit for bringing proceedings has been observed as a mandatory procedural requirement, even though the General Court does not appear to do so systematically in proceedings concerning access to documents.

> 36. For this reason, it is not improper for an applicant to refuse to accept an extension of the processing time-limits. Given the current state of EU law and the related case law, a prudent applicant must rather insist on the time-limits being observed if, from the outset, he does not intend to rule out an action being brought at a later stage.

Concluding on this point, it seems that the judicature is called upon both by applicants and institutions more to provide guidance on how to manage cumbersome applications than to provide a definition of the same. Applicants and institutions are not looking for a number to set a threshold that will determine a priori whether a document is lengthy or not. Ultimately, what they need from the judicature is the exercise of wisdom in the criterion chosen to reconcile the widest expression of the right of access to documents with the procedural feasibility of the same.

iii. Categories, Documents of a Kind

On another front, the judicature (without the law) promoted an alternative tactic for the institutional management of applications for 'lengthy documents or for a large number of documents' and/or for applications framed in a general manner.

For this purpose, the idea that certain *categories* of documents should be singled out in institutional explanations for refusals was advertised in *WWK UK v Commission*.[104] At that time it was understood that notwithstanding the fact that applications often came forth (and still do) framed in a general manner such as 'access to *all documents* concerning X', the institutions were required, in their responses to applicants, to provide itemised (ie document(s) by document(s)) explanations for refusal. In addition, the imposed itemisation and differentiation of explanations would be tied to a necessary, and prior, task of *categorisation* of the documents contained in the global file by the institutions. It is also interesting to see that there are accounts in the case law of applicants applying for access 'to the file' because it is clear that they believe that a file contains many documents hitherto unknown to them.[105]

> Case T-105/95 *WWF v Commission*
>
> 64 It is important, nevertheless, to point out that the Commission cannot confine itself to invoking the possible opening of an infringement procedure as justification, under the heading of protecting the public interest, for refusing access to the entirety of the documents identified in an application made by a citizen. The Court considers, in effect, that

[104] Case T-105/95 *WWF v Commission* [1997] ECR II-00313.

[105] Case T-237/02 *TGI v Commission* [2006] ECR II-05131, para 33:

> It follows, moreover, from Regulation No 1049/2001 that 'access to the file' and 'access to a document' are not equivalent concepts and that the right of access to a document presupposes an application describing the document sought so that it can be identified. That regulation does not create a right for citizens enabling them to inspect the files of the organ concerned in order to find therein documents of possible interest to them, an even more inevitable conclusion if applications for access to documents are not supported by reasons. In this case, the applicant has confined itself to claiming, tersely, access to 'all the documents' concerning the alleged State aid procedure cited, which is not surprising, since the applicant itself admits that it is seeking documents hitherto unknown to it.

> the Commission is required to indicate, at the very least by reference to categories of documents, the reasons for which it considers that the documents detailed in the application which it received are related to the possible opening of an infringement procedure. It should indicate to which subject-matter the documents relate and particularly whether they involve inspections or investigations relating to a possible procedure for infringement of Community law.

As a result, it became clear that following the ruling in *WWF*,[106] the institutions would be bound to categorise any file by drawing up a table of contents displaying subtitles of the type: reports; notes; expert testimony, telegrams; correspondence.

Moreover, for each category identified, an explanation needed to be given (on the basis of the various exceptions contained in the Code of Conduct) as to why that set of documents, grouped as a homogenous category, could not be disclosed. This called for two steps in the response-oriented procedural requirements imposed on institutions: first, that they explain that a certain document had been categorised into subheading X of a table of contents (when a large number of documents was requested). Second, that an explanation be provided with regard to what exception (in the Code or Regulation) might apply to category X. Therefore, the equation to be expected for each document sought was, at the least: 'category X, exception Y'.

This specification of the judicature increases the workload of the institution, but it incontestably confers robustness to the answers offered up. In the face of such an articulate institutional provision of arguments, the public would find it difficult to criticise the institution for not having given careful consideration to applications. In this manner the institutions and their public are drawn closer together because there is substantive dialogue between them. Institutional practice and the judicial criterion to assess the same would thus be aligned with the public's own understanding of the many parts (ie documents) that constitute 'a file'.

In the practice post-*WWF*, a recurrent categorisation of *documents* is observable.[107] Indeed in *VFK*,[108] 11 categories were singled out. At a later stage in the case law the judicial requirement of an *itemised* categorisation of documents (with regard to the structure of replies to applicants) would be significantly watered down. In fact, in certain circumstances the defiling of the categorisation requirement has been tolerated to such an extent that there are legitimate doubts that it survives at all.

It might be said that the dilution began with regard to refusals to grant access to administrative and investigative files[109] compiled by the institutions, more often than not the Commission. In practice, When applicants applied for 'all documents with regard to file X' the institutions tentatively answered that 'all documents with regard to file X' are covered (in their entirety) by exception Y. Whilst this type of answer seems to concern only the devising of which exception is applicable, in fact

[106] Case T-105/95 *WWF v Commission* (n 106).
[107] Case T-124/96 *Interporc* [1998] ECR II-231, para 54.
[108] Case T-2/03 *VFK* (n 45) paras 17–20.
[109] Case T-168/02 *IFAW Internationaler Tierschutzfons GmbH v Commission* [2004] ECR II-04135.

an attentive reading of the same brings to light that *a* file (once taken to represent a compilation of several categories of documents is deftly peddled as *a* category of document in its own right.[110]

The judicature, for its part, affirmed that specific reasoning:

Case C-514/07P *LPN*

64 [...] the documents relating to the [file concerning the] pre-litigation stage of an infringement procedure constitute a single category of documents and no distinction should be made on the basis of the type of document forming the file or of the author of the documents in question.

In sum, whilst in the past the judicature had imposed itemisation within institutional replies (regardless of whether applications addressed to the institutions had been framed in a general manner), in this second stage the general manner in which applications of applicants are framed[111] becomes the catalyst of institutional refusals that, in turn, are framed generally and are upheld by the courts.

a. 'In their Entirety' as a Double Shroud

Worth noting separately is the fact that when the institutions allege that the contested documents (all the documents in a file) are in their entirety[112] related to an exception, the phrase 'in their entirety' implies a double layer.

In fact, in the first place it designates the link between each and every document in a file to the same, specific, exception. The link to an exception immediately inhibits full disclosure and, traditionally, the judicature would then require that the possibility of partial access be considered.

At the same time, the same phrase 'in their entirety' has concomitantly been read as an automatic tool to dispense the institutions from the requirement to carry out the partial access test.

Case T-29/08 *LPN v Commission*

113 There are however a number of exceptions to the Commission's obligation to examine specifically and individually the documents to which access has been requested.

[110] The concept of the file as a single category of document has also been applied in three other specific circumstances, namely all documents in the administrative file concerning procedures for reviewing State aid, all the documents exchanged between the Commission and the notifying parties or third parties in the context of merger control procedures, and all the pleadings lodged by an institution in proceedings pending before the courts.

[111] Case C-514/011P *LPN* (n 67) para 47: 'All these cases shared the characteristic that the application for access in question covered not just one document but a set of documents' [which] (para 48) 'enables the institution concerned to deal with a global application and to reply thereto accordingly'.

[112] Case T-29/08 *LPN v Commission* [2011] ECR II-06021, para 109: 'it must be established whether, in this case, the Commission satisfied its obligation to examine whether the documents concerned were in fact covered, in their entirety, by the exception provided for under Article 4(2), third indent, of Regulation No 1049/2001, read in conjunction with Article 6(1) of Regulation No 1367/2006'.

Case C-514/011P *LPN* (n 67) para 9 '"partial access" for the purposes of Article 4(6) of Regulation No 1049/2001 was not possible in the case of those documents since the exception invoked applied to all of those documents'.

114 It has repeatedly been held that, since the purpose of the concrete, individual examination which the institution must in principle undertake in response to a request for access made under Regulation No 1049/2001 is to enable the institution in question to assess, on the one hand, the extent to which an exception to the right of access is applicable and, on the other, the possibility of partial access, such an examination may not be necessary where, due to the particular circumstances of the individual case, it is obvious that access must be refused or, on the contrary, granted. Such could be the case, inter alia, if certain documents were either, first, manifestly covered in their entirety by an exception to the right of access or, conversely, manifestly accessible in their entirety, or, finally, had already been the subject of a concrete, individual assessment by the Commission in similar circumstances (*Verein für Konsumenteninformation v Commission*, cited in paragraph 102 above, paragraph 75, and *API v Commission*, cited in paragraph 101 above, paragraph 58).

This establishes that the consideration of partial access is dispensed with with regard to each and every single document bundled in the file.

b. The Burden of Specificity

With such a position the judicature co-ascribes the burden of specificity to both players, but first and foremost it is ascribed to the applicant. Consequently, the level of specificity and/or categorisation that an applicant may expect from the institution is closely correlated to the degree of specificity with which the applicant has *ex ante* framed his/her own application.

It is interesting to observe in the case law how applicants have picked up on this subtlety. It is not by chance that in *ClientEarth*,[113] the applicant takes the time to make the point that its individual application (for access to documents) was not framed in a general manner, and to seek distance *in casu* from other situations in which applications had (possibly) been less adequately framed.[114]

Case C-612/13P *ClientEarth v Commission*

52 ClientEarth claims, first, that it applied for access to specific documents, not to a whole administrative file relating to infringement proceedings, nor even to a set of documents described in general terms. Further, its application concerned, not one category of documents to which similar general considerations applied, but studies in two distinct categories, namely (i) those relating to infringement proceedings which had been commenced and (ii) those not connected with any such proceedings.

As late as 16 July 2015, the judicature held firm in its concession to the institutions that varied types of documents, if related to investigative duties, within certain areas of the activity of the Union, might be treated as a single bundle (category). In consequence, access to these documents may be refused as pertaining to a single item.[115]

[113] Case C-612/13P *ClientEarth v Commission* [not yet reported].

[114] As, for example in *LPN* (n 67) and Case C-139/07P *Commission v TGI* (n 84).

[115] Moreover the Court has clearly indicated that it will validate this line of reasoning for (at least) 5 specific areas: (1) (all) documents in the administrative file relating to a procedure for reviewing State Aid: Case C-139/07P *Commission v TGI* (n 84); (2) (all) the pleadings lodged by an institution in court proceedings: Joined Cases C-514/07P, C-528/07P & C-532/07P *Sweden and Others v API and Commission*,

However, the applicant in *ClientEarth*[116] was rewarded for the degree of detail and/or breakdown employed as per the structure of the application for access, and was successful in obtaining from the judicature that refusals, when covering distinct[117] categories of documents (as was the case namely for categories (i) and (ii) quoted above) need to provide an individual reasoning, at the least, as per each category.

In sum, with the blessing of the judicature, many different documents may be grouped as a single category and treated (ie disclosed or refused) together on the basis of the same reasoning. Applicants should be wary of this and, whenever it is feasible, should consider breaking down their applications into separate categories. Still, and in the case that it is the institution that categorises the documents, applicants should also strive to check that any refusal has been organised into individual reasoning(s) as per each identified category.

D. Presuming Harm: Shelters that Keep out Public Scrutiny

Intricately woven together with the subtle (or not so subtle) new capaciousness (an entire file) breathed into the concept of category of document by the judicature are the so-called presumptions of harm in disclosure.

The figure of the presumption was introduced into the access litigation by paragraph 50 of the ECJ's ruling in the *Turco* appeal, which directly followed a previous paragraph (paragraph 49) which required a concrete document-by-document appraisal:

> Joined Cases C-39/05P and C-52/05P *Sweden and Turco v Council*
>
> 49 If the Council decides to refuse access to a document which it has been asked to disclose, it must explain, first, how access to that document could specifically and effectively undermine the interest protected by an exception laid down in Article 4 of Regulation No 1049/2001 relied on by that institution and, secondly, in the situations referred to in Article 4(2) and (3) of that regulation, whether or not there is an overriding public interest that might nevertheless justify disclosure of the document concerned.
>
> 50 It is, in principle, open to the Council to base its decisions in that regard on general presumptions which apply to certain categories of documents, as considerations of a generally similar kind are likely to apply to requests for disclosure relating to documents of the

para 94; (3) (all) the documents exchanged between the Commission and notifying parties or third parties in the course of merger control proceedings: Case C-404/10P *Commission v Editions Odile Jacob*, para 123; (4) (all) the documents concerning an infringement procedure in its pre-litigation stage: Case C-514/11P and C-605/11P *LPN and Finland v Commission* (n 67) para 65; (5) (all) the documents relating to a proceeding under Art 101 TFEU: Case C-365/12P *Commission v EnBw*, para 93.

[116] Case C-612/13P *ClientEarth v Commission* (n 113).

[117] Case C-612/13P Opinion of AG Villalon, para 52: 'Accordingly, it is my view that ClientEarth is right to complain of an infringement of the third indent of Article 4(2) Regulation No 1049/2001, inasmuch as studies that were not followed immediately by infringement proceedings were wrongly included within the concept [single category] of "investigation"'. The AG's Opinion was embraced by the judgment at paras 79 and 80.

same nature. However, it is incumbent on the Council to establish in each case whether the general considerations normally applicable to a particular type of document are in fact applicable to a specific document which it has been asked to disclose.

Whilst the principal forum for discussion of presumptions is Chapter 5,[118] there are four points that are important to approach at this stage.

The first point is that although a presumption may target a single document,[119] as a general rule it targets whole categories[120] of documents. The second point is that since an entire file may be considered equivalent to a single category, the same presumption might apply to entire files. The third point is that (as a rule) there is no room for partial access when a presumption applies. Consequently, if and when contested documents come under the presumption's wing, the institutions are not required to read the contested documents at all.[121] The fourth and final point is that as consequence of the last three points just discussed, the contested documents (that have not been read by the applicant) may be refused without ever having been read by the institution either.

The purpose of having made these four points is that since we have gone to such lengths to explain what a document *is*, it is just as important to close the present chapter by noting how the contested documents in the access litigation are, more often than not, read by no one.

E. Ruling on Empty, Documents Seen by No One

We are well aware that it is almost unthinkable that the entire procedural arch[122] of an access to documents litigation could unfold before our eyes without the contested documents ever having been read by anyone. However, if we consider the policy's players, one by one, it happens. In the first place, any applicant's access to the contested documents is barred, *tout court*, until institutions disclose the same. After all, that is the entire point of being an applicant: persons apply for documents because they have never read (watched or heard) them beforehand.[123]

Secondly, as discussed earlier, the institutions may choose not to examine the contested documents at all (if a presumption of harm is deemed to apply).

[118] Ch 5 pertains to the substantive analysis of the exceptions to the general principle *access unless*...

[119] Case T-456/13 *Sea Handling v Commission* [not yet reported] para 58 (available only in French): 'Toutefois, ladite présomption a été reconnue comme applicable également lorsqu'un seul document avait fait l'objet d'une demande d'accès (voir, en ce sens, arrêt du 25 octobre 2013, Beninca/Commission, T-561/12, EU:T:2013:558, points 1, 24 et 32)'.

[120] For alternative wording, see Case T-223/12 *Ntouvas v ECDC*, para 34: 'range of documents'.

[121] As seen above the phrase that alleges a presumption to apply to a file 'in its entirety' is woven over two layers. The first layer means: any and all document(s) in the file. The second layer means: to any and every part of any document.

[122] In the form of an example: application/refusal/confirmatory request/refusal/action for annulment/public hearing/dismissal/appeal/public hearing/dismissal or affirmation.

[123] *cf Svenska* (n 60) (in which regardless of the fact that the applicant had obtained access to the contested documents from another source the action was admissible) and likewise in *Petrie* (n 54) para 24 and *Dennekamp* (n 3) (in which because some of the names had publicly come to light the Court excluded them from the (useful) scope of the action).

Thirdly, and finally addressing the judicature's role, the EU courts are empowered to order—at their discretion—measures of inquiry/organisation which include the production of the contested documents, albeit for the eyes of the court, only.[124]

In sum, the applicant wants to read the contested documents but is impeded from doing so. The institutions may always read them yet are allowed not to. The judicature that holds the power to demand to see them—more often than not—does not order their production. The sum of these three conditions when they come together, confine the access litigation entirely to theory, to conjecture and to abstractness of reasoning. The main point, however—that no one reads the contested documents—is absent from the discussions of the doctrine and is hardly ever challenged in the case law. On this point precisely, a relatively recent ruling of the ECJ delivered in Case C-576/12P *Jurašinović v Council*[125] provides a clear analysis of the *status quo*, and is well worth spending a moment on.

In very broad lines, when applicants have complained to the ECJ about the (first instance) judicature's failure to order the production and/or examine the contested documents, the main argument has been that applicant's right(s) to a fair trial are infringed. Here, at the head of the discussion, the ECJ has been quick to reaffirm the discretionary nature of the measures of inquiry and organisation of procedure.

Case C-576/12P *Jurašinović v Council*

> 23 As regards the merits, it is necessary to ascertain whether, as Mr Jurašinović submits, the General Court was obliged to order production of the documents requested in order to give judgment in the action for annulment.
>
> 24 It must be stated in that regard that no rule of procedure of the General Court imposes such an obligation.
>
> 25 Indeed, as the Council correctly points out, the provisions of the Rules of Procedure of the General Court concerning measures of organisation of procedure and measures of inquiry—in particular Articles 64(3)(d), 65(b) and 67(3) thereof—merely provide that the General Court, may, in certain circumstances, find it necessary to acquaint itself with a document to which public access has been denied and ask the institution concerned to produce that document.

The natural consequence of this is that in every case in which the EU judicature does not choose to order the production of the contested documents, institutional decisions to refuse access (to the documents) are legitimately annulled or upheld solely on the basis of the validity of the (institutional) reasons offered up.

Case C-576/12P *Jurašinović v Council*

> 26 It should also be made clear in that regard that the lawfulness of a decision refusing access to documents, such as the decision at issue in the present case, must as a rule be assessed by reference to the reasons on the basis of which it was adopted rather than by reference solely to the content of the documents requested.

124 The judicature must consult the documents *in camera* so that the parties themselves do not have access to them; the Rules of Procedure of the General Court, Art 67(3).

125 Case C-576/12P *Jurašinović v Council* [not reported].

This is of course a harsh version of the access to documents policy. A judicature that is complacent with the fact that the contested documents might not be read (at all) is taking risks. We are well aware that many persons (to whom access has been refused) would desist at this point.

Most people (including practitioners) that we have discussed this issue with, initially display considerable difficulty in coming to terms with this status quo. They find little solace in an analytical discussion that seems far removed from what they individually believe any access policy must lay down as a minimum requirement: that someone necessarily must (prove to have) read the documents before a refusal is final. Nonetheless, we believe that on this crucial point the practice of EU access cannot be understood without a raw analytical discussion of its legal framework unhindered by pre-judgement. We return to the first argument of this book. This policy must be discussed *de lege data* (for what it is), harsh or not. Preparedness makes the applicant (and the institutions) more objective, and only then, more incisive.

i. Just a Little Sunshine in the Rain[126]

However stark the predicament (no obligation for the judicature to see the documents) a crack in the door is left open. True, it imposes a (another) burden on the applicant: to protest (from the stage of the first pleading) that being at the basis of the refusal, the specific exception(s) relied on *in casu* by the institution were not applicable to the contested documents. On the condition that that burden is discharged,[127] the ECJ derives an actual judicial obligation: an order of production (of the contested documents) must be addressed by the court to the refusing institution, to ensure the applicant's judicial protection.

Case C-576/12P *Jurašinović v Council*

> 27 It is true that, when an applicant challenges the lawfulness of a decision refusing him access to a document on the basis of one of the exceptions provided for by Article 4 of Regulation No 1049/2001, claiming that the exception relied on by the institution concerned was not applicable to the document requested, the General Court is obliged to order production of the document and to examine it, if it is to ensure the applicant's judicial protection. Indeed, if it has not itself consulted the document concerned, the General Court will not be in a position to assess in the specific case whether access to the document could validly be refused by that institution on the basis of the exception relied on or, consequently, to assess the lawfulness of a decision refusing access to that document (see, to that effect, Case C-135/11 P *IFAW Internationaler Tierschutz-Fonds v Commission* [2012] ECR, paragraph 75).

[126] This title is inspired by P Leino, 'Just a Little Sunshine in the Rain: The 2010 Case Law of the European Court of Justice on Access to Documents' (2011) 48 *Common Market Law Review* 1215, 1238.

[127] See, for a case in which there is a concomitant allegation by the institution that a presumption is applicable, Case T-623/13 *Union Almacenistas de Hierros de Espana v Commission* [not yet reported] paras 105–08.

V. CONCLUSIONS

Interestingly another case discussed before the General Court, Case T-214/13 *Rainer Typke v Commission*, has moved into appeal status before the ECJ on 18 September 2015. It now holds the reference C-491/15P. As in *Dufour*, it concerns access to databases, which suggests that within the definition of 'document' a subheading related to databases is being forged in the case law of the EU judicature.

The statutory definition of 'document' is pliant, as we have seen. The policy's object fanned out from the Code of Conduct to Regulation 1049/2001. Today, medium (one of whatever type), once confined to the conveying of written text containing data in the general direction of the public, is now equivalently permitted to act as a vehicle for something broader: content. Still, the definition's broader ambit under Regulation 1049/2001 is markedly theoretical.

Overall, the malleability of the concept of 'document' has given applicants ample choice of lexicon when putting their applications for access into words. Still, it is the same looseness that has also allowed the institutions to artfully argue their way around—and away from—the policy's intended object. The document may be disclosed only in part, the document is no longer held by the EU, the institution is unsure of whether the document exists, although the institution holds the information no such document exists.

More importantly even, because 'document' is a word without quantitative or qualitative boundaries, its central position in the law has paved the way for the judicature to throw a blanket ban over an ever-larger[128] part of this game.

As to the crude point that the contested documents are often read by no one, it paints a dismal portrait of the policy: applicants grope, institutions pay them no heed, and the judicature rules on empty.

Happily, that is only one vision, one angle, one standpoint. One must still take into account that the EU access policy does not stand alone. It must be read together with other EU policies and rules. The discussion of documents has another branch that regards what happens when the qualitative specific content of a document calls for the concurrent application of other rules that possibly contrast with Regulation 1049/2001.

In order to conclude which rule will prevail within each specific contest, it will be necessary to turn to Article 4(1) to (3) of Regulation 1049/ 2001 and begin an entirely new discussion in Chapter 5.

[128] The growth of presumptions of harm.

5

Exceptions

I. INTRODUCTION—THE UNDERTONES OF 'NO'

'NO' ALWAYS HURTS. There has yet to be a sane person who does not cringe in disappointment when a request is refused. So, precisely because refusal is so unwelcome, its study becomes central to a discussion, the focal point of which is precisely how institutions respond to a request for access to documents.

So far we have clarified what it is that applicants may request from institutions and what it is that institutions might refuse them: documents.[1] Now it is time to address the different issue of *when* and *why* institutions may refuse[2] to disclose documents.

When institutions believe that a certain document must be withheld from the public, they frame that refusal under one of several so-called 'exceptions', the building blocks of a menu[3] that allows the EU institutions to keep documents insulated from public scrutiny. Thus, within the access policy, 'No' is no monotonous term. It is actually rare that a refusal will simply state 'No'.[4] In most cases refusals make explicit that it is 'No because x' or 'No because y'.

II. A HISTORICAL PERSPECTIVE

There is still considerable difficulty in understanding the overall scheme of the exceptions that govern access. True, it always was (and still is) both intricate and layered.

[1] See Ch 4.

[2] This chapter will serve first to discuss the many possible exceptions (or grounds) at the basis of explicit refusals to requests for access. Secondly, turning to a related but as yet undeveloped topic, we will touch upon the principal lines of the relationship that exists today between the EU rules on access to documents and the EU rules on access to environmental information. Thirdly, we will address the need for the harmonious interpretation of Regulation 1049/2001 with other rules of EU law in areas other than the environment. Within a fourth part of this chapter we have chosen to engage in a separate discussion on the interplay of exceptions and the so-called 'private' interests that are at stake when any request for access is considered.

Before overall conclusions are drawn, further discussion will serve to distinguish timely and single explicit refusals from late and/or multiple explicit refusals to the same request. This last part, in particular, will bridge the discussion to Ch 6, in which implicit refusals are considered.

[3] Currently, all the statute-based exceptions to public access to documents of the EU are listed under Art 4 of Regulation 1049/2001 and under Art 6(2) of Regulation 1367/2006.

[4] With the exception of instances of legal silence (Regulation 1049/2001, Art 8); see Ch 6.

Furthermore, the case law method does not help. On the one hand, the judicature tends to quote (and rely on) paragraphs that rule(d) the past as if the legal framework of 1993[5] had never moved on in 2001. On the other hand, the judicature has come to converge on a criterion regarding the type of examination that the institutions must make of the contested documents before refusing them, which is far removed from the instructions laid down in the law.[6] 'No' has thus taken on a rather aloof connotation.

In order to understand what is valid today (2016), it is therefore essential to contrast the legal structure of 1993 with that of 2001, for the sake of ascertaining what still might be held on to, and what must be left behind.

After we describe the background to and the structure of the policy, we will look at the mandatory exceptions of 1993, how that context was revised in 2001, and how it must be differently understood and applied since then. We will then proceed in the same way with regard to the discretionary exception of 1993.

A. From 1993 to 2001 and Beyond

The text of the 1993 Code of Conduct that listed the exceptions to access was short and (deceptively) simple:

> 1993 Code of Conduct
>
> (Mandatory Exceptions)
>
> The institutions *will* refuse access to any document whose disclosure *could* undermine:
>
> — The public interest (taken to overarch 6 sub-types of situations): public security, international relations, monetary stability, court proceedings, inspections and investigations.
> — Individuals and their privacy.
> — Commercial and industrial secrecy.
> — The Community's financial interests.
> — The confidentiality of the person who supplied the information (at the request of the same).
> — The confidentiality of the Member State who supplied the information (as required by national legislation).
>
> (Discretionary Exception)
>
> The institution *may* also refuse access in order to protect the institution's interest in the confidentiality of its proceedings.

[5] See below for a discussion of the case law. The EU courts, eg, have continued to resort, well beyond 2001, to the same words that protected investigations between 1993 and 2001; Case T-105/95 *WWF UK v Commission* [1997] ECR II-00313, para 63: 'the type of confidentiality the Member States are entitled to expect'. This in spite of a novel framework for investigations post-2001.

[6] Indeed, as we will see, Art 4(6) of Regulation 1049/2001 has been practically annihilated.

i. 1993: The Background

Upon a close reading of other excerpts of the 1993 text together with the specific articles on exceptions, it might be said that there were two priors to the structure of the access policy.

ii. Cornerstone 1: A Policy for Internal Documents

The first cornerstone, which does not always come across clearly, was that the access policy, at its core, concerned public access to the internal[7] documents of the EU. These are documents that are not yet finalised or that are not intended for publication:

> Code of Conduct 1993
>
> The public will have the widest possible access to documents held by the Commission and the Council.
>
> 'Document' means any written text, whatever its medium, which contains existing data and is held by the Council or the Commission.

By contrast, the access policy was not purposefully constructed to cater for any published documents. Nonetheless, if requests were to arise for those, the applicant would simply be told where to find them. Such cases were not governed by any access policy: they were governed by the prior status quo of the document, ie public.

iii. Cornerstone 2: a Policy for Documents Authored by the EU

The second cornerstone was that any document requested from the institutions would have had to have been drawn up by the EU. If, conversely, it was authored by any other entity, under the Code of Conduct that document fell outside the policy's reach:

> Code of Conduct 1993
>
> Where the document held by an institution was written by a natural or legal person, a Member State, another Community institution or body or any other national or international body, the application must be sent direct to the author.

iv. The Structure: Mandatory v Discretionary Secrecy

With regard to the structure of the policy, it was split down the middle into two distinct halves. The EU rules, on the one hand, validated refusals meant to impede public access to internal documents that, in spite of the existence of an access policy,

[7] See Ch1. The main institutional task between 1993 and 2001 was to sift out applications according to the criterion of whether they sought documents from the EU that were already published (so that the applicant might be told where to obtain them) or, more crucially, internal documents. This second category was taken to mean 'documents which are not yet finalised or not intended for publication, irrespective of the confidentiality rating'; European Commission, *Access to Commission Documents: A Citizen's Guide* (OPOCE, 1997) 15.

still had to be kept covert. The first half of the policy was all about mandatory secrecy since this had to be assured in six cases (listed above). What is interesting is that it was established to protect a very wide range of interests, encompassing both the public and the private sector. These six counter-interests to access came to be known as the mandatory exceptions.

On the other hand, the policy also validated refusals meant to impede public access to different internal documents that, in spite of the existence of an access policy, *might* be kept covert. Within this second context, secrecy was neither called for nor obvious; it was an institutional choice, a mere possibility. This discretionary secrecy could have been preferred in one context only (listed above). By contrast to the former exceptions, this particular institutional counter-interest to access came to be known as the discretionary exception.

Therefore, between 1993 and 2001, within the legislative text that governed access the difference between the words 'will' and 'may' was crucial. It drew a line between the outer bounds of the policy (beyond which access could not be granted) and the degree of voluntary institutional engagement with the access policy. Thus, for the first six cases and six sub-types of the first case it was written: 'the institutions will[8] refuse'. By contrast, only in the case of confidentiality of the EU proceedings was 'the institutions may[9] also refuse' written into the law.

III. 1993: WHAT WAS MANDATORY

Before we proceed it is important to say that in 1993 it was inconceivable that the EU would offer the public an entire access policy and that, at the same time, there would be even the slightest of chances that documents would not be read by the institutions before being refused.

And so, in the rear of the policy an unwritten presumption stood: that before the institutions would even dare to make statements about whether a document could be released or not (thereby correlating a document to an exception), the former would have been examined (ie read). This unwritten presumption of correct correlation, in fact, translates the natural reaction of most persons to institutional statements: when an institution refuses access to a document alleging that the same is covered by a certain exception, whilst one does not really *know* if the allegation is correct or well grounded, one *presumes* that the allegation is correct and well grounded.

With regard to the mandatory class of exceptions to access, in 1993, the wording of the Code, albeit clear, called for an impeccable command of grammar. Where a mandatory exception applied, it addressed an order of non-disclosure to the institutions—since ('will') a modal auxiliary verb, indicating obligation, was employed—and thus, the former enjoyed no discretion to counter it:

1993 Code of Conduct, Mandatory Exceptions

The institutions *will* refuse access to any document whose disclosure *could* undermine

[8] Decision 93/731 and Decision 94/90: 'Documents *shall* not be granted ... where their disclosure could undermine'.

[9] Decision 94/90: 'They *may* also refuse access in order to protect the institution's interest in the confidentiality of its proceedings'.

Because of the verbal connotation ('will'), there were clearly two explicit (written) presumptions[10] at work.

First, an absolute[11] presumption of preponderance of the (confidentiality to be accorded to) interests protected by those exceptions could be read. To that effect, the interest in keeping the contested documents under a shroud of confidentiality always takes precedence over any utility (public and/or private) that might be derived from the disclosure of the same. Because of the presumption, the institutions were not obliged (of their own motion) to consider the benefits of disclosure.[12]

Secondly, another written presumption came in tandem with the first. It sprang from another verbal option ('could') and was related to harm in disclosure. In fact, since the grounding phrase in the Code was 'the institutions *will* refuse documents whose disclosure *could* undermine' and not 'whose disclosure [actually] undermines', the verbal use of the conditional waived the requisite of an *actual* harm-based evaluation. As such, the rule established as prohibited any disclosure held to be even *potentially* harmful.

In all, the protection of the interests listed in the exceptions resulted in their unfailing prevalence over whatever it was they should prevail over. Notably, in 1993, time after time it was understood that the mandatory exceptions prevailed over both the *private* interests of the person who had requested the documents and the *public* interest in the betterment of institutional accountability to the public.

At the core of a mandatory exception lay the belief that—in spite of the existence of an access policy—there was no need to take other interests[13] into account:

Case T-105/95 *WWF UK v Commission*

38. The Commission goes on to add that the exceptions in the Code of Conduct are distinguished according to their mandatory or discretionary character. The Commission points out that when it relies upon a mandatory exception it has no need to engage in an

[10] What is a (legal) presumption? It is permission from the law to assume that something (usually a prerequisite) has been fulfilled and/or complied with although we are not sure that that is so. On occasion, the law allows players (persons and institutions) to act on the basis of such presumptions. This means that decisions may be taken without certainty that one or more prerequisites (to the decision) have been met.

Moreover, the law allows for presumptions of two types. The first type of presumption allowed is an absolute presumption (*jure et de jure*). In these cases there is no room for (interested) parties to demonstrate that what has been assumed is in fact not true. By contrast, the second type of presumption allowed is a rebuttable one (*juris tantum*). Where it appears, it gives room to the players of any procedure to demonstrate that what has been assumed in first light is actually not true.

[11] As opposed to presumptions that are rebuttable.

[12] However, even that limitation to access had to be reconciled with the requirement that the contested documents be categorised; Case T-105/95 *WWF UK v Commission* (n 5) para 30.

[13] Also, Case T-20/99 *Denkavit Nederland v Commission* [2000] ECR II-3011, para 39.

As a last comment, within the access policy, the expression 'public interest' is considered under many dimensions. On the one hand, at present, access' vocabulary ubiquitously employs the expression 'public interest in disclosure'. On the other hand, as noted above, there are many other (and conflicting) public interests that call for non-disclosure. Namely, the Code listed 6: public security, international relations, monetary stability, court proceedings, inspections and investigations. In addition, potential harm to privacy, commercial and industrial secrecy, the Community's financial interests, as well as requests for confidentiality from suppliers of information or stemming from Member State legislation, whilst not qualified as public interests, would equally embody imperative arguments to refuse disclosure.

> exercise of balancing its interests against those of the person who has requested access to the documents. It argues that, having regard to the nature of the interests involved under the heading of mandatory exceptions, the balance of interests was in effect struck at the time when the Code of Conduct was adopted.

As we mentioned in the beginning of the section, in the rear, both presumptions (the absolute presumption of preponderance and the presumption of harm in disclosure) rested on a third, underlying and implicit (ie unwritten) presumption: that, before deciding to refuse documents to any applicant, the institutions would have undertaken a correct and faithful triage of the contested documents.

In other words, throughout the access policy it is always assumed that there is a measure of fit between the contested documents and the exception that the institutions have prima facie relied on to refuse access to the same to the applicant.

The judicature would, over time qualify this presumption of correct correlation as rebuttable. In other words, the judicature came to admit that it is possible that the institutions (sometimes) err[14] when they correlate contested documents to exceptions.[15] Nonetheless, the valid operation of the presumptions of preponderance and harm was completely dependent on a correct, *ex ante*, correlation between the contested documents and the exception relied on.

Therefore, and albeit to a large extent unnoticed by many of the policy's addressees, an intricate and subtle trio, correlation, preponderance and harm were at the basis of—and governed the procedure inherent to—the deceptively straightforward policy established by the 1993 Code of Conduct.

A. 1993–2001: *WWF* and *Hautala*: The Reasons behind the Requirement Categorisation and the Advent of a Necessary Analysis of the Feasibility of Partial Access

It was in this extremely restrictive context that the pre-Regulation 1049/2001 case law on mandatory exceptions developed. The leading case on mandatory exceptions is *WWF UK v Commission*.[16] A further case on disclosure of documents related to investigations but contextualised with the author's rule is *Petrie v Commission*.[17] Finally, the *Hautala v Council* proceedings, that practically call the curtain on the case law derived from the 1993 Code of Conduct, temper the presumption of preponderance of confidentiality with a criterion of proportionality and thereby formalise the possibility of partial access.

[14] Case T-105/95 *WWF UK v Commission* (n 5); Case C-353/99 P *Council v Hautala* [2001] ECR I-9565.

[15] Nevertheless, concomitantly, the judicature failed to identify clearly which actor of the access policy is called to disprove the presumption.

[16] Case T-105/95 *WWF UK v Commission* (n 5).

[17] Case T-191/99 *Petrie et al v Commission* [2001] ECR II-3677.

i. WWF

With regard to *WWF UK* and as early as 1995, the relationship between circumstances covered by a mandatory exception—such as the existence of an investigation—and the allegation that such an exception might apply to an extensive set of documents (the entirety of an investigative file) was discussed. In that particular case, the investigation (taken as an activity) was completed, but the institution had yet to take a final decision as to its outcome.

Moreover, the Commission had refused access to a large number of documents, alleging that the contested documents were covered by two[18] exceptions.

> Case T-105/95 WWF UK
>
> 63. In this regard, the Court considers that the confidentiality which the Member States are entitled to expect of the Commission in such circumstances warrants, under the heading of protection of the public interest, a refusal of access to documents relating to investigations which may lead to an infringement procedure, even where a period of time has elapsed since the closure of the investigation.
>
> 64. It is important, nevertheless, to point out that the Commission cannot confine itself to invoking the possible opening of an infringement procedure as justification, under the heading of protecting the public interest, for refusing access to the entirety of the documents identified in a request made by a citizen. The Court considers, in effect, that the Commission is required to indicate, at the very least by reference to categories of documents, the reasons for which it considers that the documents detailed in the request which it received are related to the possible opening of an infringement procedure. It should indicate to which subject-matter the documents relate and particularly whether they involve inspections or investigations relating to a possible procedure for infringement of Community law.

This ruling, in particular, shows how, since the very inception of the case law derived from the 1993 Code, even where a document was clearly related to a mandatory exception, that (mere) connection was not sufficient to alone ground a valid refusal.

On this very point, the ruling opened a discussion around categories of documents. It is a principal cornerstone of the access history and establishes (that there is to be) a hands-on relationship between the institutions and the contested documents once a request for disclosure is made.

It is true that the Court's first preoccupation was that the institutions clearly explain to applicants exactly which and how many of the contested documents fall under which exception.

But it is equally important to note that in fact, such a task increased the possibility that the institution might find that some categories of document within a file, or even some documents, a priori, formally classified as overarched by a certain category might not undermine any interest protected by a mandatory exception.

[18] Although we are focusing on the mandatory framework, it is important to note that the concrete outcome of *WWF* was overshadowed by the circumstance that the institutions had failed to clarify whether all of the documents were covered at once by both the exceptions relied on or not.

This would be the case if, upon examination of the 'entire file', some documents contained therein were found not to be covered by any of the exceptions.

Therefore, it is commonly accepted that as early as 1995 the ECJ called on the institutions to check and verify (on a case-by-case basis) the presumption[19] written nowhere: because the key to the access procedure was a real (ie actual) connection between the contested documents and the exception that the institutions had prima facie relied on to refuse them.

One way to look at it is to assume that the judicature sought to render accessible documents that had been dropped into an investigative file either by mistake or by inappropriate association with the (secrecy inherent to an) investigation.[20] The applicant thus enjoyed a better chance that the request for disclosure might be satisfied, at least in part.[21]

The practical effects of the categorisation requirement emerge from an attentive reading of the early case law. In fact, it was not uncommon for the institutions to hand out some (harmless) documents, although they were related to (ie involved) investigations. What was also clear was that the institutions themselves acknowledged (in practice) that the information these particular documents contained, if released, and albeit involving an investigation, would not undermine any asserted interest. The sensitivity of the Court, taking the form of a minimum imposition, and the (hands-on and generous) practice of the institutions, paved the way for what was later to be known in the case law as 'partial access'.[22]

ii. Hautala

Not surprisingly, in July 1999, the procedural requirement of the consideration of the feasibility of partial access[23] was born into a mandatory exception,[24] the protection of international relations.[25]

[19] See especially the discussion on this point as per the 2001 framework (section V).

[20] Another possible reading, but one that has an echo only in the case law and not within Regulation 1049/2001's Art 4(6), is that it is quite naïve to hold that, by way of the categorisation requirement, the judicature only sought to render accessible documents that had been dropped into an investigative file either by mistake or by inappropriate association with the investigation. In *WWF*, the expression of the last sentence of para 64 'related to a possible procedure for infringement' read within the context of the first sentence of para 64, could, in the alternative, be interpreted as meaning both indispensable to the investigation and sensitive. In this manner, that burden of categorisation (a minimum imposition) would have obliged the institutions to examine each document covered by the exception, on the basis of a concrete harm test, whereupon, and in addition, the institutions would be in the condition to blank out harmful passages.

[21] This logic would become the foundation for the later 'partial access'.

[22] *Hautala* (n 14).

[23] Also discussed, from a different perspective, in Ch 4.

[24] An exception today regulated under Regulation 1049/2001, Art 4(1).

[25] Yet, however meritorious, the burden of categorisation imposed on the institutions was ultimately of little avail to applicants. The institutions could—and did—divide investigative files into a standardised categorisation and then state, in regard to every category, that its entirety was related to and involved an investigation. Finally, this traditional institutional tactic would take on more serious proportions and consequences within the post-2001 framework, under which investigations are framed under Art 4(2).

Partial access means two things. First, it means that the institution satisfies itself that a document (initially refused) may be disclosed, because upon examination of the same the institution is sure that the document itself or parts of the same are (after all) not covered either by the exception relied on in first light, or by any other exception. Secondly, it means that for documents or parts of documents indeed covered by an exception the institution will consider if blanking out (ie redacting) the sensitive passages is feasible.

a. Two Levels of Categorisation

The combined requirements of *WWF* and *Hautala*, however, imply that institutions face a difficult task. A preliminary, categorisation serves a first purpose, which is to establish a prima facie relationship between documents and exceptions (which of the contested documents are in principle covered by each exception relied on).

Yet once that has been achieved, a second categorisation is necessary.[26] It concerns the sort of documents related to each exception.

This second categorisation, which needs to be undertaken with regard to each pile of documents previously ascribed per exception, serves to predict the different thresholds of harm posed by each different sort of related document (notes, letters, reports, etc) to the asserted counter-interest (which competes with an interest in disclosure). This is because, necessarily, the examination of the contested documents with a view to concluding as to the feasibility of partial access is dedicated to rebutting another presumption: that disclosure of the contested documents will undermine an asserted (counter-)interest.

This means that in 1993, even when the contested documents had been preliminarily assessed as harmful vis-à-vis one of the interests protected by an exception (a mandatory one, which left no room for access), the institutions were still obliged (via case law, *WWF*) to check if any of the contested documents had been incorrectly connected to a certain exception, and/or if any of the harmful documents contained any harmless passages. Later, and in addition,[27] the feasibility of blanking out the harmful passages would also have to be considered.

However, and in spite of this new figure (partial access) that imposed on the institutions that they make an effort to crack the hard shell of the mandatory class, the mandatory class of documents remained highly insulated from public scrutiny.

[26] This has, accordingly, been required by the judicature.

[27] Partial access, born into a *mandatory* exception—it is never redundant to restate the context of its genesis— pre-Regulation 1049/2001 requiring the blanking out of harmful passages, also carried over as an *ex lege*, mandatory, general and pervasive institutional burden of triage of documents into Regulation 1049/2001, Art 4(6).

iii. Petrie, *The Redundancy (or not) of the Author's Rule*

The substantial degree of insulation that the mandatory exceptions offered in 1993 is well illustrated by the *Petrie*[28] proceedings. The case emphasises how (all) exceptions construed pre-Regulation 1049/2001 actually enjoyed a double insulation from access. The fact that the insulation was double would, of course, be extremely relevant within the mandatory context, since that context was, of itself, already greatly restrictive.

Under the framework laid down by the 1993 Code another compelling argument in favour of non-disclosure had to be contextualised with this already robust protection of multiple interests: namely the author's rule. It functioned both as an independent and/or redundant argument whenever documents requested originated from a third party. In fact, as we have mentioned earlier (cornerstone 2), a connection criterion of authorship to any third party would—of itself—trump any request for disclosure. Thus, the institutions of the EU were not even under the obligation to consider releasing documents of that type.

In *Petrie*, the case concerned a request for access to an investigative file in which (practically) the entirety of the documents used by the institution to conduct the investigation was not EU-originating.

As such, the author's rule[29] placed them well outside the confines of the 1993 Code's influence. In these cases, no categorisation (of the non-EU documents) was imposed other than, at the most, a division into EU-originating and non-EU originating documents. Subsequently, only the implications of the EU originating documents' disclosure would be considered, and, if the disclosure of the latter could undermine the investigation, their release was prohibited.

Because investigations were at the time harboured under the public interest exception (mandatory, without a balancing test), no deference to any opposing interest in disclosure was possible. It was neither called for nor allowed.

In sum, under the 1993 Code of Conduct, documents already insulated from disclosure due to the (mandatory, without a balancing test) context into which they were born were further shrouded by the (possibly redundant) author's rule. Still, their governance was subject to three tasks, all of which were incumbent on the institutions.

B. 1993: Synopsis of Tasks Incumbent on the Institutions within the Mandatory Context

First, a categorisation of requested documents per applicable exception was required as a minimum rule. Secondly, the prediction of the level of harm posed by the release

[28] Case T-191/99 *Petrie et al v Commission* (n 17).

[29] The fact that it was not the EU that had authored the documents.

of any document, at least per sort of document (notes, letters, reports) within the pile per exception, was a requirement that the Court also wished to be satisfied. Thirdly, and finally, the governance of the mandatory exceptions (post-*Hautala*,[30] that is) was subject to the consideration of the possibility of partial access.[31]

Table 5.1: 1993 Code of Conduct: Mandatory Exceptions and Institutional Burdens

Prior 1, Internal document
Prior 2, Author's rule
1. Categorisation of documents in regard to connection with each exception asserted.
2. Within pile 1, prediction of thresholds of harm posed by release of each category/type of documents sought and the exception that they threatened.
3. Consideration of whether partial access was feasible.

i. Relevance of Temporal Sequence: Petrie *and* Hautala

Before we conclude the discussion on the mandatory exceptions of the 1993 Code of Conduct, it is important to emphasise the importance of the temporal sequence of the rulings that came forth as a consequence of both the *Hautala* and the *Petrie* proceedings.

On the one hand, Case T-14/98 *Heidi Hautala v Council* was lodged on 13 January 1998 and ruled on 19 July 1999. The respective appeal, Case C-353/99P *Council v Heidi Hautala*, was lodged on 22 November 1999 and ruled on 6 December 2001. On the other hand, Case T-191/99 *Petrie v Commission* was lodged on 25 August 1999 and ruled on 11 December 2001. The *Petrie* ruling (of the CFI) post-dates the *Hautala* ruling (of the ECJ) by a mere five days.

When the *Petrie* proceedings were lodged, partial access, as a (new) landmark of the access procedure, advertised as a victory for applicants, was already on display on the CFI's website, and had been there for at least one month. Moreover, it is difficult to envisage that over the 16 months it took to issue the *Petrie* ruling, one section of the first instance judicature did not have the time to acquaint itself with such a momentous new development ruled by another section of the same court.

True, the applicant in *Petrie* did not pursue the argument of partial access. But it is even more of a loss to the public at large that the first instance judicature did not care (of its own motion if necessary) to draw on *Hautala*[32] to reset the governance of

[30] *Hautala* (n 14).

[31] Such a model was all the more relevant from *Hautala* onwards, rendered on 19 July 1999, whereby the consideration of partial access became a procedural imposition on the institutions.

[32] Albeit limited to the first instance gravitas of Case T-14/98 *Hautala v Council* and in spite of possible *ultra petita* criticism.

public access to documents linked to the mandatory exceptions to the new standards of the case law.[33]

That is precisely what the ECJ did a mere five days later. It embedded partial access (both halves of the figure, disclosure of documents not covered *and* redaction of documents covered, if feasible) deep into the highest degree of insulation that the 1993 Code of Conduct had to offer (the exception is harboured today under Article 4(1) of Regulation 1049/2001).

As a final comment, partial access (when confirmed by the ECJ a mere two weeks before the 1993 Code would forever disappear from the law of the EU) should not to be understood as part of a heritage that was fraying. On the one hand, it was but the inevitable and necessary development of *WWF*. On the other hand, and although most would think that this goes without saying, regardless of which exception encompassed the contested documents, it compelled the institutions to read[34] the same, attentively.

IV. 1993: WHAT WAS DISCRETIONARY

Moving into the second half of the structure of the 1993 Code of Conduct, as we have noted, in 1993 a discretionary exception had also been included in it. It concerned institutional confidentiality, or institutional 'space to think'.

1993 Code of Conduct

> The institution *may* also refuse access in order to protect the institution's interest in the confidentiality of its proceedings.

Within the discretionary context too a very subtly[35] outlined presumption of preponderance is discernible. However, here (in contrast to what occurred within the mandatory context) the presumption is rebuttable. What is established is an optional (ie discretionary) preponderance of the interest of the confidentiality of institutional proceedings over other prospective interests that applicants might attempt to assert. In addition, clearly only the institutions were put in a position to (choose to) disprove the presumption.

Case T-105/95 WWF UK

> 38 When a discretionary exception is invoked, the balancing of interests (the institution's interests in confidentiality of proceedings against those of the person who has requested access to the documents) is undertaken at that point.

[33] Moreover, the first instance judicature had received a sign. Regulation 1049/2001, published in May 2001 and applicable from 3 December 2001, had moved investigations into Art 4(2), removing them from the greater insulation of Art 4(1).

[34] *cf* Case T-29/08 *LPN v Commission* [2011] ECR II-06021, para 113.

[35] The subtlety is in fact marked in such a way that it functions as a serious obstacle to the understanding of the provision's significance.

A. The Relevance of Personal Interests, if Notorious

It is important to recall that in 1993 access was—and still is—an impersonal[36] right. This meant that applicants were not bound to offer reasons for seeking documents. But, in 1993 it was equally true that in regard to situations in which only institutional confidentiality was at stake, alongside the interest that any anonymous citizen[37] might have in disclosure, particular private interests, if well known[38] had to be taken into account. The consideration of notorious particular interests was a requirement stemming from the permissive redaction of the exception of a discretionary nature (eg the institutions *may* refuse) in conjunction with the self-imposed[39] standards of governance of that discretion by the institutions.

Case T- 111/00 *British American Tobacco*

> 42. As regards, first of all, the assessment of the applicant's interest, it should be borne in mind that, under Decision 94/90, any person may request access to any unpublished Commission document, without being required to give a reason for the request (*Svenska Journalistförbundet v Council*, paragraph 65). One consequence of that situation is that, where it has no information on the particular reasons underlying a request for access, the institution concerned cannot be criticised, when it comes to balance the various interests at stake for the purpose of application of the non-mandatory exception, for assessing the applicant's interest by reference to the interest that any citizen might have who asks for access to the institution's documents, and without taking into account particular interests of which, by definition, it is unaware.
>
> 43. However, in the circumstances of the present case, the Commission cannot contend that it was unaware of the applicant's intentions in submitting its request for access to the minutes in question. As is clear from the documents before the Court (see paragraphs 7 and 8 of the present judgment), that request was preceded by steps which the applicant took in order to put its case opposing the decision taken by certain Member States to treat expanded tobacco as 'smoking tobacco' within the meaning of Article 5(1) of Directive 95/59 and, consequently, to make it subject to the regime provided for in Directive 92/12 concerning products subject to excise duty. The aim of the applicant's request, in view of the implications that such treatment would have for it from both a tax and administrative point of view, was thus to ascertain what positions were adopted on that question within the committee.
>
> 44. Against that background, the Commission clearly could not have been unaware of the applicant's interest in being able to ascertain not only the substance of the discussions but also the identities of the delegations voicing the opinions expressed.

[36] See Ch 2. There is no link to direct and individual concern.

[37] An impersonal interest or *erga omnes* standard as quoted by B Driessen, *Transparency in EU Institutional Law* (Alphen aan den Rijn, Kluwer, 2012); see Ch 2.

[38] *Hautala v Council* (n 14); Case T-204/99 *Olli Mattila v Council* [2001] ECR II-02265 paras 106–07; and Case T-111/00 *British American Tobacco* [2001] ECR II-02997, paras 42–50.

[39] See Case T-105/95 *WWF UK v Commission* (n 5) para 38.

45. Next, it must be observed that that interest could not be regarded as irrelevant to the balancing of the interests at stake.

But for this difference—that here the presumption of preponderance was always rebuttable, and that it was necessary for the institutions to undertake a balancing of interests—the discretionary framework was governed by the three presumptions that ruled the mandatory exceptions as well: correlation, preponderance and harm.

B. Governance Similar to that Inherent to the Mandatory Exception

As a consequence, the governance of the discretionary exception was also no different from the governance of the mandatory context of the 1993 Code either. Let us begin by stating that if the categorisation of requested documents was imposed in regard to mandatory exceptions as a necessary institutional burden, that same burden was—all the more so—ascribable to the domain of the discretionary exception. Moreover the requirement of the establishment of involvement[40] between the documents sought and the exception asserted applied equally to this peculiar shade of 'No'.

The same may be said of partial access. If, as a procedural burden imposed on the institutions, it was born into the mandatory exception of the protection of international relations, then, forcibly, it carried over—still under the 1993 Code of Conduct—into the less severe domain of the protection of institutional 'space to think'.

This signified, first, that the categorisation of documents, and, secondly, that the verification of any documents attached to one of the single independent exceptions, and thirdly, the consideration of the possibility of partial access, were also at the forefront of institutional governance of the contest between the advantages stemming from a broad implementation of the access policy and the interest in institutional confidentiality.

C. 1993: Synopsis of Tasks Incumbent on the Institutions within the Discretionary Context

In sum, under the 1993 Code, when offered the option to disclose or to hold back documents that could undermine their internal 'space to think', the institutions needed to discharge the burden of reasoning refusals along a double standard. First, by complying with the duties inherent to mandatory exceptions; subsequently, by further demonstrating that 'a balance (of competing interests, public and/or private, and the latter only if notorious) had 'been struck' or that a 'balancing test' had been employed.

[40] Indispensable to and sensitive.

Table 5.2: 1993 Code of Conduct: Discretionary Exceptions and Institutional Burdens

Prior 1, Internal document
Prior 2, author's Rule
1. Categorisation of documents
2. Establishment of relation of pertinence between documents sought and exception asserted.
3. Consideration of whether partial access was feasible.
4. Balancing institutional space to think against competing interests of the person who had requested access to the documents — interest of any citizen in accessing the documents — particular interests of the requesting parties, if notorious.

D. 1993: Mandatory v Discretionary, Summation

What is 1993 as a first structure of the access policy? First, two cornerstones existed in the foreground to that structure: the prequisite that the contested documents would be internal documents and the exclusionary impact of the author's rule. Secondly, all depended on whether the contested document concerned either half of the (theoretical) dichotomy put into place: mandatory or discretionary. If it fell under the second half, a balancing of competing interests would have to be struck.

Thirdly, and for both the mandatory and discretionary halves of the dichotomy, the (obviously institutional) task of categorisation had to be discharged.

Fourthly, the feasibility of partial access needed to be assessed. Moreover, the latter assessment implied two levels of analysis: on the one hand, whether parts of the documents were (after all) not covered by any exceptions and, on the other hand, for all documents and/or parts of documents that were indeed encompassed within an exception, whether redaction was feasible.

The entire structure was profoundly changed in 2001.

V. WHAT CHANGES IN 2001?

In 2001 many changes come forth. As we will see the tendency is that less insulation is (or should be) afforded to all (kinds of) documents held by the EU. In addition, the author's rule is hacked down and so is the entire concept of a Discretionary Framework[41] for exceptions. The new scheme for exceptions is now mandatory

[41] It is important to point out that some doctrine, even post-Regulation 1049/2001, continues to rely on the mandatory/discretionary distinction to distinguish Art 4(1) from Arts 4(2) and (3) of Regulation 1049/2001. See eg D Curtin and J Mendes, 'Article 42' in S Peers, T Hervey, J Kenner and A Ward (eds), *The EU Charter of Fundamental Rights, A Commentary* (Munich/Oxford/Baden-Baden, Beck/Hart/Nomos, 2014) and also L Coudray, *La transparence et l'accès aux documents, Traité de Droit Administratif Européen* (Brussels, Bruylant, 2014) 699–712. We propose a different terminology since in all 3 articles the wording employed is 'shall'. This is, however, a mere detail of terminology and one option.

across the board, yet within it a new trilogy is born. The changes are extensive and deep but often difficult to pinpoint. The cloudiness that surrounds them will, as we will see, lead to production of case law that is alarmingly eclectic in content.

A. 2001: Less Insulation?

Given the pre-2001 context, if Regulation 1049/2001 was to signify a betterment of the right of public access to documents—the Regulation coming forth to detail a Treaty-based right[42]—first and foremost, the mandatory framework, the most severe domain of protection of interests that competed with access (ie without any balancing test against the advantages arising from disclosure) would have to be retracted. Formally, it was.

B. Cornerstone 2 (the Author's Rule) Falls

Certainly implying retraction, the new framework abandoned the author's rule. In consequence any document held by the EU, regardless of whether it was authored—or not—by the institutions, turned into a legitimate target of applications for access.

i. The Discretionary Framework Falls

Regulation 1049/2001 also abandons the old dichotomy of mandatory and/or discretionary exceptions. Whilst notionally, the Regulation still capitalises on the same list of independent exceptions drawn up in 1993, the new structure chose a different (univocal) approach to exceptions: all become mandatory.[43]

However, at the same time, it creates a new trilogy within the new mandatory status—three different levels of insulation for the exceptions—and describes each level respectively in Article 4(1), 4(2) and 4(3).

ii. The New (Mandatory) Trilogy

a. Article 4(1): Mandatory with no Balancing Test

Only five[44] mandatory exceptions that are to be governed without a balancing test[45] are still listed in Article 4(1). They are further sub-classified as (a) the public interest, subdivided as regards: public security, defence and military matters, international relations, the financial, monetary or economic policy of the Community

42 Enshrined in the Treaty of Amsterdam.
43 See, above, proviso made (n 42).
44 Against 9 in 1993.
45 Now against an overriding interest in disclosure.

or a Member State; and (b) privacy and integrity of the individual, in particular in accordance with Community legislation regarding the protection of personal data. This particular mandatory exception, albeit absent any literal reference (in Regulation 1049/2001) to a balancing test, must be read in conjunction with Regulation 45/2001.[46]

b. Article 4(2): Mandatory with a (New) Balancing Test

As another sign that insulation against disclosure was withdrawing, four independent exceptions, once overarched by this (mandatory without a balancing test) standard of the Code of Conduct, were not included under Regulation 1049/2001's Article 4(1).

Regulation 1049/2001 reshuffles[47] exceptions once construed as mandatory without a balancing test (court proceedings, commercial and industrial interests and inspections and investigations) into the only moderately severe status of Article 4(2).[48]

In doing so, and regarding investigations in particular, the new rules now, literally, protect against harm to the 'purpose of' investigations whilst the old rules protected against harm to the investigations and inspections as such. In addition, and still on this point, audits are joined as an independent exception alongside inspections and investigations. Currently, these three independent[49] exceptions co-exist within the same indent of Article 4(2).[50]

[46] Although we have chosen not to address the theme *Privacy v Access* in a dedicated chapter or section, the pivotal issue around cases related to personal data is whether the names of persons belong, or not, exclusively to the private sphere. Litigation here is always about (disclosure of) the names of persons who attend meetings, or the names of expert consultants and/or expert witnesses. What is important to point out is that after years of undisputed reign of the *Bavarian Lager* appeal in which it had been established that such names could not be disclosed, the EU judicature has turned the page abruptly: eg Case C-615/13P *ClientEarth and PAN Europe v EFSA* [not yet reported]. For more on this point, and in particular as to the role of the European Data Protection Supervisor (EDPS), see Ch 7. For an overview of the case law on privacy and personal data, see V Tilli, 'Transparency, an Everlasting Challenge' in *Constitutionalising the EU Judicial System, Essays in Honour of Pernilla Lindth* (Oxford, Hart, 2012).

[47] Driessen, *Transparency in EU Institutional Law* (n 37) 107:

> The Commission proposal leading to Regulation 1049 added 'audits' and, separately, 'infringement proceedings including the preparatory stages thereof'. The first addition survived, but the later exception was deleted. The Commission made a Declaration at the time of the adoption of the Regulation, noting that this would not change its Practice in this matter, meaning that it continues to consider such proceedings covered by the exception. Following a Presidency proposal, the Council added the words 'the purpose of'. This restriction of the Scope of the exception was accepted by the Parliament.

[48] Henceforth subject to the balancing test of possible concurrence with overriding public interests; see Joined Cases C–514/11 P and C–605/11P *LPN & Finland v Commission* [not reported].

[49] The independence of exceptions that co-exist aloonside one another within indents has been argued by AG Maduro in Case C-39/05P and C-52/05P *Sweden and Turco v Council* [2008] ECR I-04723.

[50] In particular, with regard to the doctrine of judicial precedent, the new positional status (ie post-2001) of these exceptions should have an exclusionary impact on many rulings. The judicial acknowledgement

In the same way, legal advice is joined as an independent[51] exception alongside court proceedings.

c. Article 4(3)

By way of Article 4(3), mandatory status was also poured over what had once been known as the discretionary exception (institutional space to think) thus completing a new trilogy. The new and different balancing test, constructed for Article 4(2), also applies to this altered category of exception.

Article 4(3) creates an area of protection for the institutional decision-making process, an exception previously called 'confidentiality of proceedings'.[52]

Although there is an abstract difference between the type of protection against non-disclosure afforded under Article 4(3) and Article 4(2), the practical differences between them have not been easy to pinpoint. Both indents call for the possible relevance of a balancing test between the public interest in the disclosure of the contested documents and the competing interests that both these indents overarch to be taken into account. Admittedly, in order for a refusal to be validated by the judicature Article 4(3) calls for arguments that '*serious* harm' will be inflicted on the institutional decision-making process if certain documents are disclosed, whilst Article 4(2) does not.

The difficulty does not lie in observing that under Article 4(3) the harm caused by disclosure must be qualified. The difficulty, of course, lies in distinguishing in practice the concept of *serious* harm from the concept of mere harm.[53]

Article 4(3) is composed of two indents, one in regard to matters 'where institutional decisions have yet to be taken' and another in regard to 'opinions for internal use' and lays down the least severe[54] prohibition of disclosure within Regulation 1049/2001's new model.

of this exclusionary impact is required to ascertain the disutility for the present of all rulings proffered (both by ECJ and CFI) before 2001 on the basis of any independent exception once harboured under Art 4(1) but now harboured under Art 4(2). Those rulings are contextually outdated and belong to another time.

Bringing this discussion down to very concrete levels, take all rulings related to inspections and investigations delivered before the advent of Regulation 1049/2001. First, in 1993 it was those exceptions as such, not merely their purpose (as now happens), that were protected. For its part, doctrine (Driessen) has stated that this particular change implies a lesser insulation (of documents) against disclosure, as opposed to the prior status quo of 1993.

This position (yet to be clarified by the judicature) is difficult to reconcile with the fact that during the period pre-Regulation 1049/2001, all rulings on investigations rested on the assumption that no other requirement (ie to consider that a balancing test be undertaken) weighed upon the shoulders of the institutions. Again, it now falls to the judicature to ascertain that the new requirement is adequately carried out and complied with.

[51] On this point, see para 28 of the Opinion of AG Maduro in Case C-39/05P and C-52/05P *Sweden and Turco v Council* (n 50).

[52] For a neat distinction between the case law pertaining to Article 4(3) and the case law pertaining to Art 4(1) and (2), see G Goddin, 'Access to Documents in Competition Files: Where do we Stand, Two Years after TGI?' (2012) 2 *Journal of European competition Law and Practice* 112–20.

[53] Very recently, Case T-395/13 *Samuli Miettinen v Council* [not yet reported] has provided more details as to this difference.

[54] It was within the realm of Art 4(3), namely in the *Access Info Europe v Council* proceedings (Case T-233/09 [2011] ECR II-01073 and C-280/11 P, 17 October 2013 [not reported]), that the

Table 5.3: 1993 Code of Conduct Discretionary and Institutional Burdens and Regulation 1049/2001 Article 4(2) and (3) Institutional Burdens

1993 Code of Conduct Discretionary exceptions Institutional burdens	**Regulation 1049/2001 Article 4(2) Institutional Burdens**	**Regulation 1049/2001 Article 4(3) Institutional burdens**
1. Categorisation of documents	1. Categorisation of documents	1. Categorisation of documents
2. Establishment of relation of pertinence between documents sought that *could* undermine exception asserted	2. Establishment of relation of pertinence between documents sought that *would* undermine exception asserted	2. Establishment of relation of pertinence between documents sought that *would seriously* undermine exception asserted
3. Consideration of whether partial access is feasible.	3. Consideration of whether partial access is feasible.	3. Consideration of whether partial access is feasible.
4. Balancing institutional space to think against competing *interests of the person* who had requested access to the documents — interest of any citizen in accessing the documents — particular interests of the requesting parties, if known	4. Balancing institutional space to think against competing public interests in disclosure that are *overriding*	4. Balancing institutional space to think against competing *public* interests in disclosure that are *overriding*

VI. A FUNCTIONAL ANALYSIS OF ARTICLE 4 OF REGULATION 1049/2001

We have just seen the historical perspective and, keeping the main changes in mind, we will now focus on their functional implications.

accountability to which the EU legislative process is expected to be subject was held to have overriding status over asserted institutional and governmental 'space to think'. On this point, see D Chalmers, G Davies and G Monti, *European Union Law, Text Cases and Materials* (Cambridge, Cambridge University Press, 2014) 419:

> The practical consequences of the ruling are immense: prior to it there was no general right of access to docs in the trilogue the crucible of EU law-making. [Refusal of documents was grounded on] the reason that it might compromise national negotiating positions. This is no longer the case. This must be as open to scrutiny as other parts of the law-making process. The reasoning is also significant. Its central thread is the characterization of the decision-making process, namely, whether it compromises diplomatic negotiations between Member States or as a legislative process. The Court of Justice characterizes it as the latter because it sees an overriding public interest, namely, the quality of EU democracy, in characterizing it in this way. This allows it to say that the process is not compromised by disclosure as the nature of the legislative process is that it should be accountable and involve public debate.

A. Still a Tale of Presumptions

Just as subtly as during the period 1993–2001, the trilogy continues to tell a very complex tale of presumptions. The presumptions are still three, and remain the same to have enveloped the 1993 Code of Conduct: correlation, preponderance and harm. However, and by contrast, under Regulation 1949/2001 they always operate together within a mandatory context.

B. A Layered Structure, the New Interplay of the Presumptions of Correlation, Preponderance and Harm

i. The First Presumption: Correlation between the Contested Documents and the Exception Relied on

The first presumption that underlies the general structure of Article 4 of Regulation 1049/2001 is a presumption of *correlation*. It leads most persons to assume that the institutions have examined the documents and thus correctly correlated them to an exception. It is important to state that although it plays the role of something that players might assume, as had already happened between 1993–2001, this presumption is unwritten, and therefore, barely perceptible.

ii. The Second Presumption: Preponderance of the Protected Interests over 'Public Interest in Disclosure'

Resting on the first presumption (ie correlation), a second presumption (*preponderance*) written into Article 4 of Regulation 1049/2001 helps distinguish the trilogy's three classes from one another.

This second presumption is directed at clarifying whether the interests protected under each class (ie Article 4(1), 4(2) and 4(3)) are (or not) always preponderant over the advantages stemming from 'a public interest in disclosure of documents'. Moreover, this second, and written, presumption appears both under the form of an absolute version as well as under the form of a rebuttable one.

An absolute version of this presumption (also called *jure e de jure*) is written into Article 4(1). Accordingly (and always if and only if the contested documents have been correctly correlated to an exception overarched by Article 4(1)), no advantage stemming from 'the public interest in disclosure' of the contested documents may override the importance of keeping the interests protected under Article 4(1)[55] safe.

Differently, a rebuttable version of this presumption (also called *juris tantum*) governs two of the three classes, namely Article 4(2) and 4(3). To this effect, both accommodate a so-called balancing test of competing interests. Ultimately, this means that, on the basis of the results of the test, the prohibition (of disclosure) that those classes of exception lay down might be overridden.

[55] However partial access remains a requirement.

The crucial point to retain is that under the presumption of preponderance, albeit only with regard to its rebuttable version (that overarches Article 4(2) and 4(3)), harm to interests protected by the exceptions is allowed. It is allowed when the interest that disclosure serves—greater accountability of the EU to the public regarding an ample variety of topics—is considered on a case-by-case basis to override the interests protected by any of the exceptions.

If we were to portray the functioning of the first two presumptions graphically we could come up with a flowchart that would look something like this:

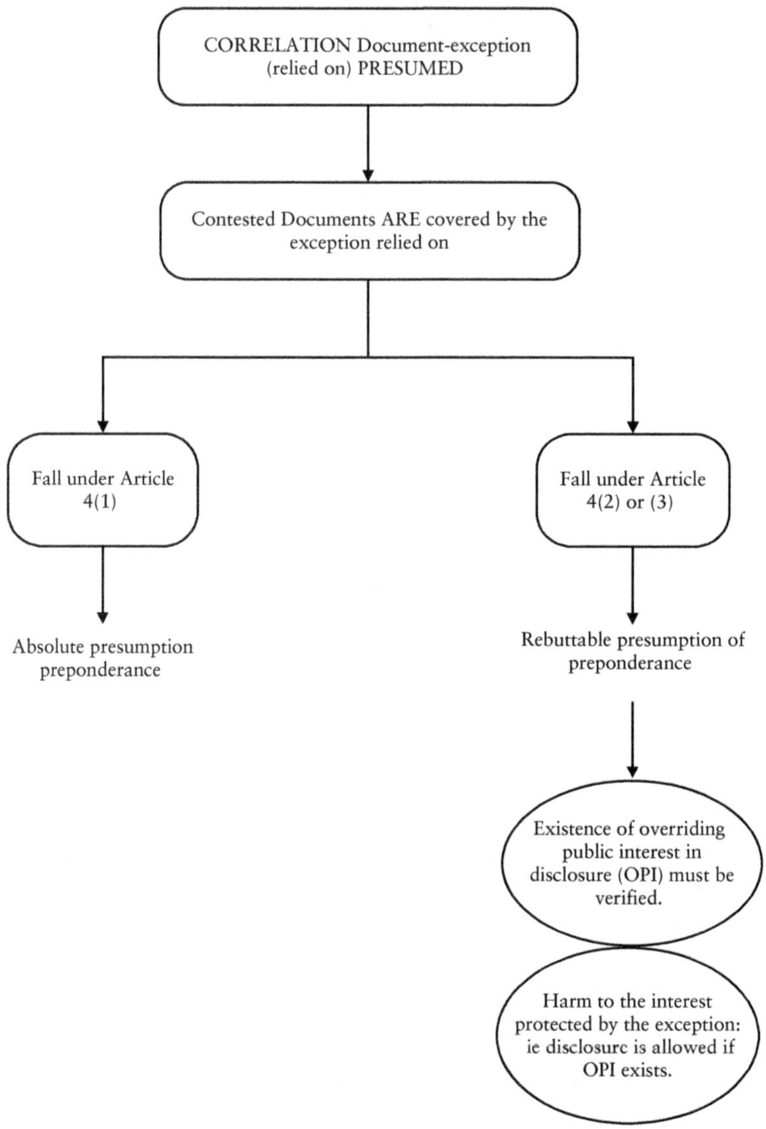

Figure 5.1: Correlation

iii. The Third Presumption: Undermining an Asserted Counter-interest (ie Harm in Disclosure) and the Feasibility of Partial Access

The scheme is not yet complete. In addition, due to the operation of a third presumption (*harm or the undermining of interests*) also written into Regulation 1049/2001, the disclosure of documents overarched by all three classes of exception (Article 4(1), 4(2) and 4(3)) must further be subject to an analysis of feasibility of partial access to documents (ie access only to some of the requested documents or to mere parts of the same).

The main point is that if the first two presumptions are true (ie the contested documents are correlated to the exception relied on and the interest in safeguarding the specific interest that the exception protects is preponderant over the public interest in disclosure) harm will ensue from disclosure. However, before this conclusion may be definitively reached, the institutions are called on to test and verify the first (and unwritten) presumption: ie actual correlation between the documents and the exception relied on.

If it folds (or, in other words, if after all the contested documents are found not to be related to the exceptions) then both the second and the third presumption—preponderance of an interest in non-disclosure and harm—fold in turn. As a consequence, the institutions are then obliged to disclose the contested documents.

This addition is obviously a legacy of the post-*Hautala* framework, and since written into Regulation 1049/2001, has become an *ex lege* command:[56]

> Partial access, as enshrined in Regulation 1049/2001, Article 4(6)
>
> If only parts of the requested document are covered by any of the exceptions, the remaining parts of the document shall be released.

The legacy, strangely, was reproduced in the law only in part. A second part of the *Hautala* legacy, the specification of a duty to blank out sensitive parts of a document, survives in the case law, but had no literal echo in Regulation 1049/2001.

On the basis of Article 4(6) of Regulation 1049/2001, as we will see, there are two concurrent tasks ascribed to the institutions:

a. First Task, Testing the Faithfulness of Preliminary Triage

Before access to documents is refused,[57] first, the institutions are bound to consider whether their first classification/triage of each of the requested documents is correct. At this point the institutions are called upon to test and verify the connection (that those very institutions presumed to exist) between the requested documents and the exceptions that the (same) institutions are planning to rely on in order to refuse access to the former.

It may be the case that some documents (or parts of documents), upon examination, might be considered not covered either by the exception first thought to overarch them or by any other exception. If the connection (document-exception(s)) folds then so does the (presumed) harm to the interest protected by the exception in question.

[56] Regulation 1049/2001, Art 4(6).
[57] ie definitively.

The reason behind Article 4(6) is that logically, if a document or part of a document is not covered by any exception, then its release does not cause harm to any interest protected by any of the exceptions. Moreover, since that is so, and since the law employs the commanding tone 'shall', the institutions are under the obligation to disclose such documents (or parts of the same). The specific duty to consider whether it is possible to grant partial access (because documents are—after all—not covered by any exception) is today a procedural requirement.

Finally, since Article 4(6) is applicable to 'any of the exceptions', the institutions must deal with this presumption regarding each of the three classes of exception. There is clearly no room for derogations. Therefore if the institution omits this analysis before refusing access to any document, the refusal becomes illegal.

Again portraying this addition graphically:

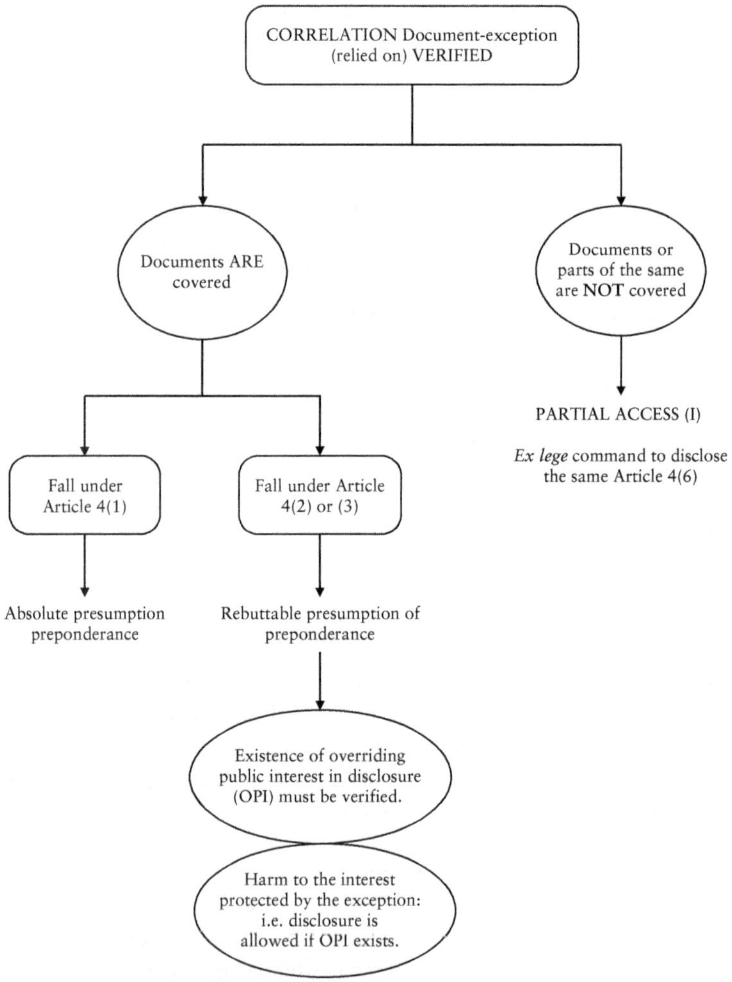

Figure 5.2: The Relevance of Partial Access

b. Second Task: Blanking out Sensitive Passages

It is important to note that, albeit not mentioned in Regulation 1049/2001, the institutional burden of the consideration of the feasibility of partial access reaches well beyond the letter of what is today Article 4(6). This is because, before access is refused, the institutions are still burdened with a second task related to partial access, originating via case law.[58] Accordingly, even if upon a first examination institutions conclude that the contested documents are, indeed, covered by any of the exceptions, they still must consider whether it is feasible to redact sensitive passages of a contested document (so that harmful passages can be blanked out). Here too, if the institutions omit to consider the feasibility of redacting, before they refuse access to a document, that refusal becomes illegal.

Case C-353/99 P *Council v Hautala*

> 29 Beside the fact that no reason has been put forward to show why an institution should be able to keep secret the items of information in a document which are not covered by the exceptions laid down in Article 4(1) of Decision 93/731, a refusal to grant partial access would be manifestly disproportionate for ensuring the confidentiality of the items of information covered by one of those exceptions. As the Court of First Instance observed in paragraph 85 of the contested judgment, the aim pursued by the Council in refusing access to the contested report could be achieved even if the Council did no more than remove, after examination, the passages in the report which might harm international relations.

What is important to note is that, under this third presumption alone (presumption of harm that is in turn based on a presumption of faithful, preliminary, triage of documents) no harm (to any protected interest) is allowed. That is exactly why the (harmful) passages must be redacted.

[58] Case T-529/09 *In't Veld v Commission*, Judgment of 4 May 2012 [not reported] para 106:

> It is clear from the very wording of Article 4(6) of Regulation No 1049/2001 that an institution is required to consider whether it is appropriate to grant partial access to requested documents and to limit any refusal to information covered by the relevant exceptions referred to in that article. The institution must grant partial access if the aim pursued by that institution in refusing access to a document may be achieved by merely blanking out the passages which might harm the public interest to be protected (Case T-264/04 *WWF European Policy Programme v Council* [2007] ECR II-911, paragraph 50; see also, to that effect Case C-353/99 P *Council v Hautala* [2001] ECR I-9565, paragraph 29).

As an attempt to portray this addition graphically:

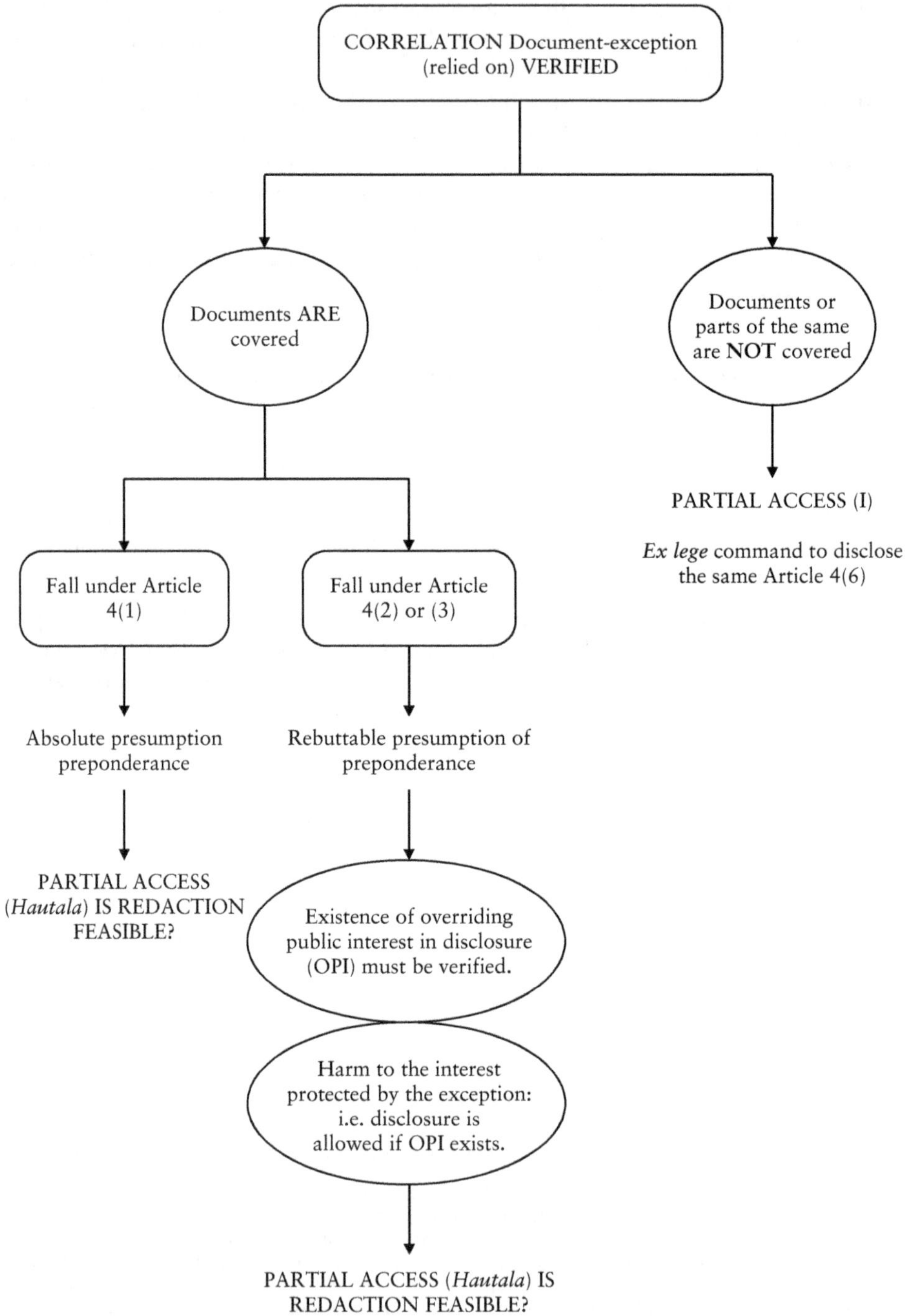

Figure 5.3: Redacting as a Requirement

c. Excessive Burden, Tempering Proportionality with Proportionality

Whilst partial access itself was derived from a need to temper refusal by way of a principle of proportionality—refusal should not assume the proportions of a blanket ban and should only be validated in regard to the documents (or to mere parts of some) whose disclosure *could* undermine the interests—that very same principle is later, in turn, drawn upon to temper partial access.

Again via case law, both institutional analytical duties (as to the feasibility of a partial disclosure because a part of a document is not covered by any exception and as to redaction when a document is covered by any exception) came to be tempered by a proportionality criterion. Proportionality is here assessed as to the administrative burden placed on the institutions.[59] If the former is found to be excessive,[60] and on the condition that it translates an accommodation of a fair solution (found between the institution and the applicant)[61] or (in absence of agreement with the applicant) as an exceptional safeguard of good administration,[62] such a burden—which takes the form of a requirement of a concrete document-by document analysis—might be whittled down or even waived altogether.[63]

C. The Loopholes of Article 4(2)

As a closing analysis of the new framework it is important to point out that Article 4(2) fails to address several issues. Moreover, all of these issues are related to the possibility that, on occasion, an overriding public interest in disclosure (OPI) exists, and what should take place if that is ascertained.

The first loophole is that Article 4(2) gives no example of what an OPI is. Secondly, it is not clear if the striking of a balance between the interests protected by the exceptions encompassed under Article 4(2) and the OPI *has to be* undertaken every time a request for access is addressed to the institutions, or whether its findings produce effects *only if and when* it is indeed undertaken. Thirdly, it is not clear *who* must identify the OPI, the applicant or the institution. Fourthly, regardless of who identifies the OPI, once identified, it is not clear *who* is to strike a balance between the interests protected by Article 4(2) and the OPI. Moreover, *when* is such a task to be undertaken? In case the burden is imposed on the applicant, is it at the moment of the initial request?[64] By contrast, if the burden is imposed on the institution is it at the moment of the first response to the applicant?

[59] Case T-2/03 *VFK* [2005] ECR II-00121.

[60] Although the finding is subject to the *ex post* control of the judicature.

[61] On the basis of Regulation 1049/2001, Art 6(3) as interpreted by *VFK* (n 59) para 96.

[62] *VFK* (n 59) para 102; and *Hautala* (n 14) para 86.

[63] *Hautala* (n 14) and *VFK* (n 60) paras 94 and 96 and 144 and 115. See s VI.D for the controversial consequences of doing without a concrete examination of the documents.

[64] O Speltdoorn, 'The *Technische Glasweke Ilmenau* Ruling, a Step Backwards in Transparency in EU Competition Cases?' in *Constitutionalising the EU Judicial System, Essays in Honour of Pernilla Lindth* (Oxford, Hart, 2012) has called our attention to the fact that in the *Ryanair* Joined Cases the GC singled out the confirmatory application of the applicant as the last viable moment in which it is feasible (for

D. The Case Law on Article 4(2)

i. Circumscribing Regulation 1049/2001 by way of an unlimited dominion of the Presumption of Preponderance

At the request of applicants that needed the loopholes filled, the judicature has dealt with Article 4(2) of Regulation 1049/2001 in a way that is eclectic, difficult to predict and significantly removed from the legal text that grounds the OPI test.

In addition, in the foreground to any ruling on Article 4(2) whilst it may seem that the judicature has made clear how, from amongst the three presumptions that operate within the article, the judges will allow the presumption of preponderance (of the interest in keeping documents confidential) to pull its full weight and more, upon a close reading of the case law however, what becomes apparent is that it is not the presumption of preponderance as enshrined in Article 4(2) that pulls its weight. Rather it is presumptions of preponderance enshrined in sectoral[65] laws (eg EU State aid rules and EU competition law) and that are extraneous to Article 4(2) that pull their weight over Article 4(2) and Article 4(6).

It is curious that this took place after a first approach in *Turco*, concerning the interpretation of the exception 'legal advice', in which it was the presumption of correlation (between the contested documents and the exception prima facie relied on) to have been given leeway. In that case, it was established that the institutions were allowed to presume (without checking) that all the documents contained in a file headed 'legal advice' were all related to the same subject matter. In consequence, significant limitations were placed on the procedural requirement of a concrete analysis of the contested documents by the institution, a requirement that until then had held as a matter of principle. It was also said that—limited to the case of legal advice—there was not a feasible distinction as to a variable nature of information contained within legal advice, that is, between disclosable parts of legal advice and non-disclosable parts of legal advice. Advocate General Maduro tried to fence off the applicability of his considerations, insisting specifically that those were not to be extended to investigations, as described in Article 4(2), nor to international relations, an exception overarched by Article 4(1). But it was to little avail.

Case C-39/05P and C-52/05P *Sweden and Turco v Council*, Opinion of AG Maduro

> 43. Thus, although there is no doubt, as the Court of First Instance ruled on another occasion, that 'the obligation for an institution to undertake a concrete, individual assessment of the content of the documents covered in the application for access is an approach to be adopted as a matter of principle ..., which applies to all the exceptions in paragraphs 1 to 3 of Article 4 of Regulation No 1049/2001, whatever may be the field to which the documents sought relate', the extent to which that requirement applies in connection with the implementation of the exception on the ground of confidentiality in respect of legal advice

the applicant) to identify the OPI. However, during the hearing of the Case T-29/08*LPN v Commission* [2011] ECR II-06021 proceedings, the GC was still willing to discuss the issue.

[65] The ECJ resists calling these laws 'special', so as not to allow the public to derive a *lex specialis* qualification of the same.

and in connection with the application of the other exceptions differs. In the latter cases, whether the disclosure of a document may actually be detrimental to the interest protected depends not only on the subject-matter of the document, but also on the nature of the information it contains. For example, it is not because a document relates to an inspection or investigation that its disclosure would automatically endanger the completion of that action and thus undermine the protection of the purpose of inspections or investigations. Likewise, the fact that a document contains information or negative evaluations about the political situation or the protection of human rights in a third country does not necessarily mean that its disclosure would affect the Union's international relations.

The ECJ was quick to adapt the considerations that the Advocate General made in regard to the sole exception of the protection of legal advice and extend them to the entirety of Article 4(2). Beginning at para 33 the ECJ dedicates an entire section of the ruling to 'the examination to be undertaken by the institution':

Case C-39/05P and C-52/05P *Sweden and Turco v Council*

35. When the Council is asked to disclose a document, it must assess, in each individual case, whether that document falls within the exceptions to the right of public access to documents of the institutions set out in Article 4 of Regulation No 1049/2001.

Therefore, the first task is to proceed to triage of documents, per exception. But the triage has to be checked:

Case C-39/05P and C-52/05P *Sweden and Turco v Council*

38 First, the Council must satisfy itself that the document which it is asked to disclose does indeed relate to legal advice and, if so, it must decide which parts of it are actually concerned and may, therefore, be covered by that exception.

39 The fact that a document is headed 'legal advice/opinion' does not mean that it is automatically entitled to the protection of legal advice ensured by the second indent of Article 4(2) of Regulation No 1049/2001. Over and above the way a document is described, it is for the institution to satisfy itself that that document does indeed concern such advice.

The ECJ goes on to state that partial access[66] must be considered (and calls for the rebuttal of the presumption of harm once the association document-exception is established):

Case C-39/05P and C-52/05P *Sweden and Turco v Council*

40 Second, the Council must examine whether disclosure of the parts of the document in question which have been identified as relating to legal advice 'would undermine the protection' of that advice.

Lastly, the ECJ insists that it is the institution that is called to rebut the presumption of preponderance (here harm is allowed, if the advantages stemming from disclosure supersede *in casu* the protected interest):

Case C-39/05P and C-52/05P *Sweden and Turco v Council*

44 Third and last, if the Council takes the view that disclosure of a document would undermine the protection of legal advice as defined above, it is incumbent on the Council to

[66] Not covered and/or if covered do not procure harm.

> ascertain whether there is any overriding public interest justifying disclosure despite the fact that its ability to seek legal advice and receive frank, objective and comprehensive advice would thereby be undermined.
>
> 45 In that respect, it is for the Council to balance the particular interest to be protected by non-disclosure of the document concerned against, inter alia, the public interest in the document being made accessible in the light of the advantages stemming, as noted in recital 2 of the preamble to Regulation No 1049/2001, from increased openness, in that this enables citizens to participate more closely in the decision-making process and guarantees that the administration enjoys greater legitimacy and is more effective and more accountable to the citizen in a democratic system.

Later in the judgment, however, the ECJ re-summarises the institutional tasks:

> Case C-39/05P and C-52/05P *Sweden and Turco v Council*
>
> 49 If the Council decides to refuse access to a document which it has been asked to disclose, it must explain, first, how access to that document could specifically and effectively undermine the interest protected by an exception laid down in Article 4 of Regulation No 1049/2001 relied on by that institution and, secondly, in the situations referred to in Article 4(2) and (3) of that regulation, whether or not there is an overriding public interest that might nevertheless justify disclosure of the document concerned.

Adding a paragraph 50 that opens the gates to the later judicial cross-stitching, in *Turco*, the ECJ allows the institutions to rely on general presumptions of correlation (and possibly also on presumptions of preponderance although that is not clear) between similar documents and one, same exception.

> Case C-39/05P and C-52/05P *Sweden and Turco v Council*
>
> 50 It is, in principle, open to the Council to base its decisions in that regard [how access to that document could specifically and effectively undermine the interest protected by an exception laid down in Article 4 of Regulation No 1049/2001] on general presumptions which apply to certain categories of documents, as considerations of a generally similar kind are likely to apply to requests for disclosure relating to documents of the same nature. However, it is incumbent on the Council to establish in each case whether the general considerations normally applicable to a particular type of document are in fact applicable to a specific document which it has been asked to disclose.

The ECJ however melts down two concepts distinguished by Advocate General Maduro and offers up a third: Advocate General Maduro had distinguished the same subject matter (correlation) of documents from the same nature of the information (linking that to preponderance) that documents contained. The ECJ, by contrast, employs the phrase 'documents of the same nature', seemingly overarching both concepts.

In addition, what is omitted from paragraph 50 is that the presumption of correlation between documents and exceptions relied on, which—since we are within the realm of Article 4(2)—in turn is the basis for a (rebuttable) presumption of preponderance (of protected interests over access), that within the specific realm of Article 4(2), leaves room for harm (to the interests protected by the exception) if the presumption of preponderance is rebutted.

Soon after that, a flurry of cases—ranging from the interpretation of the exception 'judicial proceedings' to all the corners of EU competition law 'investigations':[67] State aid, mergers, concerted practices and leniency, and finally touching upon investigations related to the protection of environment[68]—also exasperated the influence of presumptions (as construed within sectoral rules) over Article 4(2).

Finally, what had been proposed by the Advocate General in *Turco* about the presumption of correlation (ie as per the subject matter of documents) was extended, by analogy, to the presumption of preponderance (ie to the nature of the information that the document contains).

It happened first in Case C-139/07P *Technische Glaswerke Ilmenau*,[69] paragraphs 54, 55 and 62 with regard to the documents in an administrative file relating to a procedure for reviewing State aid. In its ruling, the ECJ speaks of general presumptions (quoting *Turco*); however, it does not refer to a presumption of association document-exception but clearly to another type of presumption: that certain documents must, in principle, be protected from public view, because by dicta of sectoral[70] law 'public access is not foreseen'.

In fact, that is nothing new unless the ECJ meant to say that, because of the way it is construed within the sectoral law, the presumption of preponderance when operating within Article 4(2) is absolute. However, discarding that interpretation, the Court is quick to affirm that the presumption is rebuttable (paragraph 62).

What is important to point out here is that, on the one hand, and under sectoral rules 'where public access is not foreseen', even if an applicant were to come up with a marvellous reason (ie overriding) for the contested documents to be made accessible to the public, the sectoral judicature would not be empowered to grant that request. Therefore, in the sectoral case law, necessarily, there are no examples of OPIs to draw from.

On the other hand, Article 4(2) also begins by saying that, in principle, and regardless of what the sectoral rules say, the contested documents will not be disclosed. What it then does—and here the novelty—is to give room for the players to seek out a reason—that the access judicature can validate—that is so pressing that anyone would agree that advantages would be had from disclosure.

We have already shown how, independently of the case law, at the rear of Regulation 1049/2001 there stands a presumption of correct correlation. It is clear that when Article 4(2) was drawn up it did not cross the mind of the legislator that the institutions would not have read the documents before making assertive statements

[67] On this point, see A Ezrachi, *EU Competition Law, An Analytical Guide to the Leading Cases* (Oxford, Hart, 2014) 532 ff.

[68] For environment-related cases, see C Banner (ed), *The Aarhus Convention, A Guide for UK Lawyers* (Oxford, Hart, 2015) 255 and 261.

[69] Case C-139/07P *Commission v Technische Glaswerke Ilmenau* [2010] ECR I-05855

[70] The ECJ does not like to qualify rules of sector as 'special law', in order that no *lex specialis* status be then derived. On this ruling specifically, see Speltdoorn, *Constitutionalising the Judicial System, Essays in Honour of Pernilla Lindth* (n 64). Again on the fact that the ECJ resists accepting the *lex specialis* status of sectoral rules, see N Harsdorf Enderndorf, 'The Road after Pfleiderer: Austrian Preliminary Reference Raises New Questions on Access to File by Third Parties in Cartel Proceedings' (2013) 34(2) *European Competition Law Review* 78–83, esp 82.

as to their content (the nature of the information contained in documents). In hindsight, it might be said that Advocate General Maduro proposed that it is not serious if (in order to ascertain correlation) the institution does not read every word of the documents but undertakes a more superficial examination, for the mere purpose of ascertaining that the document is what it asserts to be (in the specific case, legal advice). The Advocate General went on to say that only in the case of legal advice could the nature of the information contained within any piece of legal advice be presumed equivalent.

However, in *TGI*[71] the Court latched on to the admissibility of a superficial nature of the examination of documents for one purpose (to ascertain correlation) and extends it to the examination for a different purpose: to ascertain preponderance. It is precisely at this point that 'No' becomes unmoored from the contest document.

From the admissibility of a superficial examination (before the institutions make assertive comments as per the documents' subject matter, nature of content and degree of sensitivity) it is but a stone's throw to stating the admissibility of no examination at all.

Case T-29/08 *LPN v Commission*

119 It is apparent from that statement of reasons that the Commission essentially relied on the principle allowing the institution concerned to dispense with a specific and individual examination of each of the documents concerned or, at least, with a detailed statement of reasons in the contested decision with regard to that examination, on the ground that all those documents obviously form part of a single category of documents falling within the scope of the exception laid down in Article 4(2), third indent, of Regulation No 1049/2001.

120 That statement of reasons is not vitiated by any error of law or of fact.

[71] Case C-139/07P *Commission v Technische Glaswerke Ilmenau* (n 69).

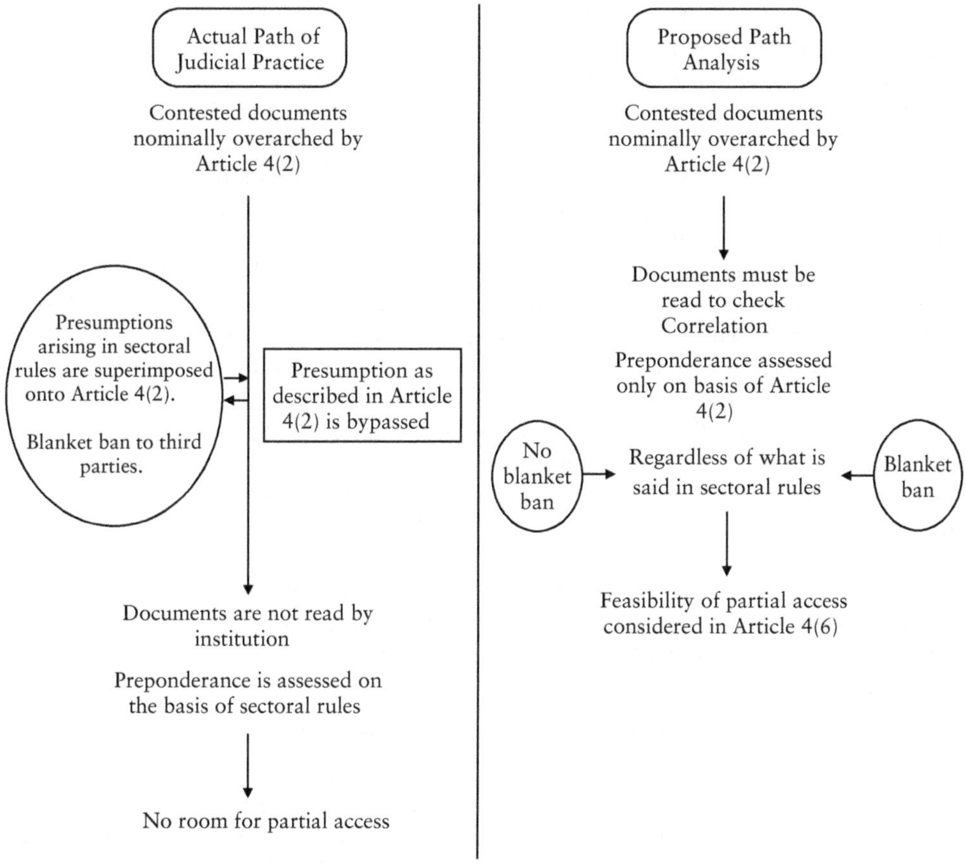

Figure 5.4: Actual Path of Judicial Practice/Proposed Path Analysis

The process is repeated *ad abundantiam*. It took place secondly, in Case C-514/07P, C-528/07P and C-532/07P *Sweden and Others v API and Commission*,[72] with regard to the pleadings lodged by an institution in court proceedings. Thirdly, in Case C-404/10P *Commission v Editions Odile Jacob*, paragraph 123, with regard to the documents exchanged between the Commission and notifying parties or third parties in the course of merger control proceedings. Fourthly, in Case C-514/11P and C-605/11P *LPN and Finland v Commission*, paragraph 65, with regard to the documents concerning an infringement procedure (related to environmental law) during its pre-litigation stage. Fifthly, in Case C-365/12P *Commission v EnBW* paragraph 93, with regard to the documents relating to a proceeding under Article 101 TFEU.

[72] Joined Cases C-514/07P, C-528/07P and C-532/07P *Sweden and Others v API and Commission* (n 48) paras 94 and 103.

Between the actual judicial path and a path having as its anchor Article 4(2), the starting point is the same: at the outset secrecy will probably be required to prevail over access. However, it is over the next steps that the two paths diverge.

Sailing down one path, the judicature has gone to great lengths to explain why it is important not to defraud the way in which the presumption of preponderance of secrecy is construed with each of the sectoral rules.[73] More often than not that path ends in a blanket ban. The blanket ban (ie 'no public access is foreseen') is then superimposed onto Article 4(2).

Conversely, a path that would not stray beyond Article 4(2) and thus would not superimpose the idiosyncrasy of presumptions, as construed sectorally, over Article 4(2) would simply require documents to be read before they are refused. Whilst in most of the cases the result would be no access (after a case-by-case examination), that simple requirement would then salvage Article 4(6).

Regulation 1049/2001 does enshrine a presumption of preponderance, but a rebuttable one. That is the difference between Article 4(1) and 4(2). Therefore, to ensure the conscionability of judicial interpretation of Article 4(2), somehow a real analysis of the advantages stemming from disclosure of (those) specific documents must be undertaken.

The result of the current judicial path has been the emergence of a sort of harmonious interpretation of Regulation 1049/2001 in general—and of Article 4(2) in particular—in the light of sectoral laws that more often than not pre-date the Regulation.

Case C-514/11P and C-605/11P *LPN and Finland*, Opinion AG Wathelet

> 64. It is clear not only from *Commission* v *Technische Glaswerke Ilmenau* but also from *Commission v Éditions Odile Jacob* and *Commission* v *Agrofert Holding* that the Court allowed general presumptions to be applied for the purpose of refusing access to documents relating to procedures for reviewing State aid or for merger control, relying, inter alia, on the existence of strict rules limiting access to the files in those procedures. In other words, although the Court, like the European Union legislature, has not introduced a hierarchy between the measures at issue, it has circumscribed the application of the general provisions of Regulation No 1049/2001 by such general presumptions, where access to documents in the administrative file would jeopardise the specific purpose of rules designed to ensure the very effectiveness of procedures for reviewing State aid and merger control.

In doing so, the judicature has encouraged an institutional practice that treats the presumption of preponderance as virtually absolute.[74]

[73] See generally K Lenaerts, 'The Principle of Transparency and its Limits in the Context of Competition Investigations' (2015) 4 *Osterreichische Zeitschrift fur Kartellrecht* 123–26; also K Jurimae, 'The Interaction between the EU Transparency Policy and The Enforcement of EU Competition Law, Who Should Strike the Balance and How Should it be Struck?' (2012) *European Competition Law Annual* 365–95; however, in this second article, at 375, the different approach of the GC is also explored and is much more nuanced.

[74] Doctrine has euphemistically employed the word more 'onerous'. On this point, see Speltdoorn (n 64).

ii. No Consideration of Partial Access

The presumption of preponderance has been flung far and wide with such conviction that, possibly in order to maintain some level of coherence with that choice (that is itself forged) the ECJ has been forced to disown partial access[75] as a procedural requirement.

> Case C-404/10P *Commission v Éditions Odile Jacob*
>
> 133 Thirdly, as regards the argument alleging incorrect interpretation of Article 4(6) of Regulation No 1049/2001 concerning the right of partial access, it must be noted that the general presumptions referred to in paragraphs 123, 130 and 131 respectively of this judgment indicate that the documents covered by them do not fall within an obligation of disclosure, in full or in part, of their content.

This, ultimately, portrays a court at war with itself.

iii. No Example of OPI and Burden of Identification Imposed on the Applicant

In addition, as another consequence of the path onto which the ECJ has settled, the burden of identifying any suitable OPI (in order to counter the exceptions of Article 4(2)) has been saddled onto the applicant, with the alarming result that to date there has been no successful[76] identification of any OPI by any applicant. Actually, to be precise, the only OPI that has been validated by the ECJ has been 'increased openness'. There could be many alternative explanations for this fact. The strongest is that Advocate General Maduro, already in *Turco* had warned that if the task of identifying the OPI were to be left to the applicant—given that the applicant had not had access to the contested documents beforehand—the task would be [sic] 'insuperable'.

iv. Something Old: Private Reasons of Private Parties

However, there is an innuendo of hope, incipient, but bright. It is related to the ECJ opening a crack in the blockade against reasons for requests. In fact, one plausible

[75] Case T-29/08 *LPN v Commission* (n 76) para 113, confirmed by the ECJ.

[76] Not even the duty of Member States to comply with Art 101 (leniency) or the principle of precaution in environmental matters (*LPN*) have managed to win the judicature over. We feel that the judicature's acknowledgement (in Case C-365/12P *Commission v EnBW Energie Baden-Wurtenberg*) that in competition law proceedings the interest in the access to a non-confidential version of documents is overriding, was not derived from an OPI test but rather, as mentioned before, from the superimposition over Art 4(2) of the presumption of secrecy as construed sectorally. In the specific case, and as the ECJ rightly singles out in para 7 of the ruling, it was the sectoral Regulation that admitted access to non-confidential versions.

> 7. Commission Regulation (EC) No 773/2004 of 7 April 2004 relating to the conduct of proceedings by the Commission pursuant to Articles 81 [EC] and 82 [EC] (OJ 2004 L 123, p. 18) provides in Article 6 thereof, entitled 'Participation of complainants in proceedings', as follows:
>
> '1. Where the Commission issues a statement of objections relating to a matter in respect of which it has received a complaint, it shall provide the complainant with a copy of the non-confidential version of the statement of objections and set a time-limit within which the complainant may make known its views in writing'.

(alternative) explanation for the lack of success in identifying any OPI is that there might be a (much too) strict textual limitation in the Regulation itself on the type of eligible interests that could come to be qualified as overriding. The version of the test as drafted in Article 4(2) is confined to the confrontation of the interests (in keeping documents confidential) protected by the exceptions laid down in Article 4(2) and (3) with a concurrent public interest in disclosure that—overriding the former—would justify disclosure of the documents. Thus, whilst the institutions are not allowed to enquire why an applicant wishes to access to a document, presently, the reverse of the coin is that applicants are not allowed to draw any benefit from putting forth or making known specific, private[77] reasons.

Joined Cases T-110/03 T-150/03 and T-405/03 *Sison v Council*, paragraphs 50–55

> 'The purpose of the Regulation [on access] is to guarantee access for everyone to public [unpublished] documents and not only access to the requesting party to documents concerning him'. And consequently 'the particular interest which may be asserted by a requesting party in obtaining access to a document covering him personally cannot be taken into account when applying the mandatory exceptions'.

v. Striking the Balance between what?

This brings us back for a moment to the question (as yet unanswered) of who is to identify the OPI, since it is intimately linked with another. Once the (alleged) OPI is identified, who is to strike a balance between competing interests in order to say which of the interests overrides the other? If we were to look back at the case law pre-Regulation 1049/2001, in these cases, balancing tests were clearly self-ascribed to the institutions.

Post-Regulation 1049/2001, after a first ruling (*Turco*) in which the ECJ had also imposed such a burden onto the institutions, today, the enforcement of that requirement has been (to say the least) co-ascribed to the applicant.

Case C-127/13 *Strack v Commission*, Opinion of AG Kokott

> 177. Mr Strack, however, raises the objection that there is an overriding public interest in the investigation of anti-dumping proceedings which justifies the transfer of that information and must be examined both by the Commission and by the General Court of its own motion.
>
> 178. That view is essentially correct. The Court has found that, in the situations referred to in Article 4(2) of Regulation No 1049/2001, the institution in question must explain whether or not there is an overriding public interest that might nevertheless justify disclosure of the document concerned. (56 Judgment in *Sweden and Turco v Council* (C 39/05 P and C 52/05 P, EU:C:2008:374, paragraph 49) It is therefore necessary to consider, of the institution's own motion, at least the most striking aspects of the individual case. (57) However,

[77] Joined Cases T-110/03 T-150/03 and T-405/03 *Sison v Council*.

at this stage, such consideration will also as a general rule turn quite significantly on particular aspects which must be raised by the applicant. (58 Judgment in *LPN and Finland v Commission* (C 514/11 P and C 605/11 P, EU:C:2013:738, paragraph 94 and the case law cited))

179. It is a fortiori true that, in court proceedings, an infringement of Article 4(2) of Regulation No 1049/2001 will fall to be considered, in connection with an examination of the overriding public interest, only if the applicant makes a complaint in that regard. If such a complaint does not concern the complete absence of such an examination, it must indicate the aspects which were not correctly assessed. It does not therefore constitute an error in law if the General Court concentrates on the applicant's submissions.

The lack of a clear justification for extending the burden to applicants is all the more serious since the OPI test is momentous. In fact, when such a test is undertaken (either by a concrete examination of the contested documents by the institution, or, on the basis of speculation, by the applicant)[78] and an overriding, public interest is found to concur, then, according to the letter of the law, the test's findings are binding.

Between who is to identify the OPI and who is to strike a balance of interests, it is principally the fact that the burden of identifying the OPI falls onto the shoulders of a player that has neither seen the contested documents and cannot argue private interests before the Court that has been difficult to accept by applicants.

On the one hand, the demonstration burden imposed on the applicant—in its present terms—might well violate the principle of practical possibility:[79]

In Joined Cases T-494/08 to T-500/08 and T-509/08 *Ryanair v Commission* at paras 75–80, The GC clarified that the General Presumption can be rebutted but only if in the applicant's confirmatory application (and not after the adoption of the refusal decision) identifies 'expressly and individually' the documents that he considers not to be covered by that presumption and he adduces sufficient evidence and arguments to that effect.[80]

[78] In this sense, see para 54 of the Opinion of AG Maduro in Case C-39/05P and C-52/05P *Sweden and Turco v Council* (n 50): 'how could he (the applicant) show the interest in disclosing a legal opinion notwithstanding the general interest in keeping it confidential when he does not know its content?' In Joined Cases C–514/11 P and C–605/11P *LPN & Finland v Commission* (n 48), the ECJ refused to give any credit to the applicant's assertion claiming that (since applicants were not aware of the content of the contested documents) the ECJ was requiring applicants to discharge that burden of proof on the basis of speculation. Also on this point, and against what was proposed in the Opinion of AG Kokott, the ECJ in Case C-127/13 P *Strack v Commission* at para 128, has ascribed such a task (of demonstrating the concurrence of an overriding public interest) to the applicant:

128 Finally, it must be observed that the appellant's criticism relating to paragraph 229 of the judgment under appeal is unfounded. First, it is clear from that paragraph that the Commission did in fact examine the existence of overriding public interests. Second, the case law of the Court provides that it is for the applicant to show that there is an overriding public interest to justify the disclosure of the documents concerned (see judgment in *LPN and Finland v Commission*, C-514/11 P and C-605/11 P, EU:C:2013:738, paragraph 94).

[79] This principle is also cherished by the EU, namely in Case C-453/99 *Courage and Crehan* [2001] ECR I-6297, paras 26 and 27; Joined Cases C-295/04 to C-298/04 *Manfredi and others* [2006] ECR I-6619, para 91; Case C-360/09 *Pfleiderer* [2011] ECR I-5161, para 28; and Case C-536/111 *Donau Chemie and Others* [2013] ECR, para 23.

[80] Speltdoorn (n 64) 469.

In fact, in *LPN and Finland*, even the ECJ could not but concur that if an applicant is not cogniscent of the content of a document refused there is no viable alternative to mere speculation.[81] Clearly, the ECJ was not proposing to condone illegal release (of information) as the basis of legitimate rebuttal. Therefore, the need to distinguish this figure from an unacceptable burden typical of *diabolica probatio* standards is urgent.

On the other hand, it is also difficult to ignore that whilst applicants face the limitation of not being allowed to offer private interests as a reason for requests within the access proceedings, when addressing any request (other than access) to institutions, and when lodging any action for annulment (other than within the access context) against any decision of which they are the addressees, private parties are compelled to offer reasons and to demonstrate a direct and individual concern.

The judicature—ever capable of changing the tide—has given a sign that it might be willing to discuss the issue further and from a different standpoint. Not so much regarding the relevance of reasons that are entirely private, but rather in regard to reasons that could be considered to spring forth simultaneously from a private and public motive.

vi. Something New? The Emergence of a Nuanced Approach in LPN and Finland v Commission*: Own Reasons of Private Parties that Act in the Public Interest*

A new concept has been coined in regard to non-governmental environmental organisations (NGOs) whose main purpose is to defend the conservation of nature. The law, acknowledging their activity—in the public interest—as meritorious, allows them first, to take (legal) form, secondly, to engage in the protection of nature and, thirdly, even to take legal action.

Environmental NGOs often request access to environmental files concerning investigations before final decisions are taken since the NGOs are often invited to submit expert comment during the process. In order to do so they claim they need access to the respective file before the investigation is completed. Or at least between the moment in which the investigative activity is completed and a definitive decision is taken by the Commission. This for the purpose of submitting a memorandum. Until now, the argument has come into direct collision with the presumption of Article 4(2) that before the investigation is completed, access to the file would undermine the purpose of the investigation.

A more difficult task is to address the issue of whether the interests that they have vowed to protect 'that the environment is not unduly harmed before the institutions are in possession of all available expertise' are their own. There is no simple answer.

'Yes' may be attempted since that particular organisation (a legal person) is the person who protects the interest (in the conservation of the environment). As such, the organisation undeniably has an interest that nature is defended. Therefore, it is also true that the organisation reaps a (moral) benefit (or stake) from a successful

[81] Case C-514/11P and C-605/11P *LPN and Finland v Commission* (n 48) para 42.

outcome of the legal proceedings. Thus, it might be said that the interest that nature is defended is—to that extent—an own interest.

But, conversely, and to the (also truthful) extent that many other persons that are apart from the organisation benefit from (the organisation's) defence of nature, then, the interest that nature is defended and the (moral) benefit (or stake) to be had from a successful outcome of the legal proceedings (lodged in the interest of the conservation of the environment), is not exclusive to the organisation, merely shared with (the rest of) the public.

A nuance has fleetingly transpired in the *LPN*[82] proceedings and may be a signal that a fresh generation of case law is in the making: to that effect a new phrase 'private parties acting in the public interest' has been offered up. It is but a crack in the wall, but it is there.

vii. Sliding Doors

Again during the *LPN* proceedings, when pressed on the point that the current (virtually absolute) interpretation of the presumption of preponderance drafted into Article 4(2) disregards the legal text's clear preference for a rebuttable framework, the ECJ, *en passant*, opened another crack into the theory of tolerance for great levels of insulation of documents encompassed by the exceptions of Article 4(2).

> Case C-514/11P and C-605/11P *LPN and Finland*
>
> 42 It follows that the system of exceptions laid down in Article 4 of that regulation, particularly in paragraph 2 thereof, is based on a balancing of the opposing interests in a given situation, that is to say, firstly, the interests which would be favoured by the disclosure of the documents in question and, secondly, those which would be jeopardised by such disclosure. The decision taken on a request for access to documents depends on which interest must prevail in the particular case.

It could mean that the future means starting from *Turco*, anew. It would not hurt that the ECJ acknowledge how in order to balance interests *someone* has to read the contested documents. Over time, it has become clear to everyone that devising the exact purpose of making the institutions read the documents has become less pressing than making sure of the simple fact that they are indeed read. Whether it is to ascertain their subject matter or the nature of the information they contain[83] is actually immaterial, one cannot go about one task without fulfilling the other.

The judicial path could thus easily slide back into Article 4(2). Therein, it suffices to require that documents are read and that correlation is verified. Once that has taken place, preponderance (of secrecy over access) could just as easily be ascertained on a case-by case-basis, regardless of what sectoral[84] rules say.

[82] ibid.

[83] Opinion of AG Maduro in Case C-39/05P and C-52/05P *Sweden and Turco v Council* (n 50) para 43.

[84] See, above.

It would at least remove what is perceived by applicants as 'unfair surprise' within litigation. Applicants that are promised to be treated on the basis of Article 4(2) are then confronted by the judicature during hearings with the argument that 'sectoral rules do not provide for access' regardless of any OPI tests. The applicants are then abruptly called upon to plead against sectoral rules that leave no room for third-party access. It is almost as if Regulation 1049/2001 had never come into existence.

Were the judicature to return to Article 4(2), the starting point would be equal to that of the sectoral rules: secrecy will possibly prevail. That notwithstanding, were the judicature not to stray from Article 4(2), the point of arrival could actually become quite different and refreshing. Article 4(2) leaves room for two possibilities that the sectoral rules squeeze out: the acknowledgement of an OPI in disclosure *and* Article 4(6).[85]

We are well aware that such an interpretation may tempt more applicants to come forth. The vision of hordes of applicants circuitously avoiding restrictive sectoral rules and banging on the door of Europe via Regulation 1049/2001 is of course a risk. Yet such applicants would only be successful if they helped call attention to the existence of OPIs, or convinced the institutions that access to mere parts of documents would hurt no one and undermine no purpose.

viii. The Tone of the Affair

Before we move on to the analysis of exceptions beyond Regulation 1049/2001 it is important to spend a few words on the (unacceptable) tone of the communication that has come to pass between applicants and institutions as per Article 4(2). It comes across clearly in Case T-181/10 *Reagens SpA v Commission*,[86] and is reported in an insightful comment by C Charalambous:[87]

> The applicant raised five pleas in law, with the first plea, it alleged that the Commission did not carry out a concrete and individual examination of all the requested documents. The Commission maintained, however that id did proceed to such an examination, even though it was not required to do so, since it was entitled to presume that the requested documents were non-accessible due to their nature.

The tone not only takes us back to the days in which the *disclosure* of documents was seen by the institutions as a favour or concession to the public; it takes us much further back. We land in a place where even the *reading* of documents is seen as a favour and a concession. And so, this last note becomes a last question on Article 4(2): after enshrinement in a Treaty and in a Charter of Fundamental Rights, is this all that the institutions and the judicature have to offer applicants?

[85] And, whilst we have repeatedly said that preponderance should be looked at only within Art 4(2) and not beyond, for the sake of argument even some quite restrictive sectoral rules point in the direction of partial access as well: C-365/12P *Commission v EnBW, Energie Baden Wurtenburg*, para 7 in which access to non-confidential versions of a decision finding infringement of Treaty rules is considered appropriate.

[86] Case T-181/10 *Reagens SpA v Commission* [not reported].

[87] C Charalambous, '*Reagens:* Access to Documents Re the Inability of an Undertaking to Pay the Fine' (2014) 5(7) *Journal of Competition Law and Practice* 466–68, 467.

ix. More Exceptions, Elsewhere

Now, to discuss other exceptions. From 2006 onwards (apart from Regulation 45/2001 which we have already mentioned), the list of exceptions to access was no longer confined to Article 4(1) 4(2) and 4(3) of Regulation 1049/2001. Another Regulation, put into place in the meantime, also requires our attention.

VII. 2006: NEW EXCEPTION—THE ENVIRONMENT

10 years ago (2006) a new protagonist was added to the list of (statute-based) exceptions that govern public access to documents held by the EU: the protection of the environment.

As a normative option, access to environmental information has been addressed by reference to two separate thresholds that should not be confused. While it is true that both resulting instruments are inspired by the Aarhus Convention[88] their individual purposes are divergent.

One threshold (the main focus of our discussion)—established under the form of a Regulation[89]—is addressed to the EU institutions. It is known as the Aarhus Regulation, which is in fact Regulation (EC) 1367/2006 on the application of the provisions of the Aarhus Convention on Access to Information, Public Participation in Decision-making and Access to Justice in Environmental Matters to Community institutions and bodies[90] dated 6 September 2006. It lays down a framework that principally seeks to facilitate a wider dimension of access to (environmental) information.

A second threshold—established under the form of a Directive[91]—has been addressed solely to the Member States and its aim is to approximate, where possible, the rules governing access to environmental information of disparate national fora.

A. For the EU Institutions—Regulation 1367/2006

The so-called Aarhus Regulation lays down a framework that principally seeks to facilitate a wider dimension of access to (environmental) information.

In its Preamble (Article 5) it clarifies that—as a normative instrument—it itself arises from the option to deal with the three pillars of the Aarhus Convention within a single piece of legislation, namely (1) access to information; (2) public participation in decision-making; and (3) access to justice in environmental matters.

[88] Although the European Community signed the Convention on Access to Information, Public Participation in Decision-making and Access to Justice in Environmental Matters as early as 1998, the process was concluded only in 2005 ([2005] OJ L 124/1).

[89] Regulation 1367/2006; see section VII.A.

[90] [2006] OJ L 264/16 (the Aarhus Regulation).

[91] Directive 2003/4/ EC on public access to environmental information [2003] OJ L 41/26.

With the proviso of acknowledgement that it is as a whole that the Aarhus Regulation is, possibly, the more important normative contribution to the access theme since Regulation 1049/2001, our discussion[92] is confined to its section (1) pertaining to access to information. In particular, to the assessment of the rules governing exceptions that the institutions may resort to when refusing access to environmental documents. Access to information in environmental matters is today governed jointly by the Preamble (paragraph 15) of Regulation 1367/2006 and by Title II of the Regulation's body: Articles 3 through 8.

It will suffice to say—as an introductory comment—that the Aarhus Regulation establishes, by default, the public interest relevance of any request for environmental information in its Article 6. It also clearly states that when decisions on disclosure are taken, certainty should be had as to whether the information contained in the documents sought by the public relates to emissions into the environment.

B. For the Member States—Directives 2003/4/EC and 90/313/EEC

On another front, within a different context, and with an entirely different purpose and methodology, attention has been paid by a first Directive 90/313/EC to existing Member State legislation on this topic. In the meantime it was repealed by Directive 2003/4/EC of the European Parliament and of the Council on 28 January 2003 on public access to environmental information.

Directive 2003/4/EC both has more exceptions to access and shields more concurrent interests to access than Regulation 1049/2001. A more restrictive perspective of access, has been—here—embraced since Member States function within a much more intense remedial context (in which courts may address injunctions to national institutions).

Thus, as the doctrine has rightly singled out

> Like Regulation 1049 the Directive foresees a list of exceptions that may preclude public access in its Article 4.
>
> This list is considerably longer than the concomitant list in the Regulation and permits refusal inter alia when the request is manifestly unreasonable, concerns material in the course of completion or unfinished documents or data, or concerns internal communications, taking into account the public interest served by disclosure. Moreover, the Member States may provide for exceptions in cases circumscribed in Article 4(2) of the Directive. This list largely corresponds to interests protected by Article 4(1) and 4(2) of Regulation 1049, but is wider in the sense that more interests are protected. Thus, it foresees an exception to protect the environment to which such information relates, such as the location of rare species.

[92] Both here and in Chs 4 and 5.

A notable exception is the protection of the confidentiality of the proceedings of public authorities where such confidentiality is provided for by law. The Court of Justice has held that:

C-204/09 *Flachglas Torgau GmbH*, Judgment of 14 February 2012 [not yet reported]

65. The condition that the confidentiality of proceedings of public authorities must be provided for by law can be regarded as fulfilled by the existence, in the national law of the Member State concerned, of a rule which provides, generally, that the confidentiality of proceedings of public authorities is a ground for refusing access to environmental information held by those authorities, in so far as national law clearly defines the concept of 'proceedings'.

Interestingly and in the opposite sense—ensuring wider access standards—than Regulation 1049/2001

Unlike the exceptions in Regulation 1049, all of the exceptions in the Directive are mitigated by the requirement that 'the public interest served by disclosure (be) weighed against the interest served by the refusal' (Article 4(2) of the Directive).

This, in essence, corresponds to the overriding public interest clause in Article 4(2) and 4(3) of the Regulation which, however, applies to all exceptions in the Directive.[93]

Although it is undoubtedly true that the Directive on access is also an important normative contribution, it would be imprudent—and maybe even reckless—to attempt to develop the EU-institutions-specific case law by recourse to it.

Regulation 1367/2006 calls for access that is wider (than the level laid down in the *de minimis* Regulation 1049/2001) for environmental files held or produced by the EU institutions. These institutions are, as a matter of principle, insulated from injunctive relief. Hence, such EU law should not be interpreted in the light of Directives, albeit governing the same subject matter, addressed solely to the Member States where, by contrast, injunctive relief thrives.

In sum, the difference in addressee involved should stand as an interpretative limitation to the EU judicature unless the disparate intensity of remedial contexts is adequately taken into account.

C. Regulation 1367/2006, Less Access: Article 6(2)

Aarhus Regulation, Article 6

Application of exceptions concerning requests for access to environmental information

2. In addition to the exceptions set out in Article 4 of Regulation (EC) No 1049/2001, Community institutions and bodies may refuse access to environmental information where

[93] Driessen (n 37) 198, para 42.

> disclosure of the information would adversely affect the protection of the environment to which the information relates, such as the breeding sites of rare species.

It is clear that Article 6(2) enlarges the menu that allows the institutions to refuse access. It is also clear why. To disclose publicly the location of breeding sites might endanger the reproductive capability of wildlife, since younglings might be disturbed, trapped or even killed. The article implies that—as is true of other situations listed in Article 4 of Regulation 1049/2001—institutions and judges must often shield counter-interests to access (here the environment, in its frailty) from the dangers of irreversible aggression.

The provision is drafted using the terms '*may* refuse' and '*would* adversely affect'. On the one hand, this indicates that a discretionary framework has been preferred. On the other, the presumable effect on the environment is qualified as an adverse one. This second part seems to imply that a, prior, abstract, harm test is to be undertaken by the refusing institution.

In sum Article 6(2) allows for less access, if necessary.

D. Regulation 1367/2006, More Access: Article 6(1)

The contribution of the Aarhus Regulation is not confined to the addition of an exception to access. Indeed, on the contrary, another of its provisions, Article 6(1), is a provision that screams for more access, and precedes Article 6(2). Still, it has to be harmoniously interpreted together with Regulation 1049/2001, and in particular with the latter's Article 4.

i. Article 6(1), First Sentence

> Aarhus Regulation, Article 6
>
> Application of exceptions concerning requests for access to environmental information
>
> *First sentence*
>
> As regards Article 4(2), first and third indents, of Regulation (EC) No 1049/2001, with the exception of investigations, in particular those concerning possible infringements of Community law, an overriding public interest in disclosure shall be deemed to exist where the information requested relates to emissions into the environment.
>
> *Second sentence*
>
> As regards the other exceptions set out in Article 4 of Regulation (EC) No 1049/2001, the grounds for refusal shall be interpreted in a restrictive way, taking into account the public interest served by disclosure and whether the information requested relates to emissions into the environment.

Article 6(1) is divided into two sentences. Regarding its first sentence, the same lays down a presumption: it determines that there is overriding public interest (in disclosure) of all documents that contain information related to emissions[94] into the environment. This is regardless of concurrent counter-interests protected by typified exceptions singled out in Article 4 of Regulation 1049/2001. However, the presumption (that an overriding public interest in disclosure exists) only trumps the counter-interests listed under the first and (part of the) third indents of Article 4(2) of Regulation 1049/2001.

Therefore, in order to devise which counter-interests are trumped, let us examine Article 4(2) in its entirety:

> Regulation 1049/2001, Article 4(2), *tout court*
>
> The institutions shall refuse access to a document where disclosure would undermine the protection of:
>
> First indent—*one exception*: commercial interests of a natural or legal person, including intellectual property
>
> Second Indent—*two exceptions*: court proceedings and legal advice
>
> Third indent—the purpose of *three exceptions*: inspections, investigations and audits
>
> unless there is an overriding public interest in disclosure.

Next let us separate out the parts of Article 4(2) (and the inherent counter-interests) that are not affected by the Aarhus Regulation's Article 6(1), first sentence.

Table 5.4: Regulation 1049/2001, Article 4(2)

Parts overarched by Article 6(1) first sentence, Aarhus: Acquire overriding public interest in disclosure where information requested relates to emissions	Parts left outside Article 6(1) first sentence, Aarhus And covered (logically) by Article 6(1) second sentence Aarhus.
First indent commercial interests of a natural or legal person, including intellectual property	
	Second Indent court proceedings and legal advice
Third indent the purpose of inspections, [...] and audits	*Third indent* Investigations, in particular those concerning the possible infringement of Community Law

[94] In such cases, there is no question of identifying any new OPI; it is the mere link to emissions that triggers the disclosable status of the documents. The definition of what emissions are has been probed in Case T-545/11 *Stichting Greenpeace NL and PAN Europe v Commission* [not yet reported] and in Case C-673/13P *Commission v Stichting Greenpeace NL and PAN Europe* [not yet reported] concerning the substance glyphosate. On these proceedings, see H Holleben, 'Judgment of the General Court of the EU on Access to Information under Substance Law: Case T-545/11, Judgement of 8 October 2012' (2013) 4 *European Journal of Risk Regulation* 565–78. However, AG Kokott, in her Opinion delivered in Case C-673/13P *Commission v Stichting Greenpeace NL and PAN Europe*, [not yet reported] has argued that

a. Article 4(2) First Indent

What is absolutely clear is that two independent exceptions listed in Article 4(2), first indent—*court proceedings, legal advice*—are not affected by Article 6(1). In other words, even if the information requested does relate to emissions into the environment, neither of the two exceptions folds automatically.

b. Part of Article 4(2) Third Indent

In addition, a single specific exception (investigations, *especially the ones related to infringement proceedings*) contained within the third indent of Article 4 of Regulation 1049/2001 is also to be withdrawn from the abovementioned presumption's area of incidence.

ii. Article 6(1), Second Sentence

This peculiar choice of normative structure in Article 6(1) first sentence warrants three remarks that are preliminary to the analysis of Article 6(1) second sentence.

First, the purpose of Article 6 of the Aarhus Regulation in its entirety is to establish a link to the entirety of Regulation 1049/2001's Article 4. Secondly, by way of the first sentence, Article 6(1) only establishes a relationship with commercial interests, inspections and audits. Thirdly, it is by way of the second sentence that Article 6(1) establishes a relationship with 'the other exceptions set out in Article 4 of Regulation 1049/2001'.

Which exceptions are those? All the exceptions in Article 4(1); the exceptions in Article 4(2) second indent; the exception that remains in Article 4(2) third indent that was not affected by Article 6(1) first sentence; all the exceptions in Article 4(3).

> Regulation 1049/2001, Article 4(1)
>
> (a) The public interest (public security, defence and military matters, international relations, the financial, monetary or economic policy of the Community or a Member State.
>
> (b) Privacy and integrity of the individual, in particular in accordance with Community legislation regarding the protection of personal data.
>
> Regulation 1049/2001, Article 4(2)
>
> The institutions SHALL refuse access to a document where disclosure WOULD undermine the protection of:
>
> — First indent (...)
> — Second Indent court proceedings and legal advice

the emissions clause may no longer enjoy automatic status. This new angle is clear from at paras 65–70 and esp at para 68: 'The emissions clause cannot thus be applicable to the information referred to in Article 63(2) of the Plant Protection Regulation. A decision on access to such information must therefore be taken pursuant to the third sentence of Article 4(2) of Regulation No 1049/2001 and Article 6(1) of the Aarhus Regulation based on an assessment of the individual case'.

The ECJ has not yet delivered judgment; however, whether it will choose to confirm this view, or not, is of utmost interest.

— Third Indent the purpose of (...), investigations and (...)

unless there is an overriding public interest in disclosure.

Regulation 1049/2001, Article 4(3)

shall be refused if *would seriously* undermine

— institution's decision-making process

unless there is an overriding public interest in disclosure.

Therefore we must look to the second sentence of Article 6(2) to understand the governance of the second indent of Article 4 of Regulation 1049/2001 'court proceedings and legal advice', and (the remaining) part of the third indent: 'investigations', particularly infringement proceedings since this part is not covered by Article 6(1) first sentence. When we examine the second sentence of Article 6(1) closely, it is clear that it determines that requests for environmental information that relate to emissions may, or not, acquire overriding public interest relevance when measured against the remnant interests (also protected by typified exceptions) in Regulation 1049/2001's Article 4.

Thus, whilst within the realm of the first sentence of Article 6(1) an overriding public interest in disclosure of documents that concern information related to emissions into the environment is always presumed to exist, within the realm of the second sentence the possibility that an overriding public interest in disclosure of documents that concern information related to emissions into the environment might override other meritorious interests protected (by the other exceptions of Article 4) must be ascertained on a case-by-case basis and by way of a balancing test.

It is also very clear that in order to protect the environment Article 6(2) calls for *less* access whilst, again to protect the environment, Article 6(1) calls for *more* access. In addition, *less* access is not aided by any absolute presumption of harm stemming from the disclosure of environmental information (related to the location of breeding sites). That provision—Article 6(2)—is written up in terms of 'may and would adversely affect'.

On the contrary *more* access is much more intensely protected by an absolute presumption of the overriding utility of disclosure of (much) information regarding emissions into the environment. That provision—Article 6(1), first sentence—is written in the assertive terms 'shall be deemed to exist where'. And even where the presumption of the utility in disclosure does not operate: the realm of 'the other exceptions in Article 4', the institutions are still required to interpret those 'other exceptions in Article 4' restrictively taking into account both the public interest in disclosure (that might or not be overriding) and the possibility that the information might relate to emissions.

iii. Play it Again?

The ECJ is not convinced. And, without a crumb of regard for the precautionary principle that governs environmental law and which is at the basis of the incursion of environmental law into the access legislation, it has proposed a *contra legem* reading of the second sentence of Article 6(1). Or, at any rate, a reading of the second sentence of Article 6(1) that is so *sui generis*, that it is impossible to concur with.

The judicature has held, first, that Article 6(1) second sentence is simply not applicable to documents related to on-going infringement proceedings. In other words, the Court attempts to peddle the theory that Article 6(1) establishes rules of accordance with all the exceptions listed in Regulation 1049/2001—including defence and military issues listed under Article 4(1)—but fails to do so regarding investigations, in particular those concerning the infringement of EU law.

The Court seemingly arrives at this conclusion since, in its view:

Case C-514/11P and C-605/11P *LPN and Finland*

The first sentence of Article 6(1) of Regulation no 1367/2006, which lays down a rule to facilitate access to documents containing environmental information, provides that that rule does not apply to 'investigations, in particular those concerning possible infringements of community law'.

It follows that infringement proceedings are regarded, by that European Union legislation, as a type of procedure which, as such, has characteristics precluding full transparency being granted in that field and which therefore has a special position within the system of access to documents.

Yet an attentive and literal reading of the provisions discussed could—just as well-sway the argument in a different direction.

In fact, it is written nowhere that just because the first sentence of Article 6(1) of Regulation 1367/2006 (when compared against Regulation 1049/2001) enhances the level of access, it follows that for any subject matter excluded from the first sentence (investigations) Regulation 1367/2006 allows the (*de minimis*) standards of Regulation 1049/2001 to be lowered.

In truth, what will always principally be at stake in litigation concerning access to any investigative file is whether the interpretation of the second sentence of Article 6(1) requires the institution to demonstrate that it has actually and specifically verified on a case-by-case basis that there are no concurrent overriding public interests that could trump the (merely putative) harm engendered by disclosure.

At the end of the day such an interpretation would merely lead to a normal, textual application of the dicta of Article 4(2) of Regulation 1049/2001.

Finally, is not at all evident that the teleology of environmental access is compatible with another statement of the ECJ: that within Article 6 of Regulation 1367/2006 there is also the intent to restrict access. Again, it is a statement that comes forth highly decontextualised and as a mere attempt to overshadow the fact that the judicature has still to help give concrete form to the more access that the Aarhus Regulation requires.

Case C-514/11P and C-605/11P *LPN and Finland v Commission*

53 Although, pursuant to Article 3 thereof, Regulation No 1049/2001, and in particular Article 4 thereof, is to apply to any request by an applicant for access to environmental information held by Community institutions and bodies, Article 6 of Regulation

No 1367/2006 adds more specific rules concerning such request for access which in part favour and in part restrict the access to the documents.

If restriction is contemplated, as we have mentioned above, restriction only applies to the disclosure of the location of breeding sites. It is not intended to be, and cannot be, disguised as a provision in any way insulating institutions and Member States from public scrutiny.

VIII. A PROCEDURE FOR 'NO'

Moving away from the problems surrounding the strength of the exceptions in Article 4 of Regulation 1049/2001 and of Article 6 Regulation 1367/2006, let us turn to the process of fighting the exceptions both outside the courts and before the courts.

A. Administrative Proceedings

First of all, requests for access must be conducted through administrative proceedings that are divided into two distinct and separate phases. Subsequently, options of recourse either to the EU Ombudsman or to the EU judicature have been put in place in order to close disputes definitively.

i. Phase 1

In a first stage, when one sends an initial application to the institutions, any adverse reply from the same—refusing access to the documents sought—may be challenged through a confirmatory application. An institutional refusal of first light is not considered to be definitive.[95] This is why a second, so-called 'confirmatory application' may be addressed to the same institution that refused access. In essence, it is a request that the institution reconsider its initial position, a second chance before conflict is irreversible.

In addition, a first set of important deadlines that must be taken into account. These concern the tempo at which communication between applicants and institutions is to proceed. Regulation 1049/2001 lays down a rhythm of successive periods of 15[96] working days for institutions to provide replies to applicants and, likewise, for applicants to choose to challenge the replies they are sent.

Moreover, the institutions might gain some extra space to think, by extending the time-limits for providing replies by an extra 15 working days. Aside from this possibility, deadlines are imperative for all and are rules of public order. In consequence,

[95] Case C-127/13P *Strack v Commission* [not yet reported] para 36, in footnotes.

[96] It was initially laid down in the implementing Decisions of the 1993 Code of Conduct as successive rounds of 30-day periods.

if an applicant allows this first deadline to lapse, the entitlement to make a confirmatory application will be lost.

What follows a confirmatory application from an applicant is that the merits of a first refusal are either affirmed, changed or reversed by the institution.

Regulation 1049/2001, Article 7—Processing of initial applications

1. An application for access to a document shall be handled promptly. An acknowledgement of receipt shall be sent to the applicant. Within 15 working days from registration of the application, the institution shall either grant access to the document requested and provide access in accordance with Article 10 within that period or, in a written reply, state the reasons for the total or partial refusal and inform the applicant of his or her right to make a confirmatory application in accordance with paragraph 2 of this Article.

2. In the event of a total or partial refusal, the applicant may, within 15 working days of receiving the institution's reply, make a confirmatory application asking the institution to reconsider its position.

3. In exceptional cases, for example in the event of an application relating to a very long document or to a very large number of documents, the time-limit provided for in paragraph 1 may be extended by 15 working days, provided that the applicant is notified in advance and that detailed reasons are given.

4. Failure by the institution to reply within the prescribed time-limit shall entitle the applicant to make a confirmatory application.

ii. Phase 2

Only at the stage that follows institutional replies to confirmatory applications[97] are further instruments made available to the applicant. Therein, if an institutional reply, explicitly, expresses refusal, the doors both to the EU Ombudsman and to the EU judicature[98] are opened.

Regulation 1049/2001, Article 8—Processing of Confirmatory Applications

1. A confirmatory application shall be handled promptly. Within 15 working days from registration of such an application, the institution shall either grant access to the document requested and provide access in accordance with Article 10 within that period or, in a written reply, state the reasons for the total or partial refusal. In the event of a total or partial refusal, the institution shall inform the applicant of the remedies open to him or her, namely instituting court proceedings against the institution and/or making a complaint to the Ombudsman, under the conditions laid down in Articles 230 and 195 of the EC Treaty, respectively.

2. In exceptional cases, for example in the event of an application relating to a very long document or to a very large number of documents, the time limit provided for in paragraph

[97] This is true whether in the first stage either an absence of reply (silence) ensued, or in the alternative, an explicit refusal was notified to the applicant.

[98] We have chosen, throughout the book, not to consider the (valid) option of recourse to the Ombudsman.

> 1 may be extended by 15 working days, provided that the applicant is notified in advance and that detailed reasons are given.
>
> 3. Failure by the institution to reply within the prescribed time limit shall be considered as a negative reply and entitle the applicant to institute court proceedings against the institution and/or make a complaint to the Ombudsman, under the relevant provisions of the EC Treaty

Again, institutions are allowed to extend the deadline for reply, once, for an extra 15 days. Other than that they are bound to reply to the applicant promptly.

Consistent with the court's assertions that an institutional refusal of first light is not considered to be definitive, only refusals that come forth in reply to a confirmatory application put an end to the administrative communication between applicants and institutions. As such, they entitle the applicant to make a complaint to the EU Ombudsman and/or to lodge an action for annulment before the EU judicature. The purpose of such an action is to request that the EU court strike down an institutional decision—'No'—that adversely affects the applicant.

B. The Choice to Go to Court

When there is a definitive reply in the letterbox, another concrete decision also constrained by time—two months—opens up for the applicant: whether or not to go to court. Within that period, the option of lodging an action for annulment of a refusal of access, before the EU judicature, will have to be considered and, eventually undertaken.

Again the deadline is imperative. Any late action would be unconditionally rejected by the courts of the EU. It would be ruled formally inadmissible[99] before its merit could even be considered. In fact, when the deadline of Article 265 TFEU lapses, the applicant is *ipso facto* disenfranchised from the right to have that (possibly) illegitimate refusal annulled. Therefore, an applicant that allows such a deadline to lapse—in a worst-case scenario—may only resume communication with the institution by way of a new, initial application for access.

i. The Effects of Annulment

Once the decision to go to court has been taken, what is the applicant to expect? Within the access context, striking down any institutional decision merely opens up a void. All situations post-annulment merely, re-open the (second stage of) the administrative procedure.

Time is brought back to the moment at which the applicant's confirmatory application has reached the institution. Consequently, the institution is bound—again—to issue a new, definitive, decision, in regard to the old request. That is, what, in the eyes of the Court, any annulment provides applicants. It brings them back in time

[99] Opinion of AG Kokott delivered in Case C-127/13P *Strack v Commission*, para 35.

and re-releases the stopwatch, the countdown for the institution to reply once more: 15 working days.

Case C-41/00P *Interporc v Commission*, Opinion of AG Léger

65 I would recall the case-law of this Court according to which, where the Court of First Instance sets aside the act of an institution, Article 176 of the Treaty requires the latter to take the measures necessary for compliance with the judgment. Both the Court of Justice and the Court of First Instance have held, in that regard, that 'the institution is required, in order to comply with the judgment and implement it fully, to have regard not only to the operative part of the judgment but also to the grounds which led to the judgment and constitute its essential basis, in so far as they are necessary in order to determine the exact meaning of what is stated in the operative part. It is those grounds which, on the one hand, identify the precise provision held to be illegal and, on the other, indicate the specific reasons which underlie the finding of illegality contained in the operative part and which the institution concerned must take into account when replacing the annulled measure.

66. However, the scope of application of Article 176 of the Treaty is limited.

67. Article 176 does not authorise this Court to issue directions to an institution where the Court has annulled a measure of that institution under Article 173 of the EC Treaty (now, after amendment, Article 230 EC).

68. It merely imposes a duty on the institution which adopted the annulled measure to ensure that any act intended to replace it is not affected by the same irregularities as those identified in the judgment of annulment. It does not, on the other hand, mean that this Court should, at the request of interested parties, determine the content of the measure intended to replace the annulled measure.

More often than not, an institutional reply refusing access will rely on a single exception from the menu at the disposal of institutions. In some cases, however, the institution may argue several exceptions at the same time.

A different and more difficult case still, is when several different exceptions are argued by the institution, in succession. That is to say, for example, one exception is volunteered at the beginning of proceedings, and while those arguments are in the process of being challenged by the applicant, the institution, later, volunteers another.

C. Successive Reasons for 'No'

Such incidents are often justified by the argument that time has moved on, and the factual circumstances surrounding the (reasons to refuse access to the) documents have changed.

i. Pick your Poison

The applicant is then burdened with multiple tasks. First, the initial explicit reasons for refusal must (continue to) be countered. If one desists, one must bear those costs. At the same time, the applicant is aware that if that (initial) lawsuit is successful, time will rewind to a moment at which the institution must provide a new answer.

And yet, the institution has done precisely that; it has anticipated the new answer to the old request.

In a certain sense, after it has been lodged, the institutions attempt to render the initial action for annulment superfluous.

The applicant is thus confronted with two problems: a first problem is if there is still any utility to be gained from pursuing the initial action for annulment to the end. The second problem is that the applicant must consider is if a challenge of the new reason—whilst an initial, previous, action for annulment is pending—is imperious.

ii. The First Problem

Once an initial explicit reason for 'No' is put forth, the applicant is always entitled to choose to conduct proceedings to their term.[100] The institutions are, in fact, being tried on a '*tempus commissi*'[101] basis. Therefore, it is the propriety of the context of each institutional reason for 'No' that will be judged. One at a time. In sum, explicit replies do not fall away in the face of late, ulterior reasons.[102]

Case T-29/08 *LPN v Commission*

100 In that regard, it must be recalled first of all that, in the context of an application for annulment under Article 230 EC, the legality of the contested measure falls to be assessed on the basis of the elements of fact and of law existing at the time when the measure was adopted (judgment of 11 March 2009 in Case T-121/05 *Borax Europe v Commission*, not published in the ECR, paragraph 48).

iii. The Second Problem

Is a challenge of a new explicit reason—whilst an initial, previous, action for the annulment of another explicit reason for 'No' is pending—imperious? Whatever the litigant's choice as to this dilemma may be, the deadline[103] for doing so is imperative. A different solution could be that the applicant request permission from the Court to amend his/her pleas in law to straddle successive reasons as well.

Case T-214/13 *Rainer Typke v Commission*

27 It should be borne in mind in this regard that, according to well-established case law, when a decision or a regulation of direct and individual concern to an individual is replaced, during the proceedings, by another measure with the same subject-matter, this is to be considered a new factor allowing the applicant to adapt his claims and pleas in law. It would

[100] Here, the *Wunenburger* jurisprudence, Case C-36/05P *Wunenburger v Commission* [2006] ECR I-10313, para 42, is held to operate, *a contrario*. See for more on this point Ch 6.

[101] Clearly, we are borrowing the expression from criminal law; we refer to the moment in which the reply is provided.

[102] And here the cutting difference between negative silences (Ch 6) and explicit replies may be gleaned; while the former capitulate in the face of late reasons, the latter stand until the end, regardless of other hurdles that arise. Both are useful, yet the latter are more resilient.

[103] This is subject to the time-limit of 2 months from the day on which the applicant gains knowledge of the same: Art 263 TFEU.

> be contrary to the principle of due administration of justice and to the requirements of procedural economy to oblige the applicant to make a fresh application. Moreover, it would be inequitable if the institution in question were able, in order to counter criticisms of a measure, contained in an application to the Courts of the European Union, to amend the contested measure or to substitute another for it and to rely in the proceedings on such an amendment or substitution in order to deprive the other party of the opportunity of extending his original pleadings to the later measure or of submitting supplementary pleadings directed against that measure.

IX. CONCLUSIONS

The deceptive simplicity of the 1993 Code of Conduct misled a significant part of the public. Access to documents did not seem important, interesting or groundbreaking. To many it was a non-topic. Was there even any strength in that Code? From 1993 until 2001 there was still a lot of talk about internal documents, most issues were still kept covert, and the litigant applicants were more concentrated on finding out whether they would be able to obtain injunctive relief from the Court rather than keen to discuss the differences between mandatory and discretionary exceptions.

With the advent of Regulation 1049/2001 many promises were made, some things changed, some got better, some became significantly worse.

First, documents to be made accessible were no longer principally the internal documents of the institutions since these became, to a large extent, specifically shielded from scrutiny by the new Article 4(3) of Regulation 1049/2001. Secondly, all (other) documents held by the EU were also overarched by the new rules. The Member States noticed quickly, since it was their documents that became the principal target of applicants. The institutions noticed (and might have experienced some relief). Applicants seem to have been slower to notice but, once they did, were eager to bring about situations in which they would cross-request the same documents both from a Member State and from an institution and then engage in comparative analysis of each of the addressee's standards of response.

Since it is no longer required that documents be read by the institutions before the former are refused, partial access, once applauded and celebrated as a victory, is often set aside by the judicature and has practically disappeared from the access scene. By contrast, Article 4(2), a provision thought to offer only a moderately severe degree of insulation of documents, has gained such support that even the mighty France (Case C-331/15P) requests the judicature to include various types of procedures under the spell of the third indent, 'investigations'.

The conservation of the environment rose and fell on the sword of the third indent of Article 4(2) as well. The ECJ has tried to convince us all that the second sentence of Article 6 of Regulation 1367/2006 ties relations with all of the exceptions in Article 4, those of Article 4(1) and 4(3) and even with some of Article 4(2), but wants to link with investigations. In consequence, access to environmental files follows a fate no different from access to all corners of investigative competition law proceedings (State aid, mergers, concerted practices etc): virtually impossible and framed in *dia-*

bolica probatio standards. It takes but a devil's wink for the principle of precaution to capitulate.

Attempting to tell this access tale is no easy task. Since the ECJ's vision of access is far removed from the promises made, both by Regulation 1049/2001 and by Regulation 1367/2006, refusal (in any of its undertones) is, in turn and more often than not, far removed from any real connection to the contested documents.

However, in spite of the many alternative situations recounted, the scheme of the many possible fates of an applicant that comes across an exception is not yet complete. It is true that it is difficult for an applicant to challenge even one exception. It is also true that challenging two or three, possibly in succession, is even more difficult. But there is one situation more difficult still: to know how to react appropriately when the institutions choose to answer by saying nothing.

6

Silence

I. INTRODUCTION—MUCH ADO ABOUT NOTHING?

THE UTILITY OF discussing the framework of silence of the EU institutions within a treatise concerning access to their internal documents could easily be misconstrued as a provocation. Most people underrate legal silence since the real silence that it is construed upon is an event that is not immediately perceptible. Legal silence advances into on-going proceedings without making any sound bites. It is also invisible. Finally, there is no case-by case notification (to applicants) of the fact that, because of it, an *ex lege* decision has been formed. All these reasons suggest that addressees may easily overlook decisions taken *ex lege*. Therefore, the discussion of their framework within a book about access is indispensable.

There are three points that need to be clarified in order to comprehend the EU courts' case law on this topic in particular and on refusals in general.

First, the discussion of the relationship between real silence and legal silence will allow us to better comprehend that any access policy is always set in place to enhance communication between an administration (here the EU) and its subjects. Therefore, it is in order to achieve this purpose that the structure of access procedures must be designed to deflect a specific threat: that the institutions might be allowed purposefully to undermine the procedure of communication by failing to respond to the requests of applicants.

Secondly, discussion will hopefully shed some light on whether it is an institutional *duty* to reply to applicants, or the *competence* to reply to applicants that endures, or not, beyond a given time frame.

Finally, the discussion of types of legal silence in particular will allow us to conclude the previous, and broader, discussion of refusals in general. In the previous chapter,[1] time was spent discussing explicit refusals to requests for access. In the present chapter we engage in the analysis of a second type of refusal, implicit refusals: silences, when they mean 'No'.

A. Giving the Emptiness in the Letter Box a Meaning

In practice, silence comes about when an applicant lodges a request for access with an institution of the EU and that institution does not reply. As a result of this institutional strategy, the applicant's letter box remains empty.

[1] See Ch 5.

No matter how many times the letter box is checked, nothing is there. Or, at least, nothing is discernible. And the applicant is thus left trapped in the anguish of interminable void. What, then, is there to gainfully discuss—from a legal point of view—when the object of the discussion is a nothingness?

Within the EU law of access, there are many ways of providing an adequate reply to a request for documents. In most cases, replies are written. However, if the law couples authentic silence with an imperative deadline, saying nothing at all is—from a legal point of view—just as acceptable. The law's paternalistic interference over what indeed is taking place produces a practical result. If institutions fail to reply in time, in lieu of an administrative decision, a substitute, automatic decision is provided by the law to the applicant. Hence, because of the advent of the decision *ex lege*, in that precise moment, authentic silence is not oblivion. Silence has meaning—ie either authorisation or refusal—and *is* an answer.

B. Positive and Negative Silence

Within administrative policies in general, the abovementioned decisions *ex lege* may emerge in two alternative forms of rules: 'positive silence' rules and/or 'negative silence' rules. Both forms are well known to the laws of the EU Member States.

In some cases the meaning 'Yes' prevails over and is ascribed to the absence of an actual reply: these are cases of positive silence. An example of this might be gleaned from hypothetical situations in which requests are addressed to institutions and where pressure is put on the institution under the form of a burden to object. In these cases, if, within a given time frame, institutions do not raise objections to propositions or requests addressed to them by applicants the same will be deemed to have been accepted or granted.

In *Torresi*,[2] Advocate General Wahl pointed out how both forms of legal silence have also found their way into EU law: 'By way of example, regarding positive silence rules, see Article 10(6) of Council Regulation (EC) No 139/2004 of 20 January 2004 on the control of concentrations between undertakings (the EC Merger Regulation)'. In fact, that particular provision states:

> Regulation 139/2004, Article 10(6)
>
> Where the Commission has not taken a decision in accordance with articles (…) within the time limits set out in paragraphs 1 and 3 respectively, the concentration is deemed to have been declared compatible with the common market

Therefore, once the deadline expires, it might be assumed that such compatibility (or, in other circumstances a right, or an authorisation) has been acknowledged.

In the aftermath of that assumption, the institution no longer needs to concern itself with the applicant's status. Positive silence saves time and resources and facilitates non-contentious relationships between applicants and institutions.

[2] In this sense, Opinion of AG Wahl, delivered on 10 April 2014, in Cases C-58/13 and C-59/13 *Torresi and Torresi v Consiglio Dell'Ordine degli Avvocati di Macerata* [not yet published] para 70.

On the contrary, in other cases the meaning 'No' prevails over and is ascribed to the absence of an actual reply: these are cases of negative silence. Within national administrative policies, access to documents in particular is structurally prone to be regulated by negative silence. The law of the EU is no exception. In *Torresi*,[3] accordingly, Advocate General Wahl points out that: 'regarding negative silence rules [in EU law], see Article 8(3) of Regulation (EC) No 1049/2001'. In fact, that particular provision states:

> Regulation 1049/2001, Article 8(3)
>
> Failure by the institution to reply [to a confirmatory application] within the prescribed time-limit [15 days] shall be considered a negative reply and shall entitle the applicant to institute court proceedings [...] or to make a complaint to the Ombudsman.

There are many reasons to prefer the negative route. At least one is that as possession is nine-tenths of the law, the applicant cannot simply proceed to waltz into the institutional premises unannounced and request to be conveyed to the archive. Someone still has to expect the applicant, open the door, accompany the applicant in, make the (right) documents available and assist in the making of copies. As an alternative, someone has to send the applicant the (right) documents by mail or e-mail.

And thus, in addition to the caution that the protection of conflicting interests requires, when beyond the expiration of any deadline the institution still needs to concern itself with the applicant, it is more prudent—and possibly preferable—to attribute the meaning 'No' to an absence of reply.

C. Negative Silence since the Implementing Decisions of the 1993 Code of Conduct

Although it was not clear from the 1993 Code of Conduct that consideration was to be given to institutional silence, the implementing Decisions of the Council and Commission stated otherwise:

> Council Decision 93/731
>
> Article 7(2). Failure to reply to an application within a month of submission shall be *equivalent to a refusal, except* where the applicant makes a confirmatory application, as referred to above, within the following month.
>
> Article 7(4). Failure to reply within a month of submission of the confirmatory application shall be *equivalent to a refusal.*
>
> Commission Decision 94/90
>
> Article 4. Failure to reply to an application for access to a document within one month of application being made constitutes an intention to refuse access. Failure to reply within one month of an application for review being made constitutes a refusal.

[3] ibid, para 70.

The access policy thus warmed to legal silence in the negative form. Therefore, since the early days, there has been room in the practice and in the case law[4] to discuss and develop thoughts about what should be done by applicants if the institutions fail to reply to an application.

Regulation 1049/2001 continued the progression of negative silence within the access policy since it embraced that procedural remedy as well. In fact, it is, as has been mentioned, certainly enshrined in Article 8(3), and is possibly also relevant (albeit *a contrario*) to the interpretation of Article 7(4). The current text is closer to the corresponding version of Commission Decision 94/90[5] than to the version adopted by the Council in Decision 93/731.[6] It is also true, as we will see below, that the EU courts have had ample opportunity to clarify the small nuances of the text that is in force today.

> Regulation 1049/2001
>
> 7(4) Failure by the institution to reply [to an application] within the prescribed time-limit [15 days] shall entitle the applicant to make a confirmatory application
>
> 8(3) Failure by the institution to reply [to a confirmatory application] within the prescribed time-limit [15 days] shall be considered a negative reply and shall entitle the applicant to institute court proceedings [...] or to make a complaint to the Ombudsman

D. Different Reactions to the Substitute Decision

Admittedly, the precise risk that the law seeks to redress here is paralysis of procedure. Legal silence may then gainfully be discussed as a procedural remedy unto itself, dissociated from implications regarding the merit of requests. However, although the law does deflect the risk of procedural paralysis, at the same time, the law neglects to address the emotional perception of this method by (some) applicants. A mere legal substitute is regarded as both more uncomfortable and as less useful than a proper reply.

When a deadline lapses, and still, a proper institutional reply does not arrive, the fact that it is the law, and not the institution, that provides a fictional reply, to which a meaning is attached, may be of little consolation. Applicants may still feel slighted. More precisely, they may feel offended by the omission. They will remonstrate and complain—to the world at large—about the rudeness of the institutions and may even go as far as pointing out that the rules on access are fraudulent since the institutions do not even bother to answer. And yet, more often than not, applicants who perceive silence in this manner will not pursue the matter further before an EU court.

[4] See eg Case T-19/96 *Carvel and Guardian Newspapers v Council* [1996] ECR II-01519 (*Carvel II*); and Case T-156/97 *Berge v Commission* [1997] ECR II-02097 (*Berge*), both regarding challenges to implied refusals whilst the 1993 Code of Conduct was in force.

[5] See text, above in this section I.C.

[6] See text, above in this section I.C.

More importantly, this impression of diminished institutional attention to an applicant's individual situation is enhanced by the fact that the institutional reply's replacement—the legal substitute provided—is not, nor could it be, reasoned. The law merely tells applicants that the institution refuses their request, yet the law, understandably, is unable to offer up reasons for 'No'.

In spite of these justified criticisms, legal silence *is* useful. Utility is not a simple term. Economic science has groomed it, but in doing so has ascribed the term so many nuances of interpretation that it would be hazardous here—in a book about the law—to use it without making a caveat. We will assume that utility simply means 'something productive'.

The point we wish to make is the following: because the legal fiction put in place by the law—a timely refusal *ex lege*—is so discreet, it is prone to be overlooked. Most persons will see silence as a nothing. Other persons, however, have recognised something in silence. Recognising such emptiness for what it is not—useless—they derive advantages from it.

II. THE ADVANTAGES OF 'NO', *EX LEGE*

The advantages of a rule of negative silence are threefold. First, it breaks the deadlock of interrupted communication. Next, it clarifies that a refusal has emerged. Finally, it affords applicants the opportunity to challenge that very refusal in a court of law.

A. The End to a Deadlock

Indeed, a first advantage that may be derived from a rule of negative silence is the end to a deadlock. In *ClientEarth*,[7] the GC clarified this point further. It held that this is only true if that silence is coupled with an imperative deadline. On that condition, at the precise moment in which a deadline lapses, a legal substitute advances

[7] Case T-278/11 *ClientEarth a.o. v Commission* [not reported], a ruling that expresses an exceptional protection of the GC of an applicant's legitimate expectations, paras 49–51:

> the multiple express undertakings made by the Commission, in its letters of 3 February, 28 February and 14 April 2011, as observed by the Court in paragraph 43 above, could have given rise to legitimate expectations, on the part of the applicants, that a final reply to the confirmatory application of 15 December 2010, was imminent. (…) that reply was not finally made until 3 February 2012, that is, the day before one year had passed after expiry of the prescribed time-limit provided in Article 8 of Regulation No 1049/2001. Therefore, the Commission clearly and seriously exceeded that limitation period. Having regard to the exceptional circumstances in which the Commission processed the confirmatory application, it is fair that the latter should pay, in addition to its own costs, three quarters of the costs incurred by the applicants. The applicants shall bear one quarter of their own costs.

This position of the GC, has, in principle—now that the point of law has been repeatedly clarified in the case law of the EU courts—been abandoned.

over authentic silence, and is considered to be a legal reply. Then, regardless of how far beyond that same moment *authentic* silence endures, the passing of the deadline completes a task and has an objective.[8] It puts a full stop to the anguish of waiting for an actual reply from the institution; the applicant is told by the law to put his/her mind at rest. In sum, both at the hand of the law, and in the eyes of the law, a reply *has* been made.

B. Clearly, the Meaning 'No'

A second advantage that may be derived from a rule of negative silence is meaning. A reply that is sent by the law to an applicant must have significance. The law resorts to a figure of fiction: the law pretends that silence means 'No'. The law gives no consideration to other possible combinations (the institution could not be bothered to answer/the institution does not care/the institution is unable to answer on time). The law of access, in particular, pretends, always,[9] that definitive silence means 'No'.

Thus, under any system that embraces negative, legal silence, when authentic silence opposes an applicant, it is as if—hence the fiction—the institution had instead, de facto, refused.

C. The Opportunity to Challenge a Definitive Refusal

Rules of negative silence do not give consideration to all forms of failure to reply. For example, they do not accord procedural relevance to silence that is provisional, in nature.

Before we proceed on this point, it is important to clarify that Regulation 1049/2001 allows applicants to apply for documents under any written form. However, it neither prescribes the form in which institutions should reply (electronic or not), nor that receipts of acknowledgement of the arrival of messages are a mandatory requirement of notifications:

> Regulation 1049/2001, Article 6
>
> Applications
>
> 1. Applications for access to a document shall be made in any written form, including electronic form, in one of the languages referred to in Article 314 of the EC Treaty and in a

[8] This classical interpretation of the function of deadlines, recently revived by AG Kokott in her Opinion in Case C-127/13P *Strack* [not yet reported], had been significantly watered down by the GC in Joined Cases T-355/04 and T-446/04 *Co-frutta II* [2010] ECR II–00001, para 59 and, according to the GC, the institution continues—beyond the deadline—to be burdened with the duty to reply explicitly in a reasoned manner. (Para 59 is quoted below in section IV.A.)

[9] It is important to keep in mind that pursuant to Case T-237/02 *Technische Glaswerke Ilmenau v Commission* [2006] ECR II-05131, paras 54–58 implied refusal only exists when the institution is put in a condition to understand what is asked of it by the applicant.

sufficiently precise manner to enable the institution to identify the document. The applicant is not obliged to state reasons for the application.

2. If an application is not sufficiently precise, the institution shall ask the applicant to clarify the application and shall assist the applicant in doing so, for example, by providing information on the use of the public registers of documents.

3. In the event of an application relating to a very long document or to a very large number of documents, the institution concerned may confer with the applicant informally, with a view to finding a fair solution.

4. The institutions shall provide information and assistance to citizens on how and where applications for access to documents can be made.

Consequently, applicants and institutions have been allowed to deal with this procedure with ample liberty. On this point, two statements are important: one is that the paper trail and the factual tempo of communications between applicants and institutions must be correctly reconstructed before an action before the courts is attempted. Another, is that proof of acknowledgement of receipt[10] of communications either in paper or electronic form,[11] although not prescribed, remains a cornerstone of the security of relationships with legal effects, and is, in case of dispute, the only way for the courts to, ex post facto,[12] ascertain the conduct of the administrative procedure.

This notwithstanding, when persons converse in a manner that is broken down into many episodes or parts, ie 'fractional communication', they increase the risk of

[10] See Joined Cases T–355/04 & T–446/04 *Co-frutta II* (n 8) para 42:

> As the Commission was not in a position to prove—in particular, by producing an acknowledgement of receipt—the date on which the applicant received the letter containing the decision of 10 August 2004, it must be held that, at the time when the action in Case T-355/04 was lodged, the applicant had an interest in bringing proceedings and that, at that date, the action was admissible.

Further on this point, a 'Note to Heads of Unit Responsible for Access to Documents Ref Ares (2014) 801872—19/03/2014' has been uploaded on the internet and consequently has come into the public domain. Therein the Commission expresses its concern with regard to the fact that 'transmission of formal replies only by email clearly does not provide for sufficient legal certainty as regards the respect of legal deadlines'; therefore, [from March 2014,] 'all negative replies (...) have to be *sent by registered mail with acknowledgement of receipt*. This is the only reliable method for getting a proof of delivery that would stand in Court'.

[11] See, on the problems arising from the lack of formality, judgment of the GC in Case T-167/10 *Europaiki Dynamiki* [not reported] paras 35–43 and esp para 49:

> In light of the content of the delivery report produced by the Commission and taking into account the statements set out by the parties in that regard, it must therefore be held that the Commission is not in a position to establish that the first contested decision was brought to the attention of its intended recipient on 27 January 2010 as it claims. There are strong indications that the document mentioned above comes from the Commission's IT system and there is no evidence enabling it to be established that the applicant's IT system guarantees proper receipt of the e-mail by its intended recipient in the same way as, for example, the intended recipient's signature or the signature of a person recognised as competent for that purpose in the event of a notification carried out by an express delivery service with acknowledgment of receipt.

[12] See order of the GC in Case T-17/10 *Steinberg* [not reported] paras 19–21 in which the applicant alleges that the Commission sent him an empty envelope.

confusion. On occasion, applicants (and institutions) send messages to one another, without clarifying context to the standard requisite, and often without clear indication if the current message is meant to be ancillary to an earlier one, or is a new or confirmatory application in its own right.[13] When one tries to make sense of a string of additions and clarifications with regard to an initial application for documents, it is enough to make one feel sorry that the world ever moved beyond the stamped letter. Those, at least, always began with 'Re your letter of date X'.

Nostalgia aside, what remains central is that, first, institutions are able to understand the first date from which documents are being asked for. Secondly, which documents are being requested? Thirdly, if an applicant asks for a list of documents, say 1–10, and the institution requests (only with regard to some, say 1, 3, 5, 7, 9) that the applicant be more precise, then (1) with regard to documents 2, 4, 6, 8, if within 15 working days (from the initial request) there is no answer from the institution, unless the applicant is willing to forego entitlement, a confirmatory application with regard to those must be made; and (2) with regard to documents 1, 3, 5, 7, 9, the applicant's response to the clarification request is, still, part of the initial application. Fourthly, the situation may be worsened if, in a message to the applicant, the institution merely extends the deadlines for a reply. That message is not a reply; it is an extension. Clearly, it is easy to lose track of where an application ends and a reply should begin.

On the assumption that the factual context and tempo context are well understood, rules of negative silence only regulate failure to reply if it is apt to express a final[14] position of an institution. Significance of finality of an institutional position is, in essence, what the applicant is here provided by the law. A meaningful final position of the institution is, thus, the necessary and sufficient condition for the applicant to be able to protest further. Indeed, definitive refusals of own pretensions are the necessary foundations on which challenges to institutional decisions must be construed. Consequently, the utility that is to be derived from a refusal *ex lege*, born of a rule of negative silence, is the subsequent option to attack a challengeable measure.

The EU courts have allocated a considerable amount of their energy in regard to the definition of 'challengeable measure'.[15] With regard to access to documents in particular, settled case law has been consistent in underlining the fact that reasoned responses to initial applications[16] were not definitive. The case law has also been

[13] See eg order of the GC 24 March 2011 in Case T-36/10 *Internationaler Hilfsfonds v Commission* [2011] ECR II-01403, paras 25–27; judgment of the GC of 19 March 2013 in Case T-301/10 *Int'Veld v Commission* [not yet published] (*Int'Veld I*) para 24.

[14] In principle, only replies to confirmatory applications are final positions of the institutions.

[15] See Case T-188/97 *Rothmans v Commission* [1999] ECR II-02463, paras 31 and 32 in contrast to Case T-106/99 *Meyer v Commission* [1999] ECR II-03273, paras 23 and 31–35 (refusal to give a reply or information); Case C-193/01 *Pitsiorlas v Council and ECB* [2003] ECR I-04837 and Joined Cases T-3/00 and T-337/04 *Pitsiorlas v Council and ECB* [2007] ECR II-04779, paras 78 and 109; Case T-47/01 *Co-frutta I* [2003] ECR II-04441, paras 29–31; Case T-237/02 *TGI I* [2006] ECR II-05131, paras 54–58. Interestingly, the order in Case T-151/03 *Nuova Agricast v Commission* [2005] ECR II-01967, paras 33 and 34 is rendered in contrast to settled case law (T-174/95 *Svenska* [1998] ECR II-02289) concerning situations in which access is attempted to documents already in the applicant's possession.

[16] See eg Case T-47/01 *Co-frutta I* (n 15) and Joined Cases T-355/04 and T-446/04 *Co-frutta II* (n 8).

consistent in underlining that, by analogy, the absences of response to initial applications were not to be considered definitive, either:

> Case C-127/13 *Strack v Commission*
>
> 36. It is clear from the case law of the Court that the procedure for access to documents held by the institutions is carried out in two stages and that the response to an initial application, within the meaning of Article 7(1) of Regulation No 1049/2001 is only the first position adopted which, in principle, cannot be subject to an appeal.

This interpretation is, moreover, supported by the text of Article 7(4) of Regulation 1049/2001.[17] Consequently, having received no answer to an initial application, if the applicant wishes to involve the EU judicature, it has always been incumbent on the applicant to have made a confirmatory application to the same institution, and to have waited for a second answer.

Settled case law notwithstanding, the judgment in *Internationaler Hilfsfonds*[18] muddied the waters. It conceded that, on occasion, an institution might express a definitive position in a reply to an initial application. Furthermore, subsequent case law (*Strack*) has also embraced that view, reinforcing the exception:

> Case C-127/13 *Strack v Commission*
>
> 36. However, exceptionally, where an institution adopts a definitive position with such a response [to an initial application], it may be subject to an action for annulment.

In the light of this proviso, it is important to state, first, that the refusals at which both judgments (*Internationaler Hilfsfonds* and *Strack*) were directed were explicit and reasoned. Secondly, that, in principle, there is no theoretical basis to apply, by analogy, the second part of paragraph of *Strack* to refusals *ex lege*. The latter do not—since they structurally cannot—include a statement of reasons. As so vividly put by the GC in *Williams*,[19] refusals *ex lege* represent 'an absolute failure to state reasons'. Therefore, there is no textual basis on which to ground any legitimate assumption proposing that the status of a silent response to an initial application is definitive. Thus, as regards the implications of legal silence, one should not stray from the terms of Regulation 1049/2001. Concluding, only a refusal *ex lege* that is a response to a confirmatory application is ever definitive.

III. DEADLINES

If refusals *ex lege* come forth upon the expiry of a deadline, it is necessary to shed light on relevant deadlines that—within the EU law of access—have a bearing on silent forms of an institutional 'No'.

[17] See above, section I.C.

[18] Judgment of 26 January 2010, in Case T-36/10 *Internationaler Hilfsfonds* (n 13) para 62, in which the ECJ acknowledged the status of final measure attaching to an explicit response to an initial application since, *in casu*, the Commission had, of its own accord, described the reply (to an initial application) as 'definitive' and, furthermore, had not reminded the applicant of the entitlement to make a confirmatory application.

[19] Case T-42/05 *Williams v Commission* [2008] ECR II-00156, paras 96–97.

A. Two Relevant Sets of Deadlines Emerge from the Rules that Govern Explicit Replies

The deadlines we will now refer to have been discussed, with regard to explicit refusals, in Chapter 5. Indeed, if we were in a world in which the institutions always managed to reply explicitly, and, of their own volition, it would not be necessary to address these deadlines once again. However, there are some relevant operational details that differ when refusal is merely implicit.

First, it is a pair of deadlines (both, 15 working days, extendable once by a further 15 working days), laid down in Articles 7 and 8 of Regulation 1049/2001, that are of relevance to this discussion. This first group of deadlines operates within what is known as the pre-litigious 'two-stage administrative procedure' of requests for access.

Secondly, another deadline, related to the time frame within which an applicant who has been addressed a definitive refusal must decide whether or not to institute proceedings against the refusing institution before the EU judicature, is also relevant to this discussion. It is currently set at two months, and is laid down in Article 263 TFEU.[20]

B. The Current Framework of Real Silence and an Imperative Deadline

Regulation 1049/2001 lays down the implications of absences of reply in the following way:

> 7(4) Failure by the institution to reply [to an application] within the prescribed time-limit [15 days] shall entitle the applicant to make a confirmatory application
>
> 8(3) Failure by the institution to reply [to a confirmatory application] within the prescribed time-limit [15 days] shall be considered a negative reply and shall entitle the applicant to institute court proceedings [...] or to make a complaint to the Ombudsman

i. The Utility of the Enabling Act in the First Stage of the Administrative Procedure

As a consequence of the current version, under Article 7(4) of Regulation 1049/2001, if within 15 working days of the registration of any applicant's request for access, the institution does not send out a reply to the applicant, then all actors involved (applicants, institutions) pretend that there is no legal obstacle to the fact that, without knowing what the institution's first opinion on access to the contested documents is, the applicant is entitled to embark on a second attempt to obtain an explicit opinion from the same institution.

[20] On disputes over the calculation of this specific deadline, see Case T-278/11 *ClientEarth a.o.* (n 7) 39.

The primary purpose of this first legal mechanism is to allow communication with the institution to proceed to a definitive stage. It is a purely facilitating mechanism. We must not, and indeed may not, assume that the institution refused.[21] The applicant is merely given a second chance to talk to the institution. An applicant who has been ignored is, in fact, reshuffled—by the law—into the position of any applicant whose initial application has been explicitly refused. The moment the deadline lapses, that moment of authentic silence simply gives rise to an enabling act on which the applicant may ground an own option:[22] the applicant's decision of whether or not to use the next rung in the ladder: a confirmatory application.

In practice, the applicant becomes entitled to re-submit the initial application, unchanged, for reconsideration by the institution.

ii. The Utility of Silences that Mean 'No' in the Second Stage of the Administrative Procedure

A different logic was construed with Article 8(3) of Regulation 1049/2001, which deals with confirmatory applications. Here, if a timely response does not arrive, everyone involved (applicants, institutions and possibly the Court) pretends first, that the institution *did* reply, and secondly, that the institution, having replied, said 'No'.

According to Article 8(3), if an institution does not respond to an applicant's second call within 15 working days, and does not provide the applicant with an explicit, definitive, institutional position as to whether the applicant may access the contested documents or not, the law does so in its stead. The law fictions a negative reply.[23] The law discharges—by default—the duty of the institution. Finally, what we conclude is that negative silence is an act. It exists not only to regulate definitively—on behalf of the institution—the status of the request for access: refused, but also to convey the applicant to the door of the Court. The applicant is thus entitled to institute court proceedings,[24] with a view to having the refusal *ex lege* annulled.

It is never too much to repeat that deadlines are imperative for applicants.[25] Therefore two months—after the negative silence is formed—is the maximum amount of time during which an applicant is allowed to consider, first, whether there

[21] Although we have defended the inapplicability—to silence—of *Internationaler Hilfsfonds* (n 13) and *Strack* (n 8), it is never redundant to look out for such an incident in future cases.

[22] As we have mentioned, this option is, concomitantly, an *ex ante* burden imposed on the applicant, that must be discharged before judicial proceedings are attempted.

[23] In Case C-127/13P *Strack* (n 8) para 33, AG Kokott qualified an implicit act of refusal as undoubtedly negative on the basis of an absolute presumption.

[24] We are not considering the alternative route of a complaint to the Ombudsman.

[25] However, this is not always true for institutions. On this point, see Case T-534/11 *Schenker v Commission* [not yet published] para 134 in contrast to para 125. See Case T-167/10 *Europaïki Dynamiki* (n 11) paras 35 and 51, in which the Court considered that applicant's challenge to a refusal to be 'out of time'.

is utility to be derived from annulling silence, and secondly to whom the utility—if it exists—is beneficial.[26]

What remains central, in any case, is that if the deadline lapses and the applicant has not lodged an action for annulment against the implicit institutional decision with the first instance court of the EU,[27] the epilogue is favourable to the institution.[28] The decision to refuse the applicant access, already definitive—since it reflects a final institutional position on access to the contested documents—also becomes definitively unsusceptible of being challenged before the judicature.

However, before we move on to discuss further issues, it should be noted that the conclusion that a 'Silence that means "No"' definitively regulates the status of a request for access is not shared by everyone. This intricate theoretical problem presupposes the clarification of a prior issue: Do any institutional tasks endure beyond imperative deadlines? And, if any do, is it only an institutional *duty* to provide a reasoned reply that endures or is it also the institutional *competence* to do so that remains?

IV. BEYOND THE DEADLINE

A. A Duty that Outlives the Time Frame of the Deadline

A first proposition of how to equate the tasks of institutions beyond the imperative deadline lingered for six years[29] and was, finally, addressed in 2010. In *Co-frutta II*, the GC held that both the duty and the competence to provide a reasoned reply to the applicant exist until the deadline and both endure beyond it. Moreover, duty and competence endure in spite of a silence that means 'No'. Consequently, negative silence does not regulate the request's status definitively. It does so only temporarily. Within this view, legal silence resembles a nothing much more than it resembles an act.

T-355/04 & T-446/04 *Co-Frutta II*

> 59 There is no legal principle which results in the administration losing its power to respond to an application, even outside the time-limits laid down for that purpose. The mechanism of an implied refusal decision was established in order to counter the risk that the administration would choose not to reply to an application for access to documents and

[26] There may be danger of a misalignment of private benefits of suit against the social benefits of suit.

[27] Case T-236/06 *Landtag Schleswig-Holstein v Commission* [2008] ECR II-00461 & C-406/06 [not yet published] & T-68/07 [not yet published] & C-281/08P [not yet published] clarify by whom a case may be commenced directly at ECJ level.

[28] The applicant is actually placed under a burden: to challenge the refusal *ex lege* by way of an action seeking annulment and/or by way of an action for damages. If none of these options is undertaken, the applicant subsequently loses any entitlement to complain (about the silence). In this sense, see Case T-456/13 *Sea Handling v Commission* [not yet published].

[29] The question was raised in Case T-355/04 *Co-frutta II* (n 8), lodged on 23 October 2004 and answered on 19 January 2010. *En passant*, Case T-355/04 was subsequently joined with Case T-446/04 *Co-frutta* (n 8).

> escape review by the courts, not to render unlawful every decision which is late. On the other hand, the administration is required, in principle, to provide—even late—a reasoned response to every application by a citizen. That approach is consistent with the function of the mechanism of the implied refusal decision, which is to enable citizens to challenge inaction on the part of the administration with a view to obtaining a reasoned response.

It is also noteworthy that the practice of the EU judicature often lent support to such an interpretation. Even today, if an applicant chooses not to challenge a refusal *ex lege*, the same applicant will not be barred[30] from instituting proceedings against an express refusal rendered even many months after the implied refusal.

As we will discuss in more detail below,[31] in such a setting, and as a consequence of the interpretation put forth, if a late (reasoned) answer follows, the applicant is bound to suffer it. In other words, with the advent of a late reply the fact that concrete reasons have been put forth is applauded to the point of overriding any (due) reprimand of the (subsequent) decision's tardiness.

B. A Late Reply is just an Option

Four years later, in *Strack*,[32] Advocate General Kokott defended a very different position. The Advocate General suggested that the definitive status of an implicit refusal (refusal *ex lege*) is upheld by an absolute presumption.

> Opinion of AG Kokott Case C-127/13P *Strack v Commission*
>
> 33. In that connection, the Court has already held that the announcement of an express, subsequent decision cannot prevent either the fiction of an implied refusal or the commencement of the time-limit for bringing proceedings. If an application has already been implicitly refused, a subsequent, express decision does not—contrary to the view of the Commission—trigger a new time-limit for bringing proceedings.
>
> 34. Where an applicant allows himself to be put off by the Commission, he risks, as a result, an action brought against a subsequent, express decision being dismissed because it is directed against a decision which merely confirms a previous decision.

Under this view, once a refusal *ex lege* comes forth, the institution is definitively (and irreversibly) presumed to have—at that defining moment—refused access. Negative silence, is thus an act, a substantive one. On the one hand, it puts an end to the duty to reply. On the other hand, what it does not do is disenfranchise institutional *competence* to reply late. In other words, only the institutional *duty to reply* is extinguished by negative silence.

[30] It is open to the EU courts to raise the issue of inadmissibility, of their own motion. However, in the Cases T-29/08 *LPN v Commission* [2011] ECR II-06021; T-17/10 *Steinberg* (n 12); and T-456/13 *Sea Handling* (n 28) the GC allowed challenges directed only at the (late) express refusal.

[31] Section IV.C. i of this chapter.

[32] Case C-127/13P *Strack* (n 8).

This new and recent interpretation does not impinge on previous and indispensable pillars of the access case law:

First, that the deadline to challenge an institutional (implicit) act—'No'—must be considered to be a rule of public order.

Next, this position is not irreconcilable with an argument in favour of acknowledgement, in such cases, of the concomitant endurance of an institutional option to provide the applicant with a second act. Beyond the deadline. A late reply as an option, along with its inherent consequences,[33] remains within the sphere of institutional discretion.

In any case, a late reasoned reply, if it takes the form of a reasoned refusal, cannot be equated as a reply to the earlier confirmatory application. It is, instead, a second institutional answer provided late, merely ancillary to a first principal legal answer—'No'—that has already been provided in reply to the applicant's confirmatory application.[34] Consequently, a late refusal *ex lege* is, at the most, an institutional confirmatory act.[35]

C. Effects on Procedure

The late (reasoned) answer—since it is merely ancillary—is not a necessary prerequisite of two important procedural requirements.

First, the advent of a late answer is not a prerequisite for the initial refusal *ex lege* to be challenged,[36] since a refusal *ex lege* may (*ipso facto*) be challenged on the basis that it breaches the institutional duty to provide reasons.

Secondly, the advent of a late answer is not a prerequisite for the period allowed for commencing proceedings (against a refusal *ex lege*) to start running. Much to the contrary, AG Kokott issues a serious warning:

> Opinion of AG Kokott Case C-127/13P *Strack v Commission*
>
> 34. Where an applicant allows himself to be put off by the Commission, he risks, as a result, an action brought against a subsequent, express decision being dismissed because it is directed against a decision which merely confirms a previous decision. He must even fear the Commission relying on the time-limit for bringing proceedings against the implied

[33] See eg the order of the GC in Case T-419/13 *Unión de Almacenistas de Hierros de España v Commission* [not yet published], in which the costs of proceedings (to challenge the refusal *ex lege*) were imposed on the institution and in which the applicant was able to subsequently challenge the late explicit reply.

[34] Logically, *a contrario*, a late granting of access does not confirm a previous 'No' *ex lege*. It overturns the previous *ex lege* decision, in principle revoking it.

[35] A pause for clarification of terminology is not wasted here. In AG Kokott's Opinion, the usage of the word 'confirmatory' both in regard to (1) the confirmatory application and to (2) the nature of the ancillary late act may cause some confusion. Therefore it is not redundant to explain that AG Kokott simply raises the point that a late reasoned refusal merely confirms what the applicant has already been told, by the refusal *ex lege*.

[36] On this specific point, see Case C-225/08P *Nuova Agricast v Commission* [2009] ECR I-00111 (*Nuova Agricast II*), order of the ECJ of 29 June 2009, para 60.

> refusal being exceeded, even though the Commission has previously repeatedly availed itself of further extensions to the processing time-limits.
>
> 35. Even if the Commission were to refrain from claiming that proceedings had been initiated out of time, or if it were to be barred from raising that objection because to do so would be to act in bad faith (*venire contra factum proprium*), the action brought would not necessarily be admissible. This is because the courts may examine of their own motion whether the time-limit for bringing proceedings has been observed as a mandatory procedural requirement, even though the General Court does not appear to do so systematically in proceedings concerning access to documents.

Subsequently, in *Sea Handling*,[37] the GC clarified the point further, using a provocative argument. The GC rebuked the applicant for not having challenged a refusal *ex lege*. Moreover, whilst not dismissing, of its own motion, the action against a subsequent, express decision, the GC stated that if the applicant chooses to ignore the refusal *ex lege* and challenge *only* the subsequent, express decisions, these, although rendered beyond the imperative deadlines of Article 8 of Regulation 1049/2001, will not be annulled on the basis of tardiness.[38]

Although we concur with the GC with regard to this approach, it would have been preferable if, when making this fundamental point, the Court had used a different expression to the one that it, *in casu*, employed. The Court held that although it would not annul the decision for tardiness, the deadlines of Article 8 had been breached, ie violated,[39] when, in truth, the argument that here excludes annulment is that such deadlines are rendered inviolable, by the earlier refusal *ex lege* that is, essentially, a timely act.

i. Challenges of Silence

Table 6.1: Challenges to Silence

Cases in which refusal *ex lege* silence is challenged		Cases in which refusal *ex lege* is left unchallenged and challenge to subsequent express decision argues breach of Articles 8(1) and (2)	
We expect costs of proceedings imposed on institution		We expect costs (for breach of deadlines) imposed on applicant	
First Instance	Appeal	First Instance	Appeal
T-196/96 *Carvel II*			
T-156/97 *Berge*			
T-355/04 & T-446/04 *Co-frutta II* (Exception)			

(continued)

[37] Judgment of the GC, of 25 March 2015 in Case T-456/13 *Sea Handling* (n 28).
[38] ibid, para 38.
[39] ibid, para 30: 'Il est constant que les délais prévus par les dispositions susvisées ont été violés'.

Table 6.1: (***Continued***)

Cases in which refusal *ex lege* silence is challenged		Cases in which refusal *ex lege* is left unchallenged and challenge to subsequent express decision argues breach of Articles 8(1) and (2)	
T-42/05 *Williams*			
T-203/06 *Eurostrategies* (holding reply)			
T-392/07 *Strack*	C-127/13P *Strack*		
T-494/08 to T-500/08 and T-509/08 *Ryanair*		T-29/08 *LPN*	
T-245/09 *Shell Hellas* (split)			
T-251/09 *Societé des Petroles Shell* (shared)			
T-359/09 *Jurašinović* (split)			
T-120/10 *ClientEarth*		T-17/10 *Steinberg*	
T-291/10 *Martin*			
T-395/10 *Stichting*			
T-449/10 *ClientEarth*			
T-14/11 *Timab*			
T-88/11 *BIA Separations*			
T-111/11 *ClientEarth* (Exception-shared)	C-612/13P		
T-211/11 *Timab* (Shared)		T-278/11 *Client Earth* (Exception)	
T-330/11 *Mastercard*			
T-341/11 *Ecologistas en Accion*			
T-362/11 *Stichting Greenpeace* (applicant did not apply for costs)			
T-418/12 *Beninca*			
T-56/13 *ClientEarth*			
T-241/13 *Typke*			
T-419/13 *Union Almacenistas*		T-456/13 *Sea Handling*	

After *Strack*, with the advent of *Sea Handling*, the pieces of silence finally fall into place, and, in hindsight, lend consistency to the case law delivered thereupon. In over 20 actions[40] lodged against silence (ie a refusal *ex lege*) none has ever reached its term without a late express refusal or late express granting of the documents

[40] Own computation.

coming forth. Moreover, with the exceptions of *Co-frutta II*, *Eurostrategies*, *Shell*, *Jurašinović*, *ClientEarth*, *Timab*, *Green Peace* and *Typke*, the GC has consistently imposed the costs on the institutions of the challenge to refusals *ex lege* on the institutions.

On the contrary, with regard to cases in which silence is not challenged, and an action for annulment is directed solely at the late express refusal, with the notable exception of *ClientEarth*, the Court has given no consideration to the de facto tardiness of the express refusal, when it rules on the imposition of costs. Consequently, costs (if such a head of claim is presented) will be imposed on the applicant.

The Court's practice suggests that if an applicant does not challenge silence, then the applicant is content to permit the refusal *ex lege* to become definitive. Thus, when a refusal *ex lege* is left unchallenged, subsequent answers, therefore, are not late. And should not be measured against the moment in which a(n express) reply was due. Lateness is not an argument that applicants are allowed to wield successfully against express refusals that are issued after legal silence.[41] Subsequent answers simply exist, as a bonus, as non-demandable additions to the timely refusal (*ex lege*).

Indeed, even *Co-frutta II* did not couple the 'duty and power to reply beyond the deadline' with any (further) deadline. It was assumed that the institutions would reply expressly (if they ever did) whenever they were ready to do so. Thus, what may be challenged in subsequent answers is not their tempo, but, conversely, only the explicit reason(s) they bring forth to justify refusal.

Therefore, if, on the one hand, the refusal *ex lege* is challenged and a subsequent answer comes forth (whilst proceedings are pending) the applicant will, in principle,[42] be authorised to amend the pleas in law, previously directed only at the refusal *ex lege*. Moreover, when the applicant challenges the refusal *ex lege*, and a subsequent answer comes forth, it is not the (de facto) belated conduct of the institution that carries weight with the Court,[43] in favour of the applicant. Rather,

[41] This position had already come forth in the order of the GC of 27 November 2011 in Case T-17/10 *Steinberg* (n 12) paras 101–02:

> Under Article 8(3) of Regulation No 1049/2001, that implicit decision could have been the subject-matter, on the part of the applicant, of Court proceedings in accordance with the provisions of Article 263 TFEU or of a complaint to the European Ombudsman. The applicant did not, however, make use of either of those opportunities, preferring to bring an action for annulment of the contested decision, by which the Commission provided an express and final reply to his confirmatory application and, therefore, implicitly withdrew the implicit decision to refuse access.
>
> Those are the only legal consequences to be drawn in the present case from the Commission's failure to reply to the confirmatory application within the prescribed period. In particular, that fact cannot render the contested decision unlawful in such a way as to justify its annulment.

However, as we have said, AG Kokott refused to qualify the subsequent reply as a reply to the confirmatory application.

[42] See, *a contrario*, when the applicant does not wish to do so, order of the GC of 9 November 2011 in Case T-449/10 *ClientEarth and Others v Commission* [not yet published] para 51.

[43] ibid, para 45:

> In view of the factual circumstances characterising the present case and, in particular, given that the Commission manifestly exceeded the time-limits under Article 8(1) of Regulation No 1049/2001 for replying to the confirmatory application, with the result that the applicants had no other choice, in order to safeguard their rights, than to bring the present action against the implied decision of refusal, the Commission must be ordered to bear its own costs and to pay those incurred by the applicants.

importance is shifted to the point that the applicant (in the challenge to the refusal *ex lege*) had been obliged to defend own procedural rights. Thus, to a great extent, it is the prior challenge of the 'absolute failure to state reasons' that lends the applicant a helping hand.[44]

On the other hand, if the applicant does not challenge the refusal *ex lege* and merely challenges a subsequent express decision (as—inter alia—happened in *LPN I*, *Steinberg* and *Sea Handling*) the temporal conduct of the institution, however 'deplorable' is, from a procedural point of view, not capable of censure by annulment.[45]

In sum, we have identified one procedural utility of negative silence: as it ensures the option that an *ex lege* definitive act may be challenged in court. We have still to discuss a second utility: crossing the Court's threshold. What utility lies in the exercise of the option: what intrinsic utility lies in an action that requests the GC to strike down silence?

V. THE PURPOSE OF STRIKING DOWN NOTHING

As we have said many times before, the access setting is one without positive injunctions. And thus, one might question the practical relevance of requesting the EU courts to remove silence since, after all, those same courts, post-annulment, are unable to order the institutions either to speak or to act.[46] Moreover, the EU courts cannot grant access to applicants of their own motion. It might seem then that, in spite of annulment, the applicant remains hostage to the capriciousness of the institutions. It is undisputed that, post-annulment, the institutions will be placed

[44] With the benefit of hindsight, there is a good explanation for the more generous nature of the GC's order in Case T-291/10 *Martin v Commission* [not reported] and in the decision of Case T-494/08 *Ryanair v Commission* [2010] ECR II-05723 (in which the applicants challenged silence) when measured against the decisions in Case T-29/08 *LPN I* (n 30), Case T-17/10 *Steinberg* (n 12) and Case T-456/13 *Sea Handling* (n 28) (in which the applicants only challenged the subsequent, express decision). It is, concomitantly, yet another argument in the sense that *Co-frutta II* (n 8) was iniquitous (since the applicant challenged silence).

[45] Judgment of the GC in Case T-456/13 *Sea Handling* (n 28) para 38. In the original language the term employed is '*deplorevoli*'. However, in French, 'Il ressort de ce qui précède que la Commission pouvait valablement prendre la décision attaquée et que cette dernière, bien que tardive, ne saurait être annulée sur la base de l'irrégularité procédurale constituée par les dépassements des délais susmentionnés, pour *regrettables* qu'ils soient'.

[46] It should be kept in mind that the lack of competence to address orders to the institutions—in annulment proceedings—was not always obvious from the courts' case law. First, the order of the ECJ of 6 December 1990 in Case C-2/88 *IMM—Zwartveld and Others* [1990] ECR I-04405, para 13, must be considered an outlier. Secondly, albeit within the boundaries of interim relief, orders that enjoin institutions *not* to disclose documents must be taken into account. Thirdly, in Case T-610/97R *Hanne Norup Carlsen, Ingeborg Fangel, Nicolas Fischer, Jørgen Erik Hansen, Marianne Henriksen, Ole Donbæk Jensen, Yvonne Petersen, Iver Reedtz-Thott, Lars Ringholm and Arne Würgler v Council of the European Union* [1998] ECR II-00485, para 34 and paras 55 and 56, an injunction was refused the applicants, merely because it would 'neutralise in advance the consequences of the judgment in the main proceedings'. Fourthly, it was only in Case T-124/96 *Interporc Im- und Export v Commission* [1998] ECR II-00231 that the argument with regard to lack of competence to enjoin was raised, and that prior rulings, Case C-15/85 *Consorzio Cooperative d'Abruzzo v Commission* [1987] 001005, para 18 and Case C-394/94 *France-Aviation*, para 42, were called on to support the statement.

under an obligation to take a new decision,[47] but it is also undisputed that it may well be the case that those same institutions will say nothing, again.[48] In spite of all these arguments, which highlight the non-practical side of the annulment of refusals *ex lege*, we believe that the exact contrary might be said: striking down silence is eminently practical.

A. What Head of Claim?

The first point we wish to address is: what should an applicant put before the judicature in a challenge to negative silence?

> I asked for a document from an EU institution yet I obtained no explicit reply within the designated deadlines. I don't know why I was refused access to the document. I was simply refused access to a document. I request the court strike down the (unreasoned) refusal.

In fact, it is arguable that the applicant should say more than this (or even be obliged to provide arguments not already put forth in the confirmatory application as to why documents should[49] be released). In fact, the structural absence of a statement of reasons in a refusal *ex lege* is—alone—sufficient to undermine the validity of such an act.[50] The EU courts are, thus, simply bound to acknowledge that no reasons are offered in that act and thus, *ipso facto*, that it breaches the requirement of Article 296(2) TFEU that 'legal acts shall state the reasons on which they are based'. Annulment is practically inevitable.[51]

[47] See Joined Cases T-355/04 and T-446/04 *Co-frutta II* (n 8) para 46.

[48] See, by analogy, Case T-124/96 *Interporc* (n 46) paras 59 and 60.

[49] Although this issue has been discussed in Ch 5, on this point it is important to take up the discussion regarding 3 points discussed in that chapter:

> 1. Regulation 1049/2001 explicitly excuses the applicant from having to provide the institutions with any (personal) reasons for an application. However, in the face of any explicit refusal, only the identification of an overriding public interest in disclosure will justify access.
>
> 2. The question of who is under the duty to identify an overriding public interest. Although more recent case law (Joined Cases C-514/11P and C-605/11P *LPN and Finland* [not reported]; *Strack* (n 8)) seems to impose this burden on the applicant, it is not clear if the institutions share the burden as well.
>
> 3. The moment in which such an identification must be made it not clear either. Possibly, the burden must be discharged within the initial application.

[50] In this sense, see Case T-42/05 *Williams* (n 19) paras 96–97.

[51] As was the case eg in the judgment of the GC in Case T-42/05 *Williams* (n 19) paras 83, 93 and 96–97. However, if an express refusal ensues an implied refusal, although proceedings against the implied refusal will be discontinued, it is clear that were it not for the subsequent, express refusal, the fate of proceedings would have been (automatic) annulment: order of the GC, Case T-120/10 *ClientEarth a.o. I*; order of the GC, Case T-291/10 *Martin v Commission* (n 44); Case T-449/10 *ClientEarth II* (n 42); order of the GC, Case T-419/13 *Unión Almacenistas* (n 33).

B. The Place (in Time) after Annulment

Annulling, or striking down a refusal *ex lege* serves to remove the implications of the earlier silence from the applicant-institution equation. Furthermore, within the access context, striking down anything (whether explicit or implicit) merely opens up a void. Therefore, a refusal born of silence is no different from an explicit refusal. As with the latter, if the former is struck down a void opens up. Moreover, it makes no difference if before the (judge-made) void comes about (by annulment) a merely fictional act/decision was in place.

Next, as has been noted, when any definitive institutional act is annulled, time is brought back to the moment in which the applicant's confirmatory application has reached the institution. Consequently, the institution is bound—again—to issue a new decision, in regard to the old request. That is, what, in the eyes of the Court, any annulment provides applicants. The stopwatch starts again in expectation of the advent of a new, again definitive, decision.

Finally, from the applicant's point of view, clearly then, there is an advantage in challenging a refusal *ex lege* before the EU judicature. The (unacceptable) alternative would be to wait, possibly in vain, for an institution to provide a late explicit answer.

One might conclude, then, that silences that mean 'No', albeit less informative about institutional reasons for refusal, are useful. As would be the case with explicit refusals, if either of these challenges were won in court, all applicants would be brought back to the same place: the moment in time from which the institution has 15 working days to decide anew, definitively.

Curiously what the challenge to silence has always brought about, empirically, is a late answer. No challenge to silence has been allowed to proceed to final judgment without a late explicit answer coming forth pending proceedings against silence.

This might be the reason why the judicature is (generally) friendly to applicants that challenge refusals *ex lege* … and (respectfully submitted) unfriendly to those who do not. The former will see the costs of proceedings imposed on the institutions, the latter will not. Moreover, the latter are not allowed to complain about the explicit refusal's lateness.

If what the judicature values is that an explicit answer—albeit late—must come forth, then it should be brought to the attention of the legislator that injunctions *de facere* 'Answer the applicant!' might be in order here.

In our view the judicature is at once, too optimistic and too severe. Too optimistic because there is no certainty that the challenge to silence will bring forth an explicit refusal. It is no more than a statistical finding, and moreover, valid for the time being. Too severe because although the late explicit answer is no less legal than a timely express decision, it is belated, inasmuch as the applicant has been on hold for many months … and, thus, from the layman's point of view it is in vain that the applicant is told by the courts that the Emperor is dressed; in the applicant's eyes the Emperor has no clothes.

Silences that mean 'No' fail the applicant severely. The applicant is burdened with lodging a timely and expensive challenge against no reason, and even if that challenge prevails in court, differently from those who challenge explicit refusals, this applicant is brought back in time to a moment in which the institution may still discharge each and any reason for 'No'.

C. In Addition: the Reputational Constraint

Still, there is another advantage that might be gleaned here. By merely threatening to, or by effectively challenging silence, the applicant imposes a reputational constraint on the popularity-thirsty institutions of the EU. An infinite loop of silences and subsequent challenges could well signify disaster for a particular applicant, but the inadequacy and the violence of such a relationship between the EU and its subjects would be projected far and wide. Many people are watching.

D. Different Points of View: Applicants' v EU Courts'

A closing comment is that applicants may have views different from the Court's in regard to what may be achieved by a challenge to silence.

In *Co-frutta II*[52] whilst the Court held that the purpose of striking down silence served to challenge inaction on the part of the administration with a view to obtaining a reasoned response, the applicant, differently, wished to reverse the flow of the tide. Instead of waiting (a little longer) for a reasoned response, the undertaking had urgency in sending the institution a message: that beyond the deadline, the institution was no longer entitled to issue a decision. The applicant argued that late decisions[53] should not be validated, since beyond the deadline, institutional competence would be lost.

Ultimately, the applicant was treated with great severity by the Court. The EU judicature ruled that applicants were bound to suffer answers given beyond the deadline. Yet one cannot help but concur that a crucial point of law was raised. Is it not the law itself that orders the applicants to put their minds at rest once the deadline for an institutional reply lapses? Is it not the law that—upon the expiry of the deadline—asks one to pretend, and act, as if, at the hand of the law, and in the eyes of the law, an adequate reply has (already) been made?

VI. OF CATS AND FOXES: HOLDING REPLIES AND LATE ANSWERS

Still on the topic of the coupling of silence and deadlines, two damaging misfits, different from one another, infiltrated the access model, and, for some time, no one seemed to be taking any notice. Cats lie low among the pigeons, and foxes cause havoc in henhouses, that much is known. What is sometimes forgotten is that in all cases in which a stranger infiltrates a model there is always a moment, at which the

[52] Joined Cases T-355/04 and T-446/04 *Co-frutta II* (n 8).
[53] Section VI.B, late answers.

imposition of damage comes about surreptitiously, the moment just before anybody notices that anything different (from a classical failure to respond) is going on at all.

A. Cat among the Pigeons: Holding Replies

The imperative punctuality—or better, the awe of deadlines—which applicants were, since the early days, bound to operate within, was not as eagerly imposed on the institutions by the EU judicature.

This might have been because the law itself provided for a form of mitigation[54] of the severity with which institutional inability to comply with deadlines should be regarded in general. It is true that the form of mitigation referred to 'exceptional circumstances'. Yet, before all else, it insinuated that exceptional circumstances might occur, and possibly would occur—inter alia because of the immoderate lack of proportion of some applicants' requests—and that consequently institutions were to be accorded some tolerance.

At the same time, it did not seem theoretically justified to accord applicants any tolerance. After all, applicants are those who ask, those who, in any case, benefit from the policy and those who, ultimately, impose administrative burdens[55] on the institutions.

> Case T-2/03 *Verein fur Konsumenten*
>
> 101 It should however be borne in mind that it is possible for an applicant to make a request for access, under Regulation No 1049/2001, relating to a manifestly unreasonable number of documents, perhaps for trivial reasons, thus imposing a volume of work for processing of his request which could very substantially paralyse the proper working of the institution. It should also be noted that, where a request relates to a very large number of documents, the institution's right to seek a 'fair solution' together with the applicant, pursuant to Article 6(3) of Regulation No 1049/2001, reflects the possibility of account being taken, albeit in a particularly limited way, of the need, where appropriate, to reconcile the interests of the applicant with those of good administration.
>
> 102 An institution must therefore retain the right, in particular cases where concrete, individual examination of the documents would entail an unreasonable amount of administrative work, to balance the interest in public access to the documents against the burden of work so caused, in order to safeguard, in those particular cases, the interests of good administration (see, by analogy, T-14/98 *Hautala v Council*, paragraph 86).

These different scales on which applicants and defendants were placed allowed a certain—relatively unnoticed—tolerance for institutional delays to form (and to occasionally transpire). It was, in fact, not uncommon for the institutions to avail themselves repeatedly of successive extensions to the processing time-limits, or, simply, to reply belatedly.[56] Over time, that generic indulgence, that permission to stray

[54] The extension of 15 working days.

[55] Case T-2/03 *Verein für Konsumenteninformation v Commission* [2005] ECR II-00121 paras 100–02; Case T-42/05 *Williams* (n 19) para 86; Case C-127/13P *Strack* (n 8) para 21.

[56] Case T-47/01 *Co-frutta I* (n 15) paras 16 and 17.

from formality, yielded an unacceptable by-product, and a treacherous figure flourished: the so-called 'holding reply'.

A holding reply is a peculiar act. More often than not it consists of a lethal sequence of seven words 'we will get back to you shortly' or, under another version 'we will get back to you as soon as possible'. Nobody knows what these words, when strung together, mean, exactly. And yet we have just spelled out two of the most common phrases employed to deal with requests in the English language.

If one allows a moment for role-play, let us imagine that one is an applicant and that one has sent a confirmatory application to an institution:

On the 14th working day after the application has been registered, the institution makes use, once, of the possibility of extending the deadline for another 15 working days.[57] You wait, patiently, as 13 more working days elapse and no reply comes forth. There are still two days left. On day 14, a letter arrives. It was actually written on day 12, and reaches you on day 14. The content of the letter is brief. The institution expresses regret that it has (once again) been unable to comply with the prescribed deadlines and adds the following phrase 'We will get back to you as soon as possible'.

What is one supposed to do? There are only 24 hours left for (legal) silence to be formed. Only two months (and one day) left within which a challenge of the (now highly probable) negative silence is feasible. One is also confronted with a more immediate fact: if two months and one day down the line is the date when the feasibility of going to court ends, then it is also true that the option of lodging an action in court is open in 24 hours (the first second after day 15).

i. Better Safe than Sorry

How soon should one request that the EU judicature strike down (legal) silence? It is highly probable that any prudent person would suggest that the applicant wait … a little. That line of reasoning embraces the view that a reply rendered post-deadline, in the wake of a 'shortly' or an 'as soon as possible'[58] will not unduly impinge on the applicant's interests. After day 1, there are, after all, two months left. Maybe a reply will arrive in the meantime and all will be resolved in a non-litigious manner.

Before all else, from a strictly legal point of view it is very important to clarify that once the period of time within which an applicant may lodge an action is opened—the time-limit for bringing proceedings commences on expiry of the time-limits for replying to the confirmatory application—the applicant is *ab initio* entitled to act in such a manner.

A holding reply would only be frank (and they never are) if—in spite of itself—it explicitly called the applicant's attention to two crucial issues.

First, that the nature of the deadline to lodge an action (against a refusal *ex lege*) in court, is imperative.

[57] Case T-203/06 *Eurostrategies v Commission* [not reported], order of 1 December 2006.
[58] Case T-19/96 *Carvel II* (n 4) para 6.

Secondly, to the fact that no holding reply—nor, for that matter any institution—is able to extend that deadline, since that deadline is a rule of public order.[59]

In the light of the courts'unequivocal qualification of deadlines as rules of public order, applicants would do well to disregard any form of holding reply, since they are not to be rebuked for exercising own procedural rights. Holding replies expose applicants to the danger of believing that the institutional statement, by inherence, extends the deadline. Yet the belief into which the applicant is (mis)led[60] is devoid of any legal basis.

In sum, holding replies are only valid,[61] if they extend a deadline, once, for a further 15 working days. Anything more ambitious is a cat, attempting to cage a particular type of pigeon into the error of waiting too long.

B. Foxes in the Henhouse: Late Answers

We have said that a holding reply is dangerous since applicants might be—out of reverential naivety—(mis)led into the error of allowing a mandatory deadline to lapse. Moreover, in regard to holding replies, there is no certainty that the institution will, ever, contact the applicant again.

On top of this, the ECJ has made it known that it is at the discretion of the judicature to reject the admissibility of a challenge that is directed only against a confirmatory act of an act that is already definitive. It could be ruled *hors delai*. The ECJ, for that matter has also left a message that the EU judicature is not inclined to this. Yet as is well known, over time, the practice of courts may change.

Therefore, less trusting applicants do institute proceedings against a refusal *ex lege*. In such cases, a main grievance is put before the Court: that the applicant has not been offered reasons for refusal, and this omission constitutes a breach of the EU Treaties.

On occasion, when such proceedings (against a refusal *ex lege*) are well underway, an act that purports to be a late, explicit, reply to the earlier confirmatory application[62] is notified to the applicant.

In the case of a positive decision, the discontinuance of proceedings is inevitable. There are no institutional reasons to be assessed against the factual background of the moment in which refusal *ex lege* came about. The only issue left to resolve then is the costs. Nowadays, they will, almost certainly, be imposed on the institution.

In the case that the late answer is a reasoned refusal, further consideration is necessary.

[59] Order of the GC in Case T-278/11 *ClientEarth a.o.* (n 7). However, *cf*, for a case in which a significant administrative burden is imposed, Case T-2/03 *Verein fur Konsumenten* (n 55) paras 14–16, 93 and 100–03.

[60] The point of applicants being misled is clearly made in Case T-278/11 *ClientEarth a.o.* (n 7) and by AG Kokott, in the Opinion of 22 May 2014, Case 127/13-P *Strack* (n 8) paras 34–41.

[61] Case T-203/06 *Eurostrategies* (n 57).

[62] Against this assumption, see AG Kokott (n 60).

i. After 'No' ex lege*: a Subsequent, Late, Reasoned Refusal*

What is in fact a late answer? Is it just a late reply to the earlier confirmatory request? Or is it a new decision that merely confirms what the applicant had already been told by the law (Article 8(3)): that access to the documents had been refused. As has been noted, the EU courts have taken two different positions on this subject.[63]

Regardless of whether the earlier position of the GC[64] or the more recent one of the ECJ[65] is adopted, a more important issue arises: when a late answer comes forth should on-going proceedings against silence be discontinued?

In truth, from the applicant's point of view, a real answer, albeit late, has finally been offered by the institution. Under this framework, no one is bound to keep up the pretence that the reasons for refusal are unknown. The applicant could now consider the real reasons offered retroactively by the institution, and subsequently take a clean decision with respect to whether these should be contested in court (by way of an enlargement of the proceedings' object or by way of independent proceedings).

ii. When the Court Takes over

Moreover, it might be added that if the applicant does not voluntarily desist from proceedings, the Court might take over *ex officio* and enforce such a solution.

Arguments in favour of *ex officio* discontinuance of proceedings, even against the wishes of the applicant,[66] are based on the assumption that the effects of annulment of silence are redundant when a reasoned answer, albeit late, comes forth. In fact, by way of a successful annulment of silence, the applicant will simply be brought back to a moment in time at which the institution would be bound to provide a new, definitive reply (to an earlier question). And, the institution, in practice, has anticipated that new answer by retroactively providing (a real) one to the earlier question.

Respectfully submitted, a magnificent muddle.

Yet, muddled as the situation may seem, other than turning back time, there is no other interest in that the silence is struck down.[67] This is not the same as denying that there might be a remnant of utility in imposing reputational costs on the institution.

For a period of time, in stark contrast to settled case law,[68] a non-formalist solution was, indeed, enforced. In *Co-frutta II*,[69] proceedings were discontinued, against

[63] One position can be read in Joined Cases T-355/04 and T-446/04 *Co-frutta II* (n 8). And the other in Case C-127/13P *Strack* (n 8).

[64] Joined Cases T-355/04 and T-446/04 *Co-frutta II* (n 8).

[65] Case C-127/13P *Strack* (n 8).

[66] Order of the GC, Case T-19/96 *Carvel II* (n 4) paras 13–15.

[67] ibid, para 16; Case T-156/97 *Berge* (n 4) paras 9–10.

[68] Case T-156/97 *Berge* (n 4) paras 9, 10 and 13.

[69] Joined Cases T-355/04 and T-446/04 *Co-frutta II* (n 8).

the applicant's wishes, and culminated in the iniquitous imposition of costs on the applicant. Doctrine qualified the incident as practically inevitable:[70]

> If the institution fails to take a confirmatory decision within the deadline, a negative decision is implied (Article 8 (3) of the Regulation): however, even though the applicant can then go to court, a subsequent decision renders the court proceeding moot. At the best, Article 8 (3) allows the applicant to pressure the institution but at the cost of initiating and withdrawing a court proceeding with little certainty that he will be able to recover the legal costs involved.[71]

The solution of *Co-frutta*[72] was decided in the wake of *First Data*[73] and *Wunenburger*[74]—which provide an insufficiently nuanced approach—and the Court grounded its reasoning on the inevitable succumbing of the party who had 'lost interest'. Today, it is still true that the principle that an express reply after an implicit reply (that has been challenged) causes an automatic[75] capitulation of the interest in having the implied refusal annulled. It remains an established pillar of the case law. Fortunately, today, on the issue of whether the applicant will be able to recover the legal costs, in the wake of *Ryanair*[76] and *Martin*[77] recovery is practically a certainty.[78]

VII. CONCLUSIONS

The sound of silence is not a pretty tune. It may be offensive to applicants. To mitigate its paralysing effects, the law conferred procedural utility to two mechanisms put in place. First, in the face of an initial absence of reply, a mere entitlement to make a confirmatory application has been included into Regulation 1049/2001. Secondly, in the face of persistent, definitive silence, the meaning 'No' comes forth. With it, the entitlement to lodge an action against silence before the EU judicature emerges.

The definition of what endures beyond silence's deadline remains contested. The EU courts have fluctuated between the insistence that there is an institutional duty to reply beyond the deadline (*Co-frutta*), and the liberating effect of the passage of time (*Strack*).

[70] Case T-19/96 *Carvel II* (n 4) paras 24 and 30–31.
[71] B Driessen, *Transparency in EU Institutional Law* (Alphen aan den Rijn, Kluwer, 2012) 255
[72] Joined Cases T-355/04 and T-446/04 *Co-frutta II* (n 8).
[73] Case T-28/02 *First Data and Others v Commission* [2005] ECR II-04119, paras 35–38.
[74] Case C-36/05P *Wunenburger v Commission* [2006] ECR I-10313, para 42.
[75] This doctrine has been mitigated in Case T-29/08 *LPN v Commission* and in Case T-402/12 *Schlyter v Commission* [not yet published], however the mitigation is limited to the field of a later additional reason offered after an express reply has already been provided.
[76] Case T-494/08 *Ryanair v Commission* (n 44).
[77] Case T-291/10 *Martin v Commission* (n 44).
[78] See eg order of the GC, 13 November 2012, in Case T-278/11 *ClientEarth a.o.* (n 7) and, in the same sense, order of the Court, 6 May 2014, in Case T-419/13 *Union Almacenistas* (n 33) paras 24 and 36.

The second position facilitates the conclusion that legal silence is an act, and, moreover a definitive one. Neither position precludes the exercise of an institutional option to provide (late) reasons for the earlier refusal. Yet, the reflection (of these alternative positions) on the amendment of the pleas in law, on the discontinuance of proceedings and on the imposition of procedural costs may vary.

What remains (relatively) uncontested is that deadlines (both for definitive replies and to commence proceedings in court) are rules of public order. Consequently, neither holding reply nor any late answer may unduly extend them. Applicants are, thus, well advised to exercise own procedural rights in a timely fashion. Doing otherwise entails the risk of being disenfranchised of the same. Regarding the governance of silence by the EU courts, the imposition of procedural costs has, especially more recently, become a benchmark of procedural conduct.

We look forward to an amendment of the courts' terminology in rulings. It needs to become more precise. The combination of *Co-frutta II*, *Strack* and *Sea Handling* have placed a heavy burden on an applicant's legal counsel. Legal counsel must convincingly explain to applicants first, that the deadlines of Article 8 of Regulation 1049/2001 are rendered *inviolable* by the rule of negative silence. Second, that it is at the cost of procedural rights that silence (refusal *ex lege*) is left unchallenged. Third, that to ignore silence will imply (in the eyes of the law) that a decision that arrives five months after an applicant is expecting it is not *late*. Fourth, that since thereby no deadline has been violated, there is no legal redress against its merely perceived tardiness.

By way of conclusion, a mechanism of judicial challenge of negative silence not only reinforces the importance of what is obtainable through the annulment of any refusal (explicit or implicit): the need for a new decision on an old request, it also imposes reputational costs on the popularity-thirsty institutions of the EU.

7

The Eccentric Actors of the Access Policy

Part I

Third Actor: The Member State—Tinker, Tailor, Soldier, Spy

THE EU MEMBER State is today, at the very least, a dichotomous place. Within that geo-political territory oblique relationships between the national and the EU dimension are forged, and thrive. As a matter of fact, citizens of the Member State are, by inherence, also subjects of the EU. Likewise, the governments of the Member States are component members of the EU. It is, therefore, practically impossible to discuss a policy of the EU without involving its underlying national players.

Nevertheless, as we are about to sketch the role of the Member States of the EU (and of other non-applicants) within the access policy, it is important to bear the order of the previous chapters of this book in mind. Throughout them, after some introductory comments on the normative development of the policy, we have discussed the position of applicants that ask EU institutions for documents. Moreover, we have ascertained that access to such documents may be granted or refused. Refusal must be grounded on the basis of exceptions that protect public and/or private interests that are direct competitors of the public interest in disclosure. Finally, we have also clarified how access to the same documents may be refused on the basis of silence.

Thus, it would appear that the actors of the access policy are merely of two kinds: applicants and EU institutions. This dual perspective of actors is reinforced by the fact that indeed most applicants are bound to the EU since those that are an EU citizen or that reside or have their registered office in a Member State are, as mentioned above, in a certain sense, its subjects. Therefore, it is conceivable that the substance of an EU policy (eg access) might be exhausted within the confines of relationships taking place exclusively between national citizens and EU institutions.

Nevertheless, applicants have other allegiances. They are also subjects of national States. It is, therefore, time to consider if the association between applicants and their State of origin and, in particular, the association between the applicant[1] and an EU Member State that is itself bound to the EU places an eccentric player into the access framework: a third actor. That discussion will be held in Part I of this chapter.

Subsequently, in Part II, we will also consider if a fourth or a fifth actor, or both, have a role to play in the access policy as well.

With regard to States, in the first place we will consider whether it is 'as such' that they are reserved any distinguishing role in the EU access policy. Secondly, we will consider if there is any special status, within the policy, reserved for States that are members of the EU.

I. MEMBERS ONLY

The first consideration—a distinctive role for the State, and merely 'as such'—has to be answered in the negative. As a matter of fact, within the seminal architecture of the Code of Conduct of 1993, in regard to States, in general, no fundamental role was assigned them. As a result, in principle only applicants and EU institutions managed requests for documents. Furthermore, conflict arising therefrom was to be dealt with by the EU judicature within the context of a direct action,[2] and/or the EU Ombudsman.

This distribution of principal roles formally ousted any State not only from the procedure pursuant to the access policy (since it was the EU institutions that answered requests) but also from the enforcement of the access policy (since the national forum was not where the judicial actions were lodged and neither was the preliminary ruling procedure employed).

Notwithstanding this overall scheme, our second consideration—a distinctive role for EU Member States—will require further examination. This is because although the policy for the most part did not require governmental input, the Member States of the EU revealed, in this regard, both an unfaltering desire and a chameleon-like ability to participate.

Our objective here is to highlight the meeting of two—often-antagonistic—aspirations. On the one hand, the aspirations of an access policy construed at the EU level that attempts to develop independently from national rules. On the other hand, the aspirations of the Member States, which seek to assert a national view of what the supranational access policy should become.

Since 1993, the EU legislator has striven to establish a certain degree of insulation of the EU access policy from national rules. For the most part, national rules on access and EU rules on access were meant to function separately. Thus, and notably, access is an area of EU law that is removed from the realm of primacy over national law.

For its part, the Member State has sought to break through the barriers set up; first, and understandably, through privileges stemming from the (now extinct)

[1] A natural or a legal person. See Ch 2. See on this topic Case C-281/08P *Landtag Schleswig-Holstein v Commission* [2009] ECR I-00199, para 24.

[2] Currently, Art 263 of the Treaty of Lisbon.

author's rule;[3] secondly, by asserting national views in situations of guardianship of EU documents; thirdly, by way of interventions[4] within proceedings initiated by a third party. Finally, still in regard to the list of instruments that Member States have deployed to influence this EU policy, the choice to appeal the adverse fate of others[5] to a higher court has been exercised. The Member State thus surfaces as the third actor of the policy. Versatile, somewhat unpredictable and resourceful.

Our discussion will proceed by contrasting periods. With regard to the period under the Code of Conduct of 1993, we will (A) examine the status of the Member State vis-à-vis the author's rule and guardianship of EU-originating documents; and (B) compare interventions against the new framework brought forth subsequent to the entry into force of Regulation 1049/2001.

II. THE MEMBER STATE UNDER THE CODE OF CONDUCT OF 1993

A. The Author's Rule and the Guardianship of EU Documents

The adoption of an author's rule by an institution (here, the EU) entails that no matter where documents are ultimately held, and no matter how many entities have a copy of the same in their possession, only the author of the documents is entitled to determine if the same are to be released into the public sphere or to be kept withdrawn from public scrutiny. Consequently, if applicants address requests for access to EU institutions concerning documents that the EU institutions hold (and use) but of which the EU institutions are not the author,[6] by way of reply these documents will be routinely refused. By contrast, a rule on guardianship means that the EU issues instructions to third persons holding EU-originating documents (or copies of the same) on the subject of how third persons are bound to proceed if applicants apply directly to them for access to EU-originating material.

i. Author's Rule

Within the Code of Conduct, the EU legislator set up a reciprocity scheme under which the origin of documents was the connection criterion to one of two alternative legal frameworks that might govern their disclosure to the public. Principally it was the nature of the author that was particularly influential over documents' status. First, from the perspective of the EU institutions, if the author of a requested document were a private party, the EU institution/s involved would redirect any applicant's request to that party. The subsequent decision—on release or withdrawal—would then be taken by the author, and (possibly) with full discretion. If the author of a

[3] See Ch 5.

[4] L Rossi, 'Choosing Exposure: A Study in Reputation of Member States in Access to EU Documents' Rules' (2009) Berkeley Program in Law and Economics, https://escholarship.org/uc/item/96d6b7fz.

[5] See Ch 8.

[6] Case T-188/97 *Rothmans v Commission* [1999] ECR II-02463, paras 17–18 and paras 56–63 in which the Commission pleaded—without success—that it was not the author of the minutes of the Customs Code Committee.

requested document was a State, an EU Member State or a national public body whilst it is true that, as before, the institutions were bound to, and did, redirect requests for access to these incoming documents to their legitimate author, by contrast, the fate of the document would be decided on the basis of national rules, notably of public order.[7]

Code of Conduct

> Where the document held by an institution was written by a natural or legal person, a Member State, another Community institution or body or any other national or international body, the application must be sent direct to the author.

Thus, whether EU Members or not,[8] States would always be offered control over the fate of self-produced/self-originating documents. Yet, they were not treated differently from any other natural or legal person that happened to fulfil the authorship criterion. Having said that, the author's rule should not be read as a symptom of a period of the access policy in which there was blind deference to national law. Actually, the opposite is true.

What the author's rule allowed the EU was a 'bread and butter' approach to incoming documents: their management was simply not a task of the EU. That relief from decisions concerning documents of others provided the Union with space and time to concentrate on its own concerns. In fact, the author's rule cannot be read in isolation from its *alter ego*: the rule of guardianship of EU documents, also directed at the Member States. The combination of both rules was, above all, the threshold to a new beginning: an era in which the EU would, alone, self-develop a policy for own documents, regardless of who held them or where they were held, thus withdrawing their fate from the long reach of national law.

ii. Guardianship

To help ensure the insulation of EU decisions from external interference, the Code clarified that any person in possession of EU documents was expected to return the courtesy of the author's rule extended to them by the EU institutions. In other words, to redirect requests from the public for these specific documents back to Brussels and/or Strasbourg. In this manner, the fate of documents originating in the EU institutions, but held by others (and, in particular by the Member States), was to be left for the institutional dome of the EU (the Council, the Commission and the Parliament) to decide.

It must not be forgotten that whilst EU Member States transmit self-produced documents to the EU, it is also true that the EU transmits large quantities of EU-originating documents to national authorities. Consequently, it is the Member State more

[7] Cases T-124/96 *Interporc* [1998] ECR II-00231, para 14 and T-92/98 *Interporc* [1999] ECR II-03521, which concerned documents drawn up by the Argentine authorities; Case T-123/99 *JT's Corporation* [2000] ECR II-03269, para 53, which concerned documents drawn up by the authorities in *Bangladesh*; and Case T-191/99 *Petrie* [2001] ECR II-3677, para 50, which concerned documents drawn up by the Italian authorities.

[8] As Argentina in *Interporc* and Bangladesh in *JT's Corporation* (n 7).

often than any other person that becomes guardian of EU-originating documents. And as the gatekeeper of the documents originating from an organisation of which it is a permanent component member, under the principle of loyal cooperation as laid down in Article 4 TEU, the Member State is required to exercise prudence.

On the whole, the expectation of reciprocal deference was a soft law rule to be governed by diplomatic common sense. Nonetheless, it gave rise to a spectacular incident between the EU and Sweden. On request from an organisation of Swedish journalists, the Swedish Government released EU-originating documents to the public. That of itself might not have been grave were it not for the concurrent, and on-going, *Svenska*[9] proceedings. Within those proceedings, the Council had refused that same organisation access to the very same documents.

The *Svenska* incident left a blemish on the relations between the EU and its component Member States. Accusations—even merely implicit ones—of disloyalty are devastating, and especially so in fields where the institutional structure of the EU requires the cooperation of other actors to manage a new policy without incidents.

An underlying tension subsisted with regard to what EU access should be and the disparities of opinion between the Member States and the EU were, moreover, both steadfast and widespread. Thus, it was urgent that the Member States find a forum for their voices. Since the route of unilateral interpretation and enforcement was untenable, the forum that was predominantly preferred was the procedure of the intervention. Without completely distracting the judicature from the concrete dispute between an applicant and an institution, it manages to accommodate healthy rivalry of opinion (between one or more national authorities and the EU institutions) with regard to the interpretation of the EU policy from which the dispute emerges.

B. Interventions

In order to clarify the context of interventions within the access policy, it is important to have in mind that within this particular context the applicant is the sole *agent provocateur* of (first instance) litigation. This is because it is the applicants that address requests to the EU institutions, and not vice versa. Consequently, it is only applicants that will possibly face the chagrin of being refused access. Therefore, from the point of view of access to justice, it is always incumbent on the applicant to complain. Institutions, by contrast, are invariably defendants[10] in first instance, since it is against their decisions that actions for annulment are directed. In fact, institutions, might, at the most, appeal first instance rulings.

Within such a setting, Member States formally submit national points of view[11] in regard to the resolution of on-going actions concerning access to documents, that are pending before the EU judicature and that oppose an applicant to an institution.

[9] Case T-174/95 *Svenska v Council* [1998] ECR II-02289.

[10] The role of institutions as defendants in first instance is discussed in Ch 3.

[11] For a general analysis of this point, see MPF Granger, 'When Governments Go to Luxembourg ... the Influence of Governments on the Court of Justice' (2004) 29(1) *European Law Review* 3–31.

This having been said, it is also natural that applicants might prefer to govern self-initiated proceedings alone. However, that is not their prerogative. In EU law, a number of natural or legal persons (including Member States and other EU institutions) may be accorded leave to intervene (and to interfere) within someone else's case.[12] Moreover, under this procedural instrument, the EU Member States are favoured over non-EU national authorities. Whilst, in principle, any person seeking to intervene is required prove a direct interest in the outcome of proceedings,[13] Member States are always[14] entitled to submit observations within any action lodged before the EU judicature.

Statute of the ECJ, Article 40

(1) Member States and institutions of the Union may intervene in cases before the Court of Justice.

(2) The same right shall be open to the bodies, offices and agencies of the Union and to any other person which can establish an interest in the result of a case submitted to the Court. Natural or legal persons shall not intervene in cases between Member States, between institutions of the Union or between Member States and institutions of the Union.

(3) Without prejudice to the second paragraph, the States, other than the Member States, which are parties to the Agreement on the European Economic Area, and also the EFTA Surveillance Authority referred to in that Agreement, may intervene in cases before the Court where one of the fields of application of that Agreement is concerned.

(4) An application to intervene shall be limited to supporting the form of order sought by one of the parties.

The invasive character of this route cannot be overstated: it is after all, intervention within litigation initiated by others. In fact, when exercising this option, the Member State 'charges' into pending proceedings, asserts the right to become cognisant of all pleadings submitted[15] and sides with one of the parties involved. If they make use of this privilege, in a dispute concerning access to documents, Member States will be able to assert national interpretation of the EU rules on access. This advantage applies both within first instance proceedings initiated by applicants versus the EU institutions and appeal proceedings.[16]

[12] Statute of the Court, Art 40(1) and 40(2). For a general framework, see K Lenaerts, I Maselis and K Gutman, *EU Procedural Law* (Oxford, Oxford University Press, 2014) 824 ff.

[13] eg order of the President of the ECJ of 6 Nov 2013 in Case C-28/13P *Gabi Thesing and Bloomberg Finance v ECB* [not reported], by which the ECJ did not acknowledge leave to intervene to Access Info Europe (AIE), on the grounds that AIE did not meet the requirements laid down in para 8 of the Statute of the ECJ, 'interest in the result of the case'.

[14] Since they are considered, alongside EU institutions, to be privileged interveners: Statute of the ECJ, Art 40(1). For further detail, see T Materne, 'La Procedure en Intervention devant la Cour de Justice de l'Union Européenne' (2013) 29 *Cahiers de Droit Européen* 77–131.

[15] It is, however, possible to secure the exclusion of access of the interveners to secret and confidential items or documents of the proceedings whose transmission to the intervener would be prejudicial to one of the parties. See the Statute of the ECJ, Art 40; the Rules of Procedure of the ECJ, Art 131(2) and 131(3); and the Rules of Procedure of the GC, Arts 50(2), 67(3) and 116(2).

[16] Appeal proceedings (discussed in Ch 8) may be initiated either by an applicant that was unsuccessful at first instance, by an EU institution whose decision to refuse access was annulled by the GC, or by any of the Member States. Within an appeal, Member States are entitled to intervene in support of either initial party to proceedings.

The privilege has a downside too. National foreign policy is exposed. Especially when a Member State supports an institution that strives to restrict access, it will hardly engender sympathy on the part of the public.[17]

From the point of view of access' beneficiaries (the applicants) what is crucial is that the applicant is then able to adequately manage the presence of the intervener/s within his/her case. Even in instances in which a Member State intervenes in favour of (the points of law submitted by) an applicant, there is always the danger that the gravitas of the Member State's foreign policy objectives might steer the outcome of the case in an unexpected direction.[18] Furthermore, if multiple Member States are attracted by a specific case,[19] hearings (tend to) become burdensome and the paperwork increases exponentially. The attention of the judicature becomes an object of a contest, arguments are often repeated to exhaustion, and allotted speaking-time for each party is inevitably watered down.

However, from a public interest point of view, the advantage of the intervention within proceedings initiated at EU level is that it makes no concession to unilateral national enforcement of EU law. The policy is then governed strictly as an EU policy, the forum for litigation remains within the monopoly of jurisdiction of the Civil Service Tribunal, the GC, and the ECJ, and thus, presiding over any development of the policy on EU access is the EU judge.

20 years into the policy, in hindsight, one might add that a selection of Member States has revealed discount rates[20] in this field. In other words, there have been points of law in defence of which the Member States are willing to pay a price for submitting what the national view on that point of law is to the EU courts. The price paid is the exposure of the national position to the public opinion. Other Member States have remained silent, choosing not to attempt to steer the EU policy. Notably, Luxembourg and Belgium, two founding Member States, remain within the group that have displayed reserve. In the same way Austria, Bulgaria, Croatia, Cyprus, Hungary, Ireland, Latvia, Lithuania, Malta, Romania and Slovakia have kept the access litigation at a distance.

From a chronological perspective, the first appearances of Member States as interveners in the access litigation featured first and foremost France in 1994,[21] closely

[17] See section iii.

[18] See, by analogy, the intervention from the European Data Protection Supervisor (EDPS) in Case T-190/10 *Egan v Parliament* [not reported] paras 25–26, in which it is clear that the applicant alleged a mismatch between its own allegations and those of the (allegedly) supporting intervener. The same had occurred in an earlier episode, Case T-2/03 *VFK* [2005] ECR II-00121, paras 50–55, in which the CFI, of its own motion, questioned the supporting interveners (BAWAG, OWAG and NoHYPOBANK) with regard to the compatibility of their arguments with the form of order (of the Commission) that they claimed to support.

[19] See inter alia Case T-174/95 *Svenska* (n 9); Case T-84/03 *Turco v Council* [2004] ECR II-04061; Case T-403/05 *MyTravel* [2008] ECR II-02027; Case T-111/07 *Agrofert* [2010] ECR II-00128; Joined Cases C-514/11P and C-605/11P *Finland and LPN* [not reported].

[20] In economics a 'discount rate' is a computation of present value. We have adopted this term to indicate the 'present value' that a Member State acknowledges for a specific point of law that is being discussed within the EU access litigation. That national discount rate will compel the Member State to intervene for or against that point of law, thereby exposing its domestic outlook on the EU access policy.

[21] In 1994, with the proviso that it is not a typical action for annulment in an access to documents context; Case 58/94 *NL v Council* [1996] ECR I-02169.

followed by the Netherlands and Denmark.[22] Sweden and the UK[23] ensued in 1995 and were followed by Finland in 1998.[24] In 1999, Spain[25] was the final Member State to submit support for points of law, before the advent of the new and different framework of Regulation 1049/2001. Moreover, under the governance of the Code of Conduct, except for the UK, the Member States within this selection were quick to position themselves either as consistently pro-applicant or as consistently pro-institution.

Within this period, the Netherlands,[26] Denmark,[27] Sweden[28] and Finland,[29] adopted a consistent pro-applicant and thus, pro-access, advocacy, whilst France,[30] by contrast, intervened consistently in favour of the defendant institutions. For its part, and making its position more difficult to read, the UK[31] fluctuated between supporting the institutions and supporting applicants.[32]

We are well aware, and it is quite clear from their submissions, that in general, Member States intervene to defend points of law. However, if we cross-reference the nationality of each applicant against that of the intervening Member State, for each case additional explanations emerge. From a different angle they shed light on interventions too. For instance, fleeting indications that national biases with regard to own citizens drive intervention could be read into the choices of the UK in *WWF UK*[33] *and Bavarian Lager*,[34] of Sweden in *Svenska*[35] and of Finland in *Hautala I.*[36]

In other words, in addition to the first abovementioned strategy (defending points of law), some Member States might choose, as a matter of policy, to intervene in proceedings just because one of their own nationals is pleading before the EU Courts. Furthermore, it would be on a case-by-case basis that the existence of positive biases (always supporting own nationals) or negative biases (always intervening against own nationals, or when national documents are involved) could be inferred.

22 In Case T-194/94 *Carvel I v Council* [1995] ECR II-02765, both Member States supported the applicant.

23 In Case T-105/95 *WWF UK v Commission* [1997] ECR II-00313, Sweden supported the applicant and the UK, the defendant institution.

24 In Case T-14/98 *Hautala I v Council* [1999] ECR II-2489, Finland supported the applicant.

25 In Case C-353/99 *Council v Hautala* [2001] ECR I-9565, Spain supported the appeal of the refusing institution (therefore the intervention is mapped as support for a defendant).

26 Cases T-194/94 *Carvel I v Council* (n 22); T-174/95 *Svenska* (n 9) and T-83/96 *Van der Wal v Commission* [1998] ECR II-00545.

27 Cases T-194/94 *Carvel I v Council* (n 22); T-174/95 *Svenska* (n 9) and C-353/99 *Council v Hautala* (n 25).

28 Cases T-105/95 *WWF UK v Commission* (n 23); T-174/95 *Svenska* (n 9); T-188/97 and T-14/98.

29 Case T-14/98 (n 28).

30 Cases C-58/94 *NL v Council* (n 21); T-105/95 *WWF UK v Commission* (n 23); T-14/98 *Hautala I v Council* (n 24).

31 The UK inaugurally supported a refusing institution in Case T-105/95 *WWF UK v Commission* (n 23) and consolidated the trend in Case T-174/95 *Svenska* (n 9). However, its next intervention, in Case T-50/96 *Primex Produkte v Commission* [1998] ECR II-03773, favoured an applicant (albeit obliquely, see note to Table 7.1 in the column concerning the UK). Support for a refusing institution was repeated in Case T-309/97 *Bavarian Lager I v Commission* [1999] ECR II-03217, yet shortly thereafter, in Case C-353/99P *Council v Hautala* (n 25) the UK supported the party who had been refused documents.

32 See Table 7.1.

33 Case T-105/95 *WWF UK v Commission* (n 23).

34 Case T-309/97 *Bavarian Lager v Commission* (n 31).

35 Case T-174/95 *Svenska* (n 9).

36 Case T-14/98 *Hautala v Council* (n 24).

Yet, there is no robust evidence to support this reading with regard to every case in which a Member State becomes involved. For example, Sweden intervened in favour of applicants that did not hold Swedish nationality. Likewise, the UK once intervened in favour of a Finnish party,[37] and against a Swedish party[38] at another moment. At any rate, the more interesting cases remain specific instances in which a Member State supports an EU institution against one of its own nationals: negative biases.

This was the case with the UK, which in *WWF UK*[39] and in *Bavarian Lager*[40] supported the Commission to the detriment of WWF UK and the Bavarian Lager Company respectively (both British subjects).[41] Here the ratio is more clear-cut. More than to a national bias, the conduct of the UK points in the direction of national nervousness.[42] After all, in both cases, the contested documents, albeit produced and held by the Commission, concern an analysis of the conduct (infringement of EU law) of that particular Member State. In these cases the Member State is in general committed to keeping the contested documents away from the public, but even more so, it is committed to keeping the contested documents away from its national subjects.

Table 7.1: Intervention of EU MS under the Code of Conduct

	Case No	Nationality of The Applicant	FR	NL	DK	SWE	UK	FIN	SP	Other Institutions A	Other Institutions D
1994	C-58/94	*NL*	D							EP	COM
	T-194/94	*UK*		A	A					EP	
1995	T-105/95	*UK*	D			A	D				
	T-174/95	*SWE*	D	A	A	A	D				
1996	T-50/96	*GER*					A[43]				
	T-83/86	*NL*		A							
1997	T-188/97	*NL*				A					
	T-309/97	*UK*					D				
1998	T-14/98	*FIN*	D			A		A			
1999	C-353/99	*FIN*			A		A		D		

nb
(i) Whether at first instance or on appeal, A = person who requests access, D = institution that refuses access.
(ii) In Case C-58/94, the A/D dichotomy, above, is not applicable.

[37] Case C-353/99 *Council v Hautala* (n 25).
[38] Case T-174/95 *Svenska* (n 9).
[39] Case T-105/95 *WWF UK v Commission* (n 23).
[40] Case T-309/97 *Bavarian Lager I v Commission* (n 31).
[41] The Bavarian Lager Company Ltd, albeit incorporated under English law, sought to import German beer into the UK. For an account of the proceedings, see C Harlow and R Rawlings, *Process and Procedure in the EU Administration* (Oxford, Hart, 2015) 131.
[42] Albeit under the regime of Regulation 1049/2001. See, by analogy, the intervention of France in Case T-402/12 *Schlyter*, in which although the applicant holds Swedish nationality, the contested documents are connected to France.
[43] In truth this case is an oblique case of support for an applicant requesting access to documents. It is clear from para 34 of Case T-50/96 (n 31) that it is connected to Case T-124/96 *Interporc v Commission* (n 7), an episode in which there were no intervening Member States. In both cases the applicant argued that the lack of access to documents weakened the rights of Interporc to full defence.

III. THE MEMBER STATE UNDER REGULATION 1049/2001

A. The Author's Rule and the Guardianship of EU Documents

Regulation 1049/2001 disrupted all equilibrium consolidated under the Code of Conduct of 1993. Principally, it extended the scope of the access policy beyond documents of which the EU was the author, to include any document held by the EU. As an inevitable consequence of the policy's larger scope and, on the cornerstone of possession, the new Regulation forged the preponderance of EU control over the author's (now forgone) control.

i. The Author's Rule is Abolished

The EU thus grabbed the fate of documents which it merely held away from the authors of the same, in an unprecedented imposition of supranational aspirations over the very national autonomy that the 1993 Code of Conduct had encouraged. The explanation offered for the *volte face* was that the author's rule had left considerable amounts of documents (ie national documents) on the basis of which EU decisions were taken, outside the EU access policy.[44] At one stroke, any authority of the Member States (or for that matter of any author) over the release of documents transmitted to the EU was set aside. Once transmitted, the release of national documents was then no longer governed by national rules. Regulation 1049/2001 would govern incoming national documents. The ghost of *Svenska*[45] was reawakened, upside down.

The principal question about the new rules was whether the EU would be able (to claim authority) to release documents that a Member State has refused the public. Whilst with one arm the EU now, greedily, brought more documents under its wing, with the other arm it established safeguards to lessen the shock. It was obvious that the EU legislator had acted on the foresight that for applicants the new Regulation's purpose might be distorted. There could be instances in which, more than assuring access to EU-originating documents, it might be (ab)used exclusively as a loophole to gain access to documents of others, which for any number of reasons happened to be held, also, by the EU. With the specific design of countering this (ab)use, provisions designed to mitigate the author's rule's disappearance had been drawn up.

First, a general safeguard—*consultation*—was established in favour of authors in general. Secondly, two additional safeguards—with regard to prior consent and to sensitive documents—were established in favour of the Member States, in particular.

[44] This was a concern of applicants, raised after *Interporc* (n 43).

[45] Case T-174/95 *Svenska* (n 9), in which Sweden released documents that the Council would have preferred to shield from public scrutiny.

ii. Consultation of Authors

Essentially, instead of total annihilation of author's privileges, in Article 4(4) of Regulation 1049/2001, a consultation of authors, replaced the old rule:

> Regulation 1049/2001, Article 4(4)
>
> As regards third-party documents, the institution shall consult the third party with a view to assessing whether an exception in par 1 or 2 is applicable, unless it is clear that the document shall, or not, be disclosed.

This new procedure,[46] applicable to contested documents held by the EU institutions and ascribable to any author[47] called (at least apparently) for mandatory consultation of the author before any document was released. Admittedly, that requirement only held unless sufficient clarity on the document's status overrode that obligation. The incumbent duty of consultation was, therefore, mandatory, in principle. Ultimately, on occasion,[48] authors might not be consulted at all before self-produced documents were disclosed to the public by a recipient institution of the EU.

iii. The Prior Consent of the Member State

However, if and when Member States were consulted by an institution, a further safeguard[49] established, in regard to Member States only, by Article 4(5) of Regulation 1049/2001, stated that the latter might, of their own volition, request that the institutions withhold a document from the public. However, only until the Member State in question was in a position to give prior consent.

[46] Case C-64/05P *Sweden v Commission* [2007] ECR I-11389, para 79: 'Moreover, Article 4(5) follows a provision, namely Article 4(4), which lays down a procedural rule, imposing an obligation to consult third parties in the circumstances it describes'.

[47] It was not immediately clear (owing to the subsequent indent of Art 4) if Art 4(4) was also intended to encompass the Member States. The ECJ replied in the affirmative in Case C-64/05P *Sweden v Commission* (n 46) para 46: 'such a right to be consulted is already possessed by the Member States to a great extent by virtue of Article 4(4) of the regulation, which lays down an obligation to "consult the third party" unless it is clear that the document shall or shall not be disclosed'.

[48] Reasoned by the clarity of the situation at hand: Case C-64/05P *Sweden v Commission* (n 46) para 68:

> Thus, for instance, according to Article 4(4) of Regulation No 1049/2001, if the institution concerned considers that it is clear that access to a document originating from a Member State should be refused on the basis of the exceptions in Article 4(1) or (2), it will refuse the request for access without even having to consult the Member State from which the document originates, whether or not that Member State has previously made a request under Article 4(5) of the regulation. In such a case it is thus obvious that the decision on the request for access is taken by the institution, having regard solely to the exceptions that derive directly from the rules of Community law.

[49] The GC in T-168/02 *IFAW Internationaler Tierschutz Fonds v Commission* [2004] ECR II-04135, para 58 refers to a '*lex specialis* governing the position of the Member State' whilst the ECJ in Case C-64/05P *Sweden v Commission* (n 46) para 43 merely uses the expression: 'Article 4(5) of Regulation No 1049/2001 places the Member States in a position that is different from that of other third parties'.

> Regulation 1049/2001, Article 4(5)
>
> A Member State may request the institution not to disclose a document originating from[50] that Member State without its prior agreement.

This second safeguard of the Member State's voice reconciled competing authorities, national and supranational, in the management of a sensitive EU policy with obvious repercussions in the national forum. Since the consultation of any author is in principle mandatory, the Member State is consistently forewarned when an own document becomes the object of request addressed to the EU institutions. Moreover, the Member State would be given an opportunity to concur—with the institutions—in the governance of the exposure of national documents to the public.

iv. 'No' and a Reason that fits Article 4(1) to (3)

The nervousness in regard to the new equilibrium exploded into the *IFAW*[51] proceedings. These concerned the possibility that the EU might release documents that Germany[52] preferred to be held back. The institutions, in *IFAW*, had consulted Germany. And Germany had said 'No'. Bluntly. Curiously, it was not the refusal as such, but its bluntness, which drove a wedge into the analysis of the new rules. Germany refused to consent to the release (by the EU) of certain documents, but had offered up no explanation of its position. Germany alleged that it was simply exercising a veto, with which Regulation 1049/2001 had endowed it.

The main virtue of the *IFAW* proceedings was that they called for examination by the EU judicature of the new balance of power in Regulation 1049/2001 with regard to the fate of documents produced by or originating from a certain actor of the access policy, and held by another.

It is true that the wording of Article 4(5) did not help. Combining the words 'may *request* (…) not to disclose (…) without its prior *consent*' in the same sentence does no justice to the requirement of clarity. Yet, it was inevitable that the right of the Member State to be consulted and the requirement that the institutions obtain the prior agreement of the Member State in order for a document to be released could not be construed as a right of (national) veto over decisions of the EU institutions. That interpretation of the safeguard would amount to reintroducing the author's

[50] In fact, under these new rules, the concept of 'origin' is broader than the concept of 'author'; Case C-64/05 *Sweden v Commission* (n 46) para 63:

> Far from referring only to documents of which the Member States are the 'authors' or which have been 'drawn up' by them, Article 4(5) of Regulation No 1049/2001 potentially concerns every document 'originating' from a Member State, in other words, as the Commission rightly submits and as was agreed at the hearing by IFAW and all the Member States which are parties to this appeal, the entirety of the documents, whoever their author may be, that a Member State transmits to an institution. In this case the only relevant criterion is the origin of the document and the handing over by the Member State concerned of a document previously in its possession.

[51] Case T-168/02 *IFAW I* (n 49) and the respective appeal in Case C-64/05P *Sweden v Commission* (n 46).

[52] Subsequently, another episode in which the Commission engaged in hostile release of documents authored by the German authorities arose: Case T-59/09 *Germany v Commission* [not reported].

rule—in regard to Member States only—which was clearly not an objective of Regulation 1049/2001.[53]

Since Regulation 1049/2001 is designed to govern the access policy at *EU* level, national interests (asserted under Article 4(5)) are never protected directly, only incidentally. When asked to consent to the release of documents, an objection from a Member State will function as a (tolerable) impediment to disclosure, only insofar as it is possible to cloak national reasons for non-disclosure under the terms of Regulation 1049/2001. Still it is not enough that this is done so merely from a formal point of view. National reasons must, from a substantive perspective, fit[54] the EU framework as well.

The safeguard is therefore not a blind yielding to national law.[55] Rather, it is based on the conviction of possible alignment between national limitations to access and the interests that may be asserted by the institutions under Article 4(1) to (3) of Regulation 1049/2001.[56] True, the Member State is invited to contribute to the application and clarification of the working of the exceptions of Article 4(1) to (3)

[53] Case C-64/05 P *Sweden v Commission* (n 46) paras 86–94.

[54] Case T-59/09 *Germany v Commission* (n 52) para 54:

> It should be noted that it is not a matter, for the institution, of imposing its view or of substituting its own assessment for that of the Member State concerned, but of preventing the adoption of a decision which it does not consider to be defensible. The institution, as author of the decision granting or refusing access, is responsible for the lawfulness of that decision. In consequence, before refusing access to a document originating from a Member State, it must examine whether the latter has based its objection on the substantive exceptions provided for in Art 4(1), (2) and (3) of Regulation No 1049/2001 and whether it has provided a proper statement of reasons with regard to those exceptions.

[55] C-64/05P *Sweden v Commission* (n 46) para 65:

> there is nothing in Regulation No 1049/2001 to support the Court of First Instance's conclusion that the Community legislature intended by Article 4(5) of that regulation to enact a sort of conflict-of-laws rule for the purpose of preserving the application of national rules, or even, as suggested by the Commission, the policies of the Member States, concerning access to documents originating from the Member States, at the expense of the specific rules laid down in that field by the regulation.

[56] The need for a measure of fit is clearly explained in paras 82–84 of the *IFAW II* judgment:

> 82 As to the discussion between the parties on the legal effects of Declaration No 35, it suffices to state that the interpretation adopted in paragraph 76 above does not in any event contradict that declaration. Although the declaration shows that the Member States, while adopting Article 255(1) EC, intended to reserve the possibility of retaining a certain control over decisions to disclose documents originating from them, it does not on the other hand give any details as to the substantive grounds on which such control might be exercised.
>
> 83 It remains to point out that, while the decision-making process thus established by Article 4(5) of Regulation No 1049/2001 requires the institution and the Member State involved to confine themselves to the substantive exceptions laid down in Article 4(1) to (3) of the regulation, it is none the less possible for the legitimate interests of the Member States to be protected on the basis of those exceptions and by virtue of the special rules for sensitive documents laid down in Article 9 of the regulation.
>
> 84 In particular, there is nothing to exclude the possibility that compliance with certain rules of national law protecting a public or private interest, opposing disclosure of a document and relied on by the Member State for that purpose, could be regarded as an interest deserving of protection

of Regulation 1049/2001. Still, even if the Member State does claim that there is an alignment of national and EU interests in the non-disclosure of the contested documents, it is ultimately the institution that—as a recipient of those documents—must assess that measure of fit. Only then may access may be refused an applicant by the EU institution. Ultimately, the decision to refuse is taken at EU level, and it is this institutional act that may be subject to the review of the EU judicature.

Finally, in our opinion, there is a very subtle and meaningful nuance between paragraphs 68 and 83 of the ruling of the ECJ in *IFAW II*.[57] On the one hand, paragraph 68[58] is directed at the final statement in Article 4(4): release of a Member State document without prior consultation, and is confined to cases in which the institution is confident that exceptions in Article 4(1) and (2) are not applicable. Moreover, the same scope of exceptions will be considered with regard to the release of documents originating from private parties when the institution decides that consultation is redundant.

By contrast, paragraph 83 of the ruling is directed at Article 4(5) and therefore determines—necessarily with regard to Member States only—that consultation with the institution (when it is carried out) is undertaken with a view to assessing whether 'the exceptions in paragraphs 1 or 2 [or 3]'[59] would, *in casu*, be applicable.[60]

v. Sensitive Documents

A further, and different, safeguard of the autonomy of the Member State from the EU access policy, takes the form of an article reserved for so-called sensitive documents held by the EU.[61] Article 9 of Regulation 1049/2001 seeks to keep

> on the basis of the exceptions laid down by that regulation (see, with respect to the legislation prior to Regulation No 1049/2001, *Netherlands and van der Wal v Commission*, paragraph 26).

[57] Case C-64/05P *Sweden v Commission* (n 46).

[58] ibid, para 68:

> Thus, for instance, according to Article 4(4) of Regulation No 1049/2001, if the institution concerned considers that it is clear that access to a document originating from a Member State should be refused on the basis of the exceptions in Article 4(1) or (2), it will refuse the request for access without even having to consult the Member State from which the document originates, whether or not that Member State has previously made a request under Article 4(5) of the regulation. In such a case it is thus obvious that the decision on the request for access is taken by the institution, having regard solely to the exceptions that derive directly from the rules of Community law.

[59] ibid, para 76:

> On the contrary, several factors militate in favour of an interpretation of Article 4(5) to the effect that the exercise of the power conferred by that provision on the Member State concerned is delimited by the substantive exceptions set out in Article 4(1) to (3), with the Member State merely being given in this respect a power to take part in the Community decision. Seen in that way, the prior agreement of the Member State referred to in Article 4(5) resembles not a discretionary right of veto but a form of assent confirming that none of the grounds of exception under Article 4(1) to (3) is present.

[60] *cf*, the law [ie Regulation 1049/20001 Article 4(4)] limits consultation with private parties to the verification that the exceptions in paras 1 and 2 (only) are not applicable.

[61] See generally D Curtin, 'Official Secrets and the Negotiation of International Agreements: is the EU Executive Unbound?' (2013) 50(2) *Common Market Law Review* 423–57.

certain documents from the public if their release could undermine essential interests of the EU or, of one or more of its Member States. In addition, special care is taken with regard to the persons responsible for processing the same.

Regulation 1049/2001, Article 9

Treatment of sensitive documents

1. Sensitive documents are documents originating from the institutions or the agencies established by them, from Member States, third countries or International Organisations, classified as 'TRÈS SECRET/TOP SECRET', 'SECRET' or 'CONFIDENTIEL' in accordance with the rules of the institution concerned, which protect essential interests of the European Union or of one or more of its Member States in the areas covered by Article 4(1)(a), notably public security, defence and military matters.

2. Applications for access to sensitive documents under the procedures laid down in Articles 7 and 8 shall be handled only by those persons who have a right to acquaint themselves with those documents. These persons shall also, without prejudice to Article 11(2), assess which references to sensitive documents could be made in the public register.

3. Sensitive documents shall be recorded in the register or released only with the consent of the originator.

4. An institution which decides to refuse access to a sensitive document shall give the reasons for its decision in a manner which does not harm the interests protected in Article 4.

5. Member States shall take appropriate measures to ensure that when handling applications for sensitive documents the principles in this Article and Article 4 are respected.

6. The rules of the institutions concerning sensitive documents shall be made public.

7. The Commission and the Council shall inform the European Parliament regarding sensitive documents in accordance with arrangements agreed between the institutions.

Differently from the prior consent safeguard of Article 4(5), Article 9 allows—inter alia—for direct protection of national interests. However, the measure is confined to areas covered by Article 4(1)(a), notably public security, defence and military matters.

The Court has had a chance to distinguish the contexts of Articles 9 and 4(5) of the Regulation,[62] and has left clear that under Article 9 the consent of the author is

[62] C-576/12P *Jurašinović v Council*, paras 46–47:

46. In that context, the fact that an institution considers a document to be 'sensitive' within the meaning of Article 9 of Regulation No 1049/2001—whilst it means that an application for access to that document must be subject to the special treatment laid down in that article [*with regard to the persons responsible for processing them*]—cannot, on its own, justify applying to that document the exceptions provided for in Article 4(1)(a) of Regulation No 1049/2001.

47. Similarly, and conversely, the mere fact that a document is not classified as 'sensitive' within the meaning of Article 9 of Regulation No 1049/2001 cannot prevent the exceptions provided for in Article 4(1)(a) thereof from applying, unless the latter provision is to be deprived of all practical effect.

logically more necessary than under Article 4(5), and is required not only in regard to release of documents but also for mere inclusion (of documents) in a register.

vi. Duties ex Guardianship Remain Constant

Whilst the author's rule faded away, its *alter ego* did not. Consequently, in spite of the loss of authority over documents (as their author), when guardian of EU-originating documents, the new rules requested that the Member State continue not to interfere unilaterally[63] in the access policy.

> Regulation 1049/2001, Recital 15
>
> Even though it is neither the object or the effect of this regulation to amend national legislation on access to documents (...) by virtue of the principle of loyal cooperation, Member States should take care not to hamper the proper application of this Regulation.
>
> Regulation 1049/2001, Article 5
>
> When a Member State receives a request for a document in its possession, originating from an institution, unless it is clear that the document shall or shall not be disclosed, the Member State shall consult with the institution concerned in order to take a decision that does not jeopardise the attainment of the objectives of this Regulation.
>
> The Member State may instead refer the request to the institution.

However, in the legal context, requests are different from orders. Furthermore, the principle of loyal cooperation is subject to limitations. In this particular context, its principal limitation is that the enforcement of the EU rules on access do not hinge on the principle of primacy of EU law. They exist independently of national law and do not require the setting aside of inconsistent national law.[64]

Thus, the incentive of 'inverted forum shopping' by applicants, already encouraged by the disappearance of the author's rule, sprang up in this context as well. In fact, when national rules on access are more generous than the EU ones—albeit within the boundaries of loyal cooperation—the Member State does gain control over EU-originating documents that have been transmitted to the Member States.

It was suddenly clear that two truths had to be reconciled. First, the institutions might release documents that the Member States would rather keep secret. Secondly, the Member States might, on the basis of national rules, release documents that the EU was not willing to share with the public.

The Advocate General who delivered the Opinion in the *IFAW* appeal proceedings[65] made a sketch of the EU and the Member State practically at each other's mercy.

[63] As had happened in Case T-174/95 *Svenska* (n 9), in which there had been a hostile release of documents by Sweden.

[64] See, however, in the field of competition law, the implications of Case C-360/09 *Pfleiderer AG v Bundeskartellamt* [2011] ECR I-05161 and of Case C-537/11 *Bundeswettbewerbsbehorde Donau Chemie AG a.o.* [not reported] and, more recently, of Directive 2014/104/EU with regard to national law.

[65] AG Maduro in Case C-64/05P *Sweden v Commission* (n 46).

In first light, the new framework caused both the Member State and the EU to lose control over self-produced documents, transmitted to and held by the other.[66]

Ultimately, and not unexpectedly, the ECJ ruled in favour of the EU: the Member States were forced to acknowledge that they 'did not hold a discretionary veto' over own documents (if they were also held by the EU). Moreover, in case of conflict, the Member States could not breach the loyalty owed to the organisation of which they were a component member.

vii. A Remnant of Authority: Interim Relief

However revolutionary, the ruling of the ECJ in *Sweden v Commission*[67] (the appeal of the *IFAW* proceedings) is silent with regard to the possibility that a Member State might deploy a request for interim relief[68] against the disclosure of documents by an institution without its consent. Indeed, the picture that comes across in its immediate aftermath is that, absent agreement, diplomatic rupture could occur.

By contrast in *Germany v Commission*,[69] a hint, that further consideration of EU predominance may be required, comes across.[70] In that case, it is apparent that the Commission, having claimed that 'the arguments put forward by the German authorities as justification for their objections to disclosure of the documents were prima facie, unfounded' informed 'the German authorities of its intention to disclose the documents at issue within a period of 10 working days'. However, as it was about to release the contested documents, the institution reminded[71] Germany that interim relief (against disclosure) might be sought. *In casu*, Germany did not rise to that challenge. Consequently, the Commission handed over the documents at issue to the requesting parties. *Ex post* disclosure, an action for annulment (for reasons of principle) was lodged against the (de facto irreversible) decision to disclose the documents.

The availability of interim relief to authors[72] of documents against hostile disclosure of the same by the EU institutions—inter alia—suggests a discreet yet visible lingering of the ghost of the author's rule over Regulation 1049/2001.

[66] ibid:

> 46. An institution may (...) grant access to a document to which the Member State has refused access, because the Community rules which the MS have agreed to impose on the institutions grant wider access to documents than the national law of the MS concerned'
>
> 47. Subject to article 5 (Cooperation) a Member State may thus disclose a document to which the community institution has refused access because its national rules on transparency are more generous.

[67] Case C-64/05P *Sweden v Commission* (n 46).

[68] Within the access policy, to that date, interim relief had only been deployed in Case T-610/97 R *Carlsen a.o. v Council* [1998] ECR II-00485 by applicants, in order to attempt to expedite access to the documents.

[69] Case T-59/09 *Germany v Commission* (n 52).

[70] ibid, paras 11, 12 and 13.

[71] In accordance with Art 5(6) of Commission Decision 2001/937/EC, ECSC, Euratom of 5 December 2001, amending its Rules of Procedure ([2001] OJ L 345, 94).

[72] Case T-59/09 *Germany v Commission* (n 52) para 3. Disclosure of the following documents was sought: '(i) a letter from the Federal Republic of Germany of 16 February 2006 in response to the Commission's letter of formal notice of 18 October 2005'.

B. Interventions—National Interpretation of the EU Rules on Access

Regulation 1049/2001 has not altered the prerogative of intervention within the access litigation. However, the abolition of the author's rule may have increased Member State's negative biases[73] towards their own citizens. This is because, under the new rules, applicants might be attempting to access documents produced by a Member State by way of Regulation 1049/2001.

As we have seen, the ECJ has ruled that there is no Member State veto regarding the disclosure of own documents held by the EU institutions,[74] and thus, access might be sought at EU level merely to trump or bypass more restrictive national rules on transparency. In these cases, what is being requested of the EU institutions is that they release information that primarily does not concern the institution. Much to the contrary, principally, the information requested concerns a Member State.

i. Those in Favour (of Access)

What remains central is that under the governance of Regulation 1049/2001 the Netherlands, Denmark, Sweden and Finland, never strayed from their pro-applicant, pro-access defence of points of law. These Member States have carefully and persistently pursued and construed expert reputations on the topic of access to documents, and are in large part responsible for significant cornerstones of the related case law.[75] Interestingly, and unless there has been significant change since 2012, the Netherlands, traditionally at the forefront of many of access' battles, made one intervention in 2002, three in 2005, and after a single intervention in 2008, has stepped back from the access litigation.[76] Estonia[77] and Greece[78] joined the selection of Member States intervening in favour of applicants. Although in the case of Greece it is possible that this occurred due to a positive bias rationale with regard to the specific case.

Portugal, Slovenia and France did make an intervention in favour[79] of access. However, the merits of the specific case were not discussed. In addition, the fact that *in casu* several EU Member States grouped together to oppose arguments (against disclosure of the contested documents) put forth by Swiss and North-American parties might mean that this case is an outlier.

Although it does not seem to unduly influence the EU judicature, an additional comment with regard to Member States that support applicants is that, on occasion, they submit interventions in support of a form of order and subsequently withdraw their interventions.[80]

[73] See Table 7.3.

[74] Case C-64/05P *Sweden v Commission* (n 46).

[75] Table 7.2.

[76] ibid.

[77] Joined Cases C-514/11P and C-605/11P *Finland and LPN* (n 19).

[78] Case T-374/07 *Pachtitis*.

[79] Case T-44/13 *AbbVie v EMA* [not yet reported]. The interventions are observable in the order of the President of the fourth chamber of the GC, 17 July 2014. Further, see Ch 8.

[80] Inter alia, Denmark in Case T-190/10 *Egan v Parliament* (n 18) para 18, and Case T-111/11 *Client Earth v Commission* [not reported] para 28; Finland in Case T-194/04 *Bavarian Lager* [2007] ECR II-04523; and Finland and Sweden in Case T-2/03 *VFK* (n 18) paras 50–55.

Finally, the cases in Table 7.2 do not represent the full set of cases that concern the Codes of Conduct and Regulation 1049/2001. Provided that we[81] have been able to compile all the cases in which a Member State has supported an applicant, those cases remain a mere fraction of the full set. The full set comprises cases in which there was intervention (for or against defendants, cases included respectively into Tables 7.2 and 7.3), and cases in which there was no intervention (not included).

Table 7.2: Interventions of the Netherlands, Denmark, Sweden and Finland under Regulation 1049/2001

	Case N°	Nationality of the applicant	NL	DK	SWE	FIN	Other MS /Inst A	Other MS/ Inst D
2002	T-168/02	GER	A	A	A			UK
	T-237/02	GER			A	A		
2003	T-84/04	IT		A	A	A		UK Comm
	T-170/03	UK		A	A		EDPS	
2004	T-161/04	BEL		A	A		EDPS	
2005	T-403/05 RENV		A	A	A	A		UK GER FR
	C-39/05P &	SWE/IT	A					
	C-52/05P	SWE /BE	A	A		A		UK SP
	C-64/05P							
2006	T-299/06					A		
2007	T-111/07	CZ		A	A	A		
	T-374/07	GRE			A		EDPS GRE	
	T-339/07	GER		A	A			
	C-139/07P	GER			A	A		
	C-514/07 &	SWE (BEL)		A		A		UK
	C-532/07							
2008	T-29/08	PT		A	A	A		UK
	T-250/08	BEL		A				UK Cou
	T-344/08	GER			A			GER FR UK
	T-362/08	GER		A	A	A		
	T-437/08	BEL			A			
	T-471/08	IRL	A	A	A	A		
	C-28/08P	UK		A		A	EDPS	
	C-506/08P	SWE (UK)		A		A		
2009	T-59/09	GER		A[82]	A	A		SP POL
	T-82/09	NL		A		A	EDPS	
	T-436/09	FR		A	A	A		Comm

(*continued*)

[81] All tables are constructed by the authors.

[82] In this case we have an instance of a Member State (Germany) that applied for the annulment of a Commission decision that granted some citizens access to documents. Therefore, *de rigueur*, the

Table 7.2: (*Continued*)

	Case N°	Nationality of the applicant	NL	DK	SWE	FIN	Other MS /Inst A	Other MS/ Inst D
2010	T-36/10	GER		A				
	T-180/10	CAN			A	A		
	T-291/10	UK		A				
	C-404/10P	FR		A	A			CZ FR
	C-447/10P	CZ		A	A	A		
2011	T-362/11	NL		A				
	C-135/11P	GER		A	A	A		
	C-208/11P	GER		A				
	C-280/11P	SP						CZ SP FR
	C-514/11 & C-605/11	PT		A	A	A	EST	GRE GER
2012	T-62/12	UK		A	A	A		
	T-306/12	IT		A	A	A		
	T-402/12	SWE			A	A		FR
2013	T-115/13							

Whether at first instance or on appeal, A = person who requests access
D = institution that refuses access

ii. Those against (an Extensive Interpretation of the Access Rules)

Displaying a very different view of the access to documents litigation, another selection of Member States made first appearances within the access to documents litigation. In 2005 Germany,[83] Italy[84] and the Czech Republic,[85] in 2009 Poland[86] and in 2011 Greece,[87] joined France and Spain who (under the Code of Conduct) had already opted for pro-institutional policies of intervention. Italy inaugurated its appearance on the access scene exposing a negative bias[88] towards an own national. An inaugural negative bias may also be attributed to the Czech Republic. However, it arises in connection with the contested documents' object[89] and not with regard to

Commission, here, plays the role of a typical applicant (A) that requests access, and Germany played the part of the typical EU institution (D) that refuses access. Hence, non-typically, support for the Commission is mapped as A, and support for the (applicant) Member State is mapped as D.

[83] Case T-403/05 *MyTravel* (n 19); Joined Cases C-514/11P and C-605/11P *Finland and LPN* (n 19); Case T-623/13 *Union Almacenistas* [not yet reported].

[84] Joined Cases T-109/05 and T-444/05 *Navigazione Libera del Golfo* [2001] ECR II-02479.

[85] In Case T-233/05 *Nomura v Commission* [not reported], the contested documents were connected to the Czech Republic.

[86] Case T-59/09 *Germany v Commission* (n 52).

[87] Case T-233/09 *Access Info v Council*.

[88] In Case T-374/07 *Pachtitis* (n 78), the applicant was Greek and, likewise, in Joined Cases T-109/05 and T-444/05 *Navigazione Libera del Golfo* (n 84), the applicant was Italian.

[89] In case T-233/05 *Nomura v Commission* (n 85), the contested documents originated from the Czech Republic.

the applicant's nationality. Subsequently, this Member State went on to consolidate its position as a pro-institutional[90] intervener. Spain also exposed negative biases.[91] In addition, other Spanish interventions have arisen.[92] Finally, Portugal, more discretely, made an oblique intervention[93] in this context.

France, conversely, sacrificed a consistent pro-institutional reputation construed under the Code of Conduct and further continued under Regulation 1049/2001[94] to come to the rescue of Edith Crésson.[95] Hereby, France exposed itself by way of an exceptional venture in the defence of an applicant, moreover, an own national. Yet, this positive bias is not without the mark of institutional solidarity; Edith Crésson, after all, was first Prime Minister[96] and, subsequently, EU Commissioner[97] for the French Republic.

The UK,[98] now easier to read than under the Code of Conduct, unequivocally abandoned the defence of applicants and consolidated the earlier tendency to side with the institutions. Again, the cases in Table 7.3 do not represent the full set of cases that concern the Codes of Conduct and Regulation 1049/2001. P Although (hopefully) we[99] have been able to include all the cases in which a Member State has supported a defendant, those cases remain a mere fraction of the full set. The full set comprises cases in which there was intervention (for or against applicants) and cases in which there was no intervention (not included).[100]

[90] Case C-404/10P *Commission v Odile Jacob* [not reported]; Case C-280/11P *Council v Access Info* [not reported]; Case T-306/12 *Spirlea* [not reported].

[91] Case T-341/11 *Ecologistas en Accion* [not reported]; Case T-603/11 *Ecologistas en Accion* [not yet reported]; and C-280/11P *Council v Access Info* (n 90).

[92] T-306/12 *Spirlea* (n 90).

[93] Case T-186/08 *LPN*. In this case, whilst not directly intervening against a national applicant in the access litigation (Case T-29/98), it did so in related proceedings (Case T-186/98). However, in both proceedings the applicant alleged that it was the lack of access to documents that impeded an appropriate defence of the environment in the public interest by LPN.

[94] See Table 7.3; Case C-506/08P *Sweden (MyTravel II)*; Case C-404/10 P *Commission v Odile Jacob* (n 90) (here, a negative bias); C-280/11P *Council v Access Info* (n 90); Case T-402/12 *Schlyter v Commission* (Swedish applicant but French documents at stake).

[95] Case C-432/04 *Commission v Crésson* [2006] ECR I-06387 is not a straightforward episode of an action for annulment of a refusal for access to documents. The access to documents incident arose within broader (disciplinary) proceedings undertaken by the Commission against Edith Crésson. In that case, according to AG Geelhoed, the ECJ, when it delivered an order of 9 September 2005, it did so rejecting 'Mrs Crésson's request to order the Commission to provide access to a number of documents related to the Commission's decision to initiate proceedings against her under Article 213(2) EC'. The access issue is further discussed in the Opinion of AG Geelhoed, delivered on 23 February 2006 at para 41 *in fine* and para 108 *in fine*. The ECJ, in the judgment delivered on 11 July 2006, for its part, states at para 48 that 'Mrs Crésson's application for the production of certain documents was rejected by the Court by Order of 9 September 2005'. Doubts could subsist that production of the documents might have been intended for the ECJ only and that might not necessarily be equivalent to a request for transmission of the same to the applicant. The text of the order itself, however, which exists only in French, states that 'l'absence de communication des [documents] n'est pas susceptible de constituer une violation des droits de la defense'. This is the reason why we have included the case in our discussion. The *Crésson* proceedings—inter alia—concerned a request that the ECJ order the Commission to grant the applicant access to documents.

[96] 1991–92.

[97] 1995–99.

[98] Table 7.3. Case T-168/02 *IFAW I* (n 51); Case T-84/03 *Turco I* (n 19); Case C-64/05 *Sweden v Commission* (n 46); Joined Cases C-514/07P and C-532/07P *Sweden and API* [2010] ECR I-08533; T-250/08 *Batchelor* [2011] ECR II-02551; C-28/08P *Commission (Bavarian Lager II)* [2010] ECR I-06055; Case C-506/08P *Sweden (MyTravel II)* (n 9); T-233/09 *Access Info* (n 87).

[99] All tables are constructed by the authors.

[100] See Table 7.3.

Table 7.3: Intervention (Czech Republic, Estonia, Germany, Greece, Italy, Spain, UK, France, Poland) under Regulation 1049/2001

	Case N°	Nationality of the applicant	CZ	EST	GER	GRE	IT	SP	UK	FR	POL
2002	T-168/02	GER							D		
2003	T-84/04	IT							D		
2004	C-423/04	FR								A	
2005	T-109/05	IT					D				
	T-233/05	UK (CZ docs)	D								
	T-403/05	UK			D				D	D	
	T-403/05 RENV				D				D	D	
	C-64/05P	SWE /BE						D	D		
2006											
2007	T-374/07	GRE				A					
	C-514/07 & C-532/07	SWE/BEL							D		
2008	C-28/08P	UK							D		
	C-506/08P	SWE (UK)			D				D	D	
2009	T-59/09	GER						D			D
	T-233/09	SP				D			D		
2010	T-359/10	SP						D			
	C-404/10P	FR	D							D	
2011	T-341/11	SP									
	T-93/11	NL			D						
	C-280/11P	SP	D					D		D	
	C-514/11 & C-605/11	PT		A	D						
2012	T-306/12	IT	D					D			
	T-402/12	SWE (FR docs)								D	
2013	T-623/13	SP			D						
2014											
2015											

iii. What Matters More? Number of Interventions or Points of Law

One could tell the story of Member State intervention by compiling the points of law that each State has supported, first under the Code of Conduct and, subsequently under Regulation 1049/2001. That methodology would, in fact, be required, if Member States fluctuated between defending applicants (those who request) and defendants (those who refuse). However, that is not the case here.

To illustrate this point, anyone who has even marginally followed the development of the EU access policy, would find it (to say the least) extraordinary if the Netherlands,[101] Denmark, Sweden or Finland ever made an intervention in support of the form of order submitted by a refusing institution. It is not by chance that (after eight years of governance of the policy by the Code(s) of Conduct followed by almost 15 years of its governance by Regulation 1049/2001) such a moment is yet to come.

In very broad lines, the alternative pro-applicant v pro-(defendant) institution is the practical translation of two forms of national political culture, which oppose one another. The first, to which Member States within the sphere of influence of Scandinavian law are partial, is extremely demanding on institutions with regard to accountability to the public. The second form aggregates Member States that prefer a zealous defence of some institutional space that is, simply, not the public's business. This is a good explanation for the fact that (except for the UK, within an earlier period and except for occasional, explicable, national biases) Member States do not fluctuate between instances in which they support an applicant (because of an interesting point of law) and instances in which they support a defendant institution (because of an interesting point of law).

Although we have opted to include intervention under a pro-applicant v pro-defendant quantitative approach, another, and quite different, point that could be explored to explain intervention, may well lie in the economic resilience of each Member State, in the distribution of available resources with regard to specific topics and national agendas, and even in the ability of the legal teams in the foreign offices to argue the topic of access to documents.

Globally, although the formidable role of Denmark, Sweden and Finland, cannot be overstated, we do not wish to raise conjecture with regard to the merits of the foreign policy of the Member States of the EU. We have written about intervention because otherwise intervention would remain, relatively unnoticed, in the background of Regulation 1049/2001. The principal attempt here was to highlight how, on the one hand, intervention is an available role that is often played by some, and, on the other hand, that applicants, institutions, and courts must take it in their stride.

[101] With regard to the Netherlands, in Case C-60/15P *Saint-Gobain v Commission* [not yet reported], it is interesting to see how the new standards of the Aarhus Regulation might lead Member States traditionally prone to intervene in favour of access to adopt a more conservative position with regard to the ability of the public to challenge other institutional and/or national decisions when national interests are at stake.

Lastly, it is also true that Member State interventions might also be addressed from another type of quantitative approach: assessing the (decreasing?) marginal utility of each successive intervention that is coherent with the previous one. In other words, and to put it bluntly, what utility lies in the successive exposure of the Member State, in quasi-compulsive assertions of the same points, once its discount rate has been adequately perceived by the EU judicature? What we mean to say is that interventions in favour of applicants from Denmark, Sweden and Finland have become a given. The same may be said (with regard to defendants) of the UK, France and Spain.

One might then wonder about many alternative scenarios: about (1) the relevance the EU judicature indeed attributes to such interventions; (2) the type of attention that a 'first appearance' intervention of, for example, Belgium would exact from the judicature; and (3) how an intervention from Denmark, Finland or Sweden, in favour of a restriction of access, would be interpreted by the judicature.

The questions are endless, and still, the excursus of a *Tinker, Tailor, Soldier, Spy* characterisation of the Member State is not complete. The State keeps more surprises up its sleeve. Member States, that are, at once, constrained guardians of EU documents and relatively powerless spectators of the management of own documents by the EU, may, as we will now discuss, play a role in the access policy, beyond intervention. They have one other option left: to take the dispensation of justice into their own hands.[102]

C. When the EU Shapes National Law

Although without the purpose of carving out yet another 'role' of the Member State in the access to documents litigation under Regulation 1049/2001, a brief reference to recent developments in EU competition law should be made. Certain incidents that occurred concurrently to the governance of access by Regulation 1049/2001 have arisen within the context of national competition proceedings. Given their predominantly national context, they are easy to overlook in this EU context of access to documents.

What is of interest here is that—quite unexpectedly—the principles governing the EU access to documents litigation have had impact within national proceedings both on the scope[103] of the national judicature's tasks and on the depth[104] of its competence.

[102] This role of the Member State—that of appellant—will be discussed in Ch 8.

[103] Case C-360/09 *Pfleiderer* and Case C-536/11 *Donau Chemie* (n 64).

[104] See Directive 2014/104/EU of the European Parliament and of the Council of 26 November 2014 on certain rules governing actions for damages under national law for infringements of the competition law provisions of the Member States and of the European Union, [2014] OJ L 349/1-19.

i. When the EU Shapes National Law: Pfleiderer, Donau Chemie *and Directive 2014/104/EU*

Up to this moment, we have discussed the role of the Member State as that of an entity that somehow attempts to impinge on the development of the EU access policy. Prior consent, guardianship, intervention and appeal[105] all make room for the national voice. The national voice, in each of these ways, strives to shape EU law.

Having done this, it is time to speak of a singular *revanche* of the EU: when first, the ECJ and, subsequently, the EU legislator, in their contribution to an EU access policy, embark on the same, now reversed, undertaking: shaping national law.

The first two incidents to suggest that the traditional insulation of the national rules on access to documents, from the EU policy on access to documents, might be under threat were two rulings of the ECJ delivered within the preliminary ruling procedure. First, Case C-360/09 *Pfleiderer*, and subsequently Case C-536/11 *Donau Chemie*. In fact, with regard to national rules on access to competition law-related leniency and settlement documents by victims of cartels,[106] EU law-derived standards[107] have been imposed onto national law via the principle of effectiveness of the protection of EU Law-derived rights.

In *Pfleiderer*, the ECJ acknowledged that with regard to requests for access to documents concerning leniency proceedings, it was for the national judge to weigh up the conflicting interests (of victims of cartels and members of the cartel that cooperated with the national authorities). Of course the ruling was confined to cases of enforcement in the Member State of EU competition law rules.

Later, in *Donau Chemie*,[108] drawing on *Pfleiderer*, the ECJ ruled further about what should take place in the national domain, when access to documents is sought to protect EU law-derived rights.[109] If national rules governing access to documents by victims wishing to institute an action for compensation for damages against members of a cartel are too restrictive, they must be set aside.

The third incident widened the hairline fracture that was already discernible in the Member State's insulation from the EU dimension of access to documents. It came about by way of Directive 2014/104/EU[110] on private enforcement of EU competition law in the Member States. The latter impinged even further on national law, this time striking at the heart of national civil procedure. Therein, and again limited to documents related to leniency proceedings and settlement submissions, in national cases concerning the private enforcement in the Member State[111] of EU competition

[105] See Ch 8.

[106] This subject has attracted extensive writing from commentators; for an overview, see N Harsdorf Endendorf and N Maierhofer, 'The Road after Pfleiderer: Austrian Preliminary Reference Raises New Questions on Access to File by Third Parties in Cartel Proceedings' (2013) *European Competition Law Review* 78–83.

[107] Stemming from the case law on effectiveness.

[108] C-536/11 *Donau Chemie* (n 64) paras 42, 43 and 49.

[109] Ex Art 101 and 102 TFEU.

[110] Directive 2014/104/EU.

[111] Directive 2014/104/EU, Art 6.

rules, the national judicature will, as of 2016,[112] be prohibited from granting applicants access to the same, on the basis of injunctions.[113] First, by removing specific information from disclosure *tout court*, the Directive redesigns the material scope of access in the Member State. The national competition authority finds clear solace in the law when refusing such documents and the right of access becomes less wide.[114] In addition, to ensure that the national judicature does not order the disclosure or disclose such documents to the public (a long-standing prerogative of the courts), the EU has chosen to interfere in national procedural law by curbing the depth[115] of judicial power also.

For the purposes of protecting the EU competition policy and its private enforcement, there is a functionalist[116] interference of the EU legislator on the traditional equilibrium between institutions (here the national competition authority) and the civil courts in the Member State. These three incidents have been discussed in Chapter 5 (Exceptions), on the basis of the principle of effectiveness, in contrast with the growing number of rebuttable presumptions of harm, which the ECJ has allowed the EU institutions to wield against applicants at the supranational EU context.

Here, they are mentioned here from a different perspective. They place a burden on the Member State, which is required to accommodate them within national law. The Member State's role, here, is one of enforcer of the EU perspective on access to documents to the detriment of centuries of refinement of national procedural rules and, of national checks and balances between the national courts, the national authorities and the national citizen.

[112] Directive 2014/104/EU, Art 21(1).

[113] Directive 2014/104/EU, Art 6: 'Member States shall ensure that, for the purpose of actions for damages, national courts cannot, at any time order a party or a third party to disclose any of the following categories of evidence: (a) leniency statements; and (b) settlement submissions'.

[114] See Ch 1.

[115] See Ch 1.

[116] Harlow and Rawlings, *Process and Procedure in the EU Administration* (n 41).

Part II

Fourth and Fifth Actors: EU Institutions—Two more Men in the Boat

The access policy's principal actors are first, applicants[117] and then, institutions.[118] As we have discussed in Part I of this chapter, in opposition to those principal actors, the Member State is an eccentric actor of the access policy. Moreover, as an intervener, the EU Member State is the policy's third actor.

This section identifies other possible interveners in proceedings. Two more exist, and both, as the EU Member State did, come to light as ancillary, eccentric actors to the access policy. Moreover, they are neither applicant, nor defendant, nor State.

The fourth actor of the access policy is, surprisingly, the EU institution. It appears, now, in a new context, as intervener. In other words, the EU institution, in contrast to its principal role, might appear either as non-defendant[119] or as non-applicant.[120]

One of the remnant roles of institutions is that of intervener in proceedings, another is of appellant of first instance decisions. The latter role, as was done with regard to State appeals, will be discussed in Chapter 8. The former, intervention, will be discussed in the present chapter.

Finally, the fifth actor of the access policy is any third party with an interest in the outcome of the case. This interested third party also appears here as a non-applicant (at first instance) and/or as a non-defendant (at first instance or appeal).

IV. FOURTH ACTOR: THE EU INSTITUTION UNDER THE CODE OF CONDUCT

A. Author's Rule and Guardianship

Inasmuch as the public did not adopt the practice of requesting from one institution the documents of another (a cross-request), with regard to institutions, the author's rule was not a protagonist of the case law. Moreover, whilst admittedly a cross-request, in that context, was conceivable, the particular applicant would have merely been redirected to the institution that had authored the documents.

One institution, the Council—in *Rothmans v Commission*[121] was, however, involved in a (negative) dispute of authorship. The episode did not arise from a cross-request of an applicant. In addition, the Council's contribution was neither

[117] See Ch 2.
[118] See Ch 3.
[119] At first instance or on appeal.
[120] On appeal.
[121] Case T-188/97 *Rothmans v Commission* [1999] ECR II-02463, as mentioned in Ch 3.

an intervention nor entirely voluntary. It was the Court of First Instance that, of its own motion,[122] requested that the Council answer questions with regard to the background of the *Rothmans* case. Thereby, the Council denied authorship of the contested documents and attributed their authorship to the Commission, which consequently was left alone to deal with the applicant's request.

Guardianship by one EU institution of another institution's documents was ineffectual with regard to access under the Codes of Conduct. At the time, and in the first place, duties arising from institutional cooperation (then Article 10 EC) and, secondly, (at its limit) the author's rule preponderance over the entire access policy, trumped even the slightest suspicion that hostile disclosure might be considered.

B. Interventions

Overall, EU institutions intervene in on-going proceedings that are taking place between other EU institutions and applicants, more often than one might expect. In doing this, as was said of the Member State, they too expose 'discount rates'.

Under the Code of Conduct only two institutions took on the role of interveners: the Commission and the European Parliament. Both institutions made interventions in *NL v Council*,[123] which is, as we have often mentioned, not a pure access to documents case. This notwithstanding, for contextual reasons[124] the Parliament sided with the Netherlands and the Commission sided with the Council. It was at the very least a signal that institutions were not afraid of opposing one another, publicly.

i. Those in Favour

It was by way of the Parliament's intervention in *Carvel I v Council*,[125] however, that it became clear that, in addition to Member States, the EU institutions might come to embrace opposing sides of the (pro-access v pro-secrecy) divide. In that case, the Parliament supported John Carvel, editor of *The Guardian*, both applicants, to the detriment of the Council, the defendant institution, against which proceedings had been commenced.

ii. No Interventions against Access

Throughout the entire period that the Code of Conduct was in force, there were no observable interventions of any institution for reasons of solidarity with another institution that happened to be refusing an applicant access to documents. Consequently, for the period governed by the Code of Conduct, the entire sample consisted of a single intervention (in favour of an applicant). One intervention, from

[122] ibid, paras 23 and 60.
[123] Case C-58/94 *NL v Council* (n 21).
[124] Addressed in Ch 1.
[125] Case T-194/94 *Carvel I v Council* (n 22).

the Parliament, is hardly sufficient to enable any robust conclusions. However there were two pieces of data, which read together, pointed in a certain direction. The first was that the Parliament had wanted a more dignified legal basis, for a right as important (to applicants) as access, since access' first breath.[126] The second piece of data was that the intervention in *Carvel I*[127] was a first appearance. Indeed, the exposure of the first discount rate is always significant as a signal that in the future we might expect the Parliament to side with applicants again.

V. THE EU INSTITUTION UNDER REGULATION 1049/2001

A. Author's Rule and Guardianship

Whilst theoretically possible since the author's rule has ceased to exist, it is unthinkable that today one EU institution would release documents of another EU institution without its counterpart's consent.[128] Institutional respect (more so even than solidarity), today governed by Article 13 TFEU, commands that hostile disclosure is not contemplated at the institutional level.

It is also true that within the access policy governed first by the Code of Conduct and subsequently by Regulation 1049/2001, the existence and disappearance of the author's rule, and its connection to guardianship of EU documents is of principal relevance to the relationship between the EU institutions and the public. This context is not aimed at managing relationships between institutions. In practice, there have been no incidents (in the case law) that prove the contrary. Until then, we may let the matter lie.

B. Interventions

Under Regulation 1049/2001, the Council and the European Data Protection Supervisor (EDPS) joined the Commission and the EP as institutional interveners.[129]

i. Those in Favour

Notably, the Parliament's inaugural signal of a pro-applicant preference[130] was consolidated. However, the consolidation came in 2012, almost 18 years later,

[126] See Ch 1.

[127] Case T-194/94 *Carvel I v Council* (n 22).

[128] This is of course different from situations such as the one that came about in Case T-193/04 *Tillack v Commission* [2006] ECR II-03995, in which it was (allegedly) an agent of the Commission that 'sold' confidential Commission documents to a member of the public.

[129] The European Chemicals Agency (ECHA) attempted an intervention in favour of the Commission, as recently as 2013 in Case C-673/13P *Commission v Stichting and Greenpeace NL and PAN Europe* [not yet reported]. However, the ECJ rejected the intervention on the grounds that the ECHA was merely 'in a similar' position to that of the Commission and was unable to prove a direct interest in the annulment of the specific decision challenged.

[130] In Case T-194/94 *Carvel I v Council* (n 22).

and is possibly the result of a positive bias. The EP that had seemingly stepped back from interventions, appeared in support of the form of order submitted by *Ms In't Veld*,[131] one of its own members.

ii. Those against

With regard to the Council and the Commission, both may be considered frequent interveners in the access litigation today, albeit the Commission more so than the Council. Although both are prone to come forward and support each other with regard to a wide range of points of law, as a matter of policy neither institution has ever used its powers of intervention in favour of (any point of law submitted by) any applicant. The discount rate of these institutions is wide: they will intervene whenever it is necessary to curb liberal interpretations of access to documents.

Individually, the Council has come forth in at least two instances: *NLG* in 2005[132] and the *Bavarian Lager* appeal in 2008,[133] each time in support of the Commission.

The Commission has been more active, coming forth at least five times to support the Council in 1994, 2003, 2004, 2009 and 2011,[134] at least once to support the ECB in 2009[135] and at least once to support the European Food Safety Agency (EFSA) in 2011.[136]

The Council and the Commission have thus gained reputations as inveterate pro-institutional interveners. Consequently, it is not to be expected that they will ever interfere against one another.

iii. Those who Fluctuate

Of quite a different order is the EDPS. First, its discount rate is clear, but extremely narrow: it principally concerns the definition of 'personal data' and/or the application of Regulation 45/2001 in conjunction with Regulation 1049/2001.[137]

[131] Case C-350/12P *Council v In't Veld* [not yet reported]; the context concerned an appeal initiated by the Council against a decision at first instance that had been favourable to that applicant.

[132] Joined Cases T-109/05 and T-444/05 *Navigazione Libera del Golfo v Commission* (n 84).

[133] Case C-28/08P *Commission v Bavarian Lager* (n 98).

[134] C-58/94 *NL v Council* (n 21); Case T-84/03 *Turco v Council* (n 19); Case T-264/04 *WWF v Council* [2007] ECR II-911; Case T-529/09 *In't Veld v Council* [not reported]; Case T-331/11 *Besselink v Council* [not yet reported].

[135] T-436/09 *Dufour v ECB* [2011] II-07727.

[136] T-214/11 *Client Earth & PAN v EFSA*.

[137] Case C-615/13P *ClientEarth & PAN v EFSA* [not yet reported] order of the President of the ECJ, 13 June 2014:

> The EDPS's role as intervener (in proceedings governed by Regulation 1049/2001) is based on Article 190 of the Rules of Procedure of the Court of Justice and Article 47(1)(i) of Regulation (EC) No 45/2001. The EDPS has a right to intervene in actions brought before the Court of Justice of the European Union, which is circumscribed within the limits deriving from the task entrusted to it. In accordance with the second subparagraph of Article 41(2) of Regulation No 45/2001, the EDPS is responsible for monitoring and ensuring the application of the provisions of that regulation and any other Union act relating to the protection of the fundamental rights

Secondly, the EDPS has intervened at least seven times in the access litigation, which makes it, alongside the Commission, the champion institutional intervener. Thirdly, its interventions have come forth in 2003,[138] 2004 (2),[139] 2008,[140] 2009,[141] 2010,[142] 2013[143] and 2014.[144] Notably, it was usual that the EDPS would side with the applicant.[145] In 2014, however, and for the first time, the EDPS sided with an institution, against an applicant.

What is of great interest here is not the position of the EDPS as such.[146] Instead, it is the abrupt reversal of a settled position from pro-applicant to pro-institution that is striking. Moreover, the topic that leads the EDPS to expose a discount rate remains identical: disclosure of names of persons when acting in a professional capacity.[147]

What changed in 2014 was the beneficiary of the EDPS' intervention. Once, such interventions would have unfalteringly favoured applicants attempting to gain access to those very names. However, as a consequence of the EDPS' appearance on the access scene in 2014, it is the institutions (EFSA also supported by the Commission) attempting to withhold those names from public scrutiny that are supported by the EDPS. This signals to applicants that it is actually possible[148] that the EDPS might (and did) intervene within proceedings with the guise of restricting their access to documents.

Whether the next intervention of the EDPS will be pro-applicant or pro-institution is unclear. This is because, differently from the Council and the Commission, the EDPS is not anchored by a pro-institutional bias. It intervenes with the sole purpose of refining the criteria according to which information connected to private life and concurrently falling within the scope of personal data is to be protected by EU law.[149]

and freedoms of natural persons with regard to the processing of personal data by a European Union institution or body, and for advising Union institutions and bodies and data subjects on all matters concerning the processing of personal data.

[138] Case T-170/03 *British American Tobacco v Commission* [not reported].

[139] Case T-161/04 *Valero Jordana* [2001] ECR II-00215; and Case T-191/04 *Bavarian Lager I* [2007] ECR II-04523.

[140] Case C-28/08P *Bavarian Lager II* (n 98).

[141] Case T-82/09 *Dennekamp* [2011] ECR II-00418.

[142] Case T-190/10 *Egan & Hackett* (n 80).

[143] Case T-115/13 *Dennekamp* (a second round of Case T-82/09 *Dennekamp* (n 141)).

[144] On 4 April 2014, see order of President of ECJ of 18 June 2014 in Case C-615/13P *ClientEarth v EFSA* (n 137).

[145] See above.

[146] The EDPS' substantive position on the relationship between Regulation 1049/2001 and Regulation 45/2001 is discussed in Ch 5 (Exceptions).

[147] Opinion of AG Villalon in Case C-615/13P *ClientEarth & PAN v EFSA* (n 137) paras 27–29.

[148] Admittedly, as we have mentioned, in *Valero Jordana*, paras 85 and 86 and *Egan and Hackett* (n 80) para 7), there had already been claims of a mismatch between the EDPS' submissions and the form of order in favour of the applicants it claimed to support. *In casu*, the GC took little heed of the alleged discrepancy; however; the EDPS' latest intervention, of 2014, in Case C-615/13P *ClientEarth v EFSA* sheds new light on this particular set of interventions.

[149] See Chapter 7, Table 7.4.

Table 7.4: Interventions of Institutions: Code of Conduct and Regulation 1049/2001

	Case No	Commission	Council	Parliament	EDPS	Others A	Others D
Code of Conduct							
1994	C-58/94 *NL v Council*	D		A			FR
1994	T-194/94 *Carvel I*			A		DK NL	
Regulation 1049/2001							
2003	T-84/03 *Turco v Council*	D				SWE DK FIN	UK
2003	T-170/03 *BAT*				A	SWE DK	
2004	T-161/04 *Valero Jordana*				A	SWE DK	
2004	T-194/04 *Bavarian Lager*				A		
2004	T-264/04 *WWF v Council*	D					
2005	T-109/05 & T-444/05 *NLG*		D				IT Caremar
2007	T-374/07 *Pachtitis*						
2008	C-28/08P *Bavarian II*		D		A	SWE DK FIN	UK
2009	T-82/09 *Dennekamp v EP*				A	DK FIN	
2009	T-436/09 *Dufour v ECB*	D				DK FIN SWE	
2009	T-529/09 *In't Veld v Council*	D					
2010	T-190/10 *Egan & Hackett v EP*				A	DK NL	

(*continued*)

Table 7.4: ***(Continued)***

2011	T-214/11 *Client Earth & PAN v EFSA*	D					
2011	T-331/11 *Besselink v Council*	D					
2011	C-280/11P *Council v Access Info Europe*			A			
2012	C-350/12 *Council v In't Veld*			A			
2013	T-115/13 *Dennekamp v EP*				A		
2014	C-615/13P *Client Earth v EFSA*	D			D		

VI. THE PRIVATE PARTY UNDER THE CODE OF CONDUCT

A. Author's Rule and Guardianship

Under the author's rule, private parties were extremely protected from hostile disclosure of own documents by the EU institutions. As we have mentioned, the disclosure of the documents of others was not an issue with regard to which the EU displayed any interest at all. However, differently from the Member States, with which closer ties exist (the *Svenska* incident notwithstanding), the control of EU institutions over the public with regard to situations of guardianship of EU documents was always frail. It was especially so from the point of view of enforcement. In spite of this there were no memorable incidents (in the case law) of hostile disclosure of EU originating documents by the public. If there were any, they were kept out of the litigation involving the Codes of Conduct and conducted before the EU courts.

B. Interventions

It was with regard to interventions, requests for interim relief and appeals that it became clear how natural or legal persons other than the applicant, are also allowed to give their contribution to proceedings that are pending before the EU courts.[150] Their intervention, however 'shall not confer the same procedural rights as those conferred on the parties, shall be ancillary to the main proceedings and shall become devoid of purpose if the case is removed from the register'.[151] Furthermore, and differently from Member States of the EU and to EU institutions, which enjoy a more privileged status,[152] third parties seeking to make an intervention must prove that they 'hold an interest in the outcome of the case, which in access to documents signifies an interest in the annulment, or the affirmance, of a specific decision refusing (the applicant) access to specified documents".

No differently from Member States and EU institutions, third parties to proceedings may be expected to intervene from two, alternative, and opposite stances. On the one hand, they might lobby the institution (before the Court), in support of the applicant, by providing arguments in favour of the disclosure of the contested documents. On the other, they might plead with the Court in support of the defendant institution encouraging the latter to withhold the contested documents from public scrutiny. No intervention of any private party came about under the Code(s) of Conduct.

[150] This section is confined to interventions of third parties within cases in which the institutions have refused documents and, consequently, the applicant has initiated proceedings against the refusing institution.

[151] Rules of Procedure of the Court of Justice 2012, Arts 129–31.

[152] However, see in Case C-615/13P *ClientEarth v EFSA* (n 137) the restriction of scope of intervention for the EDPS clarified by the Order of the President of the ECJ, 13 June 2014. Also in this sense, see the rejection by the ECJ of the prospective intervention of the European Chemicals Agency (ECHA) within Case C-673/13P *Commission v Stichting and Greenpeace NL and PAN Europe* (n 131).

VII. THE PRIVATE PARTY UNDER REGULATION 1049/2001

A. Author's Rule and Guardianship

With regard to the extinction of the author's rule, the lesser protection of incoming documents to scrutiny by the public very possibly led natural and legal persons who for a variety of reasons transmitted documents to the EU institutions to adopt a much more cautious, or even risk-averse, attitude. This fact has also very possibly led the institutions (that need information from the public to carry out the tasks with which they are entrusted) to find new ways in which it can assure those who give information that the same will only be disclosed (to an applicant) if the institution has no other option. Therefore, knowing when not to disclose information becomes just as essential to the public interest as the respect for the need of some public access to documents.

With regard to guardianship (by private parties) of EU documents, there are diverse procedural rules[153] that lay down obligations of non-disclosure addressed to third parties that hold documents of the EU. On the basis of the same and, for example, with regard to procedural documents related to pending cases, in theory, and when forewarned that a party to proceedings might be contemplating disclosure of procedural documents to third parties, the institutions may always request that the Court prescribe measures of organisation of procedure to 'remind third persons of those same obligations'. However, in practice, it also comes across that outside situations in which the private party has no wish to antagonise the EU judicature (because it is also party to on-going proceedings and subject to the control of the Court), to a large extent the institutions must rely on third parties' good faith. It suffices to say that today the EU is in a difficult position whenever it seeks to impede *ex ante* (or to obtain redress *ex post*) the hostile release of EU-originating documents by private parties and/or their dissemination on the internet, for example.

i. Consultation of Authors

Still, it is true that under the present framework EU institutions, in principle,[154] consult authors before disclosing incoming documents to the public.

ii. Prior Consent

Consultation notwithstanding, differently from situations in which Member States are the authors of incoming documents,[155] in general the law does not bind the EU institutions to manage private parties' consent with regard to disclosure of documents. However, this institutional freedom (from prior consent) may fall away when

[153] On this point, see the order of the President of the GC in Case T-812/14R *BPC Lux a.o. v Commission* [not yet reported] paras 11, 14 and 15.

[154] Regulation 1049/2001, Art 4(4).

[155] ibid, Art 5.

the subject matter of the contested documents calls for the concurrent application of other legislative instruments.[156]

iii. Interim Relief

Finally, private parties that are authors[157] of incoming documents held by the EU may, and do, deploy interim relief[158] against disclosure of own documents and/or request confidential treatment of the same, before the same are disclosed to the public. Such options tend to arise in cases involving business secrets and/or competition law,[159] when for instance, on the basis of Regulation 1049/2001, a competitor requests the EU institutions for access to documents originating from another firm.[160]

Cases such as the ones just mentioned must, however, be distinguished from a 'false friend' rooted in EU competition law: applications for confidential treatment of information allegedly covered by business secrecy, when such requests are not governed by Regulation 1049/2001.[161]

B. Interventions

With regard to interventions of private parties in the access to documents proceedings, the scenario described with regard to the Code of Conduct became

[156] As eg with regard to cases covered by Regulation 45/2001, Art 5(d).

[157] The persons who produced a document held by the EU.

[158] Persons may seek that an order of non-disclosure (*non-facere*) is addressed by the EU judicature to the institutions.

[159] The odd case out is Case T-216/01R *Reisebank v Commission* [2001] ECR II-03481 in which the pro-disclosure interim relief (suspension of the operation of institutional decision not to disclose documents) was not granted. This led the applicant to appeal the order of the GC to the ECJ in Case C-477/01P (R) *Reisebank v Commission* [2002] ECR I-02117. The ECJ did not reverse the decision of the GC.

[160] Case T-44/13R *Abbvie v EMA* (n 79), in which interim relief against disclosure was sought and, on appeal, Case C-389/13P (R) *EMA v Abbvie* [not reported]. The main proceedings concerned an application for annulment of decision EMA/748792/2012 of 14 January 2013, granting a third party access, under Regulation (EC) No 1049/2001, to certain documents. Several undertakings sought to impede the European Medicines Agency (the EMA) from granting access to information submitted in a dossier in respect of an application for a marketing authorisation for the medicinal product Humira, which is intended for the treatment of Crohn's disease. Whilst the GC granted Abbvie temporary relief, and ordered the EMA not to release the contested documents (a *non-facere* instruction), the ECJ, on appeal by the EMA, set the GC's order aside.

> Case T-73/13R *Intermune UK a.o. v EMA* [not reported], and on appeal, Case C-390/13P (R) *EMA v Intermune* [not reported]. The main proceedings concerned an application, in essence, for suspension of operation of EMA Decision EMA/24685/2013 of 15 January 2013, granting a third party (Boehringer Ingelheim GmbH, a competitor undertaking of the applicants) access to certain documents (containing information submitted (by Intermune) as part of an application for authorisation to place the medicinal product Esbriet on the market), pursuant to Regulation (EC) No 1049/2001, inasmuch as that information was not yet within the public domain. Whilst the GC granted Intermune temporary relief and ordered the EMA not to release the contested documents (a *non-facere* instruction), the ECJ, on appeal by the EMA, set the GC's order aside.

[161] eg Case T-462/12R *Pilkington Group Ltd v Commission* [not reported], in which the undertaking deployed interim relief to suspend the operation of a Commission decision rejecting confidential

rather different under Regulation 1049/2001. First, and notably, the overwhelming majority of interventions of private parties in the access to documents litigation governed by Regulation 1049/2001 support the refusing institutions. Second, and no less notably, no private party has been allowed to intervene in favour of an applicant challenging an institutional refusal to disclose documents on the basis of Regulation 1049/2001.

i. Interventions Seeking to Impede Access

An intervention against disclosure is easily confused with interim relief[162] against disclosure, and/or applications for confidential treatment[163] of documents, since all three tactics share the same purpose: that the documents are withheld from public scrutiny. The distinguishing factor between them is that whilst (ideally) interim relief and applications for confidential treatment are submitted *ex ante* disclosure, interventions occur *ex post* institutional refusal to disclose documents, and post-commencement (by the person seeking access) of a challenge in court of that very refusal.

In sum, with regard to interventions seeking to impede access, we may expect two types of actors: in the first place, authors, who have been informed by the institutions that a third party is seeking access to their documents, and have been assured of institutional refusal, might subsequently intervene in support of the refusing institution if and when any applicant challenges that refusal. In addition, persons otherwise connected to the contested documents (and who wish to keep that information from public scrutiny) might do the same.

Between 2002 and 2012 in cases governed by Regulation 1049/2001 and pertaining to the field of competition law, at least nine[164] cases bear the mark of private parties seeking to impede access to contested documents were observed. An additional case that, alone, excited eight objections to the release of documents from private parties,[165] came forth in 2013. However, albeit also related to risk of adverse effects on the commercial interests of a natural or legal person, it arises principally in connection with the concept of emissions into the environment and to the joint application of Regulation 1049/2001 and Regulation 1367/2006 (Aarhus).

ii. Competition Law

The more specific subject matter of the interventions of private parties (that have come forth in support of refusing institutions) pertaining both to Regulation 1049/2001

treatment of certain information. The GC granted Pilkington that temporary relief by order of 11 March 2013. On appeal from the Commission, the ECJ in Case C-278/13P(R) *Commission v Pilkington*, by order of 10 September 2013, confirmed that the suspension should hold. As a result (as long as the order was in force) the Commission was unable to release that information to the public.

[162] See section VII.A.iii of this chapter.

[163] See section VII.A.iii of this chapter

[164] See section VII.B.ii of this chapter.

[165] Case C-673/13P *Stichting Greenpeace NL and Pesticide Action Network (PAN) Europe v Commission* (n 129).

and competition law has been one of four types: State aid, cartels, concentrations or tenders.

a. State Aid

A beneficiary of State aid (declared incompatible with the common market), unable to access the State aid file under the specific sectoral rules, deploys Regulation 1049/2001 in order to attempt access. A competitor of that beneficiary intervenes in support of the Commission's refusal to grant access. In the alternative, a competitor of an undertaking that was given State aid attempts to access the file. The beneficiary of the State aid supports the Commission's refusal.[166]

b. Cartels

An applicant that has fallen victim[167] of a cartel requests access to the Commission's file on that same cartel. The purpose of the request is to collect evidence to subsequently or concurrently lodge an action for damages against the members of the cartel. Interveners in these cases will be the members of the cartel, who support the Commission's refusal to grant access to the competition file.[168]

c. Concentrations

An applicant seeking to challenge a Commission decision declaring a certain concentration compatible with the common market, seeks access to that specific file, whilst one of the initial parties to the concentration seeks, by intervention in support of the Commission, to impede access to the file.[169]

[166] Respectively Case T-237/02 *Technische Glasweke Ilmenau (TGI)* [2006] II-05131, in which Schott Glass, the intervener (who supported the Commission), was TGI's competitor; and in Case T-109/05 and T-444/05 *Navigazione Libera del Golfo* (n 84) in which Caremar, intervener, was the beneficiary of State aid.

[167] Other cases of EU law display a similar structure to those described above, but do not include the discussion of the rules laid down by Regulation 1049/2001. Again they are 'false friends' of cases governed by Regulation 1049/2001. eg cases concerning access to documents to specific infringement files by complainants may be discussed exclusively on the basis of other, more detailed, procedural rules. Amongst hundreds, if not thousands, of examples within competition law, a case with a special twinkle involved both the UK and Luxembourg counterparts of the De Beers Company. Both undertakings rushed to intervene in Joined Cases T-104/07 and T-339/08 *BVDG v Commission* [not reported] with the objective of impeding BVDG's access to their file. However, those proceedings were governed exclusively by Regulation 773/2004 relating to the conduct of proceedings by the Commission pursuant to Arts 81 and 82 of the EC Treaty (today Art 101 and 102 TFEU).

[168] This structure is observable in Case T-2/03 *VFK* (n 18) in which the interveners, three banks (NoHypo BAWAG and OWAG) were members of the Lombard cartel; in Cases T-344/08 [not reported] and C-365/12P *EnBW* [not reported] (in first instance and appeal) in which Siemens AG and ABB, interveners, were also cartel members; in Case T-437/08 *CDC* [2011] ECR II-08251 where Evonik Degussa, intervener, was a member of the cartel; and finally, in Case T-534/11 *Schenker* [not yet reported] all of 7 members of an aviation cartel, sporting 6 different nationalities (Koninklije Luchtvaart Maatschappij (Netherlands); Martinair (Netherlands); Societé Air France (France); Cathay Pacific Airways (China); Air Canada (Canada); Lufthansa Cargo AG (Germany); Swiss Int'l Airlines AG (Switzerland), gathered in support of the Commission in its refusal to grant the applicant access to the infringement file.

[169] Cases T 237/05 [2020] ECR II-02245 and C-404/10P *Ed O Jacob* [not reported] (first instance and appeal), a case in which Lagardère SCA supported the Commission's refusal to grant access to the file;

d. Tenders

An applicant seeking to challenge both the rejection of a tender it submitted in response to an invitation by the Commission, and the awarding of the contract to another tenderer requests access to the documentation of the tenderer's file. The party who was awarded the contract seeks to impede access to the same file, by supporting the Commission's refusal.[170]

iii. Emissions into the Environment and the Aarhus Regulation

A very recent episode, related to information on glyphosate, within which the relevance of the Aarhus Regulation within the access policy is discussed,[171] excited eight interventions in support of the Commission (one of which was rejected), and one in support of the applicant (which was rejected). Interestingly, in this particular case the ECJ has clearly organised the triage of the prospective interveners into two categories.

The first category encompasses 'representative associations which have as their object the protection of their members' interests in cases raising questions of principle liable to affect those members'.[172]

The second category into which the ECJ qualified other potential interveners targets 'persons who can establish only an indirect interest in the result of the case by reason of similarities between their situation and that of one of the parties'.[173]

likewise, in Cases T-111/07 [2010] ECR II-00128 and C-477/10P *Agrofert* [not reported] (first instance and appeal) PK Orlen supported the Commission in its refusal to grant access.

[170] Case T-437/05 *Brink Security* [2009] ECR II-03233, in which G4S, which was awarded the contract (for which Brink Security had bid), supported the Commission in its refusal to grant access.

[171] Case C-673/13P *Stichting Greenpeace Nederland and PAN Europe* v *Commission* (n 129). Concretely it is the appeal of a first instance ruling in which the GC annulled a refusal of the Commission to grant access to a Draft Assessment Report issued by the Federal Republic of Germany for the active substance glyphosate:

> Inter alia, inasmuch as that decision refuses access to the parts of that volume containing information relating to emissions into the environment, the European Commission seeks to have set aside the judgment of the General Court of the European Union in *Stichting Greenpeace Nederland (SGNL) and PAN Europe* v *Commission* (T-545/11), by which the General Court annulled the Commission's decision of 10 August 2011 refusing to grant SGNL and PAN Europe access to volume 4 of the Draft Assessment Report issued by the Federal Republic of Germany as rapporteur Member State for the active substance glyphosate under Council Directive 91/414/EEC of 15 July 1991 concerning the placing of plant protection products on the market (OJ 1991 L 230, p. 1).

[172] With regard to this criterion, *in casu*, the ECJ allowed the interventions of 7 applicants: the European Crop Protection Association (ECPA); CropLife International (CLI); European Crop Care Association (ECCA); European Chemical Industry Council (CEFIC); a joint intervention of CropLife America, Inc (CLA); the National Association of Manufacturers of the United States of America (NAM); and the American Chemistry Council, Inc (ACC). Worthy of note is that the last 3 interveners are USA-based.

[173] These persons were unable to prove a direct interest in the annulment of the specific act under challenge. With regard to this criterion, the ECJ, *in casu*, rejected the applications for leave to intervene of the European Chemicals Agency (ECHA), which sought to support the Commission.

The Court equally rejected the application of Rogesa Roheisengesellschaft Saar Mbh. Rogesa, incidentally, was the only prospective intervener (from a total of 9) that had sought to support the applicant's form of order. In support of its application to intervene, Rogesa argued that the appeal raised the same issues as those before the GC in Case T-643/13 (an action for annulment brought by Rogesa against a

At the outset, because they avoid 'multiple individual interventions which would compromise the effectiveness and proper course of the procedure'[174] representative associations more easily earn the sympathy of the courts when applying for leave to intervene in favour of an applicant.

However, failing to prove a direct interest in the annulment of the contested decision is an insurmountable obstacle to intervention regardless of whether the prospective intervener is a representative association or not. Moreover, given that similarity of context is not a sufficient ground on which to plead a right to intervene, for all private parties the standard of demonstration of an interest in the outcome of proceedings—that have as their purpose the annulment or the affirmance of an institutional refusal to grant someone else a document—is high.

iv. Interventions in Support of an Applicant Requesting Access

The multiple obstacles that a private party faces when attempting to meet the requirements laid down in EU law, before a right to intervene in someone else's case is acknowledged them by the EU judicature, is possibly the best explanation for the fact that in over 20 of EU access to documents rules, not a single intervention in support of a requesting applicant has been allowed.[175]

C. Intervention as an (Im)perfect Alternative to Own Proceedings under Regulation 1049/2001

Coming back to the rejection of leave to intervene in *SGNL* for Rogesa,[176] the prospective intervener in that case alleged that it had (elsewhere) requested different

Commission decision of 25 September 2013 whereby the Commission refused access to information relating to the determination of the 10% most efficient installations in the steel industry, which served as the basis for defining the principles for setting *ex ante* benchmarks in accordance with Art 10a(2) of Directive 2003/87). At para 14 the Court clarified that:

> By invoking the alleged affect that the judgment in the present appeal could have on a decision contested in a separate case, Rogesa invokes an interest which does not concern the subject-matter of the dispute itself, namely the access to volume 4, and is for that reason merely an indirect interest.

[174] Case T-193/04 *Tillack v Commission* (n 128) para 25.

[175] The right to intervene in support of an applicant was acknowledged to the International Federation of Journalists (IFJ) in Case T-193/04 *Tillack v Commission* (n 128). However, whilst undeniably an access to documents case, it is a case that is not related to Regulation 1049/2001.

At stake was a 'compensation claim' for an alleged accusation of bribery made by the EU in a press release on the basis of suspicions of an illegal sale of confidential EU documents by a Commission civil servant to a journalist who proceeded to publish them. It is in fact a case of serious hostile release of documents by private parties. In his pleadings Tillack, the applicant journalist, had requested that the Court 'order the Commission to produce an unexpurgated version of complaints against him'. The Commission having done so, the Court did not rule on that point.

In addition, by way of interim relief (Case T-193/04R) the applicant journalist, Martin Tillack, sought to impede the transmission of information (seized during the search of his home) from the national authorities to OLAF (European Anti Fraud Office). In both actions, leave to intervene in his support was acknowledged, to the IFJ on the basis that the latter was a 'representative association'.

[176] Case C-673/13P *Commission v Stichting and Greenpeace NL and PAN Europe* (n 129).

documents under Regulation 1049/2001. Furthermore, it alleged that within the proceedings concerning the challenge to the refusal to disclose documents (directed at Rogesa) similar arguments (to those at stake in *SGNL*) were being discussed. In terms of structure, this would be the case of any applicant that, having been refused access to documents, for example, on the grounds that the same were related to an on-going investigation protected by Article 4(2) of Regulation 1049/2001, requested to intervene in any another pending cases in which Article 4(2) was being discussed.

No one knows what, concretely would take place if Rogesa, when applying for leave to intervene in *SGNL*, could truthfully have made different allegations. For example, to have coincidentally applied for, and also have been refused, the same documents as the applicant in *SGNL* (thereby securing an interest in the documents). The same uncertainty would hold if Rogesa having requested the same documents as the applicants in *SGNL* and having been refused the same, had equally lodged an own action for annulment against that refusal (thereby securing—in separate proceedings—an interest in the outcome of an identical case).

This question is far from being merely academic. In fact, a recent episode of a pro-applicant prospective intervention (rejected by the ECJ) almost touches upon the point. In that case, the prospective interveners did not state that they had made a request for the same documents. They merely alleged that it would be very easy to do that.

In *Thesing and Bloomberg*,[177] three private parties applied for leave to intervene, in support of the applicants. The interventions of two of the three private parties, Media Legal Defence Initiative (MLDI) and Guardian News and Media Ltd (GNM), were rejected due to a technicality.[178] The third private party that applied to intervene was Access Info Europe (AIE).[179]

There were no impeding procedural technicalities that might, prima facie, impede this particular intervention. AIE however, was required, as is any prospective intervener, to prove that it is a person establishing an interest in the result of the case. With regard to this burden, AIE claimed that:

> it is a non-profit non-governmental association whose object is, according to its Articles of Association, the promotion and protection of the right of access to information in Europe as a means for the defence of civil liberties and the rights of man, in order to encourage public participation in decision making and to hold governments accountable. AIE points

[177] Case T-59/10 and Case C-28/13P *Gabi Thesing and Bloomberg v ECB* (n 13).

[178] Case 28/13P *Gabi Thesing and Bloomberg v ECB* (n 13) para 4:

> Concerning the applications for leave to intervene submitted by MLDI and GNM, it should be noted that those applications were submitted not by a lawyer, but by an employee carrying out the duties of senior legal counsel for MLDI and senior legal adviser for GNM. Under Article 130(3) of the Rules of Procedure of the Court, applicable to appeal procedures pursuant to Article 190(1) thereof, the intervener must be represented in accordance with Article 19 of the Statute of the Court. Under the third paragraph of Article 19, parties other than the institutions and the Member States referred to in the first and second paragraphs of that article must be represented by a lawyer. Since MLDI and GNM are among those parties, it follows that their respective applications for leave to intervene were not submitted in accordance with Article 130(3) of the Rules of Procedure and they should be dismissed as inadmissible.

[179] A (non-representative) association governed by Spanish law, established in Madrid, Spain.

out that it works regularly with journalists and assists them to obtain access to documents of the institutions of the European Union and, in particular, of the ECB.[180]

The ECJ proceeded to recall settled case law on the concept of an interest in the result of the case, which requires a direct, non-abstract and existing interest to be proved. But even more important to our discussion is that the ECJ clarified again how 'the mere fact of being in a similar situation gives the applicant for leave to intervene only an indirect interest in the result of the case'.

First, as the ECJ had already clarified with regard to the rejection of the application for leave to intervene of the undertaking Rogesa,[181] the term 'similar' might concern an applicant that has elsewhere requested different documents (from the contested ones) but whose (separate) case involves the discussion of similar issues and arguments to those being discussed in another pending case within which that same person applies for leave to intervene.

By contrast, in *Thesing* and *Bloomberg*[182] the fundamental question focused on the legitimacy to intervene in the proceedings of any person that might potentially apply for the same documents as the contested ones. The term 'similar', in this second sense, concerns anyone who is also entitled to request access to the documents of the ECB.

In sum, the question raised before the ECJ was whether intervention is a perfect alternative to initiating own proceedings for access to the same documents.

The ECJ was quick to reject such interpretation, and, albeit discreetly, made the point that to allow such a practice would render challenges of refusals ungovernable. Clearly, the abstract structure of such a case would become: one document, one applicant, and unlimited interveners.

Case C-28/13P *Thesing and Bloomberg*

13 In that regard, it should be recalled that Regulation (EC) No 1049/2001 as is apparent from recital 4 in the preamble and from Article 1, is intended to give the fullest possible effect to the right of public access to documents held by one of those institutions. Thus, under Article 2(1), that regulation grants the right of access to documents to '[a]ny citizen of the Union, and any natural or legal person residing or having its registered office in a Member State'. Therefore, the circle of persons who may request access to those documents is, in principle, unlimited.

14 As a result of the very wide access to the documents of those institutions, the promotion of such access is not such as to confer on associations such as AIE a right of intervention as representative associations.

15 Furthermore, even if AIE, like Mrs Thesing, but independently of her, had the right to request access to the same documents to which Mrs Thesing requested access, in view of the case law referred to in paragraph 10 of the present order, it would in principle not have a direct interest in the result of the case between Mrs Thesing and the ECB for the purposes of the second paragraph of Article 40 of the Statute of the Court.

[180] Case C-28/13P *Gabi Thesing and Bloomberg v ECB* (n 13) para 6.
[181] Case C-673/13P *Commission v Stichting and Greenpeace NL and PAN Europe* (n 129).
[182] Case C-28/13P *Gabi Thesing and Bloomberg v ECB* (n 13).

Keeping this context in mind, in the absence of clarifying case law, and although at this point we may only speculate, it would seem that any prospective intervener who is not a representative association and who wishes to support an applicant in order to assert an interest in the outcome of proceedings must comply with certain prior conditions.

Surely, at least an application for access to the same documents must have been submitted to one of the institutions of the EU. In addition, possibly, that application must have also been refused. Finally, and again possibly, a challenge in court against that same refusal must have been lodged. Rogesa failed the first condition since it did not apply for the same documents. AIE failed all of the conditions since it failed to make a concrete application for access at all.

Speculation notwithstanding, there is always the risk that having met the three conditions the prospective intervener will have another scenario to consider: that the EU judicature would opt to join the cases as an alternative to allowing cross-interventions. By way of conclusion to this point, in refusing to equate the circle of potential interveners in cases governed by Regulation 1049/2001 to the circle of Regulation 1049/2001's potential applicants, it is quite clear in *Thesing and Bloomberg* that, for the first time, the EU judicature appears concerned with an indeterminate and unlimited circle of customers.[183] An excessive number of applications or applications for an excessive number of documents might call the governability of the access to documents litigation into question. True, the EU judicature can do little to curb unlimited applications for documents,[184] but it is trying to prevent onlookers (of the access litigation) from intervening 'just because they *care*'. To do otherwise would signify an invitation to the world to interfere in each and every open case.

D. Reversing the Instrumentality: Interest in the Documents as a Facilitator of Interest in the Outcome of the Case

Up to this moment intervention has always been considered under the perspective of a person (a Member State, an institution, a private party) that wishes to interfere in a case governed by Regulation 1049/2001. Therein the classical liaison between Regulation 1049/2001 and intervention rests on the subsequent assertion of two different interests ascribed to two different masters. First, an applicant holds an interest in the contested documents just because he/she applied for them. Second, another person holding an interest in the outcome of the (applicant's) case is allowed to intervene within the former's challenge of an institutional refusal to disclose the contested documents.

[183] This concern was also voiced, outside the confines of Regulation 1049/2001, in Case T-193/04R *Tillack v Commission* (n 128) para 25:

> It should be noted, finally, that the adoption of a broad interpretation of the right of associations to intervene is intended to facilitate assessment of the context of cases whilst avoiding multiple individual interventions which would compromise the effectiveness and proper course of the procedure.

[184] See Chs 2, 3 and 4.

Before we conclude this chapter, the discussion of a different liaison alleged to exist between Regulation 1049/2001 and intervention is called for. Those who defend such a liaison allege that the status of applicant under Regulation 1049/2001 would facilitate that same person's intervention within distinct proceedings. This is not a replay of the arguments put forth by AIE in *Thesing and Bloomberg*.[185] The new allegation has been made to support intervention (of a person seeking documents) within proceedings of EU law that are not of the 'access to documents' type.

This new and tentative approach, describing the status of applicant[186] as an instrumental tactic of intervention elsewhere, was proposed by Schenker (a victim of a cartel). It sought in essence and ingeniously to bridge a great divide of EU law that opposes the concept of interest in the documents to the concept of interest in the outcome of the case.

The proposition of Schenker to the ECJ was meant to capitalise on the different positions of the undertaking, Schenker, first, within a pure access to documents case, *Schenker v Commission*,[187] and, secondly within four cases (C-596/11P; C-598/11P; C-600/11P and C-602/11)[188] that opposed the Commission and individual members of an airfreight cartel.

i. The Interests of Principal Actors and Interveners in Schenker v Commission

At the outset, *Schenker v Commission* is no different from any typical case in which a victim of a cartel requests the Commission to allow it to access that cartel's infringement file. What is distinguishing in this case is that the undertaking was seeking access to that file via Regulation 1049/2001. The institution refused access and the applicant initiated proceedings against the institution (Case T-534/11).

Not surprisingly, the seven members of the cartel applied for leave to intervene in the proceedings in support of the refusing institution. Since the documents in the infringement file concerned them personally, the cartel members easily established an interest in the outcome of the (access) proceedings and were allowed to intervene (within Case T-534/11) in support of the refusing institution. It must not be forgotten that, for its part, from the moment in which it had applied for the contested documents, Schenker had secured and established (within Case T-534/11) an interest in the contested documents.[189]

[185] Albeit with the proviso that in these new cases (C-596/11P; C-598/11P; C-600/11P, and C-602/11) an own application for the contested documents by the prospective intervener had been made (in Case T-534/11 *Schenker v Commission* (n 168)).

[186] Under Regulation 1049/2001.

[187] Case T-534/11 *Schenker v Commission* (n 168).

[188] Cases T-28/11 and C-596/11P *Commission v Koninklije Luchtvaart Maatschappij*; T-38/11 and C-598/11P *Commission v Cathay Pacific*; T-40/11 and C-600/11P *Commission v Lan Airlines a.o.*; T-46/11 and C-602/11P *Commission v Deutsche Lufthansa, Lufthansa Cargo, Swiss Int'l Airlines.*

[189] Regulation 1049/2001, Art 6.

ii. The Interests of Principal Actors and (Potential) Interveners in the Cases opposing the Commission and the Members of the Airfreight Cartel

In parallel, Schenker, always in the role of victim, attempted access to the infringement files by way of a different tactic. It applied for leave to intervene in the separate and on-going infringement proceedings that the Commission had initiated against each member of the cartel.[190] In this second context, Schenker's application to intervene was not governed by Regulation 1049/2001 and was governed by rules on interventions in general. Accordingly, Schenker had to prove an interest in the outcome of the infringement proceedings. In fact, as Schenker did, any victim of the cartel in the same situation would allege that it was seeking to intervene in order to collect information that would subsequently enable it to institute compensation proceedings against the cartel members. However, the ECJ, *in casu*, considered those reasons insufficient to ground an intervention.

It should not be forgotten that the ECJ, possibly, considered that the Commission and the members of the cartel should be left alone to reconcile their differences. It is obvious that first, even the threat of Schenker's mere spectatorship would have inhibited the cartel members. Furthermore, the looming possibility of a subsequent claim for compensation would have impeded them from voluntarily disclosing precious data (about their own behaviour) to the Commission.

iii. No Equating Different Interests

What is of particular interest to this discussion is that Schenker incidentally attempted to gain leverage over the ECJ within the infringement proceedings by calling the Court's attention to the fact 'it is the only victim of the cartel in question which has filed an application for access to the documents of the administrative procedure carried out by the Commission'. Therefore, it is also the only victim to have (elsewhere) established 'an interest in the contested documents'.

The ECJ, unmoved, declared Schenker's personal and separate application for access to (the same) documents as irrelevant towards the consideration of conditions that might root in favour of leave to intervene in any *Commission v (member of cartel)* case. As the ECJ stated,

> it is sufficient to point out that (filing an application for access to documents) is not capable of distinguishing Schenker from any other person interested in gaining access to the documents of that procedure. Pursuant to Regulation 1049/2001, any person may submit such an application for access to documents of the institutions of the European Union at any time.[191]

In fact, under Regulation 1049/2001, the demonstration of an interest in the contested documents is waived for any applicant. Consequently, that interest, albeit an acknowledged one, cannot be equated within distinct proceedings to proof of an

[190] See n 168 above.

[191] Case C-602/11P(I) *Schenker v Deutsche Lufthansa a.o.* [not reported] order of 8 June 2012.

interest (therein) in the outcome of the case. This second concept is a condition that requires demonstration before any authorisation to intervene in someone else's case may be granted.

VIII. CONCLUSIONS

By way of conclusion, in regard to the period 1993–2001, the Code of Conduct of 1993 allowed the Member State to participate in the access policy in four ways: as author, as guardian, as intervener or as appellant. Authorship brought authority. Guardianship brought the duty of loyalty to the EU to the forefront of national foreign policy. The instruments of intervention and appeal shed light on the national interpretation proposed for the EU policy; it was submitted and exposed, all in one.

The casting of a complex role for the Member State was not completed in 1993. The rules of 2001 moulded it even further, less power here, more accountability there, and as always, at the forefront of the equation, the importance of diplomatic common sense.

The Member State's freedom is much more curbed under Regulation 1049/2001, and the centre of discussion of the EU access policy shifts to measures that shield the Member State and the EU from one another. The Member State becomes a little less powerful as author of documents, suffers no change as guardian of the documents of EU institutions, and is allowed to play both roles of intervener and appellant to clarify the barrier between EU law and the national perspective on it. Whilst Article 5 of Regulation 1049/2001 protects the EU from undue interference of the Member State in the EU access policy, three other provisions (Articles 4(4); 4(5) and 9) of the same framework protect Member States from undue interference of the EU in the national policy on access.

Still, despite such shielding efforts to keep the policies separate, very recently, national law has suffered a significant setback. In fact, in regard to national rules on access—to competition law-related leniency and settlement documents—by victims of cartels,[192] EU law-derived standards[193] have been imposed onto national law via the principle of primacy.

The EU thus becomes ultimately responsible for the release of any document upon which EU decisions are based whether the document is self-produced or not. On the one hand, the new rules knowingly oust the Member State yet, on the other, they give rise to twisted incentives. The change encourages inverted forum shopping. In fact, if the EU rules on access are more generous than national rules, and a certain national document has been transmitted to the EU, an applicant that has been refused access under national law might nevertheless obtain access to the same document by way of a request addressed to the EU authorities. Regulation 1049/2001—designed as the front door to EU documents—becomes a back door to the quest for national documents.

[192] Set up in breach of EU rules.
[193] Stemming from the case law on effectiveness.

Possibly the most striking point of the discussion on intervention is that a selection of Member States has self-aligned either along a pro-institutional track, or along the alternative pro-applicant/pro access option.

With regard to the EU institutions the Council and the Commission have gained reputations as inveterate pro-institutional interveners. Conversely, the Parliament has consolidated its initial indication that it might come to be a pro-applicant intervener. Differently, the EDPS has cast an image of intervener that is solely bound to the pursuit of points of law.

With regard to private parties they, understandably intervene against disclosure only to pursue self-interest in the reserve of certain information. So far no private party has succeeded in intervening—within a Regulation 1049/2001 context—in favour of a requesting applicant. That, of itself, is a finding that makes the global discussion on intervention worthwhile. However, it is not a finding that necessarily supports a more generous setting (than the existing one) for interventions in favour of access. Applicants that plead for documents before a judicature that cannot grant them disclosure on the basis of injunctions are already subjected to the unwarranted interference of interveners filtered by the EU judicature on the basis of the strict criterion of 'interest in the outcome of the case'. To subject the discussion of applicants' cases to an incalculable number of contributions from strangers would oust the applicants away from the courts and render the procedure of Regulation 1049/2001 inoperative.

A final, and spectacular, diversification of the role of one type of intervener is to be found in the off chance that a Member State, will of its own volition and independently of parties to proceedings, appeal a first instance ruling before the ECJ (State appeals). This discussion will be held in Chapter 8, in which State appeals will be contrasted with appeals from applicants and from institutions.

8

Appeals

I. INTRODUCTION—A SECOND CHANCE TO RULE (THEM) ALL

IF NO ONE appeals any ruling of the General Court, the ECJ will be refused admittance to the access game.[1] That is, in itself, thought-provoking. However, the exercise would be merely academic. In fact, the EU access to documents policy is marked with a considerable number of appeals to the ECJ requesting that it exercise judicial review over rulings of the GC.[2]

The present chapter seeks to single out the prospective initiators of appeals. It therefore covers all actors: the applicants, the defendant institutions and, in the practice of access, (most of) the interveners.

Statute of the ECJ, Article 56:

(1) An appeal may be brought before the Court of Justice, within two months of the notification of the decision appealed against, against final decisions of the General Court and decisions of that Court disposing of the substantive issues in part only or disposing of a procedural issue concerning a plea of lack of competence or inadmissibility.

(2) Such an appeal may be brought by any party which has been unsuccessful, in whole or in part, in its submissions. However, interveners other than the Member States and the institutions of the Union may bring such an appeal only where the decision of the General Court directly affects them.

It should not be forgotten that, dwelling principally on intervention, the previous chapter was confined to examining the role of the policy's 'eccentric' actors. In that chapter we raised the point that intervention—within proceedings initiated by

[1] In addition, we would have to disregard the ECJ's role with regard to (1) cases related to access' legal basis such as Case C-58/94 *NL v Council* [1996] ECR I-02169 and Case C-387/00 *Parliament v Council* [not reported]; (2) cases discussed directly before the ECJ and which touch upon the access theme such as Case C-432/04 *Commission v Crésson* [2006] ECR I-06387 and Case C-406/06 *Landtag Schleswig Holstein* [not reported]; (3) preliminary rulings that touch upon the access theme such as Case C-321/96 *Mecklenburg* [1998] ECR I-03809; Case C-345/06 *Heinrich* [2009] ECR I-01659; Joined Cases C-92/09 and C-93/09 *Schecke and Eifert v Land Hessen* [2010] ECR I-11063; Case C-360/09 *Pfleiderer v Bundeskartellamt* [2011] ECR I-05161; Case C-536/11 *Bundeswettbewebshorde v Donau Chemie* [not reported]; Case C-636/11 *Berger v Bayern* [not reported]; Joined Cases C-372/12 and C-141/12 *M and S* (personal data) [not reported]; Case C-212/13 *Rynes* (personal data) [not yet reported] and Case C-72/15 *Rosneft v Her Majesty's Treasury a.o.* [in progress].

[2] As we have mentioned, the GC in turn also functions as a court of appeal of the decisions rendered by the Civil Service Tribunal; see Case F-111/11 *Van der Aat a.o. v Commission* [not yet reported] and the respective appeal, Case T-304/13P [not yet reported].

others—might be seen as an (im)perfect alternative to beginning own proceedings aimed at obtaining access to the same documents.[3]

Appeals might, in turn, be seen either as an (im)perfect alternative or as a complement to something else: intervention:

Statute of the ECJ, Article 56

(3) With the exception of cases relating to disputes between the Union and its servants, an appeal may also be brought by Member States and institutions of the Union which did not intervene in the proceedings before the General Court. Such Member States and institutions shall be in the same position as Member States or institutions which intervened at first instance.

If that is so, it is clear that the EU access policy implies many layers of options for actors. However, the answer to why actors opt for one or the other is difficult to devise even on a speculative basis. What we are left with is observation. Not of *why* actors opt. Merely of *who* makes those options, *which* options they do make and, finally, *what comes about* as a result.

Appeals emerge after defeat. In the language of law this is lack of success or defeat. When an applicant is unsuccessful at first instance it means (in this book, and by default) that an institutional refusal to disclose documents on the basis of Regulation 1049/2001 has been affirmed by the GC, in whole or in part. Conversely, when it is the refusing institution that is unsuccessful it means (in this book, and again by default) that an institutional refusal to disclose documents has been annulled by the GC, again in whole or in part. Moreover, when it is the institutions that are defeated and they decide not to challenge the first instance ruling there is still a subsequent burden that the former must discharge: provide a new answer to an old request.

In any case, whilst both parties always leave the court more informed about the standing legal framework of EU access to documents, it is also true that, proceedings being a contest, inevitably one of them and sometimes both leave the court disconsolate.

One way for the multiple actors of the access policy (applicants, refusing institutions and interveners) to react to the rejection of their pleas by the GC is to desist and allow the ruling of the GC to settle, which takes a mere two months.[4] The alternative is to lodge an appeal for review by the ECJ. With regard to the latter option, tenacity is, of course, burdensome. The law[5] must be discussed again. In addition, closure, which has almost certainly taken around three years,[6] will be put off for another 15 months at least.

[3] The point was raised with clarity in the attempted intervention of Access Info Europe within Case C-28/13P *Thesing and Bloomberg* [not reported].

[4] Statute of the ECJ, Art 56(1) above.

[5] Only exceptionally would the facts be reassessed. See, on this specific point, Opinion of AG Kokott in Case C-127/13P *Strack v Commission* [not yet reported] para 129: 'complaints based on findings of fact and on the assessment of those facts in the contested judgment are admissible on appeal where the appellant contends that the General Court has made findings which the documents in the file show to be substantially incorrect or that it has distorted the evidence before it'.

[6] Roughly, the average length of first instance proceedings (own computation).

Finally, there is only social utility in any appeal if, subsequently, reversal[7] of the challenged decision comes about. On the contrary, *ex post*, from a social point of view affirmation of a first instance decision is redundant: if the higher court affirms what the baseline court had already stated years before, ultimately the appeal proceedings prove to have been a waste of time and resources for everyone involved.

For any appellant, individually, an appeal is first and foremost a second life that is breathed into a failed expectation. For the EU, as an international organisation, appeals give the judicature a second chance to rule on the evolution in law of a balance of interests that affects a vast number of parties. However, there being no recourse beyond the ECJ, whilst expectations concerning access to documents may, and on occasion do, live twice before the EU judicature, it is at the most twice that these are given any consideration.

From the point of view of singling out its prospective initiators, the structure of an appeal may come in many forms. The simplest is when one party only (either the applicant or the defendant in first instance), having lost at first instance, appeals the decision of the GC to the ECJ for review. In these cases the victor in first instance is compelled to take part in the appeal and exercises passive resistance in defence of the status quo proposed by the GC.

Another possibility is that a cross-appeal comes about. Here, both the applicant and the defendant at first instance are uncomfortable with the outcome of the earlier proceedings. Therefore, each complains to the ECJ about the same or different points of law that each would prefer to be resolved in a different manner. In addition to the applicant and defendant in first instance, Member States who intervened therein[8] have lodged appeals on occasion. Finally, and spectacularly, a Member State that has seemingly been indifferent to the entire first instance process may emerge from the shadows and request the ECJ to reverse a proposition of the GC.

The ECJ is thus faced with a formidable task: to be the executor of the second chance to rule (them) all, definitively.

II. APPEALS OF THE MEMBER STATES

Because of its disposition to participate in the EU access to documents litigation in multiple ways, the most complex prospective appellant amongst the actors of the EU access policy is the Member State. As we mentioned in Chapters 2 and 7, within the EU access policy Member States do not self-identify as applicants and, therefore, when they do they participate within first instance proceedings, in principle,[9] they

[7] S Shavell, *Foundations of Economic Analysis of Law* (Cambridge, MA, Belknap Press of Harvard University Press, 2004) Ch 4, 'Litigation and the Legal Process' 391–416 explores the 'misalignment or divergence of the private incentives [respectively, to bring suit and to engage in litigation] and the social optimal incentive to do so'. The reasoning may gainfully be applied to the decision to bring an appeal.

[8] Although the possibility exists (under the Statute of the ECJ, Art 56(2) above) no intervening institutions or any intervening private party has ever done so.

[9] With exceptions such as Case T-59/09 *Germany v Commission* [not reported] in which the Member State sought to discuss the substantive grounds on the basis of which it might request the EU institutions not to disclose (national) documents.

do so as interveners. Nonetheless, it is still open to the Member States to make other incursions into someone else's case and interfere therein beyond intervention.

A. State Intervention Followed by State Appeal

Accordingly, although chosen much less frequently than the route of mere intervention, it is not unusual that having intervened within first instance proceedings a Member State will appeal the corresponding ruling.

i. Side-by-Side Appeals of Intervening Member States under the Code of Conduct

This route was first taken within the access context in 1998 in the *Netherlands and Van der Wal v Commission* proceedings.[10] The Netherlands,[11] having intervened in support of the applicant in first instance,[12] appealed the judgment of the CFI to the ECJ,[13] and did so independently from the applicant. One week later, the applicant at first instance also lodged an independent appeal.[14] Both actions were joined as Cases C-174/98P and C-189/98P, *Kingdom of the Netherlands and Gerald van der Wal v Commission*, and decided together.

Still on this point, when a Member State's appeal of a first instance judgment is subsequently accompanied by a side-by-side appeal from the applicant at first instance, or when a Member State that had been intervener in first instance independently appeals a judgment that has already been appealed by an unsuccessful party, one might be led to think that national choice redundant. There is, manifestly, some redundancy. In the first place, one appellant[15] is sufficient to permit review by a higher court. Secondly, if the Member State's objective is to defend points of law, it may pursue it just as efficaciously by intervening[16] within the defeated party's appeal.

In stating as much, we are not oblivious to two important counter-arguments. First, besides reinforcing the defence of points of law raised by the applicant, the Member State might, by way of a side-by-side appeal, question additional[17] points. Secondly, on an *ex ante* own independent appeal, the Member State might not know whether or not the unsuccessful applicant/institution will pursue the matter further.

[10] Joined Cases C-174/98P and C-189/98P *Netherlands and Van der Wal v Commission* [2000] ECR I-00001, concerning access to communications between the Commission and the national courts within the competition policy.

[11] The Kingdom of the Netherlands was, in fact, already the great initiator of the access to documents litigation by way of Case C-58/94 *Kingdom of the Netherlands v Council of the European Union* [1996] ECR I–02169.

[12] Case T-83/96 *Gerald van der Wal v Commission* [1998] ECR II-00545.

[13] 11 May 1998.

[14] On 19 May 1998, and within which the Netherlands intervened in support of the applicant.

[15] Either the defeated applicant at first instance or the Member State.

[16] See Ch 7.

[17] As opposed to interveners who are limited to supporting the form of order of one of the parties and must take the case as they find it. On this point, see Ch 7.

ii. Side-by-Side Appeals of Intervening Member States under Regulation 1049/2001

With Regulation 1049/2001 already in force, in 2005 it was Sweden that appealed other GC rulings to the ECJ.[18] First, it appealed the *Turco*[19] ruling. This was the result of proceedings with which that Member State was familiar, Sweden having been intervener at first instance. By exercising this option Sweden brought about the consolidation of the route of State appeals, introduced into the access policy by the Netherlands seven years earlier.

Moreover, as had happened with the Dutch State appeal under the Code of Conduct,[20] the applicant in *Turco* also appealed the corresponding ruling to the ECJ. Accordingly, the access to documents policy was to be marked by another side-by side appeal: one from the applicant at first instance and another from the intervening Member State.

Still in 2005, Sweden had a further contribution to make to the story of access. It raised the role of appellant Member State another notch.

iii. Isolated Appeals: Appeals (of Intervening Member States) with Regard to Rulings that the Principal Actors of First Instance Will Pursue no Further

Sweden's further contribution in 2005 was an appeal of the *IFAW*[21] ruling of the GC. Because of it, the distinguishing character of this national prerogative, and especially its irreplaceable utility, discernibly emerged.

Take any first instance proceedings within which there has been a State intervention. If the succumbing principal party is unwilling to pursue the matter further, the solution proposed by the ruling of the GC will become definitive. Here, one role of the intervening Member State at first instance might be to make sure that a solution held to be unsatisfactory is carried over into the higher court for review. There is no redundancy now.

In fact, the applicant in *IFAW* chose not to appeal the ruling of the GC. Thus, the corresponding appeal proceedings told the story of an isolated appeal from an intervening Member State. In hindsight, it might be said that were it not for Sweden the arguments put forth within the first instance proceedings, not only by Sweden, but also both by the applicant and by the Commission, would have been definitively settled according to the propositions of the GC.

The appeal in *IFAW* becomes, then, a symbolic explanation of what Member State intervention and State appeal signify at their core: a national opportunity to pursue

[18] Case T-84/03 *Turco* [2004] ECR II-04061; and Case T-168/02 *IFAW* [2004] II-04135.

[19] Concerning the necessity of a concrete examination of the contested documents by the institutions before the request to access the same is refused.

[20] Cases C-174/98P and C-189/98P *Netherlands and van der Wal v Commission* (n 10).

[21] Concerning the prior agreement of a Member State before own documents are disclosed. Again, an incident taking place post-Regulation 1049/2001: C-64/05P *Sweden v Commission* [2007] ECR I-11389, an appeal of Case T-168/02 *IFAW v Commission* (n 18), in which Sweden had supported the applicant. IFAW, albeit unsuccessful at first instance, did not lodge an appeal to the ECJ.

argument (that concerns the EU access policy) beyond the principal actors' wishes and/or capabilities and, possibly, in spite of the principal actors' shortcomings.

And if from a structural point of view, *IFAW* had been impressive enough—the Member State that soldiers on, alone—the next two incidents did not disappoint either.

Before we discuss the next two Swedish incidents, it is important to note that in July 2015, a Member State long-removed from the access litigation made a come-back: the French Republic. France chose to appeal[22] the *Schlyter*[23] ruling of the GC. The French attitude excites attention, of course, yet it comes as no surprise. First, the contested documents had been notified to the Commission by the French authorities, and France's track record in the access litigation always presupposes a national connection. Secondly, the appeal's design is to restrict access, another constant trend of this particular Member State. Thirdly, France had already gone to the trouble of intervening in the first instance proceedings and obviously had sharp[24] arguments prepared already.

B. State Appeal without Prior Intervention, a New Practice under Regulation 1049/2001: Side-by-Side and Isolated Appeals

Under Regulation 1049/2001 a new practice of the Member States came about. State appeals of first instance rulings were pursued in spite of no prior intervention of the appellant Member State within the corresponding proceedings. Again, the privileged status of EU Member States comes to light:[25] before a State appeal is considered it is not required that the prospective appellant has first been defeated and/or intervener at first instance.

i. No Prior Intervention, Side-by-Side State Appeals

A first type of State appeal without prior intervention came about in 2007 when Sweden proceeded to appeal the GC's ruling in *API v Commission*.[26] Within the access procedure this was a novelty. However, within those specific proceedings,

[22] Case C-331/15P *France v Schlyter* [in progress].

[23] Case T-402/12 *Carl Schlyter v European Commission* [not reported].

[24] The main ground of appeal and chagrin is that albeit having conceded in 2014 in Case T-306/12 *Spirlea v Commission* that the EU pilot procedure may be classified as an 'investigation' within the meaning of the third indent of Art 4(2) of Regulation 1049/2001, the GC is now refusing to extend that reasoning to the specific procedure laid down by Directive 98/34. The extreme insulation accorded to exceptions encompassed under Art 4(2) of Regulation 1049/2001 is without doubt the most contentious issue of the access policy, if that is the point now being discussed. *France v Schlyter* are proceedings worth watching.

[25] From a theoretical point of view, while it is still conceivable that an institution of the EU might attempt the same feat, it is not feasible for a private party to do so. Art 56(3) of the Statute of the ECJ does not open this route for private parties who were interveners at first instance.

[26] Concerning access to Commission pleadings drawn up for judicial proceedings, see Case C-514/07P *Sweden v API and Commission* [2010] ECR I-08533. The case's reference is quite infelicitous since it seems to suggest that Sweden and API are opponents. However, that is not the case.

two cross-appeals ensued, one from the applicant, the other from the Commission.[27] The State's option to appeal the ruling might have had a spill-over effect onto the other parties enabled to do the same. If a stranger is going to re-discuss their case, the principal actors at first instance ensure that their own dissenting voices are heard by the ECJ. The *API* appeal came to be of side-by-side structure, and was, finally, a triple appeal.

ii. No Prior Intervention, Isolated State Appeals

A different and no less striking type of State appeal was inaugurated in 2008 within the *MyTravel*[28] proceedings. The novelty this time was twofold. On the one hand, Sweden appealed the first instance ruling without having intervened within any prior phase of the corresponding proceedings. True, because of the precedent of *API*,[29] that tactic was already known to be feasible. However, this time the applicant, MyTravel, failed to appeal the ruling to the ECJ. The appeal became isolated for two reasons. First, Sweden had not taken part in the earlier proceedings; secondly, Sweden came before the ECJ alone.

MyTravel charges the brushstrokes in a portrait of the Member State as a lone suitor of a new balance, of the interests that compete within the EU access to documents policy, to which only one, entire, nation is privy. When in the face of a first defeat applicants back down, a quixotic actor might emerge from the shadows. The Member State will, in its own name and pursuing the national angle on EU matters, petition the ECJ to readjust the GC's criteria by way of judicial review.

Possibly, at the heart of State appeals of cases in which applicants desist is the knowledge that more often than not Member States' litigation structures are more resilient than those of individuals. In fact, lack of (individual) success at first instance can be both financially and morally crippling of individual incentives to fight for own rights that could also benefit a multitude of other players. Once it is accepted that many individual pretensions would well be worth pursuing further for the sake of the general good, appealing against someone else's lack of success provides an answer to the following dilemma: how to pursue a meritorious pretension into appeal, when the applicant backs down.

It must not be forgotten that when an applicant does desist, and only a Member State appeals, the evaluation of the demerit of a first instance ruling is issued only from a national perspective. Accordingly, in this setting the Member State does not merely interfere within someone else's cause. In truth, the Member State completely

[27] The Swedish appeal, Case C-514/07P, was lodged on 20 November 2007, whilst both API's appeal, Case C-528/07P, and the Commission's cross-appeal, Case C-532/07P, were lodged on 27 November 2007.

[28] For a case concerning documents pertaining to court proceedings and to the control of concentrations, see Case C-506/08P *Sweden v MyTravel and Commission* [2011] ECR I-06237. Once again, the case reference is misleading (see n 26). In this case, neither was there an appeal by the applicant at first instance (MyTravel) and nor had Sweden intervened in the first instance proceedings: T-403/05 *MyTravel v Commission* [2008] ECR II-02027.

[29] See section II.B.i above.

takes over someone else's battle. Regardless of whether the applicant or an institution will or will not appeal a first instance ruling, on the basis of a national evaluation of that very ruling's effects, and of its own volition the Member State takes the case before the highest (and final) level of the EU judicature: the ECJ.

Moreover, in the aftermath of successful State appeals, that State also becomes the purveyor of a new equilibrium for access—not just a warrior, but a general of the policy too.

C. The Netherlands, Sweden and Finland, again

In 2011, Finland broke the Swedish monopoly of State appeals within the access policy under Regulation 1049/2001. It appealed the ruling delivered in *LPN v Commission*,[30] proceedings in which it had intervened. That appeal was of side-by-side structure, since after having obtained legal aid[31] to do so the applicant appealed the first instance ruling to the ECJ as well.

The most recent State appeal within the access policy concerns the *Spirlea* proceedings.[32] In 2014, two appeals were lodged with the ECJ, one by the applicant and one by Sweden—intervener at first instance—giving rise to a side-by-side challenge of the ruling of the GC.

By way of conclusion, State appeals are yet another area in which a formidable role must be acknowledged to the Netherlands, to Sweden, and to Finland. Again, infinite questions arise. What might explain Denmark's absence? What might explain that no Member State has ever appealed a ruling of the GC in order to secure less access? Is it because if the defeated institution failed to appeal the first instance ruling on a side-by-side basis, the Member State might come across as too exposed? In such conditions the Member State would lead the appeal alone, uncertain of whether there would be follow-on interventions in support of its (national) form of order. Of course it would be extremely interesting to observe, but it has not occurred to date.

Are the answers to these questions at all important?

Having paid due tribute to the Member States that have made a contribution to the access policy, we again emphasise that this role of the Member State—State appeals—was not discussed from the point of view of merits of national foreign policy. Again, the principal attempt was to highlight how, on the one hand, a State appeal is an available role that is often played by some, and on the other hand, that applicants, institutions and courts must take it in their stride.

[30] Case T-29/08 *LPN v Commission* [2011] ECR II-06021, concerning presumptions of harm applicable to the disclosure of environmental information. The subsequent appeal, Case C-605/11P *Finland v LPN and Commission* [not reported], became, after joinder, *Finland and LPN v Commission*, which is more comprehensible.

[31] Order of the President of the ECJ, of 10 November 2011, Case C-514/11AJ *LPN v Commission* [not published].

[32] Case C-562/14P *Sweden v Spirlea and Commission* [not reported], concerning presumptions of harm applicable to EU pilot proceedings.

III. APPEALS OF THE INSTITUTIONS

As far as the practice in the access policy is concerned, appeals of institutions are not intricate from a structural point of view. There are so far no appeals from intervening institutions to be mentioned.[33] In fact, where institutional appeals have occurred, only institutions that were defendants at first instance have lodged these.

Institutional appeals will therefore be discussed here only as an option of one of the principal actors of the access policy: institutions that were defendants at first instance and that invariably[34] had refused to disclose documents to the public.

A. Institutional Appeals under the Code of Conduct

Institutional appeals are not common. In fact, under the Code of Conduct only a single case arose: *Council v Hautala*.[35] The challenge served, if nothing else, to confirm that a new cornerstone of the access policy was steadfast: partial access.

> Case C-353/99P *Council v Hautala*
>
> Article 4(1) of Decision 93/731 must be interpreted as meaning that the Council is obliged to examine whether partial access should be granted to the information not covered by the exceptions, and to annul the contested decision on finding that the Council had not made such an examination since, in its opinion, the principle of access to documents applied only to documents as such and not to the information contained in them.

Moreover, the ruling brought about a distinction between the concept of *document* and *information* (contained therein). The appeal brought no solace[36] to the institution that, as a consequence, saw its duties increase. From then on for each document requested by a member of the public, even when prima facie covered by an exception, time would have to be spent considering whether short(er) passages of (the contested) text[37] could be released without causing undue harm.

[33] This does not mean that a more diversified approach to institutional appeals will not emerge in the future. There are, in fact, areas of EU law that are very close to the access policy in which this has already taken place. eg, with regard to Regulation 1367/2006 (the Aarhus Regulation), albeit confined to the topic of internal review, in Case T-396/09 *Vereniging Milieudefensie and Stichting v Commission* [not reported] the Commission had been supported by the Netherlands (Member State to which an exemption had been granted), the Parliament and the Council. Subsequently, the Council (Case C-401/12P) and the Parliament (Case C-402/12P) appealed the corresponding first instance ruling. The Commission followed suit (Case C-403/12P). These three appellants were supported by the Czech Republic. Moreover, the applicants at first instance responded with a cross-appeal. The appeal proceedings were dismissed by the judgment of the ECJ, Grand Chamber, of 15 January 2015, for lack of *locus standi* of the applicant at first instance.

[34] With the exception of the EMA in Cases C-389/13P(R) and Case C-390/13P(R).

[35] Case C-353/99 *Council v Hautala* [2001] ECR I-09565.

[36] In other words, no measure of success.

[37] In most cases the contested documents are printed text.

B. Institutional Appeals under Regulation 1049/2001

i. Seeking to Restrict Access

Greater success embraced the institutional appeals lodged under Regulation 1049/2001, although it was not until 2007 that another institutional appeal appeared on the access horizon.

ii. Presumptions of Harm

Commission v TGI[38] was the first of a series of five memorable victories for institutions. This particular strand of cases anchored presumptions of harm into the access policy. When the former are applicable they exempt the institutions even from examining the contested documents before their disclosure to the public is considered.[39] In this way the material scope of access is scaled down.

The next step in this chain was the Commission's (cross-)appeal of the *API* judgment.[40] Subsequently, *Commission v Odile Jacob*[41] and *Commission v Agrofert*[42] came about. Still, *Commission v EnBW*[43] was lodged, to the detriment of applicants. Only by way of *Council v Access Info Europe*,[44] in which the institution's appeal was unsuccessful, and later with the more recent *Council v In't Veld*[45] was the trickle of these presumptions into the policy somewhat curbed.

iii. Names of Persons Acting in a Professional Capacity

On another topic, in 2008 the institutions, on appeal, achieved another momentous restriction of the scope of the EU access policy. The ECJ's ruling in *Commission v Bavarian Lager*,[46] in spite of strenuous objection from the European Data Protection Supervisor (EDPS),[47] awarded a victory to the Commission and shielded the 'names of persons (that are acting in a professional capacity)' from public scrutiny. The ruling was not without controversy[48] and was revised in 2016.[49]

[38] Case C-139/07P *Commission v TGI* [2010] ECR I-05885 on the subject of State aid.

[39] See Ch 5.

[40] Case C-532/07P *Commission v API*, concerning documents prepared for judicial proceedings.

[41] C-404/10P *Commission v Odile Jacob* [not reported], concerning merger control.

[42] C-477/10 *Commission v Agrofert* [not reported], concerning merger control.

[43] C-365/12P *Commission v EnBW* [not reported], concerning cartels.

[44] C-280/11P *Council v Access Info Europe* [not reported], concerning the institutions' decision-making process.

[45] C-350/12P *Council v Int'Veld* [not reported], concerning international relations.

[46] Case C-28/08P *Commission v Bavarian Lager* [2010] ECR I-06055.

[47] See Ch 7.

[48] See Ch 5.

[49] The Opinion of AG Villalon in Case C-615/13P *ClientEarth and PAN Europe v EFSA* [not yet reported] para 55 and cross-reference 20 revived the solution proposed for *Bavarian Lager* by AG Sharpston, that—at the time—was not followed by the ECJ. The ECJ confirmed the AG's views and the relationship between access to names and privacy has gained (a new) life beyond *Bavarian Lager*.

iv. Environmental Information

The public's growing interest in environmental information is also an area of access that worries the institutions.[50] Recently, *Commission v Stichting Greenpeace Nederland and PAN Europe*,[51] an institutional appeal on this subject matter has, so far, excited a crowd of interveners (in support of the Commission), some of whom are from the United States. This display of American interest, among other important conclusions that may be inferred from this, is a sign of the EU access policy's global vocation.

v. Seeking More Access (and Institutional Independence)

Although to date this has been rare, it is true that on occasion institutional appeals seek to obtain leave from the ECJ both to disclose more information and to do so on the basis of more institutional discretion. This is the case of two institutional appeals of the European Medicines Agency (the EMA). In both *EMA v Abbvie*[52] and *EMA v Intermune UK*,[53] the EMA sought and secured permission from the ECJ to disclose documents to the public that it had been ordered by the GC to hold back.

C. The Council, the Commission and the EMA, only

Only the Council and the Commission have appealed first instance rulings with the purpose of removing a piece of their world from public access to documents. Other EU institutions, even those familiar with the process of intervention such as the European Parliament and the EDPS, have displayed reserve in this matter. For its part the EMA has played a pilot role in the field of institutional appeals. It has signalled that the pursuit of less access is not the only choice that is open.

IV. APPEALS OF PRIVATE PARTIES

The appeals of private parties share institutional appeals' lack of intricacy. Therefore, in principle the former will be confined to cases of disappointed applicants in first instance retrying their pro-access arguments before the ECJ.[54]

However, it is also true that specific private parties (authors and/or persons other than applicants at first instance for which the contested documents are connected) could theoretically appear in a different light in cases involving interim relief.

[50] See Ch 5

[51] See Ch 7; Case C-673/13P *Commission v Stichting Greenpeace Nederland and PAN Europe.*

[52] Case C-389/13P (R) (n 34).

[53] Case C-390/13P(R) (n 34).

[54] Cases in which access is equally sought, and which involve interim relief, appear under a very similar form to this default framework. In fact, in Case T-216/01R and, on appeal Case C-477/01R *Reisebank*, the appellant challenged a failure of the GC to suspend the operation of an institutional decision of the Commission refusing disclosure of documents.

Therefore whilst, in general, private parties always appeal to obtain more access, certain parties may appeal to the ECJ in order to secure a shroud over the contested documents (when such arguments have failed before the GC).[55]

A. Slippery Fish

There is great heterogeneity in private parties,[56] which makes them a very elusive subject to plot as a single actor. Each and every individual situation reconfigures this option. Thus, it is difficult, if not virtually impossible, to give a coherent narrative of the development of private parties' incentives to appeal. Such appeals, albeit concerning common topics, do not arise (as is true of institutional appeals) from any concerted and coherent behaviour. That would only be the case if several appeals lodged by private parties with incidence on the same topic would have been pursued preponderantly with the aim of furthering access of persons (in general), to, say, competition proceedings or to environmental information.

Choices to re-discuss the law are fuelled by a preponderantly self-serving drive to satisfy personal needs. And although an exception (to the self-centredness of the conduct)[57] might be made for representative associations or for other associations, private parties appeal on the basis of disparate and haphazard circumstances and backgrounds. Financially strained persons, for example, might be dependent on the prior securing of legal aid[58] before they attempt an appeal.

This having been said, appeals come about in all areas within which a first instance battle is lost. It is worth noting, nonetheless, in spite of the fact that there might well be a degree of substance in every appeal that the nucleus of a significant proportion of these appeals is 'absorbed' by procedural issues.[59] In certain cases this will cause a convoluted knot of cases to build up with a succession of appeals of first instance

[55] These different models come forth when interim relief is concerned. First, at the basis of these cases, usually—at first instance—one applicant will apply to the GC for the (urgent) suspension of the operation of an institutional decision, ie a decision to disclose documents or, in the alternative, a decision to refuse documents. Secondly, the GC will then either grant these suspensions or not. In either case the GC will issue orders.

With regard to appeals of the same, if an appellant seeks to restrict access, that party will challenge orders of the GC that fail to suspend an institutional decision to grant access. (Suppose here that the appellant is not the applicant who requested documents, but rather is the author of the same, and concomitantly is the party who applied to the GC for the suspension of an institutional decision to grant access.)

[56] See comments in Ch 2 about heterogeneity even in the Civil Society category.

[57] Again this has a bearing on the concept of private parties that act in the public interest; see Ch 5.

[58] Statute of the ECJ, Arts 115–18.

[59] eg the concept of challengeable measure in Cases T-106/99 and C-436/99 *Meyer*; in Cases T-141/05, C-362/08P, T-141/05 Renv T-36/10 and C-208/11P, C-554/11P *Int'l Hilfsfonds*; the effects of a holding reply in Cases T-203/06 and C-122/07P *Eurostrategies*; the concept of legal person in Cases T-236/06 and C-406/06P; T-68/07 and C-281/08P *Landtag Schleswig Holstein*; concept of new facts that justify review in Cases T-443/07 and C-225/08P *Nuova Agricast*; representation by a lawyer that is not a third party in Cases T-452/10 and C-573/11P *ClientEarth*.

orders, and referrals back to the first instance, to unfold.[60] Moreover, it is not infrequent that the dead weight of the technicality will cause the appeal to derail[61] before any consideration is actually given to the legality of the refusal or of the intention to disclose documents, the background to the origin of every dispute.[62] Other than that, it is mainly international relations,[63] presumptions of harm[64] and the environment[65] that seem to attract the doubled efforts of private parties in their quest for access to documents.

B. Because you Lost and you have the Money to Keep on Going

In sum, it seems to us that in most cases applicants appeal because they lost at first instance and have the resources to continue the contest. Applicants who request documents from EU institutions are the preponderant type of player of this policy. They act as a first catalyst. Without an initial request there is no story to tell. No answer need come forth, no reasons to appeal it. Conversely, when requests are made and answered, and challenged before the baseline of the EU judicature, in the face of defeat an appeal might be called for. At this point, applicants at first instance share with defendant institutions and Member States (and possibly with others too) the power to apply for judicial review of first instance rulings. Notwithstanding this sharing of power, the preponderance of the role of the persons who made requests in the first place also transpires with regard to appeals, as (again on the basis of a very rough estimate)[66] more than 50 per cent of all appeals have been lodged and discussed upon demand of the former.

[60] As in Cases T-3/00 and C-193/01P followed by T-337/04P and C-84/08P *Pitsiorlas v Council and ECB*; in Cases T-236/06 and C 406/06P; T-68/07 and C-281/08P *Landtag Schleswig Holstein*; and also in T-141/05, C-362/08P, T-141/05Renv and C-554/11P *Int'l Hilfsfonds*.

[61] Rules of Prcedure of the ECJ, Art 119: 'Where the appeal is, in whole or in part, clearly inadmissible or clearly unfounded, the Court may at any time, acting on a report from the Judge-Rapporteur and after hearing the Advocate General, by reasoned order dismiss the appeal in whole or in part'.

[62] The stockpile of these incidents is a precious repository of the criteria favoured by the EU judicature in the design of a procedural law of access to documents. It teaches applicants, institutions and interveners in particular, but more importantly, onlookers in general, how to calibrate any planned approach to the process. eg in Case C-626/10P *Joséphidès v Commission and EACEA* [2011] I-00169, with regard to the issue of the competence of executive agencies to handle confirmatory requests. Also, in Case C-576/12P *Jurasinovic* [not reported], the issue of whether the EU judicature must actually consult the contested documents stole the show. Further, in Case C-573/11P *ClientEarth* [not yet reported], it was the fact of whether the lawyer was too close to the applicant or not that absorbed the discussion.

[63] Cases T-188/98 and C-239/00P *Kuijer*; Cases T-204/99 and C-353/01P *Mattila*; Cases T465/09 and C-576/12P *Jurasinovic*; Cases T-93/11 and C-399/13P *Stichting Corporate Observatory*.

[64] With regard to pleadings of the Commission prepared for court proceedings, see Cases T-36/04 and C-528/07P *API*; with regard to the concrete examination of documents, see Cases T-84/03 and C-52/l *Turco*; with regard to environmental information, see Cases T-29/08 and C-514/11P *LPN*.

[65] In Cases T-476/12 and C-60/15P *Saint-Gobain*.

[66] Own computation.

V. CONCLUSIONS

Conclusions that bring this work to its end must now be drawn with regard first to appeals of the Member States, subsequently to appeals of institutions and, finally, to appeals of private parties.

With regard to our first task, the discussion in Chapter 7 clarified how interventions are paternalistic and invasive of any applicant's space. Admittedly, interventions at first instance are allowed since Member States are privileged actors within the EU framework. Still, and ultimately, interventions are allowed to make the debate richer, to lay diversified argument before the EU judicature. Articulate case law on access serves neither Member State, defendant institution, nor applicant, exclusively. First and foremost it serves the EU.

The current chapter casts light on an even more intense mode of interference in litigation. One of the Member States may choose to appeal any first instance ruling rendered vis-à-vis any individual. In this regard, it might have been assumed that the abolition of the author's rule would have promoted an increase in (the rate of) appeal of Member States. Especially so in regard to first instance cases in which the contested documents were national documents held by the EU, and whose outcome was favourable to applicants.[67] Empirically this has not been confirmed.

It might be because, first, the Member State might have unsuccessfully deployed interim relief (against hostile disclosure) available at the moment in which the Member State is consulted by the institution. As a result, the Member State's expectations with regard to any further intervention of the EU judicature might not be high. Secondly, the Member State might already have voiced its concerns by way of intervention at first instance. Finally, it is also possible that the Member State is 'just not interested' in pursuing this route.

Surprisingly, until 2015 when France appealed *Schlyter*, State appeals have come forth only from Member States that tend to support applicants seeking access, this in spite of the absence of injunctions in the EU system. It suggests that appeals are not pursued 'so that the applicant will be given the documents'. Rather they are pursued in order for a more adequate explanation for refusal to come forth.

Whether or not State appeal is an (im)perfect alternative to State intervention is hard to say. The former is certainly less frequent than the latter, but also much more spectacular. As to why one is chosen over the other, we might have to ask the Member State directly.

With regard to our second task, institutional appeals are not frequent, have to date usually been led by the Council or the Commission, and are prone to arise with the purpose of securing presumptions of harm in as many areas of EU law as the ECJ will allow.

With regard to our third task, private parties appeal because they have failed in first instance and also because they have the financial resources to continue the contest. We have attempted to identify who applicants are in Chapter 2. However, why they request documents, why they challenge refusals and, finally even why they

[67] eg one might have expected an appeal from the UK within the *Bavarian Lager* proceedings.

appeal, is an enigma. Beyond the legal arguments that they do provide, not surprisingly the motivations behind their appeals of rulings of the GC remain a closed book. We may not blame the applicant. It is, ultimately, the fault of Regulation 1049/2001,[68] which from the start has allowed them to hide the true nature of the quest for documents. The exemption of having to provide reasons expunges any consideration of motive from the scrutiny of the judicature. Ultimately, motive may not be taken into consideration. The discussion is purely legal.

As a final note, the global vocation of the EU access policy is apparent again. The pursuit of an infinite public—signalled since access' first appearance also hits its mark, within appeal proceedings. Alongside actions at first instance, appeals also open a second chance for interventions, from near and from far. Applicants and interveners that come from abroad (USA, Canada, Israel, Switzerland, China) reveal that many people are watching from beyond the EU (also). True, some care but do not act. Others, risking exposure in the process, go to the extent of asserting interests in the outcome of EU appeal proceedings initiated by someone else. The ECJ thus becomes a global courtroom, adjudicating on interests held by persons that operate inside, but also well beyond the European frontier.

[68] Regulation 1049/2001, Art 6.

Epilogue to Public Access to Documents in the EU

BECAUSE WE CALLED this book a Herculean task, we spoke to a specialist on Art History and enquired about the mythical figure's troubles. The specialist is a medical doctor versed in painting as well as music who looked to art for his own solace when he was not busy mending broken souls. We asked him how many had Hercules labours been. For a naïve moment we hoped that the answer would be ten. Had it been so, we could have latched each labour to a chapter. And in that case we might have written 10 chapters instead of eight. We also asked him if at the end (of the labours) Hercules had stopped. And rested.

The doctor smiled.

'Hercules cannot rest', he said.

He explained how unrest is exactly what this character is about. The labours come attached to *parergas*, minor sequences of troubles that are endless.

Thus, when one takes up a Herculean labour one is required (as was Hercules) to conquer dust, heat, thirst and tiredness. And also to suffer cuts and bruises as well as to carry the weight of the story that must be told. Finally, there will always be more labours that will have to be dealt with.

Like case law. It never ends.

However, it does pause. If at no other moment, at least, in principle, case law enjoys a pause over the Summer Holidays.

So, after the final chapter, we imagined a halfway house for the Hero to retire, just for a fleeting moment, between one case and another.

At the end Hercules stops

Having discharged himself of so many troubling questions

Pays no heed to murmurs that there are more to come

New cases, different angles, words yet to reconcile

In the thirst of tiredness, he stops listening

Drops to his knees
Feels only an aching head,
Swollen hands
Blistered feet
And folds into a shade
Where children sleep.

Annexes

Annex 1—Code of Conduct—Concerning Public Access to Council And Commission Documents (93/730/EC).

Annex 2—Regulation (EC) No 1049/2001 of the European Parliament and of the Council of 30 May 2001 regarding public access to European Parliament, Council and Commission documents.

Annex 3—Regulation (EC) No 45/2001 of the European Parliament and of the Council of 18 December 2000 on the protection of individuals with regard to the processing of personal data by the institutions and bodies of the Community and on the free movement of such data.

Annex 4—Regulation (EC) No 1367/2006 of the European Parliament and of the Council of 6 September 2006 on the application of the provisions of the Aarhus Convention on Access to Information, Public Participation in Decision-making and Access to Justice in Environmental Matters to Community institutions and bodies.

Annex 1

CODE OF CONDUCT

CONCERNING PUBLIC ACCESS TO COUNCIL AND COMMISSION DOCUMENTS (93/730/EC)

THE COUNCIL AND THE COMMISSION,

HAVING REGARD to the declaration on the right of access to information annexed to the final act of the Treaty on European Union, which emphasizes that transparency of the decision-making process strengthens the democratic nature of the institutions and the public's confidence in the administration, HAVING REGARD to the conclusions wherein the European Councils in Birmingham and Edinburgh agreed on a number of principles to promote a Community closer to its citizens, HAVING REGARD to the conclusions of the European Council in Copenhagen, reaffirming the principle of giving citizens the greatest possible access to information and calling on the Council and the Commission to adopt at an early date the necessary measures for putting this principle into practice,

CONSIDERING it desirable to establish by common agreement the principles which will govern access to Commission and Council documents, it being understood that it is for each of them to implement these principles by means of specific regulations, WHEREAS the said principles are without prejudice to the relevant provisions on access to files directly concerning persons with a specific interest in them; WHEREAS these principles will have to be implemented in full compliance with the provisions concerning classified information; WHEREAS this code of conduct is an additional element in their information and communication policy,

HAVE AGREED AS FOLLOWS: **General principle** The public will have the widest possible access to documents held by the Commission and the Council. 'Document' means any written text, whatever its medium, which contains existing data and is held by the Council or the Commission.

Processing of initial applications

An application for access to a document will have to be made in writing, in a sufficiently precise manner; it will have to contain information that will enable the document or documents concerned to be identified. Where necessary, the institution concerned will ask the applicant for further details. Where the document held by an institution was written by a natural or legal person, a Member State, another Community institution or body or any other national or international body, **the application must be sent direct to the author**.

In consultation with the applicants, the institution concerned will find a fair solution to comply with repeat applications and/or those which relate to very large documents. The applicant will have access to documents either by consulting them on the spot or by having a copy sent at his own expense; the fee will not exceed a reasonable sum. The institution concerned will be able to stipulate that a person to whom a document is released will not be allowed to reproduce or circulate the said document for commercial purposes through direct sale without its prior authorization. Within **one month** the relevant departments of the institution concerned will inform the applicant either that his application has been approved or that they intend to advise the institution to reject it.

Processing of confirmatory applications

Where the relevant departments of the institution concerned intend to advise the institution to reject an application, they will inform the applicant thereof and tell him that he has one month to make a confirmatory application to the institution for that position to be reconsidered, failing which he will be deemed to have withdrawn his original application. If a confirmatory application is submitted, and if the institution concerned decides to refuse to release the document, that decision, which must be made within a month of submission of the confirmatory application, will be notified in writing to the applicant as soon as possible. The grounds for the decision must be given, and the decision must indicate the means of redress that are available, i.e. judicial proceedings and complaints to the ombudsman under the conditions specified in, respectively, Articles 173 and 138e of the Treaty establishing the European Community.

Exceptions

The institutions **will** refuse access to any document whose disclosure could undermine:

- the protection of the public interest (public security, international relations, monetary stability, court proceedings, inspections and investigations),
- the protection of the individual and of privacy,
- the protection of commercial and industrial secrecy,
- the protection of the Community's financial interests,
- the protection of confidentiality as requested by the natural or legal persons that supplied the information or as required by the legislation of the Member State that supplied the information.

They **may** also refuse access in order to protect the institution's interest in the confidentiality of its proceedings.

Implementation

The Commission and the Council will severally take steps to implement these principles before 1 January 1994.

Review

The Council and the Commission agree that the code of conduct will, after two years of operation, be reviewed on the basis of reports drawn up by the Secretaries-General of the Council and the Commission.

Annex 2

REGULATION (EC) NO 1049/2001 OF THE EUROPEAN PARLIAMENT AND OF THE COUNCIL OF 30 MAY 2001

regarding public access to European Parliament, Council and Commission documents

THE EUROPEAN PARLIAMENT AND THE COUNCIL OF THE EUROPEAN UNION,

Having regard to the Treaty establishing the European Community, and in particular Article 255(2) thereof,

Having regard to the proposal from the Commission(1),

Acting in accordance with the procedure referred to in Article 251 of the Treaty(2),

Whereas:

(1) The second subparagraph of Article 1 of the Treaty on European Union enshrines the concept of openness, stating that the Treaty marks a new stage in the process of creating an ever closer union among the peoples of Europe, in which decisions are taken as openly as possible and as closely as possible to the citizen.

(2) Openness enables citizens to participate more closely in the decision-making process and guarantees that the administration enjoys greater legitimacy and is more effective and more accountable to the citizen in a democratic system. Openness contributes to strengthening the principles of democracy and respect for fundamental rights as laid down in Article 6 of the EU Treaty and in the Charter of Fundamental Rights of the European Union.

(3) The conclusions of the European Council meetings held at Birmingham, Edinburgh and Copenhagen stressed the need to introduce greater transparency into the work of the Union institutions. This Regulation consolidates the initiatives that the institutions have already taken with a view to improving the transparency of the decision-making process.

(4) The purpose of this Regulation is to give the fullest possible effect to the right of public access to documents and to lay down the general principles and limits on such access in accordance with Article 255(2) of the EC Treaty.

(5) Since the question of access to documents is not covered by provisions of the Treaty establishing the European Coal and Steel Community and the Treaty establishing the European Atomic Energy Community, the European Parliament, the Council and the Commission should, in accordance with Declaration No 41 attached to the Final Act of the Treaty of Amsterdam, draw guidance from this Regulation as regards documents concerning the activities covered by those two Treaties.

(6) Wider access should be granted to documents in cases where the institutions are acting in their legislative capacity, including under delegated powers, while at the same time preserving the effectiveness of the institutions' decision-making process. Such documents should be made directly accessible to the greatest possible extent.

(7) In accordance with Articles 28(1) and 41(1) of the EU Treaty, the right of access also applies to documents relating to the common foreign and security policy and to police and judicial cooperation in criminal matters. Each institution should respect its security rules.

(8) In order to ensure the full application of this Regulation to all activities of the Union, all agencies established by the institutions should apply the principles laid down in this Regulation.

(9) On account of their highly sensitive content, certain documents should be given special treatment. Arrangements for informing the European Parliament of the content of such documents should be made through interinstitutional agreement.

(10) In order to bring about greater openness in the work of the institutions, access to documents should be granted by the European Parliament, the Council and the Commission not only to documents drawn up by the institutions, but also to documents received by them. In this context, it is recalled that Declaration No 35 attached to the Final Act of the Treaty of Amsterdam provides that a Member State may request the Commission or the Council not to communicate to third parties a document originating from that State without its prior agreement.

(11) In principle, all documents of the institutions should be accessible to the public. However, certain public and private interests should be protected by way of exceptions. The institutions should be entitled to protect their internal consultations and deliberations where necessary to safeguard their ability to carry out their tasks. In assessing the exceptions, the institutions should take account of the principles in Community legislation concerning the protection of personal data, in all areas of Union activities.

(12) All rules concerning access to documents of the institutions should be in conformity with this Regulation.

(13) In order to ensure that the right of access is fully respected, a two-stage administrative procedure should apply, with the additional possibility of court proceedings or complaints to the Ombudsman.

(14) Each institution should take the measures necessary to inform the public of the new provisions in force and to train its staff to assist citizens exercising their rights under this Regulation. In order to make it easier for citizens to exercise their rights, each institution should provide access to a register of documents.

(15) Even though it is neither the object nor the effect of this Regulation to amend national legislation on access to documents, it is nevertheless clear that, by virtue of the principle of loyal cooperation which governs relations between the institutions and the Member States, Member States should take care not to hamper the proper application of this Regulation and should respect the security rules of the institutions.

(16) This Regulation is without prejudice to existing rights of access to documents for Member States, judicial authorities or investigative bodies.

(17) In accordance with Article 255(3) of the EC Treaty, each institution lays down specific provisions regarding access to its documents in its rules of procedure. Council Decision 93/731/EC of 20 December 1993 on public access to Council documents(3), Commission Decision 94/90/ECSC, EC, Euratom of 8 February 1994 on public access to Commission documents(4), European Parliament Decision 97/632/EC, ECSC, Euratom of 10 July 1997 on public access to European Parliament documents(5), and the rules on confidentiality of Schengen documents should therefore, if necessary, be modified or be repealed,

HAVE ADOPTED THIS REGULATION:

Article 1

Purpose

The purpose of this Regulation is:

(a) to define the principles, conditions and limits on grounds of public or private interest governing the right of access to European Parliament, Council and Commission (hereinafter referred to as "the institutions") documents provided for in Article 255 of the EC Treaty in such a way as to ensure the widest possible access to documents,
(b) to establish rules ensuring the easiest possible exercise of this right, and
(c) to promote good administrative practice on access to documents.

Article 2

Beneficiaries and scope

1. Any citizen of the Union, and any natural or legal person residing or having its registered office in a Member State, has a right of access to documents of the institutions, subject to the principles, conditions and limits defined in this Regulation.

2. The institutions may, subject to the same principles, conditions and limits, grant access to documents to any natural or legal person not residing or not having its registered office in a Member State.

3. This Regulation shall apply to all documents held by an institution, that is to say, documents drawn up or received by it and in its possession, in all areas of activity of the European Union.

4. Without prejudice to Articles 4 and 9, documents shall be made accessible to the public either following a written application or directly in electronic form or through a register. In particular, documents drawn up or received in the course of a legislative procedure shall be made directly accessible in accordance with Article 12.

5. Sensitive documents as defined in Article 9(1) shall be subject to special treatment in accordance with that Article.

6. This Regulation shall be without prejudice to rights of public access to documents held by the institutions which might follow from instruments of international law or acts of the institutions implementing them.

Article 3

Definitions

For the purpose of this Regulation:

(a) "document" shall mean any content whatever its medium (written on paper or stored in electronic form or as a sound, visual or audiovisual recording) concerning a matter relating to the policies, activities and decisions falling within the institution's sphere of responsibility;
(b) "third party" shall mean any natural or legal person, or any entity outside the institution concerned, including the Member States, other Community or non-Community institutions and bodies and third countries.

Article 4

Exceptions

1. The institutions shall refuse access to a document where disclosure would undermine the protection of:

(a) the public interest as regards:
    — public security,
    — defence and military matters,
    — international relations,
    — the financial, monetary or economic policy of the Community or a Member State;
(b) privacy and the integrity of the individual, in particular in accordance with Community legislation regarding the protection of personal data.

2. The institutions shall refuse access to a document where disclosure would undermine the protection of:

— commercial interests of a natural or legal person, including intellectual property,
— court proceedings and legal advice,
— the purpose of inspections, investigations and audits,

unless there is an overriding public interest in disclosure.

3. Access to a document, drawn up by an institution for internal use or received by an institution, which relates to a matter where the decision has not been taken by the institution, shall be refused if disclosure of the document would seriously undermine the institution's decision-making process, unless there is an overriding public interest in disclosure.

Access to a document containing opinions for internal use as part of deliberations and preliminary consultations within the institution concerned shall be refused even after the decision has been taken if disclosure of the document would seriously undermine the institution's decision-making process, unless there is an overriding public interest in disclosure.

4. As regards third-party documents, the institution shall consult the third party with a view to assessing whether an exception in paragraph 1 or 2 is applicable, unless it is clear that the document shall or shall not be disclosed.

5. A Member State may request the institution not to disclose a document originating from that Member State without its prior agreement.

6. If only parts of the requested document are covered by any of the exceptions, the remaining parts of the document shall be released.

7. The exceptions as laid down in paragraphs 1 to 3 shall only apply for the period during which protection is justified on the basis of the content of the document. The exceptions may apply for a maximum period of 30 years. In the case of documents covered by the exceptions relating to privacy or commercial interests and in the case of sensitive documents, the exceptions may, if necessary, continue to apply after this period.

Article 5

Documents in the Member States

Where a Member State receives a request for a document in its possession, originating from an institution, unless it is clear that the document shall or shall not be disclosed, the Member State shall consult with the institution concerned in order to take a decision that does not jeopardise the attainment of the objectives of this Regulation.

The Member State may instead refer the request to the institution.

Article 6

Applications

1. Applications for access to a document shall be made in any written form, including electronic form, in one of the languages referred to in Article 314 of the EC Treaty and in a sufficiently precise manner to enable the institution to identify the document. The applicant is not obliged to state reasons for the application.

2. If an application is not sufficiently precise, the institution shall ask the applicant to clarify the application and shall assist the applicant in doing so, for example, by providing information on the use of the public registers of documents.

3. In the event of an application relating to a very long document or to a very large number of documents, the institution concerned may confer with the applicant informally, with a view to finding a fair solution.

4. The institutions shall provide information and assistance to citizens on how and where applications for access to documents can be made.

Article 7

Processing of initial applications

1. An application for access to a document shall be handled promptly. An acknowledgement of receipt shall be sent to the applicant. Within 15 working days from registration of the application, the institution shall either grant access to the document requested and provide access in accordance with Article 10 within

that period or, in a written reply, state the reasons for the total or partial refusal and inform the applicant of his or her right to make a confirmatory application in accordance with paragraph 2 of this Article.

2. In the event of a total or partial refusal, the applicant may, within 15 working days of receiving the institution's reply, make a confirmatory application asking the institution to reconsider its position.

3. In exceptional cases, for example in the event of an application relating to a very long document or to a very large number of documents, the time-limit provided for in paragraph 1 may be extended by 15 working days, provided that the applicant is notified in advance and that detailed reasons are given.

4. Failure by the institution to reply within the prescribed time-limit shall entitle the applicant to make a confirmatory application.

Article 8

Processing of confirmatory applications

1. A confirmatory application shall be handled promptly. Within 15 working days from registration of such an application, the institution shall either grant access to the document requested and provide access in accordance with Article 10 within that period or, in a written reply, state the reasons for the total or partial refusal. In the event of a total or partial refusal, the institution shall inform the applicant of the remedies open to him or her, namely instituting court proceedings against the institution and/or making a complaint to the Ombudsman, under the conditions laid down in Articles 230 and 195 of the EC Treaty, respectively.

2. In exceptional cases, for example in the event of an application relating to a very long document or to a very large number of documents, the time limit provided for in paragraph 1 may be extended by 15 working days, provided that the applicant is notified in advance and that detailed reasons are given.

3. Failure by the institution to reply within the prescribed time limit shall be considered as a negative reply and entitle the applicant to institute court proceedings against the institution and/or make a complaint to the Ombudsman, under the relevant provisions of the EC Treaty.

Article 9

Treatment of sensitive documents

1. Sensitive documents are documents originating from the institutions or the agencies established by them, from Member States, third countries or International Organisations, classified as "TRÈS SECRET/TOP SECRET", "SECRET" or "CONFIDENTIEL" in accordance with the rules of the institution concerned, which protect essential interests of the European Union or of one or more of its Member States in the areas covered by Article 4(1)(a), notably public security, defence and military matters.

2. Applications for access to sensitive documents under the procedures laid down in Articles 7 and 8 shall be handled only by those persons who have a right to acquaint themselves with those documents. These persons shall also, without

prejudice to Article 11(2), assess which references to sensitive documents could be made in the public register.

3. Sensitive documents shall be recorded in the register or released only with the consent of the originator.

4. An institution which decides to refuse access to a sensitive document shall give the reasons for its decision in a manner which does not harm the interests protected in Article 4.

5. Member States shall take appropriate measures to ensure that when handling applications for sensitive documents the principles in this Article and Article 4 are respected.

6. The rules of the institutions concerning sensitive documents shall be made public.

7. The Commission and the Council shall inform the European Parliament regarding sensitive documents in accordance with arrangements agreed between the institutions.

Article 10

Access following an application

1. The applicant shall have access to documents either by consulting them on the spot or by receiving a copy, including, where available, an electronic copy, according to the applicant's preference. The cost of producing and sending copies may be charged to the applicant. This charge shall not exceed the real cost of producing and sending the copies. Consultation on the spot, copies of less than 20 A4 pages and direct access in electronic form or through the register shall be free of charge.

2. If a document has already been released by the institution concerned and is easily accessible to the applicant, the institution may fulfil its obligation of granting access to documents by informing the applicant how to obtain the requested document.

3. Documents shall be supplied in an existing version and format (including electronically or in an alternative format such as Braille, large print or tape) with full regard to the applicant's preference.

Article 11

Registers

1. To make citizens' rights under this Regulation effective, each institution shall provide public access to a register of documents. Access to the register should be provided in electronic form. References to documents shall be recorded in the register without delay.

2. For each document the register shall contain a reference number (including, where applicable, the interinstitutional reference), the subject matter and/or a short description of the content of the document and the date on which it was received or drawn up and recorded in the register. References shall be made in a manner which does not undermine protection of the interests in Article 4.

3. The institutions shall immediately take the measures necessary to establish a register which shall be operational by 3 June 2002.

Article 12

Direct access in electronic form or through a register

1. The institutions shall as far as possible make documents directly accessible to the public in electronic form or through a register in accordance with the rules of the institution concerned.

2. In particular, legislative documents, that is to say, documents drawn up or received in the course of procedures for the adoption of acts which are legally binding in or for the Member States, should, subject to Articles 4 and 9, be made directly accessible.

3. Where possible, other documents, notably documents relating to the development of policy or strategy, should be made directly accessible.

4. Where direct access is not given through the register, the register shall as far as possible indicate where the document is located.

Article 13

Publication in the Official Journal

1. In addition to the acts referred to in Article 254(1) and (2) of the EC Treaty and the first paragraph of Article 163 of the Euratom Treaty, the following documents shall, subject to Articles 4 and 9 of this Regulation, be published in the Official Journal:

(a) Commission proposals;
(b) common positions adopted by the Council in accordance with the procedures referred to in Articles 251 and 252 of the EC Treaty and the reasons underlying those common positions, as well as the European Parliament's positions in these procedures;
(c) framework decisions and decisions referred to in Article 34(2) of the EU Treaty;
(d) conventions established by the Council in accordance with Article 34(2) of the EU Treaty;
(e) conventions signed between Member States on the basis of Article 293 of the EC Treaty;
(f) international agreements concluded by the Community or in accordance with Article 24 of the EU Treaty.

2. As far as possible, the following documents shall be published in the Official Journal:

(a) initiatives presented to the Council by a Member State pursuant to Article 67(1) of the EC Treaty or pursuant to Article 34(2) of the EU Treaty;
(b) common positions referred to in Article 34(2) of the EU Treaty;
(c) directives other than those referred to in Article 254(1) and (2) of the EC Treaty, decisions other than those referred to in Article 254(1) of the EC Treaty, recommendations and opinions.

3. Each institution may in its rules of procedure establish which further documents shall be published in the Official Journal.

Article 14

Information

1. Each institution shall take the requisite measures to inform the public of the rights they enjoy under this Regulation.

2. The Member States shall cooperate with the institutions in providing information to the citizens.

Article 15

Administrative practice in the institutions

1. The institutions shall develop good administrative practices in order to facilitate the exercise of the right of access guaranteed by this Regulation.

2. The institutions shall establish an interinstitutional committee to examine best practice, address possible conflicts and discuss future developments on public access to documents.

Article 16

Reproduction of documents

This Regulation shall be without prejudice to any existing rules on copyright which may limit a third party's right to reproduce or exploit released documents.

Article 17

Reports

1. Each institution shall publish annually a report for the preceding year including the number of cases in which the institution refused to grant access to documents, the reasons for such refusals and the number of sensitive documents not recorded in the register.

2. At the latest by 31 January 2004, the Commission shall publish a report on the implementation of the principles of this Regulation and shall make recommendations, including, if appropriate, proposals for the revision of this Regulation and an action programme of measures to be taken by the institutions.

Article 18

Application measures

1. Each institution shall adapt its rules of procedure to the provisions of this Regulation. The adaptations shall take effect from 3 December 2001.

2. Within six months of the entry into force of this Regulation, the Commission shall examine the conformity of Council Regulation (EEC, Euratom) No 354/83 of 1 February 1983 concerning the opening to the public of the historical archives of the European Economic Community and the European Atomic Energy Community(6) with this Regulation in order to ensure the preservation and archiving of documents to the fullest extent possible.

3. Within six months of the entry into force of this Regulation, the Commission shall examine the conformity of the existing rules on access to documents with this Regulation.

Article 19

Entry into force

This Regulation shall enter into force on the third day following that of its publication in the Official Journal of the European Communities.

It shall be applicable from 3 December 2001.

This Regulation shall be binding in its entirety and directly applicable in all Member States.

Done at Brussels, 30 May 2001.

For the European Parliament

The President

N. Fontaine

For the Council

The President

B. Lejon

(1) OJ C 177 E, 27.6.2000, p. 70.

(2) Opinion of the European Parliament of 3 May 2001 (not yet published in the Official Journal) and Council Decision of 28 May 2001.

(3) OJ L 340, 31.12.1993, p. 43. Decision as last amended by Decision 2000/527/EC (OJ L 212, 23.8.2000, p. 9).

(4) OJ L 46, 18.2.1994, p. 58. Decision as amended by Decision 96/567/EC, ECSC, Euratom (OJ L 247, 28.9.1996, p. 45).

(5) OJ L 263, 25.9.1997, p. 27.

(6) OJ L 43, 15.2.1983, p. 1.

Annex 3

REGULATION (EC) NO 45/2001 OF THE EUROPEAN PARLIAMENT AND OF THE COUNCIL OF 18 DECEMBER 2000

on the protection of individuals with regard to processing of personal data by the Community institutions and bodies and on the free movement of such data

THE EUROPEAN PARLIAMENT AND THE COUNCIL
OF THE EUROPEAN UNION,

Having regard to the Treaty establishing the European Community, and in particular Article 286 thereof,

Having regard to the proposal from the Commission(1),

Having regard to the opinion of the Economic and Social Committee(2),

Acting in accordance with the procedure laid down in Article 251 of the Treaty(3),

Whereas:

(1) Article 286 of the Treaty requires the application to the Community institutions and bodies of the Community acts on the protection of individuals with regard to the processing of personal data and the free movement of such data.

(2) A fully-fledged system of protection of personal data not only requires the establishment of rights for data subjects and obligations for those who process personal data, but also appropriate sanctions for offenders and monitoring by an independent supervisory body.

(3) Article 286(2) of the Treaty requires the establishment of an independent supervisory body responsible for monitoring the application of such Community acts to Community institutions and bodies.

(4) Article 286(2) of the Treaty requires the adoption of any other relevant provisions as appropriate.

(5) A Regulation is necessary to provide the individual with legally enforceable rights, to specify the data processing obligations of the controllers within the Community institutions and bodies, and to create an independent supervisory authority responsible for monitoring the processing of personal data by the Community institutions and bodies.

(6) The Working Party on the Protection of Individuals with regard to the Processing of Personal Data set up under Article 29 of Directive 95/46/EC of the European Parliament and of the Council of 24 October 1995 on the protection of individuals with regard to the processing of personal data and on the free movement of such data(4) has been consulted.

(7) The persons to be protected are those whose personal data are processed by Community institutions or bodies in any context whatsoever, for example because they are employed by those institutions or bodies.

(8) The principles of data protection should apply to any information concerning an identified or identifiable person. To determine whether a person is identifiable, account should be taken of all the means likely to be reasonably used either by the controller or by any other person to identify the said person. The principles of protection should not apply to data rendered anonymous in such a way that the data subject is no longer identifiable.

(9) Directive 95/46/EC requires Member States to protect the fundamental rights and freedoms of natural persons, and in particular their right to privacy with respect to the processing of personal data, in order to ensure the free flow of personal data in the Community.

(10) Directive 97/66/EC of the European Parliament and of the Council of 15 December 1997 concerning the processing of personal data and the protection of privacy in the telecommunications sector(5) specifies and adds to Directive 95/46/EC with respect to the processing of personal data in the telecommunications sector.

(11) Various other Community measures, including measures on mutual assistance between national authorities and the Commission, are also designed to specify and add to Directive 95/46/EC in the sectors to which they relate.

(12) Consistent and homogeneous application of the rules for the protection of individuals' fundamental rights and freedoms with regard to the processing of personal data should be ensured throughout the Community.

(13) The aim is to ensure both effective compliance with the rules governing the protection of individuals' fundamental rights and freedoms and the free flow of personal data between Member States and the Community institutions and bodies or between the Community institutions and bodies for purposes connected with the exercise of their respective competences.

(14) To this end measures should be adopted which are binding on the Community institutions and bodies. These measures should apply to all processing of personal data by all Community institutions and bodies insofar as such processing is carried out in the exercise of activities all or part of which fall within the scope of Community law.

(15) Where such processing is carried out by Community institutions or bodies in the exercise of activities falling outside the scope of this Regulation, in particular those laid down in Titles V and VI of the Treaty on European Union, the protection of individuals' fundamental rights and freedoms shall be ensured with due regard to Article 6 of the Treaty on European Union. Access to documents, including conditions for access to documents containing personal data, is governed by the rules adopted on the basis of Article 255 of the EC Treaty the scope of which includes Titles V and VI of the Treaty on European Union.

(16) The measures should not apply to bodies established outside the Community framework, nor should the European Data Protection Supervisor be competent to monitor the processing of personal data by such bodies.

(17) The effectiveness of the protection of individuals with regard to the processing of personal data in the Union presupposes the consistency of the relevant rules and procedures applicable to activities pertaining to different legal contexts. The development of fundamental principles on the protection of personal data in the fields of judicial cooperation in criminal affairs and police and customs cooperation, and the setting-up of a secretariat for the joint supervisory authorities established by the Europol Convention, the Convention on the Use of Information Technology for Customs Purposes and the Schengen Convention represent a first step in this regard.

(18) This Regulation should not affect the rights and obligations of Member States under Directives 95/46/EC and 97/66/EC. It is not intended to change existing procedures and practices lawfully implemented by the Member States in the field of national security, prevention of disorder or prevention, detection, investigation and prosecution of criminal offences in compliance with the Protocol on Privileges and Immunities of the European Communities and with international law.

(19) The Community institutions and bodies should inform the competent authorities in the Member States when they consider that communications on their telecommunications networks should be intercepted, in keeping with the national provisions applicable.

(20) The provisions applicable to the Community institutions and bodies should correspond to those provisions laid down in connection with the harmonisation of national laws or the implementation of other Community policies, notably in the mutual assistance sphere. It may be necessary, however, to specify and add to those provisions when it comes to ensuring protection in the case of the processing of personal data by the Community institutions and bodies.

(21) This holds true for the rights of the individuals whose data are being processed, for the obligations of the Community institutions and bodies doing the processing, and for the powers to be vested in the independent supervisory authority responsible for ensuring that this Regulation is properly applied.

(22) The rights accorded the data subject and the exercise thereof should not affect the obligations placed on the controller.

(23) The independent supervisory authority should exercise its supervisory functions in accordance with the Treaty and in compliance with human rights and fundamental freedoms. It should conduct its enquiries in compliance with the Protocol on Privileges and Immunities and with the Staff Regulations of Officials of the European Communities and the conditions of employment applicable to Other Servants of the Communities.

(24) The necessary technical measures should be adopted to allow access to the registers of processing operations carried out by Data Protection Officers through the independent supervisory authority.

(25) The decisions of the independent supervisory authority regarding exemptions, guarantees, authorisations and conditions relating to data processing operations, as defined in this Regulation, should be published in the activities report. Independently of the publication of an annual activities report, the independent supervisory authority may publish reports on specific subjects.

(26) Certain processing operations likely to present specific risks with respect to the rights and freedoms of data subjects are subject to prior checking by the independent supervisory authority. The opinion given in the context of such prior checking, including the opinion resulting from failure to reply within the set period, should be without prejudice to the subsequent exercise by the independent supervisory authority of its powers with regard to the processing operation in question.

(27) Processing of personal data for the performance of tasks carried out in the public interest by the Community institutions and bodies includes the processing of personal data necessary for the management and functioning of those institutions and bodies.

(28) In certain cases the processing of data should be authorised by Community provisions or by acts transposing Community provisions. Nevertheless, in the transitional period during which such provisions do not exist, pending their adoption, the European Data Protection Supervisor may authorise processing of such data provided that adequate safeguards are adopted. In so doing, he should take account in particular of the provisions adopted by the Member States to deal with similar cases.

(29) These cases concern the processing of data revealing racial or ethnic origin, political opinions, religious or philosophical beliefs or trade-union membership and the processing of data concerning health or sex life which are necessary for the purposes of complying with the specific rights and obligations of the controller in the field of employment law or for reasons of substantial public interest. They also concern the processing of data relating to offences, criminal convictions or security measures and authorisation to apply a decision to the data subject which produces legal effects concerning him or her or significantly affects him or her and which is based solely on automated processing of data intended to evaluate certain personal aspects relating to him or her.

(30) It may be necessary to monitor the computer networks operated under the control of the Community institutions and bodies for the purposes of prevention of unauthorised use. The European Data Protection Supervisor should determine whether and under what conditions that is possible.

(31) Liability arising from any breach of this Regulation is governed by the second paragraph of Article 288 of the Treaty.

(32) In each Community institution or body one or more Data Protection Officers should ensure that the provisions of this Regulation are applied and should advise controllers on fulfilling their obligations.

(33) Under Article 21 of Council Regulation (EC) No 322/97 of 17 February 1997 on Community statistics(6), that Regulation is to apply without prejudice to Directive 95/46/EC.

(34) Under Article 8(8) of Council Regulation (EC) No 2533/98 of 23 November 1998 concerning the collection of statistical information by the European Central Bank(7), that Regulation is to apply without prejudice to Directive 95/46/EC.

(35) Under Article 1(2) of Council Regulation (Euratom, EEC) No 1588/90 of 11 June 1990 on the transmission of data subject to statistical confidentiality to the Statistical Office of the European Communities(8), that Regulation does not derogate

from the special Community or national provisions concerning the safeguarding of confidentiality other than statistical confidentiality.

(36) This Regulation does not aim to limit Member States' room for manoeuvre in drawing up their national laws on data protection under Article 32 of Directive 95/46/EC, in accordance with Article 249 of the Treaty,

HAVE ADOPTED THIS REGULATION:

CHAPTER I

GENERAL PROVISIONS

Article 1

Object of the Regulation

1. In accordance with this Regulation, the institutions and bodies set up by, or on the basis of, the Treaties establishing the European Communities, hereinafter referred to as "Community institutions or bodies", shall protect the fundamental rights and freedoms of natural persons, and in particular their right to privacy with respect to the processing of personal data and shall neither restrict nor prohibit the free flow of personal data between themselves or to recipients subject to the national law of the Member States implementing Directive 95/46/EC.

2. The independent supervisory authority established by this Regulation, hereinafter referred to as the European Data Protection Supervisor, shall monitor the application of the provisions of this Regulation to all processing operations carried out by a Community institution or body.

Article 2

Definitions

For the purposes of this Regulation:

(a) "personal data" shall mean any information relating to an identified or identifiable natural person hereinafter referred to as "data subject"; an identifiable person is one who can be identified, directly or indirectly, in particular by reference to an identification number or to one or more factors specific to his or her physical, physiological, mental, economic, cultural or social identity;
(b) "processing of personal data" hereinafter referred to as "processing" shall mean any operation or set of operations which is performed upon personal data, whether or not by automatic means, such as collection, recording, organisation, storage, adaptation or alteration, retrieval, consultation, use, disclosure by transmission, dissemination or otherwise making available, alignment or combination, blocking, erasure or destruction;
(c) "personal data filing system" hereinafter referred to as "filing system" shall mean any structured set of personal data which are accessible according to specific criteria, whether centralised, decentralised or dispersed on a functional or geographical basis;

(d) "controller" shall mean the Community institution or body, the Directorate-General, the unit or any other organisational entity which alone or jointly with others determines the purposes and means of the processing of personal data; where the purposes and means of processing are determined by a specific Community act, the controller or the specific criteria for its nomination may be designated by such Community act;
(e) "processor" shall mean a natural or legal person, public authority, agency or any other body which processes personal data on behalf of the controller;
(f) "third party" shall mean a natural or legal person, public authority, agency or body other than the data subject, the controller, the processor and the persons who, under the direct authority of the controller or the processor, are authorised to process the data;
(g) "recipient" shall mean a natural or legal person, public authority, agency or any other body to whom data are disclosed, whether a third party or not; however, authorities which may receive data in the framework of a particular inquiry shall not be regarded as recipients;
(h) "the data subject's consent" shall mean any freely given specific and informed indication of his or her wishes by which the data subject signifies his or her agreement to personal data relating to him or her being processed.

Article 3

Scope

1. This Regulation shall apply to the processing of personal data by all Community institutions and bodies insofar as such processing is carried out in the exercise of activities all or part of which fall within the scope of Community law.

2. This Regulation shall apply to the processing of personal data wholly or partly by automatic means, and to the processing otherwise than by automatic means of personal data which form part of a filing system or are intended to form part of a filing system.

CHAPTER II

GENERAL RULES ON THE LAWFULNESS OF THE PROCESSING OF PERSONAL DATA

SECTION 1

PRINCIPLES RELATING TO DATA QUALITY

Article 4

Data quality

1. Personal data must be:

(a) processed fairly and lawfully;
(b) collected for specified, explicit and legitimate purposes and not further processed in a way incompatible with those purposes. Further processing of personal data for historical, statistical or scientific purposes shall not be considered

incompatible provided that the controller provides appropriate safeguards, in particular to ensure that the data are not processed for any other purposes or used in support of measures or decisions regarding any particular individual;
(c) adequate, relevant and not excessive in relation to the purposes for which they are collected and/or further processed;
(d) accurate and, where necessary, kept up to date; every reasonable step must be taken to ensure that data which are inaccurate or incomplete, having regard to the purposes for which they were collected or for which they are further processed, are erased or rectified;
(e) kept in a form which permits identification of data subjects for no longer than is necessary for the purposes for which the data were collected or for which they are further processed. The Community institution or body shall lay down that personal data which are to be stored for longer periods for historical, statistical or scientific use should be kept either in anonymous form only or, if that is not possible, only with the identity of the data subjects encrypted. In any event, the data shall not be used for any purpose other than for historical, statistical or scientific purposes.

2. It shall be for the controller to ensure that paragraph 1 is complied with.

SECTION 2

CRITERIA FOR MAKING DATA PROCESSING LEGITIMATE

Article 5

Lawfulness of processing

Personal data may be processed only if:

(a) processing is necessary for the performance of a task carried out in the public interest on the basis of the Treaties establishing the European Communities or other legal instruments adopted on the basis thereof or in the legitimate exercise of official authority vested in the Community institution or body or in a third party to whom the data are disclosed, or
(b) processing is necessary for compliance with a legal obligation to which the controller is subject, or
(c) processing is necessary for the performance of a contract to which the data subject is party or in order to take steps at the request of the data subject prior to entering into a contract, or
(d) the data subject has unambiguously given his or her consent, or
(e) processing is necessary in order to protect the vital interests of the data subject.

Article 6

Change of purpose

Without prejudice to Articles 4, 5 and 10:

1. Personal data shall only be processed for purposes other than those for which they have been collected if the change of purpose is expressly permitted by the internal rules of the Community institution or body.

2. Personal data collected exclusively for ensuring the security or the control of the processing systems or operations shall not be used for any other purpose, with the exception of the prevention, investigation, detection and prosecution of serious criminal offences.

Article 7

Transfer of personal data within or between Community institutions or bodies

Without prejudice to Articles 4, 5, 6 and 10:
1. Personal data shall only be transferred within or to other Community institutions or bodies if the data are necessary for the legitimate performance of tasks covered by the competence of the recipient.
2. Where the data are transferred following a request from the recipient, both the controller and the recipient shall bear the responsibility for the legitimacy of this transfer.

The controller shall be required to verify the competence of the recipient and to make a provisional evaluation of the necessity for the transfer of the data. If doubts arise as to this necessity, the controller shall seek further information from the recipient.

The recipient shall ensure that the necessity for the transfer of the data can be subsequently verified.
3. The recipient shall process the personal data only for the purposes for which they were transmitted.

Article 8

Transfer of personal data to recipients, other than Community institutions and bodies, subject to Directive 95/46/EC

Without prejudice to Articles 4, 5, 6 and 10, personal data shall only be transferred to recipients subject to the national law adopted for the implementation of Directive 95/46/EC,

(a) if the recipient establishes that the data are necessary for the performance of a task carried out in the public interest or subject to the exercise of public authority, or
(b) if the recipient establishes the necessity of having the data transferred and if there is no reason to assume that the data subject's legitimate interests might be prejudiced.

Article 9

Transfer of personal data to recipients, other than Community institutions and bodies, which are not subject to Directive 95/46/EC

1. Personal data shall only be transferred to recipients, other than Community institutions and bodies, which are not subject to national law adopted pursuant to Directive 95/46/EC, if an adequate level of protection is ensured in the country of the recipient or within the recipient international organisation and the data are transferred solely to allow tasks covered by the competence of the controller to be carried out.

2. The adequacy of the level of protection afforded by the third country or international organisation in question shall be assessed in the light of all the circumstances surrounding a data transfer operation or set of data transfer operations; particular consideration shall be given to the nature of the data, the purpose and duration of the proposed processing operation or operations, the recipient third country or recipient international organisation, the rules of law, both general and sectoral, in force in the third country or international organisation in question and the professional rules and security measures which are complied with in that third country or international organisation.

3. The Community institutions and bodies shall inform the Commission and the European Data Protection Supervisor of cases where they consider the third country or international organisation in question does not ensure an adequate level of protection within the meaning of paragraph 2.

4. The Commission shall inform the Member States of any cases as referred to in paragraph 3.

5. The Community institutions and bodies shall take the necessary measures to comply with decisions taken by the Commission when it establishes, pursuant to Article 25(4) and (6) of Directive 95/46/EC, that a third country or an international organisation ensures or does not ensure an adequate level of protection.

6. By way of derogation from paragraphs 1 and 2, the Community institution or body may transfer personal data if:

(a) the data subject has given his or her consent unambiguously to the proposed transfer; or
(b) the transfer is necessary for the performance of a contract between the data subject and the controller or the implementation of pre-contractual measures taken in response to the data subject's request; or
(c) the transfer is necessary for the conclusion or performance of a contract entered into in the interest of the data subject between the controller and a third party; or
(d) the transfer is necessary or legally required on important public interest grounds, or for the establishment, exercise or defence of legal claims; or
(e) the transfer is necessary in order to protect the vital interests of the data subject; or
(f) the transfer is made from a register which, according to Community law, is intended to provide information to the public and which is open to consultation either by the public in general or by any person who can demonstrate a legitimate interest, to the extent that the conditions laid down in Community law for consultation are fulfilled in the particular case.

7. Without prejudice to paragraph 6, the European Data Protection Supervisor may authorise a transfer or a set of transfers of personal data to a third country or international organisation which does not ensure an adequate level of protection within the meaning of paragraphs 1 and 2, where the controller adduces adequate safeguards with respect to the protection of the privacy and fundamental rights and freedoms of individuals and as regards the exercise of the corresponding rights; such safeguards may in particular result from appropriate contractual clauses.

8. The Community institutions and bodies shall inform the European Data Protection Supervisor of categories of cases where they have applied paragraphs 6 and 7.

SECTION 3

SPECIAL CATEGORIES OF PROCESSING

Article 10

The processing of special categories of data

1. The processing of personal data revealing racial or ethnic origin, political opinions, religious or philosophical beliefs, trade-union membership, and of data concerning health or sex life, are prohibited.

2. Paragraph 1 shall not apply where:

(a) the data subject has given his or her express consent to the processing of those data, except where the internal rules of the Community institution or body provide that the prohibition referred to in paragraph 1 may not be lifted by the data subject's giving his or her consent, or
(b) processing is necessary for the purposes of complying with the specific rights and obligations of the controller in the field of employment law insofar as it is authorised by the Treaties establishing the European Communities or other legal instruments adopted on the basis thereof, or, if necessary, insofar as it is agreed upon by the European Data Protection Supervisor, subject to adequate safeguards, or
(c) processing is necessary to protect the vital interests of the data subject or of another person where the data subject is physically or legally incapable of giving his or her consent, or
(d) processing relates to data which are manifestly made public by the data subject or is necessary for the establishment, exercise or defence of legal claims, or
(e) processing is carried out in the course of its legitimate activities with appropriate safeguards by a non-profit-seeking body which constitutes an entity integrated in a Community institution or body, not subject to national data protection law by virtue of Article 4 of Directive 95/46/EC, and with a political, philosophical, religious or trade-union aim and on condition that the processing relates solely to the members of this body or to persons who have regular contact with it in connection with its purposes and that the data are not disclosed to a third party without the consent of the data subjects.

3. Paragraph 1 shall not apply where processing of the data is required for the purposes of preventive medicine, medical diagnosis, the provision of care or treatment or the management of health-care services, and where those data are processed by a health professional subject to the obligation of professional secrecy or by another person also subject to an equivalent obligation of secrecy.

4. Subject to the provision of appropriate safeguards, and for reasons of substantial public interest, exemptions in addition to those laid down in paragraph 2 may be laid down by the Treaties establishing the European Communities or other legal instruments adopted on the basis thereof or, if necessary, by decision of the European Data Protection Supervisor.

5. Processing of data relating to offences, criminal convictions or security measures may be carried out only if authorised by the Treaties establishing the European Communities or other legal instruments adopted on the basis thereof or, if necessary, by the European Data Protection Supervisor, subject to appropriate specific safeguards.

6. The European Data Protection Supervisor shall determine the conditions under which a personal number or other identifier of general application may be processed by a Community institution or body.

SECTION 4

INFORMATION TO BE GIVEN TO THE DATA SUBJECT

Article 11

Information to be supplied where the data have been obtained from the data subject

1. The controller shall provide a data subject from whom data relating to himself/herself are collected with at least the following information, except where he or she already has it:

(a) the identity of the controller;
(b) the purposes of the processing operation for which the data are intended;
(c) the recipients or categories of recipients of the data;
(d) whether replies to the questions are obligatory or voluntary, as well as the possible consequences of failure to reply;
(e) the existence of the right of access to, and the right to rectify, the data concerning him or her;
(f) any further information such as:
  (i) the legal basis of the processing operation for which the data are intended,
  (ii) the time-limits for storing the data,
  (iii) the right to have recourse at any time to the European Data Protection Supervisor,

insofar as such further information is necessary, having regard to the specific circumstances in which the data are collected, to guarantee fair processing in respect of the data subject.

2. By way of derogation from paragraph 1, the provision of information or part of it, except for the information referred to in paragraph 1(a), (b) and (d), may be deferred as long as this is necessary for statistical purposes. The information must be provided as soon as the reason for which the information is withheld ceases to exist.

Article 12

Information to be supplied where the data have not been obtained from the data subject

1. Where the data have not been obtained from the data subject, the controller shall at the time of undertaking the recording of personal data or, if a disclosure to a third party is envisaged, no later than the time when the data are first disclosed, provide

the data subject with at least the following information, except where he or she already has it:

(a) the identity of the controller;
(b) the purposes of the processing operation;
(c) the categories of data concerned;
(d) the recipients or categories of recipients;
(e) the existence of the right of access to, and the right to rectify, the data concerning him or her;
(f) any further information such as:
    (i) the legal basis of the processing operation for which the data are intended,
    (ii) the time-limits for storing the data,
    (iii) the right to have recourse at any time to the European Data Protection Supervisor,
    (iv) the origin of the data, except where the controller cannot disclose this information for reasons of professional secrecy,

insofar as such further information is necessary, having regard to the specific circumstances in which the data are processed, to guarantee fair processing in respect of the data subject.

2. Paragraph 1 shall not apply where, in particular for processing for statistical purposes or for the purposes of historical or scientific research, the provision of such information proves impossible or would involve a disproportionate effort or if recording or disclosure is expressly laid down by Community law. In these cases the Community institution or body shall provide for appropriate safeguards after consulting the European Data Protection Supervisor.

SECTION 5

RIGHTS OF THE DATA SUBJECT

Article 13

Right of access

The data subject shall have the right to obtain, without constraint, at any time within three months from the receipt of the request and free of charge from the controller:

(a) confirmation as to whether or not data related to him or her are being processed;
(b) information at least as to the purposes of the processing operation, the categories of data concerned, and the recipients or categories of recipients to whom the data are disclosed;
(c) communication in an intelligible form of the data undergoing processing and of any available information as to their source;
(d) knowledge of the logic involved in any automated decision process concerning him or her.

Article 14

Rectification
The data subject shall have the right to obtain from the controller the rectification without delay of inaccurate or incomplete personal data.

Article 15

Blocking

1. The data subject shall have the right to obtain from the controller the blocking of data where:

(a) their accuracy is contested by the data subject, for a period enabling the controller to verify the accuracy, including the completeness, of the data, or;
(b) the controller no longer needs them for the accomplishment of its tasks but they have to be maintained for purposes of proof, or;
(c) the processing is unlawful and the data subject opposes their erasure and demands their blocking instead.

2. In automated filing systems blocking shall in principle be ensured by technical means. The fact that the personal data are blocked shall be indicated in the system in such a way that it becomes clear that the personal data may not be used.

3. Personal data blocked pursuant to this Article shall, with the exception of their storage, only be processed for purposes of proof, or with the data subject's consent, or for the protection of the rights of a third party.

4. The data subject who requested and obtained the blocking of his or her data shall be informed by the controller before the data are unblocked.

Article 16

Erasure

The data subject shall have the right to obtain from the controller the erasure of data if their processing is unlawful, particularly where the provisions of Sections 1, 2 and 3 of Chapter II have been infringed.

Article 17

Notification to third parties

The data subject shall have the right to obtain from the controller the notification to third parties to whom the data have been disclosed of any rectification, erasure or blocking pursuant to Articles 13 to 16 unless this proves impossible or involves a disproportionate effort.

Article 18

The data subject's right to object

The data subject shall have the right:

(a) to object at any time, on compelling legitimate grounds relating to his or her particular situation, to the processing of data relating to him or her, except in the cases covered by Article 5(b), (c) and (d). Where there is a justified objection, the processing in question may no longer involve those data;

(b) to be informed before personal data are disclosed for the first time to third parties or before they are used on their behalf for the purposes of direct marketing, and to be expressly offered the right to object free of charge to such disclosure or use.

Article 19

Automated individual decisions

The data subject shall have the right not to be subject to a decision which produces legal effects concerning him or her or significantly affects him or her and which is based solely on automated processing of data intended to evaluate certain personal aspects relating to him or her, such as his or her performance at work, reliability or conduct, unless the decision is expressly authorised pursuant to national or Community legislation or, if necessary, by the European Data Protection Supervisor. In either case, measures to safeguard the data subject's legitimate interests, such as arrangements allowing him or her to put his or her point of view, must be taken.

SECTION 6

EXEMPTIONS AND RESTRICTIONS

Article 20

Exemptions and restrictions

1. The Community institutions and bodies may restrict the application of Article 4(1), Article 11, Article 12(1), Articles 13 to 17 and Article 37(1) where such restriction constitutes a necessary measure to safeguard:

(a) the prevention, investigation, detection and prosecution of criminal offences;
(b) an important economic or financial interest of a Member State or of the European Communities, including monetary, budgetary and taxation matters;
(c) the protection of the data subject or of the rights and freedoms of others;
(d) the national security, public security or defence of the Member States;
(e) a monitoring, inspection or regulatory task connected, even occasionally, with the exercise of official authority in the cases referred to in (a) and (b).

2. Articles 13 to 16 shall not apply when data are processed solely for purposes of scientific research or are kept in personal form for a period which does not exceed the period necessary for the sole purpose of compiling statistics, provided that there is clearly no risk of breaching the privacy of the data subject and that the controller provides adequate legal safeguards, in particular to ensure that the data are not used for taking measures or decisions regarding particular individuals.

3. If a restriction provided for by paragraph 1 is imposed, the data subject shall be informed, in accordance with Community law, of the principal reasons on which the application of the restriction is based and of his or her right to have recourse to the European Data Protection Supervisor.

4. If a restriction provided for by paragraph 1 is relied upon to deny access to the data subject, the European Data Protection Supervisor shall, when investigating the

complaint, only inform him or her of whether the data have been processed correctly and, if not, whether any necessary corrections have been made.

5. Provision of the information referred to under paragraphs 3 and 4 may be deferred for as long as such information would deprive the restriction imposed by paragraph 1 of its effect.

SECTION 7

CONFIDENTIALITY AND SECURITY OF PROCESSING

Article 21

Confidentiality of processing

A person employed with a Community institution or body and any Community institution or body itself acting as processor, with access to personal data, shall not process them except on instructions from the controller, unless required to do so by national or Community law.

Article 22

Security of processing

1. Having regard to the state of the art and the cost of their implementation, the controller shall implement appropriate technical and organisational measures to ensure a level of security appropriate to the risks represented by the processing and the nature of the personal data to be protected.

Such measures shall be taken in particular to prevent any unauthorised disclosure or access, accidental or unlawful destruction or accidental loss, or alteration, and to prevent all other unlawful forms of processing.

2. Where personal data are processed by automated means, measures shall be taken as appropriate in view of the risks in particular with the aim of:

(a) preventing any unauthorised person from gaining access to computer systems processing personal data;
(b) preventing any unauthorised reading, copying, alteration or removal of storage media;
(c) preventing any unauthorised memory inputs as well as any unauthorised disclosure, alteration or erasure of stored personal data;
(d) preventing unauthorised persons from using data-processing systems by means of data transmission facilities;
(e) ensuring that authorised users of a data-processing system can access no personal data other than those to which their access right refers;
(f) recording which personal data have been communicated, at what times and to whom;
(g) ensuring that it will subsequently be possible to check which personal data have been processed, at what times and by whom;
(h) ensuring that personal data being processed on behalf of third parties can be processed only in the manner prescribed by the contracting institution or body;
(i) ensuring that, during communication of personal data and during transport of storage media, the data cannot be read, copied or erased without authorisation;

(j) designing the organisational structure within an institution or body in such a way that it will meet the special requirements of data protection.

Article 23

Processing of personal data on behalf of controllers

1. Where a processing operation is carried out on its behalf, the controller shall choose a processor providing sufficient guarantees in respect of the technical and organisational security measures required by Article 22 and ensure compliance with those measures.

2. The carrying out of a processing operation by way of a processor shall be governed by a contract or legal act binding the processor to the controller and stipulating in particular that:

(a) the processor shall act only on instructions from the controller;
(b) the obligations set out in Articles 21 and 22 shall also be incumbent on the processor unless, by virtue of Article 16 or Article 17(3), second indent, of Directive 95/46/EC, the processor is already subject to obligations with regard to confidentiality and security laid down in the national law of one of the Member States.

3. For the purposes of keeping proof, the parts of the contract or the legal act relating to data protection and the requirements relating to the measures referred to in Article 22 shall be in writing or in another equivalent form.

SECTION 8

DATA PROTECTION OFFICER

Article 24

Appointment and tasks of the Data Protection Officer

1. Each Community institution and Community body shall appoint at least one person as data protection officer. That person shall have the task of:

(a) ensuring that controllers and data subjects are informed of their rights and obligations pursuant to this Regulation;
(b) responding to requests from the European Data Protection Supervisor and, within the sphere of his or her competence, cooperating with the European Data Protection Supervisor at the latter's request or on his or her own initiative;
(c) ensuring in an independent manner the internal application of the provisions of this Regulation;
(d) keeping a register of the processing operations carried out by the controller, containing the items of information referred to in Article 25(2);
(e) notifying the European Data Protection Supervisor of the processing operations likely to present specific risks within the meaning of Article 27.

That person shall thus ensure that the rights and freedoms of the data subjects are unlikely to be adversely affected by the processing operations.

2. The Data Protection Officer shall be selected on the basis of his or her personal and professional qualities and, in particular, his or her expert knowledge of data protection.

3. The selection of the Data Protection Officer shall not be liable to result in a conflict of interests between his or her duty as Data Protection Officer and any other official duties, in particular in relation to the application of the provisions of this Regulation.

4. The Data Protection Officer shall be appointed for a term of between two and five years. He or she shall be eligible for reappointment up to a maximum total term of ten years. He or she may be dismissed from the post of Data Protection Officer by the Community institution or body which appointed him or her only with the consent of the European Data Protection Supervisor, if he or she no longer fulfils the conditions required for the performance of his or her duties.

5. After his or her appointment the Data Protection Officer shall be registered with the European Data Protection Supervisor by the institution or body which appointed him or her.

6. The Community institution or body which appointed the Data Protection Officer shall provide him or her with the staff and resources necessary to carry out his or her duties.

7. With respect to the performance of his or her duties, the Data Protection Officer may not receive any instructions.

8. Further implementing rules concerning the Data Protection Officer shall be adopted by each Community institution or body in accordance with the provisions in the Annex. The implementing rules shall in particular concern the tasks, duties and powers of the Data Protection Officer.

Article 25

Notification to the Data Protection Officer

1. The controller shall give prior notice to the Data Protection Officer of any processing operation or set of such operations intended to serve a single purpose or several related purposes.

2. The information to be given shall include:

(a) the name and address of the controller and an indication of the organisational parts of an institution or body entrusted with the processing of personal data for a particular purpose;
(b) the purpose or purposes of the processing;
(c) a description of the category or categories of data subjects and of the data or categories of data relating to them;
(d) the legal basis of the processing operation for which the data are intended;
(e) the recipients or categories of recipient to whom the data might be disclosed;
(f) a general indication of the time limits for blocking and erasure of the different categories of data;
(g) proposed transfers of data to third countries or international organisations;

(h) a general description allowing a preliminary assessment to be made of the appropriateness of the measures taken pursuant to Article 22 to ensure security of processing.

3. Any change affecting information referred to in paragraph 2 shall be notified promptly to the Data Protection Officer.

Article 26

Register

A register of processing operations notified in accordance with Article 25 shall be kept by each Data Protection Officer.

The registers shall contain at least the information referred to in Article 25(2)(a) to (g). The registers may be inspected by any person directly or indirectly through the European Data Processing Supervisor.

SECTION 9

PRIOR CHECKING BY THE EUROPEAN DATA PROTECTION SUPERVISOR AND OBLIGATION TO COOPERATE

Article 27

Prior checking

1. Processing operations likely to present specific risks to the rights and freedoms of data subjects by virtue of their nature, their scope or their purposes shall be subject to prior checking by the European Data Protection Supervisor.

2. The following processing operations are likely to present such risks:

(a) processing of data relating to health and to suspected offences, offences, criminal convictions or security measures;
(b) processing operations intended to evaluate personal aspects relating to the data subject, including his or her ability, efficiency and conduct;
(c) processing operations allowing linkages not provided for pursuant to national or Community legislation between data processed for different purposes;
(d) processing operations for the purpose of excluding individuals from a right, benefit or contract.

3. The prior checks shall be carried out by the European Data Protection Supervisor following receipt of a notification from the Data Protection Officer who, in case of doubt as to the need for prior checking, shall consult the European Data Protection Supervisor.

4. The European Data Protection Supervisor shall deliver his or her opinion within two months following receipt of the notification. This period may be suspended until the European Data Protection Supervisor has obtained any further information that he or she may have requested. When the complexity of the matter so requires, this period may also be extended for a further two months, by decision of the European Data Protection Supervisor. This decision shall be notified to the controller prior to expiry of the initial two-month period.

If the opinion has not been delivered by the end of the two-month period, or any extension thereof, it shall be deemed to be favourable.

If the opinion of the European Data Protection Supervisor is that the notified processing may involve a breach of any provision of this Regulation, he or she shall where appropriate make proposals to avoid such breach. Where the controller does not modify the processing operation accordingly, the European Data Protection Supervisor may exercise the powers granted to him or her under Article 47(1).

5. The European Data Protection Supervisor shall keep a register of all processing operations that have been notified to him or her pursuant to paragraph 2. The register shall contain the information referred to in Article 25 and shall be open to public inspection.

Article 28

Consultation

1. The Community institutions and bodies shall inform the European Data Protection Supervisor when drawing up administrative measures relating to the processing of personal data involving a Community institution or body alone or jointly with others.

2. When it adopts a legislative proposal relating to the protection of individuals' rights and freedoms with regard to the processing of personal data, the Commission shall consult the European Data Protection Supervisor.

Article 29

Obligation to provide information

The Community institutions and bodies shall inform the European Data Protection Supervisor of the measures taken further to his or her decisions or authorisations as referred to in Article 46(h).

Article 30

Obligation to cooperate

At his or her request, controllers shall assist the European Data Protection Supervisor in the performance of his or her duties, in particular by providing the information referred to in Article 47(2)(a) and by granting access as provided in Article 47(2)(b).

Article 31

Obligation to react to allegations

In response to the European Data Protection Supervisor's exercise of his or her powers under Article 47(1)(b), the controller concerned shall inform the Supervisor of its views within a reasonable period to be specified by the Supervisor. The reply shall also include a description of the measures taken, if any, in response to the remarks of the European Data Protection Supervisor.

CHAPTER III

REMEDIES

Article 32

Remedies

1. The Court of Justice of the European Communities shall have jurisdiction to hear all disputes which relate to the provisions of this Regulation, including claims for damages.

2. Without prejudice to any judicial remedy, every data subject may lodge a complaint with the European Data Protection Supervisor if he or she considers that his or her rights under Article 286 of the Treaty have been infringed as a result of the processing of his or her personal data by a Community institution or body.

In the absence of a response by the European Data Protection Supervisor within six months, the complaint shall be deemed to have been rejected.

3. Actions against decisions of the European Data Protection Supervisor shall be brought before the Court of Justice of the European Communities.

4. Any person who has suffered damage because of an unlawful processing operation or any action incompatible with this Regulation shall have the right to have the damage made good in accordance with Article 288 of the Treaty.

Article 33

Complaints by Community staff

Any person employed with a Community institution or body may lodge a complaint with the European Data Protection Supervisor regarding an alleged breach of the provisions of this Regulation governing the processing of personal data, without acting through official channels. No-one shall suffer prejudice on account of a complaint lodged with the European Data Protection Supervisor alleging a breach of the provisions governing the processing of personal data.

CHAPTER IV

PROTECTION OF PERSONAL DATA AND PRIVACY IN THE CONTEXT OF INTERNAL TELECOMMUNICATIONS NETWORKS

Article 34

Scope

Without prejudice to the other provisions of this Regulation, this Chapter shall apply to the processing of personal data in connection with the use of telecommunications networks or terminal equipment operated under the control of a Community institution or body.

For the purposes of this Chapter, "user" shall mean any natural person using a telecommunications network or terminal equipment operated under the control of a Community institution or body.

Article 35

Security

1. The Community institutions and bodies shall take appropriate technical and organisational measures to safeguard the secure use of the telecommunications networks and terminal equipment, if necessary in conjunction with the providers of publicly available telecommunications services or the providers of public telecommunications networks. Having regard to the state of the art and the cost of their implementation, these measures shall ensure a level of security appropriate to the risk presented.

2. In the event of any particular risk of a breach of the security of the network and terminal equipment, the Community institution or body concerned shall inform users of the existence of that risk and of any possible remedies and alternative means of communication.

Article 36

Confidentiality of communications

Community institutions and bodies shall ensure the confidentiality of communications by means of telecommunications networks and terminal equipment, in accordance with the general principles of Community law.

Article 37

Traffic and billing data

1. Without prejudice to the provisions of paragraphs 2, 3 and 4, traffic data relating to users which are processed and stored to establish calls and other connections over the telecommunications network shall be erased or made anonymous upon termination of the call or other connection.

2. If necessary, traffic data as indicated in a list agreed by the European Data Protection Supervisor may be processed for the purpose of telecommunications budget and traffic management, including the verification of authorised use of the telecommunications systems. These data shall be erased or made anonymous as soon as possible and no later than six months after collection, unless they need to be kept for a longer period to establish, exercise or defend a right in a legal claim pending before a court.

3. Processing of traffic and billing data shall only be carried out by persons handling billing, traffic or budget management.

4. Users of the telecommunication networks shall have the right to receive non-itemised bills or other records of calls made.

Article 38

Directories of users

1. Personal data contained in printed or electronic directories of users and access to such directories shall be limited to what is strictly necessary for the specific purposes of the directory.

2. The Community institutions and bodies shall take all the necessary measures to prevent personal data contained in those directories, regardless of whether they are accessible to the public or not, from being used for direct marketing purposes.

Article 39

Presentation and restriction of calling and connected line identification

1. Where presentation of calling-line identification is offered, the calling user shall have the possibility via a simple means, free of charge, to eliminate the presentation of the calling-line identification.

2. Where presentation of calling-line identification is offered, the called user shall have the possibility via a simple means, free of charge, to prevent the presentation of the calling-line identification of incoming calls.

3. Where presentation of connected-line identification is offered, the called user shall have the possibility via a simple means, free of charge, to eliminate the presentation of the connected-line identification to the calling user.

4. Where presentation of calling or connected-line identification is offered, the Community institutions and bodies shall inform the users thereof and of the possibilities set out in paragraphs 1, 2 and 3.

Article 40

Derogations

Community institutions and bodies shall ensure that there are transparent procedures governing the way in which they may override the elimination of the presentation of calling-line identification:

(a) on a temporary basis, upon application of a user requesting the tracing of malicious or nuisance calls;
(b) on a per-line basis for organisational entities dealing with emergency calls, for the purpose of answering such calls.

CHAPTER V

INDEPENDENT SUPERVISORY AUTHORITY: THE EUROPEAN DATA PROTECTION SUPERVISOR

Article 41

European Data Protection Supervisor

1. An independent supervisory authority is hereby established referred to as the European Data Protection Supervisor.

2. With respect to the processing of personal data, the European Data Protection Supervisor shall be responsible for ensuring that the fundamental rights and freedoms of natural persons, and in particular their right to privacy, are respected by the Community institutions and bodies.

The European Data Protection Supervisor shall be responsible for monitoring and ensuring the application of the provisions of this Regulation and any other

Community act relating to the protection of the fundamental rights and freedoms of natural persons with regard to the processing of personal data by a Community institution or body, and for advising Community institutions and bodies and data subjects on all matters concerning the processing of personal data. To these ends he or she shall fulfil the duties provided for in Article 46 and exercise the powers granted in Article 47.

Article 42

Appointment

1. The European Parliament and the Council shall appoint by common accord the European Data Protection Supervisor for a term of five years, on the basis of a list drawn up by the Commission following a public call for candidates.

An Assistant Supervisor shall be appointed in accordance with the same procedure and for the same term, who shall assist the Supervisor in all the latter's duties and act as a replacement when the Supervisor is absent or prevented from attending to them.

2. The European Data Protection Supervisor shall be chosen from persons whose independence is beyond doubt and who are acknowledged as having the experience and skills required to perform the duties of European Data Protection Supervisor, for example because they belong or have belonged to the supervisory authorities referred to in Article 28 of Directive 95/46/EC.

3. The European Data Protection Supervisor shall be eligible for reappointment.

4. Apart from normal replacement or death, the duties of the European Data Protection Supervisor shall end in the event of resignation or compulsory retirement in accordance with paragraph 5.

5. The European Data Protection Supervisor may be dismissed or deprived of his or her right to a pension or other benefits in its stead by the Court of Justice at the request of the European Parliament, the Council or the Commission, if he or she no longer fulfils the conditions required for the performance of his or her duties or if he or she is guilty of serious misconduct.

6. In the event of normal replacement or voluntary resignation, the European Data Protection Supervisor shall nevertheless remain in office until he or she has been replaced.

7. Articles 12 to 15 and 18 of the Protocol on the Privileges and Immunities of the European Communities shall also apply to the European Data Protection Supervisor.

8. Paragraphs 2 to 7 shall apply to the Assistant Supervisor.

Article 43

Regulations and general conditions governing the performance of the European Data Protection Supervisor's duties, staff and financial resources

1. The European Parliament, the Council and the Commission shall by common accord determine the regulations and general conditions governing the performance of the European Data Protection Supervisor's duties and in particular his or her salary, allowances and any other benefits in lieu of remuneration.

2. The budget authority shall ensure that the European Data Protection Supervisor is provided with the human and financial resources necessary for the performance of his or her tasks.

3. The European Data Protection Supervisor's budget shall be shown in a separate budget heading in Section VIII of the general budget of the European Union.

4. The European Data Protection Supervisor shall be assisted by a Secretariat. The officials and the other staff members of the Secretariat shall be appointed by the European Data Protection Supervisor; their superior shall be the European Data Protection Supervisor and they shall be subject exclusively to his or her direction. Their numbers shall be decided each year as part of the budgetary procedure.

5. The officials and the other staff members of the European Data Protection Supervisor's Secretariat shall be subject to the rules and regulations applicable to officials and other servants of the European Communities.

6. In matters concerning the Secretariat staff, the European Data Protection Supervisor shall have the same status as the institutions within the meaning of Article 1 of the Staff Regulations of Officials of the European Communities.

Article 44

Independence

1. The European Data Protection Supervisor shall act in complete independence in the performance of his or her duties.

2. The European Data Protection Supervisor shall, in the performance of his or her duties, neither seek nor take instructions from anybody.

3. The European Data Protection Supervisor shall refrain from any action incompatible with his or her duties and shall not, during his or her term of office, engage in any other occupation, whether gainful or not.

4. The European Data Protection Supervisor shall, after his or her term of office, behave with integrity and discretion as regards the acceptance of appointments and benefits.

Article 45

Professional secrecy

The European Data Protection Supervisor and his or her staff shall, both during and after their term of office, be subject to a duty of professional secrecy with regard to any confidential information which has come to their knowledge in the course of the performance of their official duties.

Article 46

Duties

The European Data Protection Supervisor shall:

(a) hear and investigate complaints, and inform the data subject of the outcome within a reasonable period;
(b) conduct inquiries either on his or her own initiative or on the basis of a complaint, and inform the data subjects of the outcome within a reasonable period;
(c) monitor and ensure the application of the provisions of this Regulation and any other Community act relating to the protection of natural persons with regard

to the processing of personal data by a Community institution or body with the exception of the Court of Justice of the European Communities acting in its judicial capacity;

(d) advise all Community institutions and bodies, either on his or her own initiative or in response to a consultation, on all matters concerning the processing of personal data, in particular before they draw up internal rules relating to the protection of fundamental rights and freedoms with regard to the processing of personal data;

(e) monitor relevant developments, insofar as they have an impact on the protection of personal data, in particular the development of information and communication technologies;

(f) (i) cooperate with the national supervisory authorities referred to in Article 28 of Directive 95/46/EC in the countries to which that Directive applies to the extent necessary for the performance of their respective duties, in particular by exchanging all useful information, requesting such authority or body to exercise its powers or responding to a request from such authority or body;

(ii) also cooperate with the supervisory data protection bodies established under Title VI of the Treaty on European Union particularly with a view to improving consistency in applying the rules and procedures with which they are respectively responsible for ensuring compliance;

(g) participate in the activities of the Working Party on the Protection of Individuals with regard to the Processing of Personal Data set up by Article 29 of Directive 95/46/EC;

(h) determine, give reasons for and make public the exemptions, safeguards, authorisations and conditions mentioned in Article 10(2)(b),(4), (5) and (6), in Article 12(2), in Article 19 and in Article 37(2);

(i) keep a register of processing operations notified to him or her by virtue of Article 27(2) and registered in accordance with Article 27(5), and provide means of access to the registers kept by the Data Protection Officers under Article 26;

(j) carry out a prior check of processing notified to him or her;

(k) establish his or her Rules of Procedure.

Article 47

Powers

1. The European Data Protection Supervisor may:

(a) give advice to data subjects in the exercise of their rights;

(b) refer the matter to the controller in the event of an alleged breach of the provisions governing the processing of personal data, and, where appropriate, make proposals for remedying that breach and for improving the protection of the data subjects;

(c) order that requests to exercise certain rights in relation to data be complied with where such requests have been refused in breach of Articles 13 to 19;

(d) warn or admonish the controller;
(e) order the rectification, blocking, erasure or destruction of all data when they have been processed in breach of the provisions governing the processing of personal data and the notification of such actions to third parties to whom the data have been disclosed;
(f) impose a temporary or definitive ban on processing;
(g) refer the matter to the Community institution or body concerned and, if necessary, to the European Parliament, the Council and the Commission;
(h) refer the matter to the Court of Justice of the European Communities under the conditions provided for in the Treaty;
(i) intervene in actions brought before the Court of Justice of the European Communities.

2. The European Data Protection Supervisor shall have the power:

(a) to obtain from a controller or Community institution or body access to all personal data and to all information necessary for his or her enquiries;
(b) to obtain access to any premises in which a controller or Community institution or body carries on its activities when there are reasonable grounds for presuming that an activity covered by this Regulation is being carried out there.

Article 48

Activities report

1. The European Data Protection Supervisor shall submit an annual report on his or her activities to the European Parliament, the Council and the Commission and at the same time make it public.

2. The European Data Protection Supervisor shall forward the activities report to the other Community institutions and bodies, which may submit comments with a view to possible examination of the report in the European Parliament, in particular in relation to the description of the measures taken in response to the remarks made by the European Data Protection Supervisor under Article 31.

CHAPTER VI

FINAL PROVISIONS

Article 49

Sanctions

Any failure to comply with the obligations pursuant to this Regulation, whether intentionally or through negligence on his or her part, shall make an official or other servant of the European Communities liable to disciplinary action, in accordance with the rules and procedures laid down in the Staff Regulations of Officials of the European Communities or in the conditions of employment applicable to other servants.

Article 50

Transitional period

Community institutions and bodies shall ensure that processing operations already under way on the date this Regulation enters into force are brought into conformity with this Regulation within one year of that date.

Article 51

Entry into force

This Regulation shall enter into force on the twentieth day following that of its publication in the Official Journal of the European Communities.

This Regulation shall be binding in its entirety and directly applicable in all Member States.

Done at Brussels, 18 December 2000.

For the European Parliament

The President

N. Fontaine

For the Council

The President

D. Voynet

(1) OJ C 376E, 28.12.1999, p. 24.

(2) OJ C 51, 23.2.2000, p. 48.

(3) Opinion of the European Parliament of 14 November 2000 and Council Decision of 30 November 2000.

(4) OJ L 281, 23.11.1995, p. 31.

(5) OJ L 24, 30.1.1998, p. 1.

(6) OJ L 52, 22.2.1997, p. 1.

(7) OJ L 318, 27.11.1998, p. 8.

(8) OJ L 151, 15. 6.1990, p. 1. Regulation as amended by Regulation (EC) No 322/97 (OJ L 52, 22.2.1997, p. 1).

ANNEX

1. The Data Protection Officer may make recommendations for the practical improvement of data protection to the Community institution or body which appointed him or her and advise it and the controller concerned on matters concerning the application of data protection provisions. Furthermore he or she may, on his or her own initiative or at the request of the Community institution or body which appointed him or her, the controller, the Staff Committee concerned or any individual, investigate matters and occurrences directly relating to his or her tasks and which come to his or her notice, and report back to the person who commissioned the investigation or to the controller.

2. The Data Protection Officer may be consulted by the Community institution or body which appointed him or her, by the controller concerned, by the Staff Committee concerned and by any individual, without going through the official channels, on any matter concerning the interpretation or application of this Regulation.

3. No one shall suffer prejudice on account of a matter brought to the attention of the competent Data Protection Officer alleging that a breach of the provisions of this Regulation has taken place.

4. Every controller concerned shall be required to assist the Data Protection Officer in performing his or her duties and to give information in reply to questions. In performing his or her duties, the Data Protection Officer shall have access at all times to the data forming the subject-matter of processing operations and to all offices, data-processing installations and data carriers.

5. To the extent required, the Data Protection Officer shall be relieved of other activities. The Data Protection Officer and his or her staff, to whom Article 287 of the Treaty shall apply, shall be required not to divulge information or documents which they obtain in the course of their duties.

Annex 4

REGULATION (EC) No 1367/2006 OF THE EUROPEAN PARLIAMENT AND OF THE COUNCIL

of 6 September 2006

on the application of the provisions of the Aarhus Convention on Access to Information, Public Participation in Decision-making and Access to Justice in Environmental Matters to Community institutions and bodies

THE EUROPEAN PARLIAMENT AND THE COUNCIL OF THE EUROPEAN UNION,

Having regard to the Treaty establishing the European Community, and in particular Article 175(1) thereof,

Having regard to the proposal from the Commission,

Having regard to the opinion of the European Economic and Social Committee([1]),

After consulting the Committee of the Regions,

Acting in accordance with the procedure laid down in Article 251 of the Treaty, in the light of the joint text approved by the Conciliation Committee on 22 June 2006([2]),

Whereas:

(1) Community legislation in the field of the environment aims to contribute *inter alia* to preserving, protecting and improving the quality of the environment and protecting human health, thereby promoting sustainable development.

(2) The Sixth Community Environment Action Programme([3]) stresses the importance of providing adequate environmental information and effective opportunities for public participation in environmental decision-making, thereby increasing accountability and transparency of decision-making and contributing to public awareness and support for the decisions taken. It furthermore encourages, as did its predecessors([4]), more effective implementation and application of Community legislation on environmental protection, including the enforcement of Community rules and the taking of action against breaches of Community environmental legislation.

(3) On 25 June 1998 the Community signed the United Nations Economic Commission for Europe (UNECE) Convention on Access to Information, Public Participation in Decision-making and Access to Justice in Environmental Matters (hereinafter the Aarhus Convention). The Community approved the Aarhus Convention on 17 February 2005([5]). Provisions of Community law should be consistent with that Convention.

(4) The Community has already adopted a body of legislation, which is evolving and contributes to the achievement of the objectives of the Aarhus Convention. Provision should be made to apply the requirements of the Convention to Community institutions and bodies.

(5) It is appropriate to deal with the three pillars of the Aarhus Convention, namely access to information, public participation in decision-making and access to justice in environmental matters, in one piece of legislation and to lay down common provisions regarding objectives and definitions. This contributes to rationalising legislation and increasing the transparency of the implementation measures taken with regard to Community institutions and bodies.

(6) As a general principle, the rights guaranteed by the three pillars of the Aarhus Convention are without discrimination as to citizenship, nationality or domicile.

(7) The Aarhus Convention defines public authorities in a broad way, the basic concept being that wherever public authority is exercised, there should be rights for individuals and their organisations. It is therefore necessary that the Community institutions and bodies covered by this Regulation be defined in the same broad and functional way. Under the Aarhus Convention, Community institutions and bodies can be excluded from the scope of application of the Convention when acting in a judicial or legislative capacity. However, for reasons of consistency with Regulation (EC) No 1049/2001 of the European Parliament and of the Council of 30 May 2001 regarding public access to European Parliament, Council and Commission documents([6]), the provisions on access to environmental information should apply to Community institutions and bodies acting in a legislative capacity.

(8) The definition of environmental information in this Regulation encompasses information in any form on the state of the environment. This definition, which has been aligned to the definition adopted for Directive 2003/4/EC of the European Parliament and of the Council of 28 January 2003 on public access to environmental information and repealing Council Directive 90/313/EEC([7]), has the same content as the one laid down in the Aarhus Convention. The definition of 'document' in Regulation (EC) No 1049/2001 encompasses environmental information as defined in this Regulation.

(9) It is appropriate for this Regulation to provide for a definition of plans and programmes taking into account the provisions of the Aarhus Convention, in parallel with the approach followed in relation to the Member States' obligations under existing EC law. 'Plans and programmes relating to the environment' should be defined in relation to their contribution to the achievement, or to their likely significant effect on the achievement, of the objectives and priorities of Community environmental policy. For the ten-year period starting from 22 July 2002, the Sixth Community Environment Action Programme establishes the objectives of Community environmental policy and the actions planned to attain these objectives. At the end of this period, a subsequent environmental action programme should be adopted.

(10) In view of the fact that environmental law is constantly evolving, the definition of environmental law should refer to the objectives of Community policy on the environment as set out in the Treaty.

(11) Administrative acts of individual scope should be open to possible internal review where they have legally binding and external effects. Similarly, omissions should be covered where there is an obligation to adopt an administrative act under environmental law. Given that acts adopted by a Community institution or body acting in a judicial or legislative capacity can be excluded, the same should apply to other inquiry procedures where the Community institution or body acts as an administrative review body under provisions of the Treaty.

(12) The Aarhus Convention calls for public access to environmental information either following a request or by active dissemination by the authorities covered by the Convention. Regulation (EC) No 1049/2001 applies to the European Parliament, the Council and the Commission, as well as to agencies and similar bodies set up by a Community legal act. It lays down rules for these institutions that comply to a great extent with the rules laid down in the Aarhus Convention. It is necessary to extend the application of Regulation (EC) No 1049/2001 to all other Community institutions and bodies.

(13) Where the Aarhus Convention contains provisions that are not, in whole or in part, to be found also in Regulation (EC) No 1049/2001, it is necessary to address those, in particular with regard to the collection and dissemination of environmental information.

(14) For the right of public access to environmental information to be effective, environmental information of good quality is essential. It is therefore appropriate to introduce rules that oblige Community institutions and bodies to ensure such quality.

(15) Where Regulation (EC) No 1049/2001 provides for exceptions, these should apply subject to any more specific provisions in this Regulation concerning requests for environmental information. The grounds for refusal as regards access to environmental information should be interpreted in a restrictive way, taking into account the public interest served by disclosure and whether the information requested relates to emissions in the environment. The term 'commercial interests' covers confidentiality agreements concluded by institutions or bodies acting in a banking capacity.

(16) Pursuant to Decision No 2119/98/EC of the European Parliament and the Council of 24 September 1998 setting up a network for the epidemiological surveillance and control of communicable diseases in the Community([8]), a network at Community level has already been set up to promote cooperation and coordination between the Member States, with the assistance of the Commission, with a view to improving the prevention and control in the Community of a number of communicable diseases. Decision No 1786/2002/EC of the European Parliament and of the Council([9]) adopts a programme of Community action in the field of public health that complements national policies. Improving information and knowledge for the development of public health and enhancing the capability to respond rapidly and in a coordinated fashion to threats to health, both of which are elements of this programme, are objectives that are equally fully in line with the requirements of the Aarhus Convention. This Regulation should therefore apply without prejudice to Decision No 2119/98/EC and Decision No 1786/2002/EC.

(17) The Aarhus Convention requires Parties to make provisions for the public to participate during the preparation of plans and programmes relating to the environ-

ment. Such provisions are to include reasonable timeframes for informing the public of the environmental decision-making in question. To be effective, public participation is to take place at an early stage, when all options are open. When laying down provisions on public participation, Community institutions and bodies, should identify the public which may participate. The Aarhus Convention also requires that, to the extent appropriate, Parties shall endeavour to provide opportunities for public participation in the preparation of policies relating to the environment.

(18) Article 9(3) of the Aarhus Convention provides for access to judicial or other review procedures for challenging acts and omissions by private persons and public authorities which contravene provisions of law relating to the environment. Provisions on access to justice should be consistent with the Treaty. It is appropriate in this context that this Regulation address only acts and omissions by public authorities.

(19) To ensure adequate and effective remedies, including those available before the Court of Justice of the European Communities under the relevant provisions of the Treaty, it is appropriate that the Community institution or body which issued the act to be challenged or which, in the case of an alleged administrative omission, omitted to act, be given the opportunity to reconsider its former decision, or, in the case of an omission, to act.

(20) Non-governmental organisations active in the field of environmental protection which meet certain criteria, in particular in order to ensure that they are independent and accountable organisations that have demonstrated that their primary objective is to promote environmental protection, should be entitled to request internal review at Community level of acts adopted or of omissions under environmental law by a Community institution or body, with a view to their reconsideration by the institution or body in question.

(21) Where previous requests for internal review have been unsuccessful, the non-governmental organisation concerned should be able to institute proceedings before the Court of Justice in accordance with the relevant provisions of the Treaty.

(22) This Regulation respects the fundamental rights and observes the principles recognised by Article 6 of the Treaty on the European Union and reflected in the Charter of Fundamental Rights of the European Union, in particular Article 37 thereof,

HAVE ADOPTED THIS REGULATION:

TITLE I GENERAL PROVISIONS

Article 1

Objective

1. The objective of this Regulation is to contribute to the implementation of the obligations arising under the UNECE Convention on Access to Information, Public Participation in Decision-making and Access to Justice in Environmental Matters, hereinafter referred to as 'the Aarhus Convention', by laying down rules to apply the provisions of the Convention to Community institutions and bodies, in particular by:

(a) guaranteeing the right of public access to environmental information received or produced by Community institutions or bodies and held by them, and by setting out the basic terms and conditions of, and practical arrangements for, the exercise of that right;

(b) ensuring that environmental information is progressively made available and disseminated to the public in order to achieve its widest possible systematic availability and dissemination. To that end, the use, in particular, of computer telecommunication and/or electronic technology, where available, shall be promoted;

(c) providing for public participation concerning plans and programmes relating to the environment;

(d) granting access to justice in environmental matters at Community level under the conditions laid down by this Regulation.

2. In applying the provisions of this Regulation, the Community institutions and bodies shall endeavour to assist and provide guidance to the public with regard to access to information, participation in decision-making and access to justice in environmental matters.

Article 2

Definitions

1. For the purpose of this Regulation:

(a) 'applicant' means any natural or legal person requesting environmental information;

(b) 'the public' means one or more natural or legal persons, and associations, organisations or groups of such persons;

(c) 'Community institution or body' means any public institution, body, office or agency established by, or on the basis of, the Treaty except when acting in a judicial or legislative capacity. However, the provisions under Title II shall apply to Community institutions or bodies acting in a legislative capacity;

(d) 'environmental information' means any information in written, visual, aural, electronic or any other material form on:

    (i) the state of the elements of the environment, such as air and atmosphere, water, soil, land, landscape and natural sites including wetlands, coastal and marine areas, biological diversity and its components, including genetically modified organisms, and the interaction among these elements;

    (ii) factors, such as substances, energy, noise, radiation or waste, including radioactive waste, emissions, discharges and other releases into the environment, affecting or likely to affect the elements of the environment referred to in point (i);

    (iii) measures (including administrative measures), such as policies, legislation, plans, programmes, environmental agreements, and activities affecting or likely to affect the elements and factors referred to in points (i) and (ii) as well as measures or activities designed to protect those elements;

    (iv) reports on the implementation of environmental legislation;

(v) cost-benefit and other economic analyses and assumptions used within the framework of the measures and activities referred to in point (iii);
(vi) the state of human health and safety, including the contamination of the food chain, where relevant, conditions of human life, cultural sites and built structures in as much as they are or may be affected by the state of the elements of the environment referred to in point (i) or, through those elements, by any of the matters referred to in points (ii) and (iii);

(e) 'plans and programmes relating to the environment' means plans and programmes,
(i) which are subject to preparation and, as appropriate, adoption by a Community institution or body;
(ii) which are required under legislative, regulatory or administrative provisions; and
(iii) which contribute to, or are likely to have significant effects on, the achievement of the objectives of Community environmental policy, such as laid down in the Sixth Community Environment Action Programme, or in any subsequent general environmental action programme.

General environmental action programmes shall also be considered as plans and programmes relating to the environment.

This definition shall not include financial or budget plans and programmes, namely those laying down how particular projects or activities should be financed or those related to the proposed annual budgets, internal work programmes of a Community institution or body, or emergency plans and programmes designed for the sole purpose of civil protection;

(f) 'environmental law' means Community legislation which, irrespective of its legal basis, contributes to the pursuit of the objectives of Community policy on the environment as set out in the Treaty: preserving, protecting and improving the quality of the environment, protecting human health, the prudent and rational utilisation of natural resources, and promoting measures at international level to deal with regional or worldwide environmental problems;
(g) 'administrative act' means any measure of individual scope under environmental law, taken by a Community institution or body, and having legally binding and external effects;
(h) 'administrative omission' means any failure of a Community institution or body to adopt an administrative act as defined in (g).

2. Administrative acts and administrative omissions shall not include measures taken or omissions by a Community institution or body in its capacity as an administrative review body, such as under:

(a) Articles 81, 82, 86 and 87 of the Treaty (competition rules);
(b) Articles 226 and 228 of the Treaty (infringement proceedings);
(c) Article 195 of the Treaty (Ombudsman proceedings);
(d) Article 280 of the Treaty (OLAF proceedings).

TITLE II ACCESS TO ENVIRONMENTAL INFORMATION

Article 3

Application of Regulation (EC) No 1049/2001

Regulation (EC) No 1049/2001 shall apply to any request by an applicant for access to environmental information held by Community institutions and bodies without discrimination as to citizenship, nationality or domicile and, in the case of a legal person, without discrimination as to where it has its registered seat or an effective centre of its activities.

For the purposes of this Regulation, the word 'institution' in Regulation (EC) No 1049/2001 shall be read as 'Community institution or body'.

Article 4

Collection and dissemination of environmental information

1. Community institutions and bodies shall organise the environmental information which is relevant to their functions and which is held by them, with a view to its active and systematic dissemination to the public, in particular by means of computer telecommunication and/or electronic technology in accordance with Articles 11(1) and (2), and 12 of Regulation (EC) No 1049/2001. They shall make this environmental information progressively available in electronic databases that are easily accessible to the public through public telecommunication networks. To that end, they shall place the environmental information that they hold on databases and equip these with search aids and other forms of software designed to assist the public in locating the information they require.

The information made available by means of computer telecommunication and/or electronic technology need not include information collected before the entry into force of this Regulation unless it is already available in electronic form. Community institutions and bodies shall as far as possible indicate where information collected before entry into force of this Regulation which is not available in electronic form is located.

Community institutions and bodies shall make all reasonable efforts to maintain environmental information held by them in forms or formats that are readily reproducible and accessible by computer telecommunications or by other electronic means.

2. The environmental information to be made available and disseminated shall be updated as appropriate. In addition to the documents listed in Article 12(2) and (3) and in Article 13(1) and (2) of Regulation (EC) No 1049/2001, the databases or registers shall include the following:

(a) texts of international treaties, conventions or agreements, and of Community legislation on the environment or relating to it, and of policies, plans and programmes relating to the environment;
(b) progress reports on the implementation of the items referred to under (a) where prepared or held in electronic form by Community institutions or bodies;

(c) steps taken in proceedings for infringements of Community law from the stage of the reasoned opinion pursuant to Article 226(1) of the Treaty;
(d) reports on the state of the environment as referred to in paragraph 4;
(e) data or summaries of data derived from the monitoring of activities affecting, or likely to affect, the environment;
(f) authorisations with a significant impact on the environment, and environmental agreements, or a reference to the place where such information can be requested or accessed;
(g) environmental impact studies and risk assessments concerning environmental elements, or a reference to the place where such information can be requested or accessed.

3. In appropriate cases, Community institutions and bodies may satisfy the requirements of paragraphs 1 and 2 by creating links to Internet sites where the information can be found.

4. The Commission shall ensure that, at regular intervals not exceeding four years, a report on the state of the environment, including information on the quality of, and pressures on, the environment is published and disseminated.

Article 5

Quality of the environmental information

1. Community institutions and bodies shall, insofar as is within their power, ensure that any information that is compiled by them, or on their behalf, is up-to-date, accurate and comparable.

2. Community institutions and bodies shall, upon request, inform the applicant of the place where information on the measurement procedures, including methods of analysis, sampling and pre-treatment of samples, used in compiling the information can be found, if it is available. Alternatively, they may refer them to the standardised procedure that was used.

Article 6

Application of exceptions concerning requests for access to environmental information

1. As regards Article 4(2), first and third indents, of Regulation (EC) No 1049/2001, with the exception of investigations, in particular those concerning possible infringements of Community law, an overriding public interest in disclosure shall be deemed to exist where the information requested relates to emissions into the environment. As regards the other exceptions set out in Article 4 of Regulation (EC) No 1049/2001, the grounds for refusal shall be interpreted in a restrictive way, taking into account the public interest served by disclosure and whether the information requested relates to emissions into the environment.

2. In addition to the exceptions set out in Article 4 of Regulation (EC) No 1049/2001, Community institutions and bodies may refuse access to environmental information where disclosure of the information would adversely affect the

protection of the environment to which the information relates, such as the breeding sites of rare species.

Article 7

Requests for access to environmental information which is not held by a Community institution or body

Where a Community institution or body receives a request for access to environmental information and where this information is not held by that Community institution or body, it shall, as promptly as possible, but within 15 working days at the latest, inform the applicant of the Community institution or body or the public authority within the meaning of Directive 2003/4/EC to which it believes it is possible to apply for the information requested or transfer the request to the relevant Community institution or body or the public authority and inform the applicant accordingly.

Article 8

Cooperation

In the event of an imminent threat to human health, life or the environment, whether caused by human activities or due to natural causes, Community institutions and bodies shall, upon request of public authorities within the meaning of Directive 2003/4/EC, collaborate with and assist those public authorities in order to enable the latter to disseminate immediately and without delay to the public that might be affected all environmental information which could enable it to take measures to prevent or mitigate harm arising from the threat, to the extent that this information is held by or on behalf of Community institutions and bodies and/or those public authorities.

The first subparagraph shall apply without prejudice to any specific obligation laid down by Community legislation, in particular by Decision No 2119/98/EC and by Decision No 1786/2002/EC.

TITLE III PUBLIC PARTICIPATION CONCERNING PLANS AND PROGRAMMES RELATING TO THE ENVIRONMENT

Article 9

1. Community institutions and bodies shall provide, through appropriate practical and/or other provisions, early and effective opportunities for the public to participate during the preparation, modification or review of plans or programmes relating to the environment when all options are still open. In particular, where the Commission prepares a proposal for such a plan or programme which is submitted to other Community institutions or bodies for decision, it shall provide for public participation at that preparatory stage.

2. Community institutions and bodies shall identify the public affected or likely to be affected by, or having an interest in, a plan or programme of the type referred to in paragraph 1, taking into account the objectives of this Regulation.

3. Community institutions and bodies shall ensure that the public referred to in paragraph 2 is informed, whether by public notices or other appropriate means, such as electronic media where available, of:

(a) the draft proposal, where available;
(b) the environmental information or assessment relevant to the plan or programme under preparation, where available; and
(c) practical arrangements for participation, including:
    (i) the administrative entity from which the relevant information may be obtained,
    (ii) the administrative entity to which comments, opinions or questions may be submitted, and
    (iii) reasonable time-frames allowing sufficient time for the public to be informed and to prepare and participate effectively in the environmental decision-making process.

4. A time limit of at least eight weeks shall be set for receiving comments. Where meetings or hearings are organised, prior notice of at least four weeks shall be given. Time limits may be shortened in urgent cases or where the public has already had the opportunity to comment on the plan or programme in question.

5. In taking a decision on a plan or programme relating to the environment, Community institutions and bodies shall take due account of the outcome of the public participation. Community institutions and bodies shall inform the public of that plan or programme, including its text, and of the reasons and considerations upon which the decision is based, including information on public participation.

TITLE IV INTERNAL REVIEW AND ACCESS TO JUSTICE

Article 10

Request for internal review of administrative acts

1. Any non-governmental organisation which meets the criteria set out in Article 11 is entitled to make a request for internal review to the Community institution or body that has adopted an administrative act under environmental law or, in case of an alleged administrative omission, should have adopted such an act.

Such a request must be made in writing and within a time limit not exceeding six weeks after the administrative act was adopted, notified or published, whichever is the latest, or, in the case of an alleged omission, six weeks after the date when the administrative act was required. The request shall state the grounds for the review.

2. The Community institution or body referred to in paragraph 1 shall consider any such request, unless it is clearly unsubstantiated. The Community institution or

body shall state its reasons in a written reply as soon as possible, but no later than 12 weeks after receipt of the request.

3. Where the Community institution or body is unable, despite exercising due diligence, to act in accordance with paragraph 2, it shall inform the non-governmental organisation which made the request as soon as possible and at the latest within the period mentioned in that paragraph, of the reasons for its failure to act and when it intends to do so.

In any event, the Community institution or body shall act within 18 weeks from receipt of the request.

Article 11

Criteria for entitlement at Community level

1. A non-governmental organisation shall be entitled to make a request for internal review in accordance with Article 10, provided that:

(a) it is an independent non-profit-making legal person in accordance with a Member State's national law or practice;
(b) it has the primary stated objective of promoting environmental protection in the context of environmental law;
(c) it has existed for more than two years and is actively pursuing the objective referred to under (b);
(d) the subject matter in respect of which the request for internal review is made is covered by its objective and activities.

2. The Commission shall adopt the provisions which are necessary to ensure transparent and consistent application of the criteria mentioned in paragraph 1.

Article 12

Proceedings before the Court of Justice

1. The non-governmental organisation which made the request for internal review pursuant to Article 10 may institute proceedings before the Court of Justice in accordance with the relevant provisions of the Treaty.

2. Where the Community institution or body fails to act in accordance with Article 10(2) or (3) the non-governmental organisation may institute proceedings before the Court of Justice in accordance with the relevant provisions of the Treaty.

TITLE V FINAL PROVISIONS

Article 13

Application measures

Where necessary, Community institutions and bodies shall adapt their rules of procedure to the provisions of this Regulation. These adaptations shall take effect from 28 June 2007.

Article 14

Entry into force

This Regulation shall enter into force on the third day following that of its publication in the *Official Journal of the European Union.*

It shall apply from 28 June 2007.

This Regulation shall be binding in its entirety and directly applicable in all Member States.

Done at Strasbourg, 6 September 2006.

For the European Parliament

The President

J. BORRELL FONTELLES

For the Council

The President

P. LEHTOMÄKI

(1) OJ C 117, 30.4.2004, p. 52.

(2) Opinion of the European Parliament of 31 March 2004 (OJ C 103 E, 29.4.2004, p. 612), Council Common Position of 18 July 2005 (OJ C 264 E, 25.10.2005, p. 18), and Position of the European Parliament of 18 January 2006 (not yet published in the Official Journal). Legislative resolution of the European Parliament of 4 July 2006 (not yet published in the Official Journal) and Decision of the Council of 18 July 2006.

(3) Decision No 1600/2002/EC of the European Parliament and of the Council of 22 July 2002 laying down the Sixth Community Environment Action Programme (OJ L 242, 10.9.2002, p. 1).

(4) Fourth Community Action Programme for the Environment (OJ C 328, 7.12.1987, p. 1), Fifth Community Action Programme for the Environment (OJ C 138, 17.5.1993, p. 1).

(5) Council Decision 2005/370/EC (OJ L 124, 17.5.2005, p. 1).

(6) OJ L 145, 31.5.2001, p. 43.

(7) OJ L 41, 14.2.2003, p. 26.

(8) OJ L 268, 3.10.1998, p. 1. Decision as last amended by Regulation (EC) No 1882/2003 (OJ L 284, 31.10.2003, p. 1).

(9) OJ L 271, 9.10.2002, p. 1. Decision as amended by Decision No 786/2004/EC (OJ L 138, 30.4.2004, p. 7).

Glossary

Appeal	Challenge, lodged before a higher court, by one of the parties to previous legal proceedings of certain points of the lower court's judgment.
Applicant	A beneficiary who requests documents from an institution.
Beneficiary	The group of person or bodies to which a right is ascribed in the abstract.
Cross-appeal	Challenge lodged before a higher court, by both (or more) parties to proceedings of certain points of the lower court's judgment.
de lege data	The law exactly as it has been laid down.
de lege ferenda	The law as we think it should be.
Incoming documents	Documents transmitted to institutions by third parties.
Injunctive relief	The ability of the courts to direct institutions to behave in a certain manner.
Internal documents	Documents drawn up by the institution and that are not intended for publication.
Lawyer or legal counsel	A legal representative, with the ability to plead before one of the national jurisdictions and who is sufficiently detached from the represented party, ie not a trustee or employee (in-house lawyer).
Legal personality	The capacity to be the titleholder of rights and duties. Quality inherent to natural persons but for bodies who wish to claim the status of legal person proof of existence (in national law) is necessary.
Orders (of the Court)	Decisions of the courts that fall short of a judgment.
Presumption	Permission from the law to assume that a prerequisite has been fulfilled although we are not sure that that is so.

Bibliography

Adamski, D, 'How Wide is "The Widest Possible"? Judicial Interpretation of the Exceptions to the Right of Access to Official Documents Revisited' (2009) 46 *Common Market Law Review* 521–49.

Amalfitano, C, 'L'accesso ai documenti in possesso della Corte di Giustizia dell'Unione Europea nell'esercizio delle sue funzioni amministrative' in *Scritti in Onore di Giuseppe Tesauro Scientifica* (Naples, Editoriale scientifica, 2014) vol 2, 781–806.

Armstrong, KA, 'Citizenship of the Union? Lessons from Carvel and the Guardian' (1996) 59(4) *Modern Law Review* 582–88.

Banner, C (ed), *The Aarhus Convention, A Guide for UK Lawyers* (Oxford, Hart, 2015) 255–61.

Barav, A, 'Opacité et Transparence, ou, le droit d'émpecher, la jurisprudence em matière d'access aux documents provenant des États Membres detenues par les institutions communautaires' in *Chemins D'Europe, Mélanges em Honneur de Jean-Paul Jacqué* (Paris, Dalloz, 2010) 29–62.

Boer, M Den, 'Steamy Windows: Transparency and Openness in Justice and Home Affairs' in V Deckmyn and I Thomson (eds), *Openness and Transparency in the European Union* (Maastricht, EIPA, 1988) 103.

Broberg, M, 'Access to Documents: a General Principle of Community Law' (2002) 27 *European Law Review* 194.

Brunmayer, H, 'The Council's Policy on Transparency' in V Deckmyn and I Thomson (eds), *Openness and Transparency in the European Union* (Maastricht, EIPA, 1988) 71.

Burca, G de, 'The Drafting of the Charter of Fundamental Rights' (2001) 26 *European Law Review* 126.

Cabral, P, 'Member State Documents in EC Law' (2006) 31(3) *European Law Review* 378–89.

Cardwell, S and Lea PJ, 'Transparency Requirements in the Course of a Legislative Procedure, Council v Access Info Europe' (2015) 21(1) *European Public Law* 61–80.

Chalmers, D, Davies, G and Monti, G (eds), *European Union Law, Text Cases and Materials* (Cambridge, Cambridge University Press, 2014).

Charalambous, C, 'Reagens: Access to Documents Re the Inability of an Undertaking to Pay the Fine' (2014) 5(7) *Journal of Competition Law and Practice* 466–48.

Chiti, E, 'Further Developments of Access to Community Information: Kingdom of the Netherlands v. Council of the European Union' (1996) 2 *European Public Law* 536.

Cotino, L, 'Theory and Reality of Public Access to EU Information' in D Curtin, AE Kellerman and S Blockmans (eds), *The EU Constitution: The Best Way Forward?* (The Hague, TMC Asser Press, 2005) 233–44.

Coudray, L, *La transparece et l'accès aux documents, Traité de Droit Administratif Européen* (Brussels, Bruylant, 2014) 699–712.

Curtin, D, 'Democracy, Transparency and Political Participation' in V Deckmyn and I Thomson (eds), *Openness and Transparency in the European Union* (Maastricht, EIPA, 1988) 115.

——, 'The Constitutional Structure of the Union: A Europe of Bits and Pieces' (1993) 30(1) *Common Market Law Review* 17–69.

——, 'Betwixt and Between: Democracy and Transparency in the Governance of the European Union' in B De Witte et al (eds), *Reforming the Treaty on European Union: The Legal Debate* (The Hague, Kluwer, 1996) 95.

——, 'Judging EU Secrecy, Amsterdam Centre for European Law' Working paper (2012) 7.

——, 'The Fundamental Principle of Open Decision Making and EU (Political) Citizenship' in D O'Keefe and P Twomey (eds), *Legal Issues of the Amsterdam Treaty* (Oxford, Hart, 1999) 71.

——, 'Official Secrets and the Negotiation of International Agreements: is the EU Executive Unbound?' (2013) 50(2) *Common Market Law Review* 423–57

—— and Meijers H, 'Access to European Union Information: an Element of Citizenship and a Neglected Constitutional Right' in N Newahl and A Rosas (eds), *The European Union and Human Rights* (The Hague, Kluwer, 1995) 77.

—— and J Mendes, 'Article 42' in S Peers, T Hervey, J Kenner and A Ward (eds), *The EU Charter of Fundamental Rights, A Commentary* (Munich/Oxford/Baden-Baden, Beck/Hart/Nomos, 2014) 1099–119.

De Leew, M, 'The Regulation on Public Access to European Parliament, Council and Commission Documents in the European Union: Are Citizens Better Off?' (2003) 28 *European Law Review* 324.

Driessen, B, *Transparency in EU Institutional Law, a Practitioner's Handbook* (Alphen aan den Rijn, Kluwer, 2012).

Dyrberg, P, 'Current Issues in the Debate on Public Access to Documents' (1999) 24 *European Law Review* 157.

Ezrachi, A, *EU Competition Law, An Analytical Guide to the Leading Cases* (Oxford, Hart, 2014).

Ferreira, S De Abreu, 'The Fundamental Right of Access to Environmental Information in the EC: A Critical Analysis of WWF-EPO v Council' (2007) 19 *Journal of Environmental Law* 399–408.

Goddin, G, 'Access to Documents in Competition Files: Where do we Stand, Two Years after TGI?' (2013) 2 *Journal of European Competition Law and Practice* 112–20.

Gomme, AB, *The Traditional Games of England, Scotland and Ireland* (London, Forgotten Books, 2012).

Granger, MPF, 'When Governments Go to Luxembourg, The Influence of Governments on the Court of Justice' (2004) 29 *European Law Review* 1–31.

Guggenbuhl, A, 'A Miracle Formula or an Old Powder in New Packaging' in V Deckmyn and I Thomson (eds), *Openness and Transparency in the European Union* (Maastricht, EIPA, 1988).

Harden, I, 'The Revision of Regulation 1049/2001 on Public Access to Documents' (2009) 2 *European Public Law* 239–56.

Harlow, C and Rawlings, R, *Process and Procedure in the EU Administration* (Oxford, Hart, 2015).

Harsdorf Endendorf, N and Maierhofer, N, 'The Road after Pfleiderer: Austrian Preliminary Reference Raises New Questions on Access to File by Third Parties in Cartel Proceedings' (2013) 34(2) *European Competition Law Review* 78–83.

Haywood, E, 'The European Policy of Francois Mitterand' (1993) 31(2) *Journal of Common Market Studies* 269–82.

Heliskoski, J and Leino, P, 'Darkness at the Break of Noon: the Case Law on Regulation No 1049/2001 on Access to Documents' (2006) 43 *Common Market Law Review* 735–81.

Jurimae, K, 'The Interaction between the EU Transparency Policy and The Enforcement of EU Competition Law, Who Should Strike the Balance and How Should it be Struck?' (2012) *European Competition Law Annual* 365–95.

Kranenborg, HR, 'Is it Time to Revise the European Regulation on Public Access to Documents?' (2006) 12(2) *European Public Law* 251–74.

Lafay, F, 'L'accès aux documents du Conseil de l'Union: contribution à une problématique de la transparence en droit communautaire' (1997) 33 Jan–Mar (1) *Revue Trimestrelle de Droit Européen* 37.

Leino, P, 'Just a Little Sunshine in the Rain: The 2010 Case Law of the European Court of Justice on Access to Documents' (2011) 48 *Common Market Law Review* 1215, 1238.

Lenaerts, K, '"In the Union we Trust": Trust Enhancing Principles of Community Law' (2004) 41 *Common Market Law Review* 317–21.

——, 'The Principle of Transparency and its Limits in the Context of Competition Investigations' (2014) 4 *Osterreichische Zeitschrift fur Kartellrecht* 123–26.

——, I Maselis, I and Gutman, K, *EU Procedural Law* (Oxford, Oxford University Press, 2014).

Lentner, GM, 'Access to Documents of the Institutions: Transparency of International Negotiations: Council of the Union v Sophie in't Veld, ECJ (First Chamber), Judgment of 3 July 2014, C-350/12P' (2014) 4 *European Law Reporter* 123–29.

Luszcz, V, 'Gunpowder for Court Battles: Litigant's Access to EU Institution Documents' (2012) 13 *EUZW* 488–94.

Maes, M, 'Le droit d'accès aux documents des institutions europénnes: ou en est la revision du règlement 1049/2001?' (2014) 3 *Revue du Droit de L'Union Européenne* 475–97.

Mandrescu, D, Access to Leniency Programme Documents Based on the Transparency Regulation: The European Commission v EnBw Energie Baden-Wurtrenberg AG' (2015) 42(3) *Legal Issues of Economic Integration* 301–15.

Materne, T, 'La Procedure en Intervention devant la Cour de Justice de l'Union Européenne' (2013) 29 *Cahiers de Droit Européen* 77–131.

Mendes, D and Curtin, J, ' Article 42' in S Peers, T Hervey, J Kenner and A Ward (eds), *The EU Charter of Fundamental Rights, A Commentary* (Munich/Oxford/Baden-Baden, Beck/Hart/Nomos, 2014) 1099–119.

Naome, C, 'The Case-Law of the Court of Justice and of the Court of First Instance on Transparency from Carvel to Hautala II (1995–2001)' in V Deckmyn (ed), *Increasing Transparency in the EU?* (Maastricht, EIPA, 2002) 147–98.

Nentwich, M, 'The EU Intergovernamental Conference 1996/1997' in A Follesdal and P Koslowski (eds), *Democracy and the European Union* (Berlin and New York, Springer, 1998) 93.

O'Keefe, D, 'Union Citizenship' in D O'Keefe and P Towney (eds), *Legal Issues of the Maastricht Treaty*, London (London, Chancery Press, 1994) 87–107.

Oberg, U, 'Public Access to Documents after the Entry into Force of the Treaty of Amsterdam: Much Ado about Nothing?' (1998) 2(8) European Integration Office On-line Papers

Osterdahl, I, 'Openness and Secrecy: Public Access to Documents in Sweden and the European Union' (1998) 23(4) *European Law Review* 336.

Peers, S, 'The New Regulation on Access to Documents: A Critical Analysis' (2001) 21(I) *Yearbook of European Law* 385–442.

Pinker, S, *The Sense of Style, The Thinking Person's Guide to Writing in the 21st Century* (New York, Penguin, 2014).

Ragenmalm, H, 'The Community Courts and Openness within the European Union' (1999) 2 *Cambridge Yearbook of European Legal Studies* 19–31.

Rossi, L, 'Choosing Exposure: A Study in Reputation of Member States in Access to EU Documents Rules' (2009) Berkeley Program in Law and Economics, Https://escholarship.org/uc/item/96d6b7fz.

—— and Geraldes, S, 'Portugal, Article 234 and Competition Law' in B Rodger (ed), *Article 234 and Competition Law, An Analysis* (The Hague, Kluwer, 2008) 528–39.

—— and Sousa Ferro, M, 'Report on Portugal' in B Rodger (ed), *Competition Law, Comparative Private Enforcement and Collective Redress Across the EU* (The Hague, Kluwer, 2014).

Schomerus, T, 'Access to Information on Legislative Proceedings: Case Note on the Judgement of the Court (2nd Chamber) of 18 July 2013, C-515/11' (2013) 10(4) *Journal for Environmental and Planning Law* 397–401.

Schwarze, J, 'Access to Documents under European Union Law' (2015) 2 *Rivista Italiana di Diritto Pubblico Communitario* 335–44.

Shavell, S, *Foundations of Economic Analysis of Law* (Cambridge, MA, Belknap Press of Harvard University Press, 2004) Ch 4, 'Litigation and the Legal Process'.

Snyder, F, 'Interinstitutional Agreements: Forms and Constitutional Limitations' in G Winter (ed), *Sources and Categories of European Union Law, A Comparative and Reform Perspective* (Baden-Baden, Nomos, 1996) 453.

Speltdoorn, O, 'The *Technische Glasweke Ilmenau* Ruling, a Step Backwards in Transparency in EU Competition Cases?' in *Constitutionalising the EU Judicial System, Essays in Honour of Pernilla Lindth* (Oxford, Hart, 2012) 439–72.

Tilli, V, 'An Everlasting Challenge for the European Union in Constitutionalising the EU Judicial System' in *Constitutionalising the EU Judicial System, Essays in Honour of Pernilla Lindth* (Oxford, Hart, 2012) 473–85.

Tourrès, V, 'Droit d'accès aux documents jurisdictionels: um pas vers la transparence? Trib EU, 27 Fevrier 2015, Breyer / Commission, aff. T-188/12' (2015) 1 *Revue des affaires europénnees* 195–204.

Vilaça, JL da Cruz, *EU Law and Integration, Twenty years of Application of Law* (Oxford, Hart, 2015).

Weiler, JH, Haltern and U Mayer, F, 'European Democracy and Its Critique, Five Uneasy Pieces' (1995) EUI Working Paper RSC No 95/11, 4.

OTHER SOURCES

Basic Texts on Transparency Concerning the Activities of the Council of the EU, February 2000, 53 (Publications Office, Luxembourg) ISBN 92–824–1831–6. The Code of 1995 is only marginally referred to in the literature.

Index

NB—Information in tables is indicated in **bold** and information in figures is indicated in *italics.*